Praise for *Ho*

"A powerful reclamation o̶ tools once used to oppress us into instruments of liberation, healing, and protection."
—**ABIOLA ABRAMS,** author of *African Goddess Initiation* and creatrix of the *Faces of Oshun Oracle* deck

"Bomani, with her trademark love, directness, expertise, and wit, creates a guidebook for those of the diaspora wanting to utilize ancestral magic to navigate hostilities while protecting and soothing themselves."
—**EDEN ROYCE,** award-winning author of *Root Magic*

"[This book] opened my eyes to the abundant ways in which Hoodoo is not only deeply intertwined with my spiritual DNA but is in fact the power that fuels it."
—**CHRISTENA CLEVELAND, PHD,** author of *God Is a Black Woman*

"*Hoodoo Saints and Root Warriors* can bring you safety, wisdom, and blessed assurance."
—**SHERRY "THAT HOODOO LADY" SHONE,** author of *Hoodoo for Everyone*

"Bomani ignites the fires of Hoodoo in an inimitable way. This book defies time. Bomani takes readers behind the multi-dimensions of historical curtains to reveal the potential for empowerment through magick that Hoodoo has always possessed."
—**STEPHANIE ROSE BIRD,** author of *365 Days of Hoodoo*

"A book that is simultaneously full of love, rich with hope, and unapologetically fierce as it provides the information we need to prepare, protect, and find our strength."
—**RHONDA ALIN,** founder of Black Women of Magick and Conjure

"A fierce and necessary volume that honors Black resistance and the power of conjure as a form of spiritual survival and political defiance. Bomani doesn't just write about resistance—she embodies it."
—**DENISE ALVARADO,** author of the *Marie Laveau Voodoo Grimoire*

"After reading *Hoodoo Saints and Root Warriors*, my heart is full, and the fire within me has been reignited."
—**MECCA,** astrologer and author, MyLifeCreated.com

"I am completely blown away by the fortitude, honesty, and beauty within Mawiyah."
—**GRANDDAUGHTER CROW,** (Dr. Joy Gray), author of *Wisdom of the Natural World*

"Bold, brilliant, and deeply transformative. This book is not only exquisitely written…but it is also a book of profound necessity."
—**ELYSE WELLES,** author of *Sacred Wild*

"These pages contain tools to help you discover how to transform your pain into power, your rage into resilience, and your silence into change."
—**ELHOIM LEAFAR,** author of *Manifestation Magic and Dream Witchery*

"Mawiyah unapologetically provides a blueprint for combating white supremacy, racism, and systemic oppression."
—**ALY KRAVETZ,** aka BronxWitch, founder and CEO of BronxWitch HeadQuarters

"An incredibly well-researched history of rarely known Hoodoo practitioners mixed seamlessly with accessible rituals for liberation."
—**MARCELITTE FAILLA HENDRED, PHD,** assistant professor in the Department of Philosophy and Religious Studies, North Carolina State University

"A map to the source of power colonization has tried to hide from us.... It's a portal to untapped power for those of us expanding our awareness of ancestral magick."
—**DR. SARAH L. WEBB,** founder of Colorism Healing

"Bomani is such a brilliant, powerful source, resource, and thought leader in our tradition....She has an incredible way of disseminating very complex spiritual technology into accessible tools."
—**JO-NÁ A. WILLIAMS,** Esq.

"[This book] encourages us to do what [our ancestors] did during hard times: stand up against those that look to oppress us."
—**ANIBAL "AB" RODRIGUEZ,** content creator, AB's Witch Journal

"Bomani's work beautifully tells the stories of our collective high ancestors who were the embodiments of revolution, freedom fighting, and endless resolve."
—**ANGÈLE PRESSLEY,** owner of Hoodoo Hussy Conjure Enterprises

"This thought-provoking book is unlike any other I have read in recent years."
—**CHRIS ONAREO,** Olóriṣà, psychic medium and host of the *We're Booked!* podcast

"A powerful testament to the resilience, brilliance, and sacred defiance of Black spiritual traditions."
—**OMISADE BURNEY-SCOTT,** founder/chief menopause steward, *Black Girl's Guide to Surviving Menopause* podcast

HOODOO SAINTS
AND
ROOT WARRIORS

About the Author

Mawiyah Kai EL-Jamah Bomani is an award-winning writer, educator, and spirit woman. Mawiyah is an eighth-generation Spiritual Disruptor, Egun Medium, Death Doula, and Priestess of OYA in the Yoruba system of spirituality. She is also editor in chief of the culture and Afrikan Traditional Spirituality e-zine *Oya N'Soro*. Mawiyah is the host of *FishHeadsinRedGravy*, a podcast dedicated to celebrating marginalized people of the esoteric/occult world. Her writings have appeared in numerous magazines, including *The Crab Orchard Review*, *Dark Eros*, and *Catch the Fire*. She has written several plays, including *Spring Chickens*, which won her the Southern Black Theatre Festival's 2012–2013 Playwright of the Year Award. She is also the Critical Mass 8 Literary Award winner and a KAT Artist Residency recipient. Mawiyah currently lives, writes, and conducts Orisa rituals, spiritual consultations, workshops, house cleansings, and divinations in both northern and southern Louisiana. Visit her at www.MawiyahKaiELJamahBomani.com.

HOODOO SAINTS AND ROOT WARRIORS

STORIES AND MAGICK FOR LIBERATION

MAWIYAH KAI EL-JAMAH BOMANI

LLEWELLYN
WOODBURY, MINNESOTA

Hoodoo Saints and Root Warriors: Stories and Magick for Liberation Copyright © 2025 by Mawiyah Kai EL-Jamah Bomani. All rights reserved. No part of this book may be used or reproduced in any manner whatsoever, including internet usage, without written permission from Llewellyn Worldwide Ltd., except in the case of brief quotations embodied in critical articles and reviews. No part of this book may be used or reproduced in any manner for the purpose of training artificial intelligence technologies or systems.

FIRST EDITION
First Printing, 2025

Cover art by Delita Martin
Cover design by Shira Atakpu
Interior illustrations by Llewellyn Art Department

Llewellyn Publications is a registered trademark of Llewellyn Worldwide Ltd.

Library of Congress Cataloging-in-Publication Data (Pending)
ISBN: 978-0-7387-7854-9

Llewellyn Worldwide Ltd. does not participate in, endorse, or have any authority or responsibility concerning private business transactions between our authors and the public.

All mail addressed to the author is forwarded but the publisher cannot, unless specifically instructed by the author, give out an address or phone number.

Any internet references contained in this work are current at publication time, but the publisher cannot guarantee that a specific location will continue to be maintained. Please refer to the publisher's website for links to authors' websites and other sources.

Llewellyn Publications
A Division of Llewellyn Worldwide Ltd.
2143 Wooddale Drive
Woodbury, MN 55125-2989
www.llewellyn.com

Printed in the United States of America

GPSR Representation:
UPI-2M PLUS d.o.o., Medulićeva 20, 10000 Zagreb, Croatia,
matt.parsons@upi2mbooks.hr

Other books by Mawiyah Kai EL-Jamah Bomani

Conjuring the Calabash
Empowering Women with Hoodoo Spells & Magick

Dedication

Oh say, can you see by the blood in the street,
that this place doesn't smile on you, colored child.
—Jill Scott

I dedicate this book to the First Nations people who inhabited the land of my birth: the Chitimacha, Atakapa, Caddo, Choctaw, Houma, Natchez, and Tunica. Thank you for fighting alongside my ancestors then, now, and in spirit. I dedicate this book to the wisest Esu I count myself fortunate to have met, Baba Asante Nalls, my teacher, mentor, and initiator—thank you for allowing my family the pleasure of existing in your world.

I dedicate this book to the Pan Afrikan ancestral mothers and fathers who fought and are fighting for the freedoms of BIPOC and AAPI people globally.*

This book is dedicated to the allies and accomplices burning the midnight oil on the road toward helping Black and Brown people end the PTSD associated with White supremacy. The fight requires all hands, not just Black and Brown fists. This book is dedicated to the memory of those spirits who sat with me drinking tea steeped in yellow dock root, hydrangea root, and elderberry. Thank you to Marie Laveau, Harriet Tubman, Mother Catherine Seals, Sojourner Truth, Anna Murray Douglass, Harriet Jacobs, Ida B. Wells, Annie Mae Aquash, Phillis Wheatley, Zora Neale Hurston, Isabelle Lockett, Sarah Jane Henry Coulter, Ernest Herrera, Lonzo Coulter, Marcus Garvey, and Baba Medahochi. Thank you for the soul medicine that quenches my thirst with each sip.

Ase and Oya blessings.

....
* I spell Afrika with a *k* to align the spelling with the language pattern heard on the continent before the arrival of the British and Portuguese. These groups polluted what they heard and inserted a *c* instead of a *k* in words like *Afrika* or *Kongo*. For more information, see "Four Reasons for Using 'K' in Afrika" by Haki R. Madhubuti and Rose Buchanan (January 27, 1994, https://soh.omeka.chass.ncsu.edu/items/show/692).

Disclaimer

This book contains advice and information detailing both the usage and formulation of herbs specifically for spellcrafting and rituals. This book is not intended to diagnose, treat, or prescribe for any illness or disease. Readers using the information in this book do so at their own risk. The author and publisher accept no liability for adverse effects. No portion of this book is meant to be used as a substitute for the advice of a licensed/board-certified therapist or physician. If you have or suspect you have a medical problem, do not attempt any of the spellcrafting listed in this book. Consult a healthcare provider before beginning any herbal regimen.

Readers are cautioned: To achieve maximum results, follow each work as it is written.

Trigger Warning

This book contains content that some readers may find troubling or triggering. This includes, but is not limited to, graphic depictions of and references to physical, emotional, and sexual abuse (including rape), as well as themes of death, suicide, and murder. Additionally, the narrative addresses self-harm, childhood trauma, and Post Traumatic Slave Syndrome. Please be mindful of these and other possible triggers. We encourage you to prioritize your well-being and seek assistance from a licensed medical or mental health professional if needed.

Contents

Preface   xvii
Introduction   1

> One: Hiding in Plain Sight   9
>
> Two: Sandy Jenkins: Salvation Magick   27
>
> Three: John Horse Seminole Wildman: Mental Fortitude   49
>
> Four: Queen Julia Brown: Protection from Overwork   71
>
> Five: St. Jean Malo: Claiming Reparations   91
>
> Six: Exu and His Holy Harlot, Pomba Gira: Healing Black Love   109
>
> Seven: Joseph and the Dirty South Headstand: Protection   135
>
> Eight: La Madama's Bridge Over Slave Waters: Financial Success and Nationalism   161
>
> Nine: St. Expedite: Hurry Up and Be Prepared   183
>
> Ten: Black Herman the Magic Man: Protecting Your Activism   203
>
> Eleven: Mother Catherine Seals: Protecting Our BIPOC Women   225
>
> Twelve: Zora Neale Hurston: Learning to Honor Our Past   249

Thirteen: Mama Healer Henrietta Lacks: BIPOC
Healthcare 277

Conclusion 299

Acknowledgments 309

Appendix A: Hoodoo Chifforobe 311

Appendix B: Patricia Ann Dean's Gumbo Recipe with a Side of Black Hawk 315

Appendix C: The Psalms 323

Appendix D: Adinkra Symbols 401

Required Reading for Spiritual Disruptors 405

Bibliography 411

Preface

Immigration and Customs Enforcement (ICE) raids, along with the war in the Gaza Strip, remind me of a powerful quote by Toni Morrison: "The very serious function of racism is distraction. It keeps you from doing your work. It keeps you explaining, over and over again, your reason for being. Somebody says you have no language and you spend twenty years proving that you do. Somebody says your head isn't shaped properly so you have scientists working on the fact that it is. Somebody says you have no art, so you dredge that up. Somebody says you have no kingdoms, so you dredge that up. None of this is necessary."

Racism has kept many of us, even in the moments of our dying breaths, trying to prove we are worthy of the title *human*. There are those in the Black community eager to proclaim, "We are not those Brown people or Muslim people, so their plight is not ours to worry about." We choose instead to stand down. We lie to ourselves, believing that if we sit in the corner quietly sipping our coffee, kissing our ankh or crucifix, our Blackness will go unnoticed. Our historical context will become whitewashed, and we will finally become honorary White people. We get so fixated on being seen that we misconstrue acceptance for respect. We miss the mark when it comes to building community and restructuring BIPOC (Black, Indigenous, and People of Color) and AAPI (Asian American and Pacific Islander) spaces that are cultural beacons of hope and promise. These spaces can and should be structured as financial and business havens, spiritual coves, medical retreats, and educational sanctuaries protected and policed by our own guards for our people. That is the work required. That is the necessary work of Pan Afrikanism. That is the lasting legacy that matters in the spirit of communities like Greenwood/Black Wall Street (Tulsa, Oklahoma); the Hayti District in Durham, North Carolina, also known as "the Black Capital of the South"; Harlem, New York, "the Black

Mecca"; U Street (Washington D.C.); Tenth Street Historic District (Dallas, Texas); the Fourth Avenue District (Birmingham, Alabama); Jackson Ward (Richmond, Virginia); Seventh Street (West Oakland, California); Sweet Auburn Historic District (Atlanta, Georgia); Bronzeville (Chicago, Illinois); Farish Street (Jackson, Mississippi); and Faubourg Treme (New Orleans, Louisiana).

I've accepted that White supremacy, with its feral child racism, is a religion—the colonizer's true religion. White supremacy is rooted in keeping non-White individuals longing for acceptance, longing for honorary membership into an esteemed religious order that would rather go up in flames than cling to an inclusive ideology. White supremacy has a god: Whiteness. It has a doctrine: privilege. And it has its iconography: hate.

We who know better and do better are the comrades wondering and hoping that today isn't the day we are forced to hide students in cupboards in our classrooms, shuffle them through windows, and tuck them beneath blankets stashed on the floor of our cars—all to keep them safe, to keep their families together. We are the accomplices refusing to stand by and watch America judge the humanity of others. I am a soldier, a comrade to all BIPOC and AAPI people. I am an accomplice to revolution and the liberation of BIPOC and AAPI people worldwide. Their hurt is my hurt. Their survival is my survival.

America, a country founded by outcasts (some criminals, others indigent, and then those evading religious persecution), now finds itself in the peculiar position of serving as judge and jury over the lives of others seeking asylum, seeking a chance to survive. What about the American Dream for those born non-Christian or LGBTQIA+ BIPOC people? What if they are a practicing Muslim? A child once lovingly thriving in Palestine? A child born into a family void of honorary Whiteness? Who decides which people become friends versus foes? White supremacy decides, and those who challenge its tenets are vetoed out of existence.

In my own life, I haven't gone a day without being victimized by the shadow of White supremacy. For example, on the very day I was asked to write this preface, I received a work email asking if I had used, or had knowledge of who was fraudulently using, the company credit card during these summer vacation months. As the only BIPOC educator employed there for sixteen years, I was singled out as a possible culprit, along with the other BIPOC people who happen to be janitors and cafeteria workers.

To be BIPOC in America is to live a life where no matter how many degrees you earn, how corporate your attire, or how well you speak, if you are non-White, you will forever be stereotyped and profiled under a gaze of constant scrutiny. In this woman's mind, there was no way I didn't either steal the credit card or possess direct knowledge of the actual thief's whereabouts. After being employed there for sixteen years with a highly effective work record, there was no amount of convincing I could offer to alter her perception of me—in opposition to the adage that "all Blacks steal." Being non-White labels me a seedy character, ungodly, and requires a warden's supervision at all times to ensure my moral compass stays intact.

I wrote this book because I was tired. I was sick and tired. I was sick with anxiety, depression, and fear. I was tired of watching other BIPOC and AAPI people bleed out, literally and figuratively, hoping and praying for a chance to experience the space to just breathe. I'm tired of holding my breath. I'm tired of looking over my shoulder, wondering if today is the day America sticks her hands into her bag of tricks and chooses a new way to peel away our freedoms, our sanity, our self-worth.

This book is a war manifesto, equipped with spiritual weapons. This book encourages us to fight for ourselves and the greater BIPOC and AAPI communities at large. This book is our machete in a darkened room. It reminds us how sweet the taste of vengeance is. This book is sharp. It is calm. This book is as menacing as it is venomous. This book is how we heal, how we grow, how we focus our intentions on liberating our soul's journey in this world and far into the next world. This book is for those who will one day stand courageously on our shoulders, unwilling to sacrifice either their purpose or their God-given humanity.

—July 2025

Introduction

Public Enemy's groundbreaking 1990 album, *Fear of a Black Planet*, imagines a world where race is no longer understood from a predominantly White perspective. The album predicts a "Blackening" of not just America, but the entire globe—a shift not even institutional racism, White supremacy, or White elitism can stop. US census projections support this idea, stating that by 2045, the United States will become a minority-majority nation, with White Americans making up 49.7 percent of the population and people of color 50.3 percent collectively.[1] This demographic shift counters the belief that virtue is inherently tied to European Whiteness. Instead, it highlights the idea that when humanity chooses love over racial divisions, the world takes on a richer, more diverse hue.

Public Enemy's Chuck D draws inspiration from Dr. Frances Cress Welsing, author of the international bestseller *The Isis Papers: The Keys to the Colors*. In 1970, while at Howard University, Dr. Welsing proposed the "color confrontation theory." She argued that racism stems from deep psychological insecurities, specifically "a profound sense of numerical inadequacy and color inferiority" White Europeans felt when encountering the vast majority of the world's people, "all of whom possessed varying degrees of color-producing capacity."[2] This "pigment envy" is the source of Whites' romanticized longing for alliances with people of color and their simultaneous persecution of them. Racism thus becomes a way of protecting White supremacist ideals, often cloaked in warped moral justifications like a belief in racial purity as divinely ordained.

Even so, Welsing argues that beneath White privilege lies a secret lust for Blackness, one that, despite repression, never quite dies out. For some, this

---

1. William H. Frey, "The US Will Become 'Minority White' in 2045, Census Projects," Brookings, March 14, 2018, https://www.brookings.edu/articles/the-us-will-become-minority-white-in-2045-census-projects/.
2. Frances Cress Welsing, "The Cress Theory of Color-Confrontation," *The Black Scholar* 5, no. 8 (1974): 32–40.

manifests as a searing conflict: a desire to subjugate people of color while also being irresistibly drawn to them.

The cover of *Fear of a Black Planet* shows Earth colliding with another, darker planet bearing the group's logo. It's a visual warning of where the world is headed, especially when people dismiss meaningful discussions about racism and progressive frameworks like critical race theory. This rejection of open dialogue feeds the distortion of BIPOC stories, the banning of books, and the silencing of marginalized voices, tactics that criminalize and dehumanize people of color. Such actions perpetuate harmful stereotypes, painting Black people as uneducated, thugs, prostitutes, baby mamas, or addicts. Over time, this hatred fuels anxiety, depression, and scapegoating, culminating in negrophobia or anti-Blackness: a pervasive fear and extreme aversion toward Black people and Black culture.[3]

Even some self-proclaimed "liberal allies" play a part in this dynamic. I've spoken with White folks who proudly declare their commitment to Black Lives Matter yet harbor private fears about equality. Some say things like, "If BIPOC people get all the rights, where does that put us White people? Does equality mean we'll all become poor? Who wins in the end, or do we all lose?" These so-called allies only want to appear to be fixing our problems. Instead of acting as accomplices in the fight against oppression, they maintain a system that keeps Black communities reliant on their "help." In this way, we miss the real promise of liberation. We wind up honoring the ports where we were dropped off but not the places the slave ships stole us from.

For some White individuals, negrophobia creates so much discomfort that they actively avoid contact with Black and Brown people, or seek to eliminate them from their surroundings altogether. Psychologists state that White people's brains don't even need direct exposure to Black people

---

3. J. L. A. Garcia, "Racism and the Discourse of Phobias: Negrophobia, Xenophobia and More—Dialogue with Kim and Sundstrom," Philosophic Exchange, 2020, https://soar.suny.edu/handle/20.500.12648/7164.

to experience feelings of panic.[4] A person's brain can create a fear response even when they're not actually in a threatening situation. In other words, after seasons of being a groomed hatemonger, you'd expect that seeing Black people—on television, on social media, in books, and so on—would incite a Manchurian candidate–like figure: a lifelong White supremacist whose sole purpose is to end the colored agenda by all means necessary.

I remember being at work during President Trump's first term. He was headed to Bossier City as part of a last-ditch effort to rally support for a Republican gubernatorial candidate. Several White coworkers approached me, laughing nervously before one confided, "The truth is, President Trump is like a father figure. He represents how I grew up; he's like the men in my life, past and present. I don't think I should be made to feel sad about that. I love the men in my family, just like I'd expect anybody else would love the men in theirs. No, these men aren't perfect, and sometimes they make me hold my breath in diverse company. But you have to understand, they're from a different time. It's hard to reconcile their upbringing with this new world full of new pronouns and constant whining. I can no more tell an apple tree to grow oranges than I can tell a White man not to live brazen in his Whiteness. Be proud of all you did to acquire this country, and even prouder of every measure you'll take to keep it."

She went on to tell me that Black Lives Matter was a sin against the Almighty because it was Black folks' way of trying to use color to build up their self-esteem. She saw it as Black folks wanting to matter more than White folks because they can be born in different hues. To think, this woman was a semester away from a doctorate in education. She was someone who dreamed of creating curriculums to transform public education into what she called "a beacon of hope."

In moments like this, I realized that simply blocking out the noise of ignorance and racism wasn't enough. I needed to create a collection of

---

4. Kim Mills, host, *Speaking of Psychology*, podcast, episode 110, "The Invisibility of White Privilege, with Brian Lowery, PhD," American Psychological Association, accessed November 7, 2024, www.apa.org/news/podcasts/speaking-of-psychology/white-privilege.

formulas that would help people of color, their allies, and their accomplices shift the paradigm toward protection, healing, and generational survival. So I decided to share the same workings that have kept me, my family, and my community sane as part of spiritual warfare for the soul. It's for those who believe without a shadow of a doubt that Black people are, as W. E. B. Du Bois stated, human beings worthy of an equitable pursuit of happy justice.[5]

My Vision

When my literary agent asked why I believed *Hoodoo Saints and Root Warriors* was necessary, I thought about a book I bought in 2020 based solely on the title: *Tarot for Troubled Times*, by Shaheen Miro and Theresa Reed. To say this book blew my mind would be the understatement of my adult life. It was the first tarot manual I saw that not only addressed social issues like racism, homophobia, addiction, gun violence, White supremacy, the separation of children from their families at the border, sexual assault, and pipeline battles fought by the Ojibwe, but also covered deeply personal issues, like divorce, death, financial struggles, social media–induced trauma, and of course that oldie but goodie, love.

If you read my first book, *Conjuring the Calabash*, you know Hoodoo is my friend, my confidant, and my protector. I depend on it fiercely, and I enjoy sharing it with others, especially those people of color who still see it as nothing short of dancing with the devil. But Miro and Reed's bold confrontation of topics no modern mystic had dared dip their toes in became my wake-up call. Their words propelled me to use this book to champion Hoodoo as a source of personal strength *and* a weapon for social change.

In these pages, you'll find formulas for transformation—ways to correct the horrors of disenfranchisement with a Hoodoo history of defiance, liberty, and humanity. I've also included testimonials from my spiritual clients to demonstrate how the works transformed their lives for the better.

---

5. W. E. B. Du Bois, *Black Reconstruction in America 1860–1880*.

Finally, this book explores Hoodoo's role as a force for communal protection and, most important, retaliation. For many, Hoodoo is a double-sided salvation. It reconnects us to the past and fosters reciprocity in the present, where skin color dictates not only how people of color may thrive, but also how and if they're allowed to survive.

What Is Hoodoo?

Hoodoo references Afrikan American folkloric practices steeped in healing, hexing, and protection. Hoodoo is conjure; it is rootwork; it is Black folks' spiritual hygiene. It is the magick that has sustained Black and Brown people since our enslavement in lands opposed to our way of life. Hoodoo is our way of communicating with the universal spirits; it is a channeling of ancestors, of gods, of goddesses, and of saints.

This book introduces the lives and legacies of the Hoodoo saints, guardians who fueled resistance and nurtured the survival of people of color across generations. Hoodoo sparked the Haitian Revolution, and in the hands of Black and Brown midwives, Hoodoo has saved the lives of countless breech babies throughout the years. Hoodoo is a gumbo of bones, roots, shoots, and herbs, all infused with the primal knowledge of Afrikans, First Nations folks, and Europeans. Hoodoo is a way of talking to the earth, who then convinces the sky not to cry as the plantation goes up in flames.

How Does Hoodoo Work?

In Hoodoo, the first step is for the conjurer to choose a sacred vessel called a *witness*. This witness, also known as a taglock in the craft, holds the essence of the person who will receive the work. It is an item the intended person has physically bonded with, usually through repeated touch. This bond is what gives the witness its spiritual charge.

Think of the witness as an anchor—a tangible object that ties the physical to the spiritual. It could be anything the person has touched or considers their personal property: pens, receipts, a toothbrush, makeup, undergarments, a hairbrush, prescription medicine bottles, letters, a used cup or soda can, a cigar or cigarette stub. Even a photo of the person printed from the internet can act as a witness. The key is to select an object that is accessible, easy to hide, and won't be missed—you don't want your witness to be someone's car, pet, or laptop!

Once they've chosen a witness, the conjurer must decide what form the work will take, whether that's a hex, a spell, an evil eye, a crossing, or a curse. Then the conjurer defines the terms of the agreement with Spirit, including what will "turn the trick," or undo the work. (To be clear, there are times a conjurer won't reverse a work even when they know how to, choosing instead to let their victim dwell in their discomfort.)

One last note: Many Hoodoo workings use graveyard dirt. When collecting graveyard dirt, be careful to obey any laws regarding graveyards or cemeteries in your community. If gathering dirt from inside a graveyard is too difficult, you can bag soil from just outside the property. Alternatively, take soil from your own yard and place it inside a mason jar with either an image of a graveyard or one of a deceased ancestor. Leave the jar outside under the night sky for nine days before using the soil in workings.

Conjure and Religion

I recently watched a lecture by Dr. Yvonne Chireau titled "Root Doctors and Hoodoo Medicine" on YouTube. During the Q&A period, she addressed a fascinating question: Did Hoodoo arise independently from religious doctrine, or did its mingling with Western religion, particularly Christianity, come before Hoodoo itself?[6] In other words, did Hoodoo need Christianity to exist, or was there already a practice of rootwork and conjure in place before the rise of Christianity in enslaved communities? Chireau pointed out that it wasn't until after Emancipation that many Black people became Christians by choice. Before this, rootwork and conjure didn't have a formal name. Instead, these practices coexisted in one humongous gumbo pot, a blend of ancestral knowledge salvaged from

----

6. Yvonne Chireau, "Root Doctors and Hoodoo Medicine," YouTube, February 18, 2022, https://youtu.be/icabuoWxPC0?si=JgZXZxfxclA4htEy.

Afrika, Indigenous First Nations spirituality, and elements introduced by European immigrants.

As Black people assimilated into Pentecostal, Holiness Spiritualist, and Catholic churches in and around New Orleans, Hoodoo went undercover as a way of "hiding in plain sight." Rootwork and conjure became a form of healing for those times when the prayers of a pastor or priest weren't enough. This evolution also shifted the perception of conjurers themselves, casting them as saints, sinners, or hellraisers depending on whether they performed their work openly inside a church or after hours under cover of darkness.

Throughout this book, you'll encounter the term *syncretism*, defined by *Merriam-Webster* as the fusion of religious beliefs, with one practice presumably overshadowing the others.[7] For enslaved people, syncretization was a way to hide their beliefs and spiritual practices from their Christian captors. Today, I like to think of syncretization as another way of hiding in plain sight for those who aren't ready to practice Hoodoo publicly but still want to fight the good fight toward liberation. In this book, we'll frame Hoodoo practices around ancient and modern-day "saints." These saints will mark locations where offerings can be placed and praise words channeled. Whether in statue form, framed behind glass, or placed inside a plastic document sleeve, the saints are guiding figures that provide a physical connection to Spirit.

The legacy of the Hoodoo saints reminds me of their unwavering courage in the face of White supremacist hatred. Each saint refused to bow down to injustice, even when the cost of resistance was blood, sweat, tears, and even death. Their miracles lie in the fact that we haven't forgotten their purpose, their fortitude, and their resolve. Because of them, we continue to find beauty and salvation while honoring the traditions they passed down to us.

---

7. *Merriam-Webster Dictionary*, "syncretism," accessed July 31, 2025, https://www.merriam-webster.com/dictionary/syncretism.

Chapter One
Hiding in Plain Sight

In Catholicism, the path to sainthood begins with an investigation into the candidate's life for evidence of heroic virtue. Then, it must be determined if the person is venerable. Finally, the candidate must be credited with performing a proven miracle.

As we delve into how we'll canonize the Hoodoo saints that follow in this book, we'll honor the legacies of Afrikan conjure traditions and blend diasporic knowledge with New World lore. In this way, we take back our Afrikan deities. We listen as the voices of these Hoodoo saints remind us whose shoulders we stand on. In their presence, we vow to never forget that no one will gift us our liberation—we have to take it, bit by bit, blow by blow, hood by hood, city by city, state by state until we're the last ones standing. Our fingers may be weary and our fingers calloused. Yet, we remain steadfast, all while choking the final breath out of White supremacy.

Syncretization

Syncretization allowed our Afrikan ancestors to hide their indigenous beliefs under the cover of worshipping Christian saints. By aligning Afrikan spirits with Catholic saints, they created a way to continue their spiritual practices while seeming to conform. This camouflage was both strategic and sacred.

Today, through these syncretized saints, devotees can connect with divine energies. By making offerings, touching sacred objects, and conversing with these spiritual forces, their petitions travel the universe to seek help from powerful patrons for causes above and beyond our human grasp.

Following is a list of syncretic matches between the Afrikan Orisas and various Catholic saints.[8]

- *Aganju:* Saint Christopher
- *Agidai:* Saint Bartholomew
- *BabaluAye:* Saint Lazarus
- *Boromu & Borosia:* Saint Elias
- *Dada & Bayani:* Our Lady of the Rosary, San Ramon Nonato, Saint Lucy
- *Elegba:* Holy Child of Atocha, Saint Anthony of Padua (Eshu Laroye), San Benito de Palermo, The Lonely Soul - Anima Sola (Alagbana), Infant of Prague, Saint Peter (Eshu Onibode)
- *Erinle:* Saint Raphael
- *Ibeji:* Saints Cosme and Damian, Idowu: the child in Our Lady of Charity's arms *(Note: The Ibejis and Idowu are sometimes associated with Faith, Hope, and Charity)*
- *Iroko:* Our Lady of the Immaculate Conception
- *LogunEde (Laro):* Saint Michael Archangel, Saint Expedite
- *Nana Buruku:* Our Lady of Mount Carmel
- *Nanu:* Saint Martha
- *Oba:* Saint Rita of Cascia, Saint Catherine of Sienna
- *Obatala:* Our Lady of Mercy (Ransom)
  - *Ayaguna:* Saint Sebastian
  - *Oshagrinan:* Saint Joseph the Worker
  - *Eruaye:* Divine Providence
  - *Oba Moro:* Jesus of Nazareth
  - *Yeku Yeku:* Santisimo
  - *Oshanla, Obanla:* Our Lady of Mercy (Ransom)
  - *Alagema:* Saint Philomena or Saint Lucy
- *Ochosi:* Saint Norbert

---

8. "Syncretism (Orisha-Saint Correspondence)," NARKIVE Newsgroup Archive, accessed July 12, 2024, https://alt.religion.orisha.narkive.com/PF8QMNbQ/syncretism-orisha-saint-correspondence.

- *Ogun:* Saint Peter, Saint Michael the Archangel (Ogun Shibiriki)
- *Oke:* Saint Roque, Saint Robert
- *Olokun:* Stella Maris (Our Lady, Star of the Sea)
- *Orishaoko:* Saint Isidor
- *Orunmila:* Saint Francis of Assisi
- *Osayin:* Saint Ambrose, Saint Sylvester
- *Oshumare:* Saint Bartholomew
- *Oshun:* Our Lady of Charity
- *Ololodi:* Our Lady of Loreto
- *Oya:* Saint Theresa of Lisieux *(in Havana),* Candlemas *(in Matanzas),* Saint Theresa of Avila
- *Shango:* Saint Barbara
- *Yembo:* Saint Anne
- *Yewa:* Our Lady of Montserrat, Saint Clare, Our Lady of the Abandoned Ones
- *Yemaya:* Lady of Regla
- *Asesu:* Saint Clare of Assisi
- *Achaba:* Saint Martha
- *Mayelewo:* Lady of Regla

What Is the Kongo Cosmogram?

The Kongo cosmogram, often referred to as the Dikenga or Yowa, is a spiritual symbol created by the Bakonga people of the Kongo region.[9] In addition to highlighting the four phases of life, the Kongo cosmogram depicts the movement of the sun and its phases, also referred to as Tendwa Nza Kongo. For generations Kongo cosmograms have been drawn on the walls of churches, at the bottom of baptismal pools, or carved into the underside of collection plates.

The literal interpretation of the Kongo cosmogram is "the turning," meaning the literal turning of each soul's existence from the spirit realm

---

9. Wyatt MacGaffey, "Constructing a Kongo Identity: Scholarship and Mythopoesis," *Comparative Studies in Society and History* 58, no. 1 (2016): 159–80, https://doi.org/10.1017/s0010417515000602.

to birth, adulthood, eldership, and regeneration through physical death. Read counterclockwise, it shows the life path of all beings as they travel through the universe.

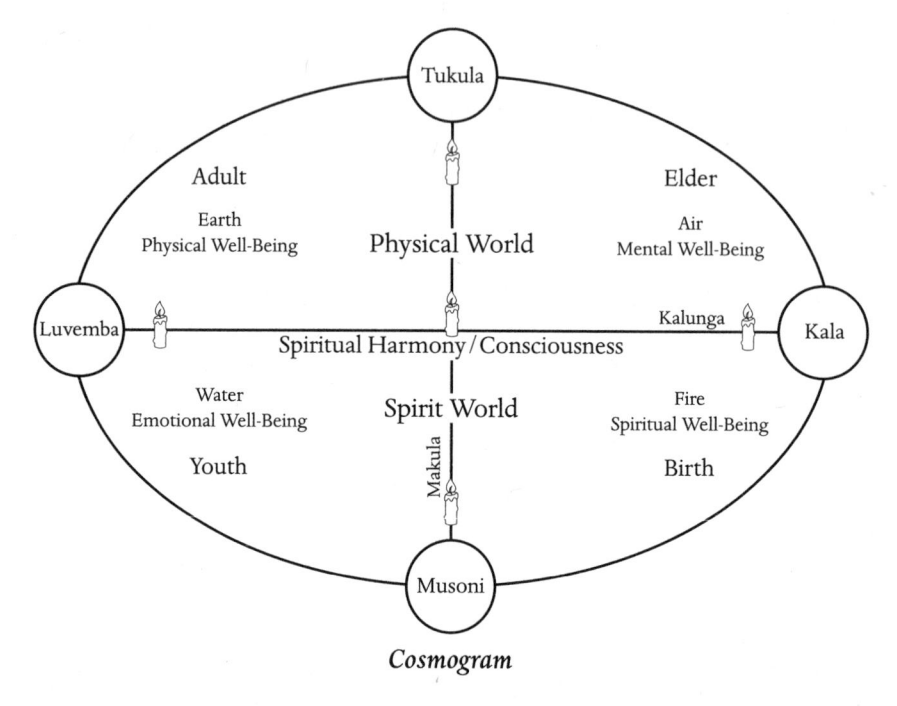

```
                      Tukula
           Adult                    Elder
           Earth                     Air
      Physical Well-Being      Mental Well-Being
                    Physical World
                                Kalunga
  Luvemba ────────────────────────────── Kala
          Spiritual Harmony / Consciousness
           Water                    Fire
      Emotional Well-Being    Spiritual Well-Being
                     Spirit World
           Youth         Makula      Birth
                      Musoni
```

Cosmogram

Tukula is the physical maturation of each body. Luvemba is the opening of the veil between worlds, a transformation into the spirit world. Makula is the ancestral council, or warehouse of seated wisdom. It's where Kala, the rebirth of birth, is allowed to manifest. Kalunga is the cosmic consciousness of both the physical world and the spiritual world, which join in lifting the veil.

Following are more key points about the Kongo cosmogram:

- The Kongo cosmogram reminds us that we're born on an ancestral continuum. We mature by evolving or devolving through personal bouts of success and hardship. We physically die so our soul can transcend this realm and move to the ancestral plain, where we assess our eternal lessons.

- Just as plants and animals adapt to the seasons, so too do humans. Our physical path is a circular one that echoes the spiritual world. All of Earth's inhabitants are interconnected, one species depending on the other. This is to fortify the ethereal consciousness vibrating in tune to a rhythm called existence. When we care for ourselves and the environment, we vibrate at a frequency of wholeness impenetrable to the ill of White supremacy.
- Through temperance we learn to navigate heartache and trauma with a genuine openness that prevents these situations from impacting our life for long. We evaluate how we arrived at tumultuous, oppressive moments, and instead of asking, "Why me?" we generate a meditative state of grace. We apologize to the part of us that views roadblocks as an excuse to unravel at the seams. We submit to Hoʻoponopono in the early stages of grief. We give into the powerful affirmation that *trouble don't last always*.
- Life is a series of quiet deaths. Ku Nseke refers to the physical world, where living beings exist. Ku Mpemba (sometimes spelled *Kumpemba*) refers to the spiritual realm. All that we learn, unlearn, and refuse to learn becomes ingrained in our DNA. As we travel through each life, we have the option of doing it all again or rejecting parts or the entire thing. Our physical demise doesn't end our commitment to balance, nor does our spiritual ability to change bodies or lives disconnect us from our human obligations to work toward personal growth and personal peace. Past-life readings and Akashic records reviews can help us decide what's trash and what can be salvaged.
- We live as fluidly as water. Our past lives reverberate, disguised as déjà vu. When these moments arise, they remind us we have access to a council of ancestors who are always watching and willing to intervene at a moment's notice. The sensation of reexperiencing events, places, or people is our ancestors' way

of saying, "We see you messing around with those trifling-ass ingrates. Fool, don't do that. Run the other way fast!"

The Process of Canonizing Hoodoo Saints

When we think of sainthood, most people imagine stained-glass windows gracing the insides of Catholic churches. I spent a large chunk of my life attending Catholic schools, so believe me, I get it.

Under Catholicism, canonization is performed to declare a person worthy of public recognition as a saint. The criteria for each person is that he or she must wait five years after their death. Next, the person's life must show verifiable proof of a holy existence. Then, heroic virtue must be proven. This means the life of the deceased influenced others, that it drew them into the folds of faith. Afterward, the deceased must show a miracle that happens in their name as a result of prayer. This is known as beatification. It happens because of devotion to a spirit believed to already be living joyously in heaven, where they're now imbued with the highest form of magick. Lastly, a second miracle must be performed, ensuring the beatification and devotion to this person are without flaw and that this person is without a doubt worthy of the honor of sainthood.

Once last note: Some saints, whether in statue or image form, customarily show up as White. In these cases, I enjoy painting or coloring the saint to match my physical aesthetic, and there's nothing remotely wrong with that. Never let the color of colonialization deter you from working with any and all saints. Keep paint, crayons, and markers in your hue in your magickal toolkit, and color that saint chocolate.

Hoodoo Canonization Instructions

Our Hoodoo canonization process deviates from the Catholic version. That's okay because it brings us closer to a spiritual healing that involves our ancestors, sheroes and heroes, ourselves, and our community.

The canonizing of Hoodoo saints is the first step in opening your sacred portal. This sacred portal is the space where the saint becomes a deified warrior, ready and willing to balance the scales for you and your loved ones. Canonization ensures that the healing physical altar established for your saint is sufficiently charged with energy to bring success to all your spiritual endeavors.

In Afrikan traditional religions, especially as they exist in the diaspora, counterclockwise circular movement has high significations and relevance to drawing down spirits. In many places, walking the dikenga is practiced today as a way of opening ritual, meditation, and connecting to God. As we canonize our saints, we will recite the psalm used to call forth the spirit as we walk counterclockwise around the outer circle.

The canonization process also includes drawing your own Kongo cosmogram. Recall that the cosmogram is an ancient ritual tool and portal designed to call forth ancestral energies. When employing the cosmogram for this purpose, we're channeling success and abundance while quieting the trauma and hardships that come with being Black in a world where racism has become America's love language.

When introducing a new saint into your spiritual work, you must first canonize them using the following instructions. Once a person has been canonized to sainthood, you're free to build an altar to them and work with them using any exercise in this book.

EXERCISE: WORKING THE KONGO COSMOGRAM

When canonizing Hoodoo saints, always begin by drawing the Kongo cosmogram. You can use chalk, markers, paint, cornmeal, or cascarilla, and you can draw your cosmogram on a sheet of paper or poster board. (I encourage newbies to start with a large poster board, either 36 x 48 inches or 40 x 60 inches.) The key is to use materials you're comfortable with, especially during your first few attempts. As you gain experience, you may gravitate toward drawing on larger surfaces, like a wooden plank, a tarp, a sheet, or the floor.

Conversely, if your life requires spiritual discretion, or if you don't have space or time to construct a large Kongo cosmogram, simply print out five cosmograms from the internet, place them in sheet protectors, then position one in the center of your floor space and the others at cardinal directions. This method will be just as effective as drawing your own.

Please note: The following canonization exercise should always precede the creation of any saint altar.

Needs:

- a Kongo cosmogram
- 5 drinking glasses
- plain water (enough to fill the glasses)
- 5 white seven-day candles
- a photo of the person being canonized
- 5 cowrie shells
- a cauldron or other fireproof receptacle
- 1–2 charcoal disks
- 1 piece each of frankincense, myrrh, and amber resin
- a shakere
- Psalm 1 (see appendix C)

For the altar:

- liquid black soap and water (enough to clean the altar space)
- a soft sponge or cloth
- Florida water in a spray bottle

Instructions:

After making or printing out your cosmogram, set it on the floor. Place a glass of water inside each of the smaller circles, then place a candle in front of each glass. Place the Hoodoo saint's photo at the center crosspoint. Drop a cowrie shell into each glass.

Working outside the cosmogram, place a lit charcoal disk inside the cauldron. Add the resin.

Sit in front of the cosmogram and begin shaking your shakere with soft, gentle taps. Breathe along with the rhythm. If you've drawn a cosmogram that's large enough to step into, take off your shoes and socks and stand barefoot at the center of it.

Hold the image of the person being canonized inside your Bible as you speak the invocations. Recite Psalm 1 nine times, then say the following:

> O great and mighty spirit, [saint's name], grant me a moment of counsel. Most holy spirit, in your presence I sit ready and willing to petition you in all your glory and divine knowing. Infuse my life with your essence so that I may rejoice in the perils of those who would condemn me to a life of misery and racial injustice. I open my home to you. May you seek refuge at my altar—this space I've paved for you in your honor. May you find it a suitable home away from home as you aid me in my struggle. Love of my love, blood of my blood, offerings shall be but a meager show of appreciation. Help me, and your story will forever be exalted. Ase, Ase, Ase. Amen, Amen, Amen.

Bow your head and continue with the shakere until you feel the unification between human and spirit essence—the alignment should start in your feet, then slowly move to the top of your head. Sitting or standing, rotate your body counterclockwise as you say, *I exalt you, [saint's name]! I exalt you, Makula! I exalt you, Luvemba! I exalt you, [saint's name nine times].*

Once finished, lie on the floor on your back in corpse pose for fifteen to thirty minutes, then douse the flame and begin assembling the saint's shrine. Leave the picture at the center crosspoint for twenty-four hours; you'll move it to your altar once it's assembled.

To build your altar, first sweep and cleanse the area with liquid black soap. Once dry, spritz the altar-to-be three times with Florida water. Let it air-dry completely before dressing it. Unless specified, all exercises can be performed on or near your altar space.

Hoodoo Dice Divination

When working with the saints, I often find myself wanting to know my daily forecast. I like to know what I'm running into just as much as I want to know the situation I left behind.

Divination with dice opens up a figurative and literal can of truths that can whip your ass into shape or have you clamoring to get back in bed. By the way, long before dice were used in divinatory practice, ancient diviners used the knucklebones of sheep or goats. This method of divination is defined by the Greek term *astragalomancy*, referencing astragaloi, the marking and cutting off of a sheep's knucklebones. These knucklebone readings, in the hands of the ancient Greeks and Romans, were mainly used to diagnose physical and mental illnesses.[10]

Today, we can use dice to diagnose all manner of illnesses and trauma, and to guide us on the path of protection and abundance. This method is a way to channel not only saints, but also the ancestral guides who are willing to search the void of our experiences and relay findings back to us through divination.

Now I'll share the basic technique and interpretations of dice divination, a heavily employed Hoodoo conjuration and an early divinatory method I teach to my students.

---

10. "A Rare Assemblage of Knuckle Bones for Gaming and Divination Discovered in the Ancient City of Maresha," The Friends of the Israel Antiquities Authority, August 18, 2022, https://www.friendsofiaa.org/news/2022/8/18/a-rare-assemblage-of-knuckle-bones-for-gaming-and-divination-discovered-in-the-ancient-city-of-maresha.

EXERCISE: DICE DIVINATION

In this exercise, you'll learn the basics of dice divination as a means of gaining knowledge and insight into one's past, present, and future.

Needs:

- 1 piece of cloth or a large black poster board (at least 2 x 2 feet)
- Hoyt's cologne
- 3 dice, each with number configurations 1–6
- 1 empty tin can

Instructions:

Set your cloth down, then add two to three drops of Hoyt's cologne to your palms. Rub them together swiftly until they're heated.

Place the dice in the can and shake them up before tossing them onto the cloth. Add the face-up numbers on each one together, noting the total. Look this number up in the following list of numerical interpretations.

Repeat two more times for a total of three linked interpretations. Think of it like stringing three sentences together to make a paragraph. As you become more proficient with readings, you'll find yourself creating longer chains in patterns of three: six, nine, twelve, and so on.

When finished, spritz your dice with Hoyt's cologne again before storing in the can to keep them spiritually charged. Storing your dice in the can also protects them from being used for anything other than divination.

Keep a record of your readings, noting how comfortable and adept you feel using dice. As you begin the journey of communicating with each saint, your dice will become an important tool in your Hoodoo arsenal.

Numerical Interpretations

Following are the basic numerical interpretations for dice divination.

* 1 = Family difficulties coming.
* 2 = Things are not what they seem.
* 3 = A pleasant surprise in the future; circumstances will change without warning.
* 4 = Unpleasant disappointments, arguments, and disagreements.
* 5 = Strangers or surprises bring happiness; plans come to fruition in new friendships.
* 6 = Misfortune or loss; a friend may ask a favor.
* 7 = You become the victim of gossip, scandal, business, money trouble, a new romance, or a difficult problem to solve.
* 8 = Take it slow; do not act in haste, distress, or difficulty; clothing as a gift.
* 9 = Love, success, reconciliation, or a gambling win.
* 10 = New beginnings, success, career, money, and legalities.
* 11 = Short-term illness; grief, a parting, a sorrow, a trip for entertainment, or a death may concern you.
* 12 = A message of importance arrives soon; seek advice for legal documents, or spend a large sum of money.
* 13 = A period of unhappiness, disappointment, or misery if you pursue current situations with no self-pity, or it will cause more problems.
* 14 = New friends bring excitement to your life. You'll receive excitement in your life, unexpected assistance from someone close/a new lover, or an admirer.

- 15 = Follow your intuition about false friends; don't be drawn in by others' troubles; no new projects for a few days.
- 16 = A short trip turns out to be both fun and profitable.
- 17 = A change in plans may be necessary; be on the lookout for advice from strangers; have water dealings with people from afar.
- 18 = Success/a wish will be obtained; expect happiness, financial success, or a rise in status.

Kongo Cosmogram and Dice Divination

In the beginning of your divinatory practice, you should use your dice by themselves. As you become more proficient and comfortable with your interpretations, you can include a cosmogram like the one in the image below. Tossing dice onto a large rendering of the Kongo cosmogram gives me even a clearer sense of the roadblocks I need to be mindful of.

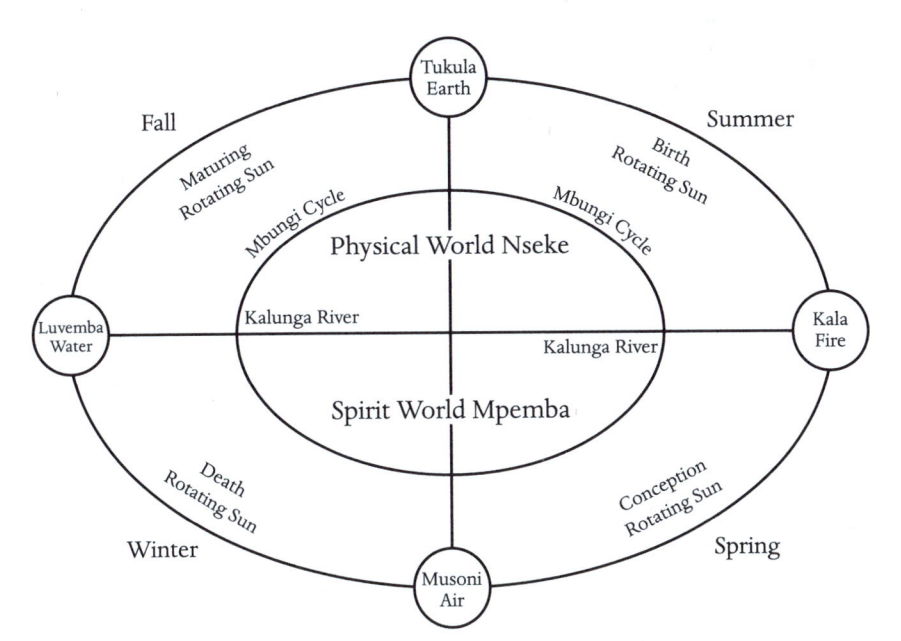

Dice Divination and the Kongo Cosmogram

I like to print and laminate my cosmograms so they have a longer life. Then, follow the dice divination instructions with the modification of tossing the dice onto your printout.

Interpretation

You'll read the dice by combining the numerical interpretations with the additional input from the Kongo cosmogram interpretations that follow.

- *Death:* (rotating sun) A rebirth, ailments looming, depression, ending of a physical life or emotional cycle.
- *Conception:* (rotating sun) A rebirth of ideas, a new chapter in your life, acceptance, or the physical birth of a child by you or someone dear.
- *Birth:* (rotating sun) An opportunity you've pooled your emotional and physical resources into is showing out proudly in your world, stepping happily into a new chapter of life, or the physical birth is near of a transformative beginning.
- *Maturing:* (rotating sun) A finality of knowing who you are and your purpose. The realization that you're not only divine, but crucial to the success of your desires. Paying closer attention to your mental and physical well-being. Letting your spiritual joy encompass all you do, leaving worry behind.
- *Luvemba:* The need to travel to a body of water, take a swim, learn to swim, or create holy water by speaking psalms over a tall, cooling glass of water. The need for a trusted person to pour water over your head, a cooling spiritual bath at the hands of another. Washing the feet of an elder to gain wisdom and add more compassion to your life. Allowing a loved one to bathe you and/or wash your feet with psalm waters.
- *Musoni:* The need to breathe more to soften your heart by giving yourself grace. It's time to take life one day at a time. Take long walks in your favorite park, on your favorite trail, or go for

a hike. Whatever you choose, take long, deep, cleansing breaths as you stroll.
- *Kala:* Life is on fire! That's a good thing; it's time to blaze through the excitement, as long as you remember to get projects finished. Feed the flames anxiety, fear, and doubt and soak in the soothing warmth of liberation. In between it all, remember to nap often.
- *Tukula:* Get outside and stand barefoot and grounded on the earth. Welcome your soul back into the folds of nature. Feel the soil between your toes, and know that you're connected to all those souls who lived in fear, in regret, in hope, and in triumph. You're not the first to be in this moment of self-discovery about yourself, your community, your nation. The knowledge you gain while standing will remind not only you but your ancestors that you're ready to assume the responsibility of being the change you want to see in the world.
- *Nseke:* (physical world) This is a reminder that you aren't fulfilling your life's commitment to the fullest. You're in a position to do something that has been on your heart for ages. Those past-life wants are coming back to haunt you.
- *Mpemba:* (spiritual world) The ancestors are channeling you—it's time to sit with your altar space and listen. It's time for a *rogacion de cabeza*, a term used in Santeria and Lukumi for the ritualized cleansing of one's head. It's time to bathe in spirit waters again and sleep in white. It's time to investigate if busybody spirits are trying to run your life. If so, it's time to cut their cord. Get those dousing rods and that photo of a trusted ancestor out, and get to inquiring, "Who's inhabiting my space?"
- *Kalunga River:* Before you go to sleep, place under your bed a jar of graveyard dirt at your head and blessed psalm water at your feet. The mind is heavy, and the rivers of uncertainty are

emerging. There are dreams that are trying to get through, so be patient and listen to all dreams, even daydreams.

- *Mbunji Circle:* The soul of your existence. Your past lives are making themselves known. They are merging, reminding you of what wasn't accomplished back then and how the carryover of an inflated ego has brought shame and shattered relationships. This is a reminder to sit with a black mirror in a darkened room. Allow the mirror to be flanked by the flickering flames of one black candle and one white candle. As you sit, speak freely to all your past lives and tell them, "Hold still, allow life to keep dancing in circles, and soon, very soon, the soft spots will heal." This is a call to sitting with a spiritual teacher for a past-life reading.
- *Winter:* This ushers in a hardening of the earth. This is a time where you shouldn't keep it real if it might result in you losing everything that matters. Watch your mouth, and watch out for folks who try to make you give a fuck when it ain't your time to give a fuck.
- *Spring:* You've grown since winter, and not only do you know who you are, but you know who's been sincere and who's been pissing at your front door and trying to convince you it's rain. You're too grown to be knuckling up and too cute to be walking around battered and bruised. Who cares what the other fool looks like after the battle?
- *Summer:* Time to go nude inside your bedroom, or if you're bold, walk the entire length of your house in the buff. It's time to free up space from all the decaying drama that has accumulated in your life. Sometimes it's other people's drama that has spilled over into your line of fire, and off and running you went. Now it's time to go to a nude beach or make one in your own house or backyard. Spend as little time as possible wearing underwear if nudity isn't your thing yet. The goal is release the junk and clutter from the body, mind, and yes, the house.

- *Fall:* I think of this as my sweat lodge or sauna time of year. It's when nature reminds me that happiness, just like sorrow, is a happening that evolves and devolves over time. There's no permanence to my joy or my anxiety. It all shall pass, and there's nothing I can do to alter what's to come. The inevitable shouldn't be met with fear but with reverence. It's time to fall back in line with loving myself, detoxing my pores, and getting a massage from a honey, lover, or friend. Even if you've never had a reiki session, now's the time to make it a top priority. Remember, the tower that falls can be rebuilt one painfully joyous brick at a time.

Patterns in Divination

When divining—and I can't state this enough—you'll have three different numerical patterns that will be read as separate interpretations before combining into one thought. As you continue to throw, your message will become more definitive. For example, let's say you're sitting with St. Joseph and you ask, "Should I rent a vacation home in Denmark or Italy?"

- *First toss* = 5 (Strangers or surprises bring happiness/plans come to fruition in new friendships.)
- *Second toss* = 17 (A change in plans may be necessary; be on the lookout for advice from strangers; have water dealings with people from afar.)
- *Third toss* = 12 (A message of importance arrives soon; seek advice for legal documents, or spend a large sum of money.)

Your reading indicates a change of plans, and that a new option will manifest by way of a new set of researched options. A stranger, either through social media or a chance in-person encounter, will connect you to a home away from home that will keep you safe from racists. You decide to heed St. Joseph's words, and instead of either option, you head to a yoga retreat in Mexico that becomes your home away from home for the next ten years or more.

Now, let's say you were using a Kongo cosmogram as a mat, and your three landing positions were Nseke, Kala, and Musoni. This trip is about rest and fulfilling a promise to the physical you. It's time away from the hustle to figure out what happened to your fire: Who stole it, and what are you going to do to get it back pronto? It's about taking those deep, cleansing breaths and getting up off your sexy butt and doing the damn thang. If you despise getting a gym membership, then use that YouTube, honey, and find a workout you can do with minimal equipment. You're reminded to get heart-happy and healthy.

The more fluent you become in deciphering dice interpretations, the more meaningful each question-and-answer session will become when petitioning the saints, not only for yourself but also your loved ones. The saints will remind you in their not-so-subtle ways to be loud, be proud, and by all means, do it in style.

Chapter Two
Sandy Jenkins:
Salvation Magick

In 1832, an enslaved Frederick Douglass became enraged after a run-in with Edward Covey, the sadistic man he was leased to.

As the story goes, unfamiliar with farming skills, Douglass often made costly mistakes. Case in point: Douglass was sent to retrieve wood from a forested area. Having been raised in the city, he had no idea how to manage a team of oxen. Under Douglass's care, the oxen broke away, destroyed the cart, and damn near killed Douglass. After gathering himself, he managed to rein in the oxen. Upon reaching Covey, he relayed the whole incident. An unsympathetic Covey answered by whipping Douglass.

Covey was known as a slave breaker, a man who beat slaves into submission for offenses ranging from running away, to destroying crops, to failing to procreate. In chapter 10 of *Narrative of the Life of Frederick Douglass*, we learn just how ruthless he was. Covey routinely overworked enslaved people, from sunup to sundown. He would feed them, but not give them enough time to ingest their meals. He also camouflaged himself among the fields of working enslaved people to spy on just how fast or slow each was working. If Covey found a slow-moving individual, he'd beat the crap out of them. One could only imagine the emotional toll it took on any enslaved person working for Covey.

On this day, Covey had set his sights on Douglass, and the men found themselves in a two-hour-long brawl. This is the moment when Sandy Jenkins, our conjurer, walked in.

Jenkins spied a battle-worn Douglass trampling through the woods, and after a brief exchange, he convinced Douglass to return to Covey's plantation with a protective root in his pocket called High John the Conqueror. This root gave Douglass the foresight to stand tall, recognizing after his scuffle with Covey that he was just as much a man as any

White man, dead or alive. The root further blessed him by giving him the patience to achieve his most significant work as a prominent Afrikan American abolitionist.

Although little is known about the life of Sandy Jenkins, what's certain is that High John the Conqueror root was his prescription for liberation. So to deepen our understanding of Jenkins, we must understand how his conjured activism in the form of High John the Conqueror root gave the lexicon of Afrikan American endurance to one of our greatest freedom orators. Were it not for the efficaciousness of Sandy Jenkins's magick, the world may have never been introduced to the determination and grit of Frederick Douglass.

Moreover, how had Sandy Jenkins eluded a sadistic tyrant like Covey? Had he been released into the wild by way of magick? Had he himself run away and performed a sort of calling to those souls buried deep within the earth? Had he gained the keys to an otherworldly ancestral protection from these mighty dead, one that shielded him from the eyes of slave catchers like Covey?

The stories I heard from elders were that Jenkins was indeed a renowned conjurer. He was a saint whose magick was so potent he could simply walk onto a plantation and carry enslaved people away to freedom. I heard there wasn't nothing Sandy couldn't do with a High John root and words older than the poopoo stains stuck to the tattered threads of America's crotchless panties. My grandfather once hinted that Jenkins had a wife whom Covey had fatally raped and mutilated for spurning his advances. As she slipped away, Jenkins promised to shortchange Covey out of every slave he acquired or even thought about acquiring. With that intention sealed, Jenkins moved deep into the woods, watching and waiting for the right moment to bring about Covey's downfall. Little did Covey know, that downfall would come in the form of Fredrick Douglass, thanks to the protection of Sandy Jenkins's magickal High John the Conqueror root.

While Douglass remained enslaved for four more years, he never again endured the weight of Covey's whip, or any man's. This is thanks to the rootwoking conjure man St. Sandy Jenkins, and the prince behind the root.

The Uncomfortable Truth about Frederick Douglass

Exploring the life of Frederick Douglass, particularly as it relates to Sandy Jenkins, raises deeply troubling questions. Many Black women, myself included, wrestle with uncomfortable truths about Douglass, specifically his alleged affairs with White women while married to freewoman Anna Murray Douglass. This discomfort grows when we consider the impact these women had on Anna, often fueled by their privilege and misogynoir. White women like Julia Griffiths, Helen Pitts, and Ottilie Assing frequently hurled insults at Anna, mocking her for her dark skin and her illiteracy.[11] They knew that because they presented themselves as antislavery advocates with money to burn, and as benefactors to all things Frederick Douglass, Anna had no choice but to hold her nose until the day they or she died.

Despite the criticism, Anna was the one who assisted Frederick with his intricate escape plan. She gave him her life savings to fund his northern travels, money earned from nine years working as a domestic. She borrowed a freedman's protection certificate so he could gain safe passage to New York. She even sold her feather bed to help him with any surprise expenses that might arise during his travels. And the sailor's disguise Frederick used to escape? She made it with her own hands.

Anna risked her life and freedom for a man she loved—a man who at the time wasn't even her husband. She also worked tirelessly to aid other enslaved people. As part of the Underground Railroad, her home provided passage for at minimum one hundred fugitive slaves. And despite being illiterate, she was heavily involved in the work of the East Baltimore Improvement Society, which provided intellectual and social opportunities for free Blacks in the area. According to Rosetta Douglass, Anna and Frederick's daughter, even though her mother had minimal reading ability, she managed the household accounts with ease.[12] From the years 1845–1847, when Frederick's abolitionist tours left Anna alone to raise their children,

---

11. Leigh Fought, *Women in the World of Frederick Douglass* (Oxford University Press, 2017).
12. Rosetta Douglass Sprague, *Anna Murray Douglass* (Self-published, 2020).

she saved every cent he sent home, relying only on her domestic's salary to cover the family's living expenses.

It was alleged that the move to New York romantically separated Anna and Frederick. Soon after, through the encouragement of benefactors, he decided he needed a more educated companion, which placed him even more squarely in the crosshairs of White female abolitionists.[13]

Writing about Anna Murray Douglass doesn't demean Frederick Douglass's role as an Afrikan American hero. Rather, it speaks to the situation so many Black women find themselves in when loving alongside charismatic, powerful men of color. Sistahs feel that some White women start seeing them as a mark early in life, believing they can take any Black man from any Black woman because their Whiteness makes them prettier and more marketable. My Black sistahs also believe that in a White supremacist world, they *are* Anna most days. And if their purpose and values don't fit a European worldview, they'll be locked out of any kind of meaningful relationship with Black men.

So hell yeah, we love Frederick. However, as BIPOC women, we recognize that Anna deserves our love even more. Were it not for Sandy Jenkins and, more importantly, High John, Douglass's story might've ended at the hands of Covey's violent and masochistic temper. And were it not for Anna sewing that sailor's uniform and providing the freedman's certificate, our dear Frederick might not have escaped to New York. Without Anna, we might not know the champion of antislavery politics, women's rights, and the Underground Railroad. I say, without Anna, no Frederick. I say, without Anna, no freedom.

The Root at the Heart of the Story

High John the Conqueror root is also known as *Ipomoea jalapa* root. It's related both to the morning glory and the sweet potato plant. To me, the smell has a nutty odor. High John is a strong laxative, so if you ingest the

---

13. Fought, *Women in the World of Frederick Douglass.*

ground root, expect to live on the toilet for a while. However, as an amulet in mojo bags, it increases luck.

Because High John the Conqueror's root resembles a man's testicles, the root is a heavy, dark-skinned favorite in sex magick, more specifically nature-sack magick: keeping a man's penis limp or under the control of a domineering lover. When the root is used in sex magick, it should be kept whole, not in chipped or powdered form. You don't want to center your magick around the idea of a man's crushed nuts or scrotum. Chips and powders are primarily used in oils, baths, and washes.

A Story about High John the Conqueror

My grandfather always said every root got a story. He'd tell us how it was wise to understand the story so you knew how to nurture either the healing side or killing side of all things in nature. Then he would go on to singing a song about trouble that always made me laugh. I remember the fine-tooth parts of it, like how folks say trouble don't last always, but live long enough and you'll always run into some kind of trouble. One day you gonna slow-drag yourself into trouble. Then he'd introduce us to High John.

High John understands how easy it is to get into trouble; to get out, you have to have a cool head and a belief in your own divinity. The story goes, there was an old man, a diviner, who lived a quiet life on a path at the foot of a densely overgrown jungle. His wilted matchbox of a house was all the home he'd ever known for seventy-seven years.

This evening had been similar to most evenings. He was anxious, euphoric, sleepy, hungry, angry, and appreciative. He was pouring his second cup of chamomile tea when he heard someone rapping at his door. It was 10:30 p.m., so he wondered who it could be. He turned the fire off on the stove, then he shoved the kettle from the front burner to the back. He used his apron to push the dry chamomile sprinkled across the table into his hands, then he blew it throughout each room on his way to the front door. When the last few sprinkles fluttered through the air, he asked, "Who is it?" Thinking he heard a familiar voice, he began sliding the latch left. The man didn't have a fear in his mind that would keep him up at night. He was the kind of man crazy enough to challenge a nightmare to a fight.

He turned his back as the hall suddenly filled with the scent of tobacco and mint. A short man came shuffling through the door wearing *Abrus precatorius* pea jewelry. There was abrus on his wrists, neck, and hanging from his earlobes. He sat in the first chair he came across, a tattered wingback in the living room. He motioned the diviner closer, then handed him a teacup from his pocket. "Might you oblige an old man with a cup of that chamomile you were enjoying?" The stranger grinned and winked, then stared around the dimly lit shotgun house.

The diviner retrieved the cup from the stranger's hand, all the while thinking, *What kind of prankster shows up at somebody's house in the wee hours of the night?* Maybe Deacon Calloway, who had only just left an hour before, was up to some kind of mischief. Calloway's soft-spoken, caramel-colored wife had been victimized under the law of paramour rights, where White rapists could make any Black woman their sexual partner regardless of marriage or the woman's wishes. Maybe he hoped to learn that the diviner's call to High John to relieve Calloway's wife's rapist of his last breath had worked. Or maybe this stranger was Calloway's way of reacquainting the stern diviner with the art of laughter, a softness he'd forgotten after laying his own wife to rest some fifteen years earlier due to stomach cancer.

After pouring the tea, the elder diviner decided to draw Calloway out of hiding: He opened the window near the alley that ran by his house, then he gathered two palmfuls of dried eucalyptus, fennel, and black pepper. He whispered an old language forgotten even by God into his hands, and then he let the herbs fly onto the alleyway. The herbs would pull Calloway into the light of the moon and make him confess the reason for his ruse.

Just as the diviner was straining his eyes, trying to separate shadows from darkness, the stranger cleared his throat. "Might I bother you for three glasses of water? My three High Johns need a bath. And don't worry about that man you sent away. He can't believe what he don't yet know. He can't be here and there. There, he's trying to see if a lifeless body comes out that White man's house. He can only be where he at, and your alley ain't where he at."

The diviner turned toward the man, who was still seated comfortably in the darkened room. He placed three glasses of water on the table next to the stranger and watched as he dropped a root into each. The roots absorbed the water, then the man scooped them up and popped them into his mouth.

"Who are you?" the diviner asked.

"Light up that reefer in the tin can buried deep within your sock drawer. Sit a spell, and I will tell you no lie."

The diviner was confused—Calloway didn't know about his reefer stash. He hid it well and only smoked on evenings when he was angriest with God for taking his wife. Still, he did as the stranger asked and rolled and lit the joint and handed it to him.

The stranger laughed. "For years, you've gotten it all right. You called it many a day, even before your bones hit the mat. You've heard it all—the details of sons hanging from trees while soft-hearted mothers beg for their lives to be avenged. Killing has a place in your magick. I've watched you with delight, Brother Diviner Talifero."

The diviner reached for the joint from the stranger's outstretched hand. "*What* are you?" he inquired with confusion.

"You ask the right question, Diviner Talifero. I'm a *what* that isn't of this world, but a *who* that is of all worlds. I'm the prince of a land across rivers of time. I am High John the Conqueror. I am the root of Hoodoo. Whatever success you've achieved is because of me; I willed it to be so. That man's wife is safe, but he has six daughters, and the White man, after being duly persecuted, will still have two brothers who will gladly take up his mantle. What you didn't know is that the dead man was grooming them to become more of a monster than he could be in ten lifetimes. Diviner Talifero, us got work to do. Us gonna devise a plan to rid the entire town of racism. Us gonna put a barrier around it so it looks like a ghost town to anyone not wearing my root wrapped in copper strung around their neck."

The diviner dropped to his knees, bowing his head. The joint fell from his mouth to the floor.

"Get up, Talifero," High John said. "We ain't got time for all that hoity-toity bullshit."

The diviner rose and listened to every detail High John the Conqueror spelled out. He was as much in awe as he was delighted to meet the man behind the mystery. The prince and the diviner waited until three minutes past midnight. They gathered tools for digging; empty jars, a few of which they filled with urine; red brick; bones from small animals; steel wool; and twine.

The first stop was a potter's field, where they retrieved soil from the grave of the eldest woman and man. Then they traveled across town to the Whites' section of town, where they gathered soil from the Confederate cemetery. They weren't satisfied with any old heap of soil; they found a general who had erased a whole territory of Black Indians from the world. As they gathered the soil, the prince saw the diviner's disgusted scowl. "Talifero, you smelling the legacy of this man. His soil reeks of anger and hatred. Top it tight; we don't need that bad blood spilling nowhere but where we put it."

The last stop was a reservation, to speak with a man who knew everything there was to know about Black Hawk and his medicine. The prince and the man hugged and spoke in a language unknown to Talifero, a mixture of Sauk and Kikongo. Once or twice they'd glance over toward Talifero and grin. The prince gave the man the jars, and the diviner watched as the prince regurgitated the three roots into the man's hands. Then the men went on sniggling, grinning, and whispering deep sighs before the prince embraced him. The man told both the prince and the diviner to close their eyes. He listened as both men chanted in the same unknown language until a cold silence filled his brain. When he opened his eyes, the diviner and the prince were back in his alley.

He and the prince mixed the soil collected from their travels. Suddenly the diviner heard footsteps—it was the Sauk man, who suddenly appeared before them with a sack across his back. Inside were the jars, each glowing as if they had been infused with otherworldly power.

The prince reached inside his mouth and pulled out an alligator tooth. He grinned and handed it to the diviner. "It's a gift from Uncle Monday. Crush it after you pray over it and add it to the juju gumbo we brewing right here." Then the Sauk man handed the prince the three roots, which the prince began pounding with a mallet.

For thirteen days the men worked. The diviner repeated Psalms 56, 71, and 89 till his mouth ran dry, and the prince and the Sauk man sang in their mysterious language. At midnight on the thirteenth day, they sprinkled their juju gumbo around the borders of town. Within a week, every racist living inside town limits, those dead and those roaming around with beating hearts, picked up what little they could carry and started walking, headed toward the moonlight. Just like that, the town became known as Liberation Nation. You can't find it on any map. You got to be wearing High John wrapped in copper strung around your neck to enter it.

Stand with your back toward the wind and whisper nine times: *The prince High John the Conqueror is coming from way over them waters. Kongo man with the root in his hands reunited with Black Hawk and Maroons from soils far and wide. His alligator general man got his troops in the bayous. Better watch your step; you might lose your head. Tarry too long, watch you wake up dead.*

Just like in my grandfather's story, modern-day Black and Brown conjurers can use High John the Conqueror to overcome obstacles, confuse their enemies, and squelch physical assaults or microaggressions before they have a chance to escalate. This root can also infuse its carriers with enough esteem to channel their ancestors as they speak out in defense of their rights. It has truly helped me gather my thoughts and find my voice, and it can and will help you, if you let it.

EXERCISE: SANDY JENKINS ALTAR AND SALVATION MAGICK

Your Sandy Jenkins altar will be devoted to salvation magick—how we utilize Hoodoo to deliver us from the difficult illusion of freedom. In a world where the media emotionally troll us while crafting a path to our demise, we need salvation magick more than ever.

Needs:

- 2–3 yards dark brown cloth
- 1 green candle
- 1 black candle
- 1 bowl of water
- 1 African violet plant
- 1 Rose of Jericho, placed inside a bowl
- a cauldron or other fireproof receptacle
- 1 charcoal disk
- 9 bay leaves
- 4 High John roots
- 3–6 tablespoons black salt
- 3–6 tablespoons asafoetida
- 3–6 dried eucalyptus bundles
- 3 pieces of frankincense resin
- 1 bowl of pinecones
- bergamot oil
- a framed 8 x 10 inch image of the Sankofa adinkra symbol (see appendix D)
- framed images of Frederick Douglass, Anna Murray Douglass
- a sheet of paper with the name "Sandy Jenkins"
- Psalm 140 (see appendix C)

Instructions:

Place the cloth over a table or on the floor. Position the candles in the center with the bowl of water in front. Place the African violet on the left of the water and the Rose of Jericho on the right. Use your decorating prowess to lay out the other items.

Place the lit charcoal disk inside the cauldron. Add the resin. Light the candles, then recite Psalm 140 nine times. Ask Frederick, Anna, Sandy, and High John to anoint your life with salvation from White rage and the White gaze. Sit with your eyes closed until the resin burns out, envisioning a future where a force field of protection stands firm between you and White supremacy.

Once the resin stops burning, your altar is open for business.

Salvation Work

After doing salvation work, some of my clients find themselves walking toward a totally new career, lover, or lease on life. Others find that their tormentors were fired, quit, or demoted. Some have even found their tormentors looking to *them* for salvation.

A friend of mine who was a psychology professor confided in me about being gangstalked by a group of coworkers. (Gangstalking is a form of daily harassment, intimidation, and persecution of an individual by a group of people.[14]) My friend had wanted to introduce Hoodoo to a small, closed group of BIPOC students as a way of teaching them about indigenous medicinal practices. But the moment she voiced the idea to her bosses, she was met with verbal abuse. It didn't end there; she quickly became the target of a wave of harassment, at work and at home. Her lunch was laced with something that smelled like roach spray. A decapitated rat painted red,

---
14. "The Dark Art of Gangstalking: Uncovering Their Methods," Stop Gangstalking Awareness Group, October 11, 2023, https://stopgangstalking.org/gangstalking-techniques/.

black, and green was placed in her purse with a note that read *Use this for Hoodoo medicine.* An envelope with a wad of shit-stained toilet paper inside was placed in her mailbox. This time the note read *Eating shit is a closed practice.*

My friend admitted that she had contemplated driving her car into rush-hour traffic just to escape the pain. We cried together, and I told her how empty the world would be without her love, especially for people grappling with trauma. She had helped numerous students dealing with parents who had turned their backs on them for being gay or trans. She was a beacon of strength for so many, and the world needed her healing.

I instructed her on the following exercise, *Walking toward Salvation*. A week after she used it, she phoned me laughing hysterically. "Heads started rolling today!" Not only was the head of her department fired, but he started singing like a lark and didn't stop until many others were fired, including three professors, two campus police officers, and two cafeteria workers. Six students were placed on probation. The university swept the whole ordeal under the rug to avoid embarrassment. They offered my friend a promotion, but she opted instead to take her hush money and go into private practice. Her current office is across the street from the university.

EXERCISE: WALKING TOWARD SALVATION

This is the exercise I instructed my friend to use.

Needs:

* pen and paper
* a pair of shoes (preferably an old pair you're retiring)
* liquid black soap and water (enough to clean both shoes)
* a soft sponge or cloth
* Florida water in a spray bottle
* Psalms 1 and 59 (see appendix C)
* a cauldron or other fireproof receptacle

* 1 stick of palo santo incense
* 2 socks
* ½ cup soil (from home, work, or wherever trouble resides), divided
* 3 tablespoons black salt, divided
* 3 tablespoons asafoetida, divided
* 2 9-inch strips of twine
* 1 black candle
* 1 black or white hand towel
* *Optional:* 2 nails

Instructions:

Write a letter to Sandy Jenkins and High John about your troubles and ask them to deliver justice to your soul. Include the names of those putting you in harm's way. Be sure to write their names nine times, forming a cross. Set the letter aside when complete.

Pick up your shoes—it's time to clean them thoroughly with black soap and water. Once they're dry, spritz them with Florida water, then recite Psalms 1 and 59 into the shoes nine times each. Set the shoes aside. Light the palo santo stick and pass the letter through the smoke on both sides. Read the letter out loud three times, then set it ablaze. Save the ashes from the letter in the cauldron.

Fill each sock with half of the soil, salt, asafoetida, and ashes from the burnt letter. Tie each sock in a knot, then strengthen the knots by tying the twine securely beneath them. Place a sock in each shoe, pushing the sock firmly up toward the toe. Light the candle, place the hand towel on the altar, then place the shoes back to back on top of the towel, pointing in opposite directions. (The shoes represent the conjure worker walking out of harm's way toward freedom.)

Time to meditate: Close your eyes and ask Sandy and High John about your situation. Sit for fifteen to thirty minutes before extinguishing the flame and heading to bed.

Repeat the meditation nightly for the next month. Incorporate the psalms as a closing to the meditation. Continue with the meditation for nine nights on, nine nights off until the situation is resolved. (*Note:* If you choose to place the shoes outside, you can nail them symbolically into the earth and perform the meditation there.)

Diving Deeper

Let's delve deeper into why BIPOC people need salvation magick by considering the story of Dr. Antoinette Bonnie Candia Bailey.

Dr. Bailey, a Black woman, worked as the vice president of student affairs at the historically Black Lincoln University of Missouri in Jefferson City in 2023. After being fired on January 3, 2024, she died by suicide five days later.

Soon after her death, friends and colleagues spoke up about the toxic workplace conditions Dr. Bailey had endured at the hands of her White superiors. Some alumni reported incidents where Dr. Bailey was set up to fail at her administrative duties. An email she wrote on the day of her death to her employers backed up their claims. In the email, Dr. Bailey referenced her mental health and accused the university's White president of bullying and harassment. "It went downhill after the FMLA and ADA documents were submitted due to my severe depression and anxiety," she wrote. "I requested to be removed under your leadership as this was causing significant attacks."[15] But even after asking for support from the university's board of curators, she was turned away, despite severe depression

---

15. Lauren Turman, "Emails Surface from LU's VP of Student Affairs Sent the Day She Died by Suicide," *KRCG*, January 12, 2024, https://krcgtv.com/news/local/emails-surface-from-lus-vp-of-student-affairs-sent-the-day-she-died-by-suicide.

and despair. She went on to write, "Lincoln is where it started for me and where it ended."

Dr. Bailey is remembered for her extensive work advocating for social justice at Lincoln. Bailey was a strong voice for BIPOC women's rights and workplace diversity.

If you or anyone you know is struggling with thoughts of suicide, contact the national Suicide and Crisis Lifeline at 988. If you or anyone you know feels they're being harassed or victimized, contact the National Center for Victims of Crimes at 855-484-2846. Finally, a database of BIPOC and AAPI therapists can be found at www.inclusivetherapists.com.

Following are several works that are often employed one after the other: *The Blues Ain't Alright Bath, Licorice Root Shoes, Glamour Warfare,* and *Sandy's Rescue Root*. These workings assist you in quelling emotional breakdowns on a deeper level. They fortify your resolve while reminding you that no form of a contrived Satan is about to steal your right to joy or your right to peace.

EXERCISE: THE BLUES AIN'T ALRIGHT BATH

You can take this spiritual bath one to two times a week as needed.

Needs:

* 3 tablespoons sandalwood oil
* 3 tablespoons vanilla extract
* 3 teaspoons licorice root powder
* 3 tablespoons powdered High John the Conqueror root
* 3 teaspoons powdered Solomon's Seal root
* Psalm 121 (see appendix C)
* 1 bar of black soap
* 1 black candle

Instructions:

Begin by running a bath as you normally would. Add the sandalwood oil, vanilla extract, licorice, High John, and Solomon's Seal. Stir counterclockwise with your dominant hand between the addition of each ingredient.

Once the water is thoroughly mixed, stand and recite Psalm 121 over the water three times, then say the following:

> *By the power of these hands, I will cleanse my soul space. I will not allow you the pleasure of stealing my truth. You will not weasel your supremacist ideology into my story of survival. I fought for this life. My encounters with the vexations of the world are messy enough without your two cents, your microaggressions blossoming into a hatred of BIPOC and AAPI people. I do not give you the authority to make me cry, to make me fear the dawning of each new day. You don't own me. I have never been your slave, your puppet, or your pet. Keep fucking with me, and you will meet High John on the road. The last whisperings you will hear will be his. He will write your name at the bottom of his shoes in blood. Ase. Ase. Ase.*

Disrobe and step into the water. Ensure that the waters saturate you from head to toe. (I sometimes use a cup, towel, or my cupped hands to make sure the water is distributed thoroughly.) Saturate your body three times, then wash your entire body with the bar of black soap three times, making sure to build up a soapy lather. Rinse, step out, and dry off.

Sit at your altar with the candle lit for fifteen minutes. Lay down your struggle, then go to bed knowing help is on the way. Sleep with your head covered in white.

EXERCISE: LICORICE ROOT SHOES

These shoes allow you to control your enemy and make them weak and meek.

Needs:

- 1 green candle
- a cauldron or other fireproof receptacle
- 1 charcoal disk
- 3 pieces of myrrh resin
- 2 sheets of paper with the Gyawu Atiko adinkra symbol (see appendix D)
- a pair of shoes you intend to wear ASAP
- liquid black soap and water (enough to clean both shoes)
- a soft sponge or cloth
- 2 teaspoons powdered licorice root, divided
- 2 teaspoons powdered High John the Conqueror root, divided
- Psalm 111 (see appendix C)
- a mason jar
- 1 whole garlic bulb

Instructions:

Light your candle and the charcoal. Place the lit charcoal inside the cauldron. Add the resin. Write the name of the person standing in the way of your salvation on the back of your Gyawu Atiko symbols nine times. Set aside.

Next, clean both shoes with black soap and water, then let dry. (I like to allow the shoes a few hours to dry, if their material warrants it.) Once the shoes are clean and dry, place half of the licorice and High John into each shoe, making sure to direct them toward the toe. Tape a Gyawu Atiko symbol to the inside of each shoe's heel. (You may need to fold or cut down the paper to make it fit.)

Whisper Psalm 111 into each of the shoes three times, then rest them on or near your altar. Snuff out the candle and allow your shoes to rest overnight; they will be ready to wear in the morning. Before you put them on, pour the powdered root mixture into the mason jar, but leave the symbols inside.

Repeat this work once a week as needed. You can use the same powdered root mixture for the entire month before sprinkling it around your front door.

EXERCISE: GLAMOUR WARFARE

This working charges jewelry for the coming week.

Needs:

* jewelry (e.g., earrings, watches, necklaces, bracelets, rings)
* 1–2 charcoal disks
* a cauldron or other fireproof receptacle
* powdered High John the Conqueror root (enough to smoke the jewelry)
* Psalm 141 (see appendix C)

Instructions:

Lay the jewelry across your altar, then place a lit charcoal disk inside the cauldron. Add several pinches of High John. As the powder smokes, recite Psalm 141 three times as you pass your jewelry through the smoke. Don't rest your jewelry on the disk; hold each piece high enough so only the smoke touches them.

After all the pieces are smoked, recite the psalm again three times, then leave the jewelry to rest overnight on your altar. Keep adding pinches of High John until it's gone, then let the charcoal disk burn out on its own before heading to bed.

EXERCISE: SANDY'S RESCUE ROOT

This work strangles your problem person or unruly situation (metaphorically!), relieving you of your anxiety.

Needs:

* a ball of steel wool
* a framed photo of the person causing you anguish or a written statement about the situation
* a large mason jar
* 1–2 cups soil (can be from your backyard or purchased from a garden store)
* a sheet of paper with the Gyawu Atiko adinkra symbol (see appendix D)
* 2 pieces of High John the Conqueror root
* 1 whole bulb of garlic
* 1 white candle
* *Optional:* Psalm 91 (see appendix C)

Instructions:

Wrap the steel wool around the photo. Fill the mason jar halfway with soil, drop in the adinkra symbol, then add more soil to fill the jar, leaving one to two inches free at the top. Push the garlic bulb into the soil until it's hidden, then seal the jar tightly.

Light the candle and place it atop the jar each night until the culprit or the situation is resolved. Allow the candle to burn as you sit and meditate on the flames for ten to fifteen minutes. During your meditation, envision the problem being cut out of your life and its residue slumping back into the earth to decompose. You can speed up your healing by reciting Psalm 91 and calling out the names of your ancestors, Sandy Jenkins, or High John.

Juju on the Fly

One of my clients, a thirty-six-year-old queer Puerto Rican man named Johnathan, was taught how to access his Akashic records. *Akasha* is a Sanskrit word meaning ether or space. These records reveal every thought, action, and wording that has existed across time and many, many lifetimes.[16] They're a library of information cataloged deep within our soul space. We access this space through a deep, meditative journey within, one that takes patience and openness to all things metaphysical.

Johnathan's Akashic records teacher had informed him that in the midst of astral travel, as he was trying to cleanse his family of generational trauma, he had unwittingly intercepted his father's misdeeds. This resulted in a deep-seated tendency to accept abuse as affection. Johnathan's father had impregnated his fourteen-year-old mother at forty years of age. After learning the child he had been raping was pregnant, he tried to strangle her. When her father came to rescue her, shooting the rapist in the back twelve times, a stray bullet hit his daughter, and she died soon after. While Johnathan was saved, he was doomed to live through years of ridicule and rejection at the hands of his grandfather.

Johnathan remembers being beaten by his grandfather, who resented the fact that he survived and his daughter didn't. At fifteen, Johnathan ran away from his grandfather's home. He met a man, a twenty-one-year-old good Samaritan who would become Johnathan's lover and eventual pimp six months later.

When Johnathan and I talked over the phone, he laughed between every sentence, claiming he just wanted White men to stop taking him for granted. He reiterated how tired he was of being treated like a dirty secret or guilty pleasure. He had a thing for bad boys, but not racists.

I told Johnathan that instead of living his days as a human punching bag, he could turn Juju on the Fly into his life's salvation. Johnathan had said on many occasions that he found tarot too tight-lipped and needed a

---

16. "Akashic Records for Beginners: Access Your Soul's Journey," The Hermit and the Page, July 19, 2023, https://thehermitandthepage.com/akashic-records-for-beginners/.

deck that knew how to spill *all* the tea. Since I love Lenormand decks, I told him we'd use that as part of his prescription instead, so it was a win for the both of us.

Lenormand cards are named after Madame Lenormand, said to be the most celebrated psychic of her time. She was rumored to have used the cards to divine for the likes of Robespierre, Marat, Empress Josephine Bonaparte, and Tsar Alexander of Russia.[17] After her death in 1843, her name was placed on a deck of cards modeled after her original deck. These cards received wide circulation around Europe and are used for divination to this day.

Lenormand decks have a total of thirty-six cards with various images. (My favorite is *Lenormand of Hope* by Erika Robinson.) We won't be learning to use the entire deck. Instead, we'll use specific cards to direct our psychic energy as a catalyst for change.

Once Johnathan employed the exercise, he was able to renegotiate his life contract and open himself up to a forever love. His true love would be receptive to his warmth and able to nurture him through the forgotten seasons of his childhood. This man, in the end, came in a melanated package as a Black music teacher.

EXERCISE: CROSSROADS JUJU

Working with Lenormand cards resets your current situation by opening a portal to other options vibrationally available to you as a part of your specific soul journey. You'll have to choose, but the options will be a pleasing respite to your anguish.

Needs:

* Hoyt's cologne
* 1 piece of High John the Conqueror root

---

17. Monica Bodirsky, "The Lenormand Oracle: History and Practice," *Spiral Nature Magazine*, October 17, 2018, https://www.spiralnature.com/magick/lenormand-oracle-history-practice/.

- 1 each of the Garden, the Crossroads, and the Woman/Man Lenormand cards (*Note:* With the Woman/Man cards, choose the one you identify with)
- a black satchel or drawstring bag
- pen and envelope

Instructions:

Add two to three drops of Hoyt's cologne to your palms. Rub them together swiftly until they're heated. Touch the High John to your forehead (your third eye chakra), kiss it, then touch it to your heart. Place the High John inside the satchel and set it aside.

Write the following on the envelope: *I am open to downloading a new form of vibrational consciousness into my life. I am ready to transcend this cycle of life. I am the soul who finds salvation.* Place the envelope inside the satchel.

Place the satchel on your altar. In the morning, put it close to your flesh. (You can attach it to your bra strap or tie it to a piece of twine or cord and wear it around your neck.) Wear the satchel for nine days on and nine days off until your life's vibration shifts.

Chapter Three
John Horse Seminole Wildman:
Mental Fortitude

Born in 1812, John Horse (also known as Juan Cabello, Juan Cavallo, and Gofer John) was an excellent marksman of mixed Afrikan and Seminole ancestry.[18] He fought along with the Seminoles during the Second Seminole War (1832–1842), also known as the Florida War, which pitted the Seminoles—a mix of both Indigenous First Nations peoples and Afrikan First Nations peoples—against the United States.[19]

Horse rose to prominence after the Seminole leader Osceola was captured by General Thomas Sydney Jesup. Serving as a warrior-diplomat, Horse (who knew how to read, write, and speak English) acted as a liaison to the Seminole chiefs, as an agent for the US government, and as a Mexican army officer. Although he fought against the United States, he often sought agreements that secured land for Indian territories. Over the course of his life he survived three wars, four assassination attempts, and many attempted kidnappings by money-hungry slave patrols.

The Black Seminoles, also called Maroons, traced their ancestry to both Afrikan and Seminole bloodlines. During the early nineteenth century, their shared resistance against oppression—both physical enslavement and colonial domination—led them to build a hidden society in the dense forests of Florida. It was from this stronghold that Horse emerged as an active soldier in the Seminole War. When the US tried to force the Seminoles from their ancestral Florida land, Horse was pivotal in uniting Afrikans and Seminoles against them. In one bold move as a war chief, Horse negotiate a signed agreement with US officials allowing Black Seminoles to live free in Florida.

....

18. "John Horse," The Great Seminole Nation of Oklahoma, accessed July 14, 2024, http://seminolenation-indianterritory.org/johnhorse.htm.
19. "Story of John Horse, a Black Seminole Warrior," ArchBalt, accessed July 14, 2024, https://www.archbalt.org/story-of-john-horse-a-black-seminole-warrior/?print=pdf.

Horse's many successes would not have been possible without the medicine of his spiritual leader and prophet, Abiaka Hadjo. The name is Muscogee and is translated as "heap at the root."[20] Abiaka used guerilla tactics, attacking enemies from seemingly nowhere, then retreating into the swamps. He not only guided battles but also administered healing to the wounded.[21]

Despite being captured and imprisoned at Castillo de San Marcos in St. Augustine as part of the Seminole War, Horse and the Black Seminoles created the largest haven for runaways in the US. Before the Civil War, they led the nation's largest slave revolt, secured the emancipation of enslaved people, and orchestrated the largest exodus of enslaved people from the Florida Everglades through Oklahoma to Mexico, where they signed an agreement to own their land free of White encroachment.

Notably, the first legal free town in North America was established in the Everglades by these communities. But their freedom came at a high price. In 1818, General Andrew Jackson moved to Florida and initiated brutal campaigns to reclaim the land for the US. His actions, unauthorized by President James Monroe, included the execution of many Seminoles and the reenslavement of Black free people. Later, as president, Jackson's Indian removal policies targeted Black Seminole communities, which led to the Second Seminole War (1835–1842), the largest and costliest Indian war.

It's estimated that enslaved Afrikans from more than 385 plantations joined the Black Seminoles, decimating the region's economy by effectively destroying cash crops and sugar mills. After relocating to Mexico, they continued to face threats from Texas slave catchers who sought to reenslave them. Under Horse's leadership, however, the Black Seminoles successfully gained legal land in Mexico, founding the community of Nacimiento de los Negros in the state of Coahuila. The settlement became a key stop on what

---

20. Tayannah Lee McQuillar, *Hoodoo Tarot: A 78-Card Deck and Book for Rootworkers* (Destiny Books, 2020).
21. "The Devil, Abiaka: The Legacy of Sam Jones—Florida Seminole Tourism," September 21, 2023, https://floridaseminoletourism.com/the-devil-abiaka-the-legacy-of-sam-jones/.

is known as the Southern Underground Railroad, aiding the escape of an estimated ten thousand enslaved people from Texas to Mexico.[22]

Today, the descendants of Black Seminoles in Mexico, known as Mascogos, celebrate their blended heritage with traditions like Juneteenth and Día de los Negroes. They eat a combo of Afrikan-Seminole and Mexican dishes, such as corn on the cob, sweet potato bread, pumpkin empanadas, pan de mortero (mortar bread), soske (corn-based atole), and asada (slow-cooked pork in hot peppers).

The exodus John Horse led remains the largest mass movement of Maroons in US history. Some believe Horse lived well into his seventies, while others believe he disappeared or died while on a reaffirmation trip in 1882, never to be heard from again. Regardless, Horse died fighting until the end, trying to protect the land and freedom of the Black Seminoles.

St. John Horse

Whenever I returned home from school in tears because some child born with alabaster-colored skin had called me blackymoe or joked that I looked like a burnt biscuit left in the oven too long, my grandfather, Ernest Herrera, always knew what to do. He had a habit of calling the herb St. John's Wort "St. John Horse," and he would carefully wrap the dry herbs in a small muslin bag. Then he would whisper into the bag, "Don't ever let what folks call you define you. Words have the potential to run you crazy if you ain't careful. Take it from John Horse, a man who spent the larger part of his life enduring all that fighting, being lied to and lied on, being scattered like leaves in June walking from state to state. I know it 'bout drove him mad. You ain't got to tell me. John Horse was marked for depression from the day of his birth, but he withstood instead of withered. All the United States government wanted him to do was to wither away and die."

Afterward, Grandfather would brew a tea with the bag and pour a cup for him and one for me. Once my nervous system was calm and my solar

---

22. Nduta Waweru, "John Horse: The Black Indian Who Was a Pain in the Butts of the US Military in Florida," Face2Face Africa, June 26, 2018, https://face2faceafrica.com/article/john-horse-the-black-indian-who-was-a-pain-in-the-butts-of-u-s-military-in-florida.

plexus manipura chakra was aligned, I had the willpower, self-esteem, confidence, and strength of character to fight the nightmares draining my energy.

My grandfather would sip until all that was left was a circular island of honey residue he eased toward the rim. He'd stick his finger in the cup and swirl it around, allowing the honey to soak his index finger before one final slurp, which made us both giggle. Then he would ask, "What kind of wild-minded man goes south when everybody what think they know reasoning say go north? I heard that man went to Mexico with a pocket full of wort so that as they traveled, they could stuff pinches under their tongue to ensure not a one of them ever lost their mind. Even heard he fed pinches to his horse after the death of her foal. It took her only about a week before she was able to gallop through Nacimiento de Los Negros. John Horse deserves all the praise as the man who saved lives and minds, even with all that hardship. John proved to be a giant among mortals." Now ain't that saintly?

EXERCISE: ST. JOHN'S MENTAL FORTITUDE ALTAR (PART 1)

Your St. John Horse altar will be dedicated to mental fortitude. Please note, this is part one of a three-part working that includes making sofkee and writing a letter.

Needs:

* liquid black soap and water (enough to clean both shoes)
* a soft sponge or cloth
* Florida water in a spray bottle
* 2–3 yards dark green cloth
* 3 straw placemats
* 1 brown candle
* 1 green candle
* 1 black candle
* a Kongo cosmogram (see page 11)

- 3 pieces of Low John root
- a sheet of paper with the Odo Nnyew Fie Kwan adinkra symbol (see appendix D)
- a framed image of John Horse
- a framed image of the Florida Everglades
- a framed image representing Mascogos culture
- a mason jar filled with water
- a mason jar filled with graveyard soil
- a bowl of prepared sofkee (see recipe on page 54)
- a cauldron or other fireproof receptacle
- 1–2 charcoal disks
- 1–3 pieces of amber resin

Instructions:

Clean your altar with liquid black soap and water. Once dried, spritz it with Florida water, let it dry again, then let it sit untouched for twenty-four hours.

Place the cloth on the altar, then center the three placemats on top. Leave enough room between each so two candles can stand beside the center mat and one candle can stand in front of it. (It's your choice which candle goes where.)

Place the cosmogram on the center mat, then set the framed image of John Horse in front of it. Place the Low John on top of the adinkra symbol and position it near the cosmogram. For the other mats, place the framed image of the Florida Everglades on one and the framed image of Mascogos culture on the other. Place the mason jars and place the bowl of sofkee on your altar near the image of John Horse. Use your discretion in placing all the other items. Place a lit charcoal disk inside the cauldron, then add the resin. Light the three candles.

Once you've prepared the altar to open sacred space for John Horse, use the instructions in part 3 to write a letter to him.

RECIPE: SOFKEE (PART 2)

John Horse's Florida Seminoles and the Miccosukee Nations dried and ground corn (maize) long before the coming of Columbus. From this maize came sofkee, also known as polenta, yellow grits, or mamaliga in Romania.[23]

In my family, we eat sofkee to honor St. John Horse and to help channel the clarity we need to accomplish our daily tasks. A pot of sofkee can keep you full for a long time. It can be made plain or flavored with pumpkin, fruit, or other spices.

Ingredients:

* 2 tablespoons olive oil
* 1 cup cornmeal or polenta (yellow grits)
* 4–5 cups water
* sea salt
* cayenne pepper

Instructions:

Preheat an oven to 350 degrees Fahrenheit. Use the olive oil to oil a deep casserole dish. Pour in the cornmeal, water, and salt to taste. Stir until evenly moistened. Place in the oven, uncovered, for one hour. Remove from the oven, stir to ensure there are no lumps, then season with more sea salt, olive oil, and cayenne pepper to taste.

---

23. Sarah Pope, "Traditional Foods of the Seminole Tribe of Florida: A Healthy Home Economist," The Healthy Home Economist, February 11, 2012, https://www.thehealthyhomeeconomist.com/traditional-foods-of-the-seminole-tribe-of-florida/.

EXERCISE: WRITING A LETTER TO JOHN HORSE (PART 3)

After building your altar, you'll write your letter to John Horse. I've provided a start below, but make sure to add information about your personal frustrations to the letter. Name your discomfort; salvation can only be had when you name the pain.

Needs:
* pen and paper
* Psalms 70, 97, and 113 (see appendix C)

Instructions:
Write the following letter, adding your own details in the areas noted.

> Dear John Horse,
>
> In 1835, at the start of the Second Seminole War, more than 1,500 American soldiers were killed. It was claimed that the Black Seminoles contended with the full military power of the United States. Your resilience speaks to your refusal to be enslaved. Today, I honor your legacy of fighting against mental strain and turmoil. Be with me, Great Warrior. Your child [your name] is forever born to liberate.
>
> [your name]

After writing the letter, read it nine times, then recite Psalms 70, 97, and 113 three times each. Reread the letter each time you use the altar, and close by reciting the psalms.

The Black Woman's Drive to Succeed

When I think of John Horse, I think of the trauma he must have endured avoiding slave catchers, eluding four attempts on his life, and surviving three wars. His anxiety had to have been through the roof!

Today BIPOC people still suffer at the hands of privileged Whites. John Horse's mental fortitude, for me, parallels the way many Black and Brown women walk through life every day. A 2015 meta-analysis indicated the association between racism and mental health is twice as strong as the link between racism and physical health. BIPOC individuals reported that, along with experiences of racism, they encountered mental health issues that included PTSD and suicidal thoughts. Research also suggested that the fear of racism is harmful in that it has the potential to undermine a person's resilience, hope, and motivation.[24] This undermining of potential also affects the health of children, adolescents, and emerging adults.

Moreover, for Black and Brown women, living at the intersection of racism and sexism is no easy feat. Let's examine the facts: 54 percent of Black women have experienced being the only or one of the only Black people in the room. When in meetings, these women often feel closely watched and that a bad decision or poor performance might reflect negatively on their entire race. Black women enroll in college at higher rates than men across races. Between 2004 and 2014, Black women with bachelor's degrees or higher increased by 24 percent. When listing their motivations, many ambitious Black women say they want to become top executives to influence their workplace cultures.[25]

Diving Deeper

Robin Boylorn, an intercultural communications professor at the University of Alabama, told the BBC that it seems impossible to be a Black woman and not be angry, after "generations of oppression, discrimination, and erasure."[26] She went on to express the sentiment, "Men are allowed to be angry as a performance of masculinity. White women are allowed to be

---

24. "Racism as a Determinant of Health: A Systematic Review and Meta-Analysis," *PLoS One* 10, no. 9 (September 23, 2015), https://doi.org/10.1371/journal.pone.0138511.
25. "Working at the Intersection: What Black Women Are Up Against," Lean In, accessed January 19, 2020, https://leanin.org/black-women-racism-discrimination-at-work.
26. Ritu Prasad, "Serena Williams and the Trope of the 'Angry Black Woman,'" *BBC News*, September 11, 2018, https://www.bbc.com/news/world-us-canada-45476500.

angry as a clarion call. So Black women should be encouraged to express their anger as well, particularly in the face of injustice."[27]

Black women are oftentimes on the receiving end of discrimination as a result of tone bias. We're dismissed as screamers and yellers who live to chastise everyone—Black men. Black children. White people. Anytime a Black woman speaks with authority or conviction, she's immediately perceived as angry, which often means a low performance score and no chance for a raise. When we speak up against workplace microaggressions, we can be verbally reprimanded for being overly ambitious and "out for ourselves." But simultaneously, as women of color, we're expected to always bring our A game. We have to be the most proficient, well versed, always capable, and forever available. The fate of our entire race relies on it.

I don't know any Black woman who hasn't been labeled an "angry Black woman" at some point. You know the stereotype: It's the hostile, aggressive, overbearing, illogical, ill-tempered, and bitter Black woman who can't play nicely in dignified company.

The angry Black woman is a trope I believe originated during the time of Afrikan enslavement. Angry women were often those who fought against rape, and those like Margret Garner, who preferred to see her daughter dead by her own hands rather than be subjected to ownership. When we examine angry Black women through the ages, it's clear the media has played a role in feeding us the idea that Black women who fight to be heard are ignorant. Television characters like *Amos 'n' Andy's* Sapphire, *The Jeffersons'* Florence, and Sheneneh from the hit sitcom *Martin* are just a few examples.

When I speak with Black women about how this trope affects their working environments, the consistent theme is that you're damned if you do speak up, and eliminated from the conversation when you don't. They feel they have no choice but to make their peace with other people's perceptions and keep aggressively moving toward success as best they can. I've had sistahs repeatedly tell me they didn't go through graduate school, medical school, or law school just to walk on eggshells.

....
27. Prasad, "Serena Williams."

One sistah credits hip-hop and Hoodoo with preparing her for the battle waged at her job every day. "I'm a mechanical engineer, a career choice I love. The White men at work used to waste no time drowning me out of every situation, but now I bring my loud and proud mouth to the conference room every day. I used to debate in college, and I was a cheerleader; getting loud don't mean nothing to me. Think about it: I'm not just fighting White men but their women, who by default always have their say over the Black chick. Fuck that. My ancestors didn't live through hell just so I could grovel. I play my hip-hop mix right before I get out of the car. I'm in the parking garage jamming. They leave that conference room knowing the biggest dick in the room ain't theirs, it's my clit."

The Georgetown Law's Center on Poverty and Inequality examined the experiences of girls between the ages of ten and fourteen with childhood racism. They found many had experienced harmful perceptions that Black girls were more mature and less in need of protection than White female students the same age.[28] Perceptions that label Black girls as having bad attitudes, being ready to fight, and being oppositionally defiant are all forms of adultification bias, a form of racial prejudice where children of minority groups, mainly Black and Brown, are treated as more mature than they actually are. Another harmful perception is that Black girls are less innocent than White girls. When Black girls express views that are contrary to the status quo, they're immediately labeled "bad" and often suspended or expelled. Black girls are three times more likely to be referred to the juvenile justice system than White girls.[29]

The following *Scream Water* ritual can and should be walked through with our young girls. As much as scream water helps to console us, it will aid them. Racism doesn't just happen to adults. So if you know of young people who are experiencing racial bias, especially as students, I encourage you to fight the fight legally, with conferences, and with magick.

....

28. P. R. Lockhart, "A New Report Shows How Racism and Bias Deny Black Girls Their Childhoods," *Vox*, May 16, 2019, https://www.vox.com/identities/2019/5/16/18624683/black-girls-racism-bias-adultification-discipline-georgetown.
29. "Black Girls Viewed as Less Innocent than White Girls, Georgetown Law Research Finds," Georgetown Law, June 27, 2017, https://www.law.georgetown.edu/news/black-girls-viewed-as-less-innocent-than-white-girls-georgetown-law-research-finds-2/.

EXERCISE: SCREAM WATER

Scream water aids in drawing out the animosity you feel whenever your leadership capabilities are questioned, your performance is criticized, or your self-advocacy is labeled "controlling" or "hyperemotional." This spritz channels your anger and frustration toward the ones who truly deserve to feel it (and trust me, they will!).

Needs:

* a bowl or pot of plain water (*Note:* The size doesn't matter so long as the water isn't spilling over the top)
* a small spray bottle or cotton balls
* mason jars (to hold any extra water not used for spritzing)
* Psalm 3 (see appendix C)

Instructions:

Hold an image in your mind of the people who've demeaned you. Recite Psalm 3 nine times (I like to bring the water to a boil first, but you don't have to), then scream the names of the offending individuals into the water. Go at it for as long as you feel the anger coursing through your veins.

Once you've determined enough is enough, pour some of the scream water into a spray bottle small enough to fit in a purse or work bag. Working discreetly, spritz the water around the individuals' spaces or any objects they regularly touch. For example, I've spritzed office floors and car doors, windshields, and tires. (*Note:* For safety's sake, I encourage young people to moisten cotton balls with this water and drop them in problematic places instead of spritzing.) Repeat once a week.

EXERCISE: SELF-AFFIRMING GODDESS TEA

Another tool that keeps me sane is this self-affirming goddess tea. It helps me to not let my anger rule the day and become the sole deciding force in my life.

This is a tea that will particularly call to you after a hard day at work. Some days, I ain't going to lie, I might down two cups before advancing to my recipe for scream water.

Needs:

* plain water
* a tea setting (cup, spoon, and saucer)
* 1–2 reusable tea bags or 2 5 x 5 inch pieces of cheesecloth and 5–9 inches of twine
* 1 tablespoon dried peppermint
* 1 tablespoon dried lemon balm
* Psalm 3 (see appendix C)
* 1 pinch ground cinnamon
* 20–30 drops Kava liquid
* honey, agave, or other sweetener

Instructions:

Set the water to boil. Add the herbs to your reusable tea bags or cheesecloth and close. Once the water boils, pour a portion into the cup, add the tea bags, and cover with the saucer. Let the tea steep for five to seven minutes. As it does, recite Psalm 3 over the covered cup nine times. After the tea has steeped, stir in the cinnamon, kava, and honey to taste. Drink this tea slowly while envisioning a woman who speaks her mind without feeding into stereotypical innuendos.

LYNEL

I had a once-upon-a-time White coworker named Holly, an imbecile hired to be overseer of operations at the school where I worked. Before I even met Holly, my boss and the vice principal were singing her praises. They went on and on about how they had found the perfect lead teacher for my special education team, a team where the two senior members were an Afrikan American woman and a Puerto Rican woman, both employed by the same school for over a decade. Yet here we were, and there was Holly. Holly, who presided over us not with wealth or educational intellect but with her White pedigree.

Here's just one example: Holly and I were asked to attend a meeting with a very wealthy White couple, evangelicals who felt that BIPOC people were better off as custodians or cafeteria workers instead of teachers. (Yes, they said as much to me on the day they were invited to tour the school.) The meeting was set two months in advance, so we all had plenty of time to prepare.

On the morning of the meeting, Holly showed up in tears. Her face was beet red, and her hair looked like she had stuck her tongue in a socket. She claimed she didn't have her work done because her home printer ran out of ink and she got in a fight with her husband. Then she started screaming profanities about suffering through a thankless marriage to an idiot.

When our boss questioned her about her appearance, she just growled and started pulling her hair out and chewing it. Then she peeled her purse from her shoulder, only to toss every item inside while hurling profanities at everyone present, including the parents. The boss again tried to calm her by telling her she understood Holly was a perfectionist. Even the parents chimed in, offering her hugs and prayers. Worst of all, when all was said and done, Holly's fuckup had magically become my fault.

I swear, were it not for your Hoodoo, I might still be out of work or in jail, because I was about to choke a bitch out. But I know going upside a bitch's head won't change how I'm viewed; it will only make matters worse. Your tea has saved me more days than I can count.

EXERCISE: TALK THAT TALK BEFORE YOU WALK THAT WALK TEA

Here's the tea I advised Lynel to use.

Needs:

* plain water
* a tea setting (cup, spoon, and saucer)
* 1–2 reusable tea bags or 2 5 x 5 inch pieces of cheesecloth and 5–9 inches of twine
* 2 teaspoons dried tulsi
* 2 teaspoons dried chrysanthemum
* 2 teaspoons dried jasmine
* honey, agave, or other sweetener
* Psalms 11 and 12 (see appendix C)

Instructions:

Set the water to boil. Add the herbs to your reusable tea bags or cheesecloth and close. Once the water boils, pour a portion into the cup, add the tea bags, and cover with the saucer. Let the tea steep for five to seven minutes. As it does, recite Psalms 11 and 12 over the covered cup three times each. After the tea has steeped, stir in honey to taste and drink slowly. The tea will help you calm down and process your decisions.

Variation:

I drink this tea in front of my John Horse altar. Between sips, I recite an incantation from a sheet of paper: *I will not be moved unless I want to pick up and go. I stand on my square, as divinely and eloquently as the next. My intelligence may be questioned by you, but never by me. You are nothing in the greater scheme of my universe. I am the treasure born* from my ancestors' toils. Money don't run me, honey. I choose to abide by the laws of truth, release, and balance.

On the back of the incantation, I draw the Ananse Ntentan (Ananse Ntotan) adinkra symbol (see appendix D). I leave the incantation on the altar until it's served its purpose, then I burn it and sprinkle the ashes under the mat outside my front door, or the mat in my car. I leave the ashes for a month before sweeping them away.

Juju on the Fly

Dawn, a twenty-one-year-old Afrikan American woman, emailed me about a riff that tore a hole through her fifteen-year friendship with Traci, a White woman of the same age.

At the predominantly Black schools they attended, there was never, as far as Dawn could remember, an emphasis on skin color, except for one time when they were in the ninth grade. Dawn described the altercation as Dorrell, a Black male student, got mad when he couldn't get play from Traci. He started drilling her about why she was at a Black school if she didn't plan on giving Black boys play. There were White schools in the city, and he questioned whether Traci was dumb, poor, or both, and so had no choice but to learn with niggahs. Dawn said Traci's eyes started swelling up. She knew she was on the verge of crying. Dawn jumped in by punching the boy in the mouth. It was that day the two girls started calling themselves sisters from another mother.

DAWN

While the three of us were sitting in the principal's office waiting for him to return from a board meeting across town, Traci kept whispering to me, "Let's not make this about me being White. Let's just say Dorrell tripped you by mistake, and you thought he was trying to make his friends laugh. You misread the whole thing."

Dorrell spoke up before I could answer. "I just asked a question, and your homegirl Dawn hit the shit out of me. Yawl dyking or something? The White girl, she your boo? That's why a brother can't get no play?"

I had to jump in. I wasn't going to allow Dorrell to go around telling the entire student body I was a lesbian and that he got that bloody mouth from trying to come between me and my White lover. No fucking way! Not when I had my eyes on Carver McDaniel. I reminded Dorrell that his brother was a senior track star, highly sought after by scouts. That meant if a racial incident got out with his little brother's name attached, it could ruin his track future.

By the time the principal turned the knob, we had fashioned a story about tripping and a slap that was way too hard, a slap that could all be explained through the exonerating tone of Traci's Whiteness. We walked out of that room free and with a firsthand view of the power of Whiteness. We even became besties, the three musketeers.

Turns out Dorrell was gay and hoping if he brought Traci home, his family would lose their shit and convince him to date anybody but a White chick. He eventually got accepted into a fashion design school. Traci and I went to a local college and decided we'd spread our wings and fly away for graduate school, like a PhD program somewhere far from the parents who still wanted to run not only our bank accounts, but our lives. We went to an HBCU for undergrad. Later, we researched PhD programs and finally settled on a lily-White site more than three hundred miles away. Dorrell kept repeating, "Be careful. Join or start a Black student union." He also warned me that Traci might change once she got around her people.

TRACI

Dawn wants the world to keep banging its head against an invisible wall just to prove Black people didn't go through a terrible set of events. She wants every White person to diversify their thinking to balance out the fact that the philosophy behind one race having the upper hand over another isn't my fault. It's not my mom's doing or my father's. They can't help that they were born White and that the White founders of America laid the framework for generations of historic imbalances. I didn't make this world, but I'd be a fool to deny myself the advantages of being me.

Dorrell was always filling Dawn's head with tales of White supremacy and how one day I was going to wake up a neo-Nazi. You want the truth? Dawn struggled to fit in. The people at the school weren't used to stuff like Black Lives Matter, which Dawn interjected into nine out of ten conversations. Like I told Dawn, you can't blame people for not seeing the correlation between their color and some form of fake privilege. I was poor too. Sometimes I wore dresses made by Dawn's mother.

There was this time when Dawn invited Dorrell to a mixer that one of the students, Delken, was having up in the mountains. The trip involved hiking, kayaking, and sleeping under the stars. I thought Dawn could show the seven others who she really was. They'd see she wasn't accepted into such a prestigious school because of affirmative action, but rather she was an overachieving Black woman fighting to be heard; she wasn't a threat. At least that's what I thought, until she let Dorrell brainwash her into a Black versus White agenda. She became this liberal attack dog, getting up every day just to trick White professors into saying something insensitive. They already thought she was a show-off—all that cabbage patching every time she aced a quiz or exam. I tried to convince her to let them see her fuck up for once.

You can imagine how pissed off I was when the cab pulled up to the bus station and out walked Dorrell carrying two duffle bags. I'll never forget it. He was dressed like a Black Paul Bunyan; all he needed was a blue ox. I know by now you get the picture that there is no love lost between Dorrell and me. I think he tolerated me because of my color. He wasn't really my friend from day one. Dawn was the bridge that was ready to be detonated. He forgot that I could've derailed his future and that of his brother.

I was fuming and fed up with Dorrell. He fucked up the entire trip, excuse my French. He did what he always does: he convinced Dawn to become Bree Newsome, tugging at these clueless White men and women's *integrity. She and Dorrell spent the trip starting fights, and when they had enough, Dorrell liberated their asses home. Yes, they were asked to leave, and nope, I didn't intercede. Dawn moved out of the apartment we were sharing, dropped out of the university, and moved in with Dorrell and his lover. She enrolled in an HBCU, and I didn't talk to her again until an education conference in Florida.*

DORRELL

Dawn is smart, way smarter than Traci, but those racists kept treating her research like it was created by artificial intelligence. She was an inmate at that school, and the wardens were having none of her Amos Wilson Alvin Poussaint shit. She was outshining White students, and a decision was made by the Whites to fade Dawn to black.

Even back in high school Traci was aware of her privilege. She played the game "blend in until you don't need to blend in." Dawn didn't do nothing out of order. We know when in the company of White folks they already got it in their head you don't belong, so you gotta work ten times harder than they do. In the end, Traci with her C average got the cushy job, a job with all them zeros behind it, and Dawn with her A+ average is praying every year for tenure. Don't get me started, but at least Dawn is happy living a life that ain't always easy. She knows she ain't killing her spirit to be something she could never morph into: a cringe-level, mediocre blondie.

After talking to Dawn, Traci, and Dorrell sporadically for over a year, I tried to make them aware of how racism was the central theme of their on-again, off-again relationship. I tried to engage Traci in an open conversation about repairing her friendship with Dawn. Part of my prescription was for her to participate in workshops that centered around White privilege. I listed several opportunities for Traci to delve deep into how White privilege had played a major role in how she was beginning to view her path for success. I had hoped for Dawn's sake, who at the time very much wanted a relationship with Traci, that Traci would not take offense to how, even growing up poor and White, she was still a beneficiary of White supremacy ideology. Traci became defensive and tried to explain that even though she was earning a six-figure salary, she had started out the same as Dawn, which in her mind meant she could never truly be someone who benefited from White privilege. She believed that her parents, like Dawn's, were high school educated, blue-collar workers who never once gained from their Whiteness.

I told Traci that on that fateful day of the fight, her words could've gotten two students expelled and ended the athletic career of another. Her words could've gotten teachers and even the principal reprimanded, and possibly enraged an entire community. A White girl crying is always heard, and she's attended to with care and precision. Traci hung up before I could say more.

After years of therapy and spiritual healing, Dawn and Dorrell were over it. Dorrell asked me for a business reading for them; he felt like spiritually, they could both use a reboot. They had forgotten how to be present for their own goals. I told them to also remember the importance of therapy, and that they needed support groups and ways to channel safe spaces as they moved away from this idea of salvaging relationships rooted in White privilege. Dorrell said his business was good, but it could be better, and it would be if he didn't have to spend so much time hyping up Dawn's broken esteem. He said he loved Dawn, but he wanted her to stop measuring herself again against Traci's achievements; he felt like that was Dawn's only problem. She was always hoping she and Traci would fall back into a friendship.

I assigned Dawn and Dorrell a reading: "White Privilege: Unpacking the Invisible Knapsack" by Peggy McIntosh. They had to journal. They also had to read articles on White supremacy, microaggressions, and workplace racism, and they had to interact with every story they read to see how every encounter made them feel and to think of ways they would change the outcomes of those stories.

EXERCISE: CELEBRATE YOUR HUBRIS

The following ritual helps increase one's self-esteem or hubris. It celebrates the need to overachieve and not "shut the fuck up," slow down, or blend in with the crowd.

Please note, this is the first part of a two-part working. Three days after celebrating your hubris, you'll make a pot of intuitive enchantment tea (see recipe on the following page).

Needs:
* plain water
* a tea setting (cup, spoon, and saucer)
* 1 tablespoon dried lemongrass
* 1 tablespoon dried elderberry
* 1 teaspoon powdered anise
* 1–2 reusable tea bags or 2 5 x 5 inch pieces of cheesecloth and 5–9 inches of twine
* 1 each of the Clouds, the Coffin, the Stars, and the Woman/Man Lenormand cards (*Note:* With the Woman/Man cards, choose the one you identify with)
* honey, agave, or other sweetener
* Psalms 3, 4, and 5 (see appendix C)

Instructions:
Set the water to boil. Add the herbs to your reusable tea bags or cheesecloth and close. Once the water boils, pour a portion into the cup, add the tea bags, and cover with the saucer. Let the tea steep for five to seven minutes while you complete the rest of the working.

Recite Psalms 3, 4, and 5 over the covered cup nine times each. Light your altar candles and ask John Horse to assist you in navigating this emotional subjugation. Place the Lenormand cards on your altar. The Woman/Man card represents you, while the Clouds represent confusion, insecurity, and the uncertainty you want removed from your life. The Coffin symbolizes the transformation required for you to heal and accept your losses and gains. The Stars card is a reminder to go after *your* dreams, not other people's, and to honor your destiny as it relates to the abundance you've inherited in this life, in this body.

After the tea has steeped, stir in honey to taste and enjoy your hubris drink.

EXERCISE: INTUITIVE ENCHANTMENT TEA (PART 2)

This tea helps you stop accommodating other folks' dreams and give you more grace in pursuing your own. Drink it over the three days immediately following the hubris ritual to promote spiritual growth and soul-level self-awareness.

Needs:

* a sheet of paper with the Abode Santann adinkra symbol (see appendix D)
* a tea setting (cup, spoon, and saucer)
* Psalms 3, 4, and 5 (see appendix C)
* plain water
* 1–2 reusable tea bags or 2 5 x 5 inch pieces of cheesecloth and 5–9 inches of twine
* 1 teaspoon dried licorice root
* 1 teaspoon powdered cranberry
* 1 teaspoon dried rose buds
* 1 tablespoon dried jasmine
* honey, agave, or other sweetener

Instructions:

Place the adinkra symbol on the saucer. (You may need to fold or cut down the paper to make it fit.) Holding the saucer, recite Psalms 3, 4, and 5 over the symbol nine times, then set it aside.

Set the water to boil. Add the herbs to your reusable tea bags or cheesecloth and close. Once the water boils, pour a portion into the cup, add the tea bags, and cover with the saucer. Let the tea steep for five to seven minutes. As it does, light your altar candles and ask John Horse to enchant your life with intuitive favor and the mindset to move beyond the mental prisons of those who would have you spend an eternity in hiding.

After the tea has steeped, stir in honey to taste and repeat the following: *The fruits of my labor deserve to be experienced. I am not bossy. I am someone who exhibits the qualities of an exceptional leader. I am the proactive go-getter this world needs but oftentimes doesn't deserve.*

All teas can be consumed two to three times per week or whenever you get the urge to navigate over, under, and straight through White privilege and its many minions.

Chapter Four
Queen Julia Brown:
Protection from Overwork

The home of Queen Julia Brown (1845–1915) is located in Frenier, Louisiana, nestled four miles northeast of Laplace in St. John the Baptist Parish. Frenier's story is one part Louisiana history and one part Hoodoo/Voodoo lore.

When I was growing up, I attended a Catholic school, and while there, our historical studies began and ended with all things Louisiana. You can imagine my excitement when in fourth grade my teacher gave us permission slips for a boat tour through the waters of the Manchac Swamp. But before we were allowed to board a tour boat, we had to study the story of Frenier.

The surname Frenier has its origins in the French province of Bourgogne. The family line can be traced back to Thibault, the lord of Freshes who, in 1358, was in service to the Duke of Burgundy.[30] However, the town also has German roots: Originally, it was called Schlosser after two German immigrants, Martin and his brother Adam. Together, the pair cleared the area forests to create a lucrative timber industry.

As time progressed, the community of Schlosser grew to over twenty-five families. This growth spurt made the timber industry competitive, but the brothers knew it would prove financial suicide if they continued. Instead, they decided to cast their financial lot in cabbage farming. Since the Louisiana soil was good for cabbage, the brothers exported sauerkraut to New Orleans. For decades this was their families' main source of income, and it made them very wealthy.[31]

....
30. "The Lost City of Frenier," *Southern Gothic* (blog), March 26, 2018, https://www.southerngothicmedia.com/blog/2018/3/24/episode-003-the-lost-city-of-frenier.
31. "Hollier on Da Bayou: Swamp Legends, Voodoo Queen of Manchac Swamp, Julia Brown," *Hollier on Da Bayou* (blog), July 24, 2018, https://hollierondabayou.blogspot.com/2018/07/swamp-legends-voodoo-queen-of-manchac.html.

But the story that put Frenier on the map has to do with a Hoodoo and Voodoo/Vodoun practitioner named Queen Julia Brown.

The Real Queen Julia

Some historical accounts say Queen Julia (also known as Julie White) was a priestess of Voodoo who lived and presided over the spiritual needs of Frenier. She was a healer renowned for her gris gris, juju, and crossings, and she spent many a day sitting on her porch, strumming her guitar while singing prophetic dirges that folks often regarded as curses. Some claimed she had sold her soul to the devil so she could see all the problems folks had swarming around their lives, and with that knowledge, Satan would cause these folks many restless nights. Once these individuals were beat down and ready to be rid of this emotional toil, they would then be led straight to the front door of Queen Julia Brown. They believed that after getting help from Julia, payment would come in the form of selling their own souls to Satan. In this way, many people feared that her second sight was a way to gather souls for the devil's army. In fact, people who came to her for healing began to whisper about her. They wondered if she was actually causing their troubles with her magick just to keep them as clients.

The dirge Brown is most noted for is the one that established the fearsome reputation she has to this day. The refrain went like this: "One day, I'm going to die and take this whole town with me."[32] On September 29, 1915, a monster of a hurricane slammed southern Louisiana for an entire day. The storm surge rose thirteen feet, with winds reaching 125 miles an hour. While many New Orleans residents were warned a few days before the direct hit, there wasn't enough time for the news to reach Frenier. When many residents made their way to what was seen as the safest location, the railroad depot, no one could predict its collapse and the deaths of the twenty-five townspeople who were huddled inside.

....

32. "Sinister Manchac Swamp and the Chilling Curse of Julia Brown," Ancient Pages, August 25, 2021, https://www.ancientpages.com/2021/08/25/sinister-manchac-swamp-and-the-chilling-curse-of-julia-brown/.

The storm washed over Southern Louisiana, leaving a death toll of close to three hundred lives lost. By October 1, 1915, the towns of Frenier, Ruddock, and Napoleon had been virtually washed away. A newspaper account described Brown's funeral on the day of the storm: "At 4 o'clock, however, the storm had become so violent that the Negroes left the house in a stampede, abandoning the courts. The corpse was found Thursday, and so was the wooden box, but the casket never had been found."[33]

I've spoken with Hoodoo and Voodoo practitioners who've heard stories passed down through their lineage about Queen Julia's well-respected ability in the area of conjuring, which made some folks very jealous. Even though she pointed folks toward safety, some took her advice and carved out their own opinions about her second sight.

Other people believe Queen Julia was a money-grubber, and when she felt she wasn't paid enough by the townspeople for all she had brought them through, she went back to the devil to conjure up that hurricane. The devil, not one known to play fair, told her that to grant her wish, he'd need her soul ASAP. Julia replied that she was so sick and tired of the townspeople and their bullshit that their eternal rest was fine with her.

Even today, guides who cruise tourists through the Machac Swamp tell the tale of Queen Julia Brown, the woman who cursed an entire town. Some swear that if you step off the boat just as the sun goes down and tiptoe toward the graveyard, you can still hear Queen Julia cackling up to the storm and singing her refrain.

My teachings on Queen Julia Brown were about a woman born Julia Bernard in Louisiana sometime around the year 1845. She went on to marry a man named Celestin Brown in 1880. Somewhere around 1900, the federal government gave her husband a 40-acre homestead. Upon Celestin's death in 1914, the homestead was transferred to Julia. Since Frenier was heavily populated with poor folks who couldn't afford to travel to New Orleans for a doctor, *traiteur* (folk healer), midwife, or two-headed woman, Julia saw

---
33. "Sinister Manchac Swamp."

a chance to help folks in need while also carving out a life as a self-made woman of privilege and merit.

I was told by my grandmother that the fear folks felt was actually shame. "They were ashamed that this woman, who had given so much, was a woman they took for granted, a woman they characterized as evil, and at the last seconds of her life, they shunned her help. They knew they owed Queen Julia Brown their lives. They knew she was a two-headed woman; she wasn't two-faced or malicious."

My grandfather said he heard she had died trying to steer the storm away from Louisiana. "The ritual went on for weeks. It required more than one conjure woman; I heard the recipe calls for three, but Julia was all they had, so the spell took a toll on her body. She was tired from a lack of sleep. Most days, her brain was so rattled that all she could do was sing that song. If nothing else, she hoped and prayed the townspeople would get scared enough of that haunting dirge to leave Frenier and never look back."

Julia Brown is exalted to sainthood because she's the quintessential healer who spent her life trying to reroute folks to safer shores. When patrons no longer flooded her porch, she turned her message into a song that could not be ignored. Her death is martyrdom, a truth that can no longer be denied: even healers need to be noticed.

I remember a saying my grandmother would whisper about women and witch hunts, how sometimes the most potent form of murder is to be overlooked, voided out in plain sight. Then she would go on to tell me about women who step into towns where no one understands their intentions, and how these women are often scapegoated as witches. The most painful of these instances happen to women who dwell in the lap of familiarity.

EXERCISE: QUEEN JULIA BROWN ALTAR

Too often in this world healers either go unnoticed or get wrongly accused of being heretics and monsters, especially in death. Create an altar to Queen Julia Brown to reverse this reality.

Needs:

* 2–3 yards black cloth
* 1 small toy train set (large enough to encircle the altar cloth)
* a large basin (should fit comfortably on your altar)
* plain water
* 2–3 drops green food coloring
* 3 small toy alligators
* 1 green candle
* 1 black candle
* a framed image of Queen Julia Brown
* a pen
* 1 3 x 5 inch index card
* glue
* 1 popsicle stick
* modeling clay
* 1 small toy guitar
* 1 small toy wooden cabin
* cabbage and cornbread, prepared
* a bowl
* Psalm 67 (see appendix C)

Instructions:

Place the cloth over a table or on the floor, then set up the train set so that it encircles it. Fill the basin with water, leaving two to three inches clear at the top. Add the food coloring, then drop the alligators in the water.

Place the candles on either side of the image of Queen Julia Brown, then write "Frenier, Louisiana" on one side of the index card and "Queen Julia Brown" on the other. Glue the cardstock to the popsicle stick. Using the modeling clay, create an oval mound sturdy enough to stand on its own. Once the glue on the cardstock has dried, stick the bottom of the popsicle stick into the clay so the card stands up like a signpost marker. Place the marker on the altar.

Prepare the cabbage and cornbread. (You can surf the internet for options or use a family recipe.) Place a portion of each in the bowl, place the bowl on the altar, then lay out the remaining items beside it. (Use your discretion as part of your placement design.) Recite Psalm 67 nine times.

Wellness and Revolutionary Resilience

A few years ago, my eldest daughter called me from Havana, Cuba, asking me to divine using opele. She was curious about the energy surrounding a young man she was interested in. She had met this young man through social media, and their talks, according to her, were sweet and intellectual. But he was beginning to show possessive views around relationships. The young man's parents had divorced when he was twelve years old over his mother's infidelity, which had destroyed his belief in family values. I threw on it and immediately my maternal grandfather, who serves as my spirit guide, whispered that the young man was surrounded by death.

As I read the opele, a gust of wind entered the room, blowing the divining chain off the table and onto the couch behind me. I glanced out the sliding glass door to the backyard while turning to retrieve the opele. Standing there was a woman in a black brocade dress with a golden veil and an opele of her own in her left hand with a skull in her right. She spoke to me telepathically, calling me by my Ifa name, Ifaniyi Aboyade Omobola Bomani. She introduced herself as Death. She laughed and dared me to look away. I remember checking my ide to make certain Death wasn't here to claim my life. She ran her claws like nails over the glass, tapping every now and then, and her words were ice cold. "You keep questioning whether or not this boy is good enough for your daughter. Try to make that opele show you what's coming. Go on, try it, but you won't like the result. What he brings is me."

She grinned and pointed to the image of my daughter. I began to feel as though someone was applying immense pressure to my forehead. It was as if someone was drilling a hole at the crown of my head and then filling my skull with water. Death's voice reverberated through the pain: "He will die by his own hands. He will take your daughter with him. I can smell the gunpowder, taste the fragments of metal shard beneath my tongue."

I was in tears and got up to grab a tissue. When I turned back toward the table, Death was gone. That reading had lasted two hours, and I felt like I had spent it in a boxing ring dodging Mike Tyson. I had a migraine that was out of this stratosphere. I was dehydrated and nauseous, and I felt as though I was walking on horribly thin air.

Immediately after phoning my daughter and relaying my encounter with Death, she was onboard with ending the relationship. She tried to have the conversation about distancing themselves rather than simply ghosting him, but he became verbally abusive and emotionally distraught. She deleted the young man from her social media, and I had to cleanse my aura and hers from this spiritual shitstorm.

Although my daughter's cleanse was virtual, it still proved extremely effective. I pulled out my ankle bells and tied them in place to aid me in grounding both our spirits to this earth. Then I took two cotton balls, one for me and one for her, saturated them with coconut oil and shea butter, then placed both at the center of my head. I tied a white scarf over my head to keep the cotton balls in place. Finally, I drank my *They'll Be Damned If You Do and Damned If You Don't Tea*. Once I felt the nausea and dehydration subside, I picked up my singing bowl and called calm to me for thirty minutes. Afterward, I crawled into bed.

Diving Deeper

My spiritual work often puts me face-to-face with spiritual entities who require energy to manifest, to communicate, and to interact with the living in ways we're comfortable with. I believe that as our brain tries to make sense of our spiritual communication with the world beyond the veil, our rational brain balks and wants to shut out all irrational scenes. This, in my opinion, affects our overall physical health. The more society develops a deeper understanding of what diviners do and take on while accessing a client's spiritual inquiries, the deeper the acceptance will be when the diviner says, "I need to protect my peace."

In fact, protecting one's peace, whether or not you're a diviner, begins with abandoning social media for a few days, seeking instead to meditate, do yoga, journal, talk to a therapist, get a massage, make a sauna date, seek out a sweat lodge or reiki, do aromatherapy, or get acupuncture.

Dr. Nedra Glover Tawwab in her article "Give Yourself Time to Heal" acknowledges that everyone on the path to healing has to trust their feelings, giving themselves the space to figure out when they're healed enough to reenter a given situation. Personally, I had to learn to trust my feelings and my personal healing process. I had to come to terms with the fact that my healing story would fit my personal commitment to self-care. My needs and my nonnegotiable boundaries were my business, and they weren't up for debate.

Ayahuasca (pronounced eye-ah-WAH-ska) is a psychedelic in plant form. It can be brewed into a tea or smoked. It has helped many users find spiritual ease while taking emotional responsibility for their current lives. It's also been a major part of my and my clients' journeys, along with ritual. Ayahuasca can be intense, and using it to revisit past traumas can feel like living through a long, terrifyingly dark night of the soul. However, it has proved to be a positive healing agent that Amazonian cultures have used for more than three thousand years in sacred rituals, magickal ceremonies, and to address psychological and physical concerns.

Many of my clients say their journey with ayahuasca allowed them to visit past traumas and to envision a new way of confronting and mastering their healing paths. After their journey, they experienced a peace and happiness, a new love for the soul within. I'm not saying ayahuasca is for everyone, but I've used it to successfully divine for many clients whose past lives have greatly scarred their current life.

If you're interested in ayahuasca medicine, here are a few highly regarded retreat centers known for their ethical practices and comprehensive support:

- Temple of the Way of Light (Peru)
- Rythmia Life Advancement Center (Costa Rica)
- Spirit Vine Ayahuasca Retreat Center (Brazil)
- Soltara Healing Center (Costa Rica)
- Nihue Rao Centro Espiritual (Peru)[34]

Allison's Story

I had an on-again, off-again client who thought her weight (five hundred pounds) meant the only man who would want her was a man in jail serving a thirty-year life sentence. At the time I began divining for Allison, she never would say what he did, only that she believed he was a victim of the school-to-prison pipeline. LaJuan was on year twelve of his sentence when Allison came to me for divination. She was thirty-six and he was forty-eight. Allison would drive 135 miles from her home to the state penitentiary for their conjugal visits. As she put it, "Ain't nothing like dick on lockdown."

Before I became her weekly diviner, Allison warned me that under no condition would she give up her relationship with LaJuan. Before him her last sexual partners were a meetup in Atlanta with a couple who practiced polyamory. This couple didn't believe she was as huge as she was (these were her words), and when it came time to get it on, the husband put a condom on a broom handle and inserted it inside of her vagina. That was three years before her volunteer work at the penitentiary teaching a GED course in English, which is where she met LaJuan.

---

34. Tomiko, "13 Best Ayahuasca Retreats around the World (July 2024)," Passports and Grub, July 1, 2024, https://passportsandgrub.com/the-best-ayahuasca-retreats/.

She would say, "Where else can a big ass Black woman find a man always ready to fuck her with no reservations?" She told me over and over how much he nurtured all of her and reminded me how LaJuan looked just like 50 Cent. Our divination sessions typically lasted ninety minutes. I would divine with Lenormand, playing cards, and bones, walking Allison through what Spirit had devoted. She would then proceed to disregard the reading and do the opposite of what Spirit had prescribed.

Against my better judgment, Allison decided to move closer to the penitentiary and eventually have a baby with LaJuan. After two years of Allison ignoring my prescriptions and then calling me at five in the morning to bitch about how God was conspiring against her, I told her to stop crying and listen. I proceeded to read the Grand Tableau spread using all thirty-six Lenormand cards. Apparently, her lover wasn't only sexing her up, but he had been a big booty boy rapist of most of the prisoners in his cell block. He also had other chunky honeys visiting him on the days she couldn't. Spirit also told Allison to get a full physical.

None of this went well with her. She once again accused me of using my reading to fat-shame her. She said I didn't want to see a fat chick getting dicked down. She accused me of being jealous and more concerned with sowing doom and gloom in her picture-perfect love life. She said I was summoning unhappiness on purpose so she'd remain a lifelong client and that she never wanted to fuck with me again. She would, however, let me stay her Facebook friend, just so I could watch her and her penitentiary lover have their baby. Then she slammed the phone down.

About a year later, I saw a jaw-dropping announcement from Allison on Facebook. Apparently, she had contracted HIV. She found out a week before a trip to Tijuana for gastric bypass surgery. I immediately pulled the card for her from Christy C. Road's *Next World Tarot*—the Lovers card came up. The image was of a clothed woman standing with a cane and staring into a mirror. As she stood there, her nude image stepped out of the mirror, a full-figured, no cane–carrying woman comforting her human reflection.

The meaning for Allison was clear: It's time to nourish the soul; it's time to examine who you are and acknowledge your worth apart from the fucked-up gaze of conniving lovers. It's time to make amends with your first lover: yourself. The nourishment becomes a physical, spiritual, and emotional transcendence that says to the soul, *You, my darling, are enough.* Validation is warranted only by the eyes in the mirror.

I took a picture of the card and texted it to Allison along with the message from Spirit. She texted back, "You were right all along, so much. Bye." Two days later, she blocked me from her contact list.

I've never enjoyed the emotional toll it takes to unravel situations. However, the longer I live and give myself healing grace, loose ends bother me less and less on the surface. Even though I felt like I flubbed with Allison, I know Alex Elle would say, "Things aren't always going to be in our favor, so when they are, we have to take what we can from these experiences and move on forward."[35]

Since the events of 2020, society has needed an emotional detox. This is due to not only the pandemic health crisis but also the rise in racial violence. We've seen a 25 percent increase in collective anxiety and depression worldwide.[36] Research shows this rise in rates of depression and anxiety has led to poor decision-making skills and thrust many into what is known as *optimism bias*.

Optimism bias is the tendency to believe our decisions are inviolable; when the opposite is proven and life backfires, we lose our shit and topple over the edge, distraught, embarrassed, and emotionally undone. On the flip side, the existential crisis of 2020 also saw a rise in folks googling the phrase *energy healing*. More people became concerned about their mental and physical health as they found that exercising at home still left them longing for conversations about self-reflection, self-love, and mindfulness.

....
35. "27 Inspirational Alex Elle Quotes on Love & Healing," Art of Poets, April 22, 2024, https://artofpoets.com/alex-elle-quotes/.
36. Jamie Ducharme, "Why the COVID-19 Pandemic Is Prompting a National Existential Crisis," *Time*, December 29, 2020, https://time.com/5925218/covid-19-pandemic-life-decisions/.

On social media platforms like TikTok, over 14 million viewers have searched the #blackhealers and #blackherbalists tags. Along with articles on websites and networks like NBC, Vox, and CNBC, this has proven to be an era of rapid expansion for BIPOC spiritualism.

Years of absorbing Allison's poor decision-making in the form of optimistic bias had pigeonholed me as a caregiver, forced to shoulder her burdens but really doing little more than coddling her desires. I was reduced to being her fairy godmother as she blindly ignored her self-destruction and barreled down the train track of exploitation at full speed. My psyche danced between anxiety, panic, and fear. These stressors could only be soothed by the cleansing waters of a potent spiritual bath crafted to fuel grace and forgiveness.

EXERCISE: SOOTHING THE SOFT SPOTS BATH

This bath releases users from suffering by proxy. It also shifts your consciousness and intuitive connectedness from community to centering your own healer's soul.

Needs:

* a pot and lid
* plain water
* ½ teaspoon dried calendula
* ½ teaspoon dried basil
* ½ teaspoon dried rosemary
* ½ teaspoon dried comfrey
* ½ teaspoon dried peppermint
* 1 orange, sliced into five sections
* 1 lemon, sliced in half
* 1 cup honey
* 1 bottle of champagne
* Psalms 67, 80, and 90 (see appendix C)

Instructions:

Fill the pot halfway with water. Add the herbs, mixing them in with your dominant hand.

Add the orange and lemon, honey, and champagne, then cover with the lid. Place both hands on top and recite Psalms 67, 80, and 90 once each.

Let the mixture sit covered for twenty-four hours under the moon. When ready to use, scoop the desired amount into your bath water. Remember to wash from head to toe. Use the wash as frequently as you like within the next nine days.

EXERCISE: THEY'LL BE DAMNED IF YOU DO AND DAMNED IF YOU DON'T TEA

This tea has helped many release the negative residue of painful work-related trauma. By purging this trauma from your life, one sip at a time, you release the sickness and historical violence that teaches us to hate our own stories.

Needs:

* a sheet of paper with the Anyi Me Aye adinkra symbol (see appendix D)
* a tea setting (cup, spoon, and saucer)
* plain water
* Psalms 6, 67, and 71 (see appendix C)
* 1–2 reusable tea bags or 2 5 x 5 inch pieces of cheesecloth and 5–9 inches of twine
* ½ teaspoon dried mullein
* ½ teaspoon dried skullcap
* ½ teaspoon dried lavender
* ½ teaspoon dried chamomile
* honey, agave, or other sweetener

Instructions:

Place the adinkra symbol on the saucer. (You may need to fold or cut down the paper to make it fit.) Holding the saucer, recite Psalms 6, 67, and 71 over the symbol three times each, then set it aside.

Set the water to boil. Add the herbs to your reusable tea bags or cheesecloth and close. Once the water boils, pour a portion into the cup, add the tea bags, and cover with the saucer. Let the tea steep for five to seven minutes. After the tea has steeped, stir in honey to taste and drink slowly.

Juju on the Fly

Coming out of the spiritual broom closet can be met with family, friends, and coworkers calling you the devil, demonic, isolated, disowned, or fired. In a country where 65 percent of the population identifies as Christian, it can be problematic to explore esoteric, indigenous, and ancestral beliefs that are publicly stigmatized.[37] It becomes easier for BIPOC folks to hide their spiritual identities than to answer the call of their ancestral beginning.

Sheba Gibbs, a sister of Puerto Rican ancestry, told me she realized at around three years of age that Espiritismo is a normal part of her family's life on both her mother and her father's side. She also understood that there was a deeper knowing that had to be observed when engaging with the outside world. "People have had the police called on them for Santeria and rituals like the ones my abuelita presided over, where a black goat was offered as an ebbo to Sango." Even though the Supreme Court has ruled that religious animal sacrifice cannot be made illegal, the practice is still controversial. "My grandparents had to move quite often before settling

---

37. "Measuring Religion in Pew Research Center's American Trends Panel," Pew Research Center, January 14, 2021, https://www.pewresearch.org/religion/2021/01/14/measuring-religion-in-pew-research-centers-american-trends-panel/.

down in New Orleans, buying a home, and choosing their godchildren with care," Sheba says.

I know from personal experience that a challenging divination can prompt a client to spin up a web of lies. They'll have the local government breathing down your throat like you're running a slaughterhouse instead of practicing a religion. I learned early to be careful to protect not only my grandparents' spiritual house, but all spiritual houses in my community.

"It can be burdensome, a heavy set of consequences that make you question validity of your faith," Sheba muses. "My Santeria and Espiritismo isn't normalized. Working in corporate America as a chemical engineer, I have to be stealthy in how much of my true self I allow people the privilege of knowing. It's assimilation as a means of survival in a country that can't handle the truth. Your Juju on the Fly series of workings (*Bitch, I'll Smoke You; Fuck Off, I'm Going to Bed Salve*; and *Queen Julia Brown Healer Dolls*) have helped me accept the ancestral guidance that walks with me with an open heart. My people survived slavery and colonization. They lived knowing that sometimes it was wisest to throw as many stones as you can hold and hide your hands."

EXERCISE: BITCH, I'LL SMOKE YOU

This exercise is what I call the spiritual power punch: a combo of workings prescribed to heal the flyest juju workers. It symbolizes living always at the crossroads of abundance with your heart aligned with women's intuition. The Woman/Man Lenormand card serves as a guide and protector in this working, offering a spiritual pathway through conflict and psychological distress.

Needs:

* 1 each of the Cross, the Fish, and the Woman/Man Lenormand cards (*Note:* With the Woman/Man cards, choose the one you identify with)
* 1 teaspoon dried passionflower

* 1 teaspoon dried catnip
* 1 teaspoon dried anise
* 1 teaspoon dried peppermint
* a bowl
* a pipe
* a lighter or matches
* 1 green candle
* 1 black candle
* 1 red candle
* Psalms 107, 63, and 25 (see appendix C)

Instructions:

Place the cards on your altar in a row in the following order from left to right: the Cross, the Fish, and the Woman/Man. Light your altar candles.

Place the herbs in the bowl and mix them together with your fingers. As you do, recite Psalms 107, 63, and 25 over the mixture. When finished, place a few pinches of the herb mixture in the pipe, light it, and smoke it. With each inhale and exhale, envision yourself as part of a healing collective that doesn't just talk the talk, but works the work by setting safe boundaries to protect ourselves from those who would disempower us. Recite the following: *The moment I enter my home, I am reclaiming my ability to reprise the role of healer, increasing awareness as I live and celebrate my whole story in its entirety.*

Smoke to your heart's content or until you feel the vibration taking up space within. This smoke blend will bring you peace, liberating all the many colonized configurations inside you.

EXERCISE: FUCK OFF, I'M GOING TO BED SALVE

I use this salve to calm my legs and feet, especially after a long day of living on other folks' time. If I feel mentally oppressed, I use the salve over my entire body, then crawl into bed with a glass of wine, kombucha, a trashy novel, and my clitoral stimulator nearby.

Needs:

* a crockpot
* 1 cup coconut oil
* 1 cup almond oil
* 2 ounces dried lavender
* 2 tablespoons dried chamomile
* 2 tablespoons dried spearmint
* 20–30 drops essential oils (cedar and lavender)
* a 9 inch x 11 inch cheesecloth
* a pot for straining
* 4 ounces beeswax
* 2 tablespoons liquid witch hazel
* small lidded glass jars (enough to store the salve)
* Psalms 25, 133, and 140 (see appendix C)

Instructions:

Add the coconut oil, almond oil, and dried herbs to the crockpot. Set to warm and let steep for two hours. When finished, use the cheesecloth to strain the herbs out of the oil, allowing the oil to collect in the straining pot.

Transfer the strained oil back into the crockpot and set to medium. Stir in the essential oils until completely blended, then add the beeswax. Continue stirring until the beeswax has melted. Remove from heat and let the mixture cool for five minutes.

Once slightly cooled, add the witch hazel and mix. Let the salve sit for five more minutes before placing small amounts into the jars for later use. Recite Psalms 25, 133, and 140 nine times each.

When you smooth the salve over your body, recite the following: *I accept that I am a healer, a lover, a fighter, but not a quitter. Smooth my life, baby. Smooth my life, baby. Smooth my life, baby.*

EXERCISE: QUEEN JULIA BROWN HEALER DOLLS

This work is performed to allow the spirit of each person needing healing to have a doll placeholder that serves as their physical representation in your space.

Needs:

* 2–3 skeins of yarn
* scissors
* 1 ball of twine
* an index card
* a pen
* a hole puncher
* a larger item that is longer than the length of your fingers (e.g., an old DVD case or a baby's shoe box top)
* Psalm 31 (see appendix C)

Instructions:

Take one end of the yarn and begin wrapping it around your outstretched fingers, excluding the thumb of your nondominant hand. Wrap the yarn twenty times to form the doll's hands. Cut the yarn away from the main skein, then cut two small pieces of twine to tie the arms at both ends. Secure the twine to create hands and snip the loops at each end to form fingers. Set the doll aside.

Next, take out the larger item you selected (e.g., an old DVD case or a baby's shoe box top). Wrap the yarn around it thirty to forty times to form the doll's body, ensuring it's at least three times as long as the arms.

Remove the doll's body from the case or box top. Tie off one section with twine to create the doll's head. Cut the loop on the opposite end that wasn't tied down with twine. Arrange the doll's body evenly. Place the arms under the doll's head and weave the flowing yarn over, between, and behind the arm section. Tie twine around the waist to hold the arms in place. This completes a female doll, which is shown in the sketch below. For a male doll, separate the lower section evenly into legs.

Healer Doll Example

Take the index card and punch two holes at opposite ends. Write your healing wish for the intended person on one side; on the other, write their name. Thread twine or yarn through the holes to create a necklace and hang it around the doll's neck.

Recite Psalm 31 nine times and allow the doll to rest at your altar. Recite the psalm nightly until the healing has moved into an advanced stage of satisfaction.

Chapter Five
St. Jean Malo:
Claiming Reparations

On June 19, 1784, Jean Saint Malo (unknown–1784) was hanged in New Orleans Square, later christened Jackson Square.[38] June 19 is marked as the day of remembrance in Louisiana, where we celebrate the life of Jean San Malo, our symbol of liberation and resistance.

In the late eighteenth century, Malo and his Cimarrons, referred to in New Orleans as Maroons, made their home in the marshes surrounding the city. Maroon communities were groupings of enslaved fugitives who established settlements near colonies of the still-enslaved living on the plantations. These Maroon communities extended from land near Virginia and North Carolina to land in Louisiana, and even as far as Jamaica. Enslaved Afrikans in Louisiana seeking to run away would scurry to the outskirts of New Orleans, their final destination being the Louisiana swampland.

A common practice when escaping the plantation was for one family member to stay behind. They not only served as a spy, but also supplied food, weapons, and any plantation tools that could serve as weapons to the Maroon society. Enslaved Afrikans also wreaked havoc on their captors in other ways, such as burning crops, stealing tools, stealing weapons, and providing herbs as a form of biological warfare in the hands of cooks working in the big house.

Jean Saint Malo, or Juan Saint Malo, was often referred to as "the bad saint" (*malo* means "bad" in Spanish). He was also named after the city of Saint-Malo, a slave port in Brittany, France.[39] Malo lived near the plantation

---

38. Cierra Chenier, "Jean Saint Malo: The Man, Maroon, & Martyr," *NOIR 'N NOLA*, July 30, 2018, https://www.noirnnola.com/post/2018/07/30/jean-saint-malo-the-man-the-maroon-the-martyr.
39. Chenier, "Jean Saint Malo."

of Pierre Frederick d'Arensbourg, near New Orleans. There's no record detailing Malo's upbringing. We do know that after his escape, it was his carpentry skills and crafting furniture that allowed him to trade weapons and gunpowder. St. Malo became the leader of nearly fifty Maroons. Their main camp was in Bas Du Fleuve, in present-day St. Bernard Parish.

Maroons lived independently with little to no White interference. They were committed to forcefully protecting their liberation. Remember, Malo was before Nat Turner's rebellion in 1831 and Charles Deslondes's in 1811. Malo's group included his wife and an unheard number of women loyal to the fight at all costs. In fact, the community was nearly evenly split between men and women. Malo's settlement cultivated corn, squash, and rice. They gathered and ground herbs. They used willow reeds to make baskets and sifters. They used cypress wood to carve vats and troughs. They gathered sassafras, berries, and palmetto roots; trapped birds; and hunted fish.[40]

Maroons were often assisted in their liberation by the region's Choctaw. This relationship between Maroons and the Choctaw is considered the original treatise that gave birth to the New Orleans Mardi Gras tradition.

Legend goes that Malo stabbed a tree near his encampment while exclaiming in French, *"Malheur au blanc qui passera ces bornes,"* or "Woe to the Whites who pass this boundary!"[41] He had a lieutenant nicknamed Knight of the Axe. This man was known to brutally split open the heads of any White man trying to recapture Afrikans.

Malo's downfall came when several White men ran into a group of Maroons on their way to barter for goods. A scuffle ensued as the White men attempted to reenslave the Maroons. After the fog cleared, four White men lay dead, and the Maroons fled to Chef Menteur.

Governor Miro believed the Maroons' audacity would spread to other plantations. Enslaved Afrikans could use Malo's courage as a call to rebellion. If four White men could be killed, then more could die. The gover-

---

40. Chris Dier, "The Legend of Jean Saint Malo," Chris Dier, June 19, 2020, https://chrisdier.com/2020/06/19/the-legend-of-jean-san-malo/.
41. Dier, "Legend of Jean Saint Malo."

nor tried to send free people of color to kill Maroons and decimate their settlements. Malo was briefed on these tactics and alerted other Maroons. The ones he couldn't alert in time were sentenced to three hundred lashes and exiled nine hundred miles away.

A bounty was put out on Malo, offering any enslaved person who could bring back Malo's head immediate freedom. Eventually, Malo was shot in the arm and captured with several Maroons near Terre Gaillarde. Other Maroons fled to the Barataria swamps upon hearing Malo was captured.

In New Orleans Voodoo, St. Maroon is described as a colored saint seen on Marie Laveau's altar. People in the know say St. Maroon is the patron of runaways and is none other than Jean Saint Malo, the Black man who challenged America to stand on truth as the home of the enslaved.

Working with St. Malo

In the years I've worked with St. Jean Malo in defense of reparations, he has helped me come to terms with my personal reckoning in the face of racial injustice. The repair, in my opinion, is continuously vetoed by those who know full well that the extent of White supremacist atrocities outweighs any debate on monetary allocation. Our foremothers and forefathers are still denied their place in a society that thrives off their labor, their blood, and their sweat. Society is still screaming *hell fucking no* to decades of activists pressuring presidential candidates, Congress, local governments, private banking, retail, and educational institutions to award the descendants of those BIPOC folks severely traumatized by racism. The legislation, H.R. 40, introduced by Representative John Conyers, D-Mich in 1989, was slated to create a commission to study slavery and discrimination in the US with the potential to formalize restitution proposals for reparations.[42] It was representative Sheila Jackson Lee who introduced the commission to study and develop reparation proposals for Afrikan American H.R. 40 in the 118th Congress during the legislative session of 2023–2024. The goal of

---

42. "H.R. 40 Is Not a Symbolic Act. It's a Path to Restorative Justice," American Civil Liberties Union, May 22, 2020, https://www.aclu.org/news/racial-justice/h-r-40-is-not-a-symbolic-act-its-a-path-to-restorative-justice.

the commission is to compile evidence of slavery's dominance with respect to the national economy, the role of the federal and state governments in supporting slavery, and discriminatory laws.[43] As of August 1, 2025, H. R. 40 was reintroduced in the 119th Congress by Representative Ayanna Pressley (D-MA) on January 3, 2025. Thus, the legislative journey of the bill has been consistently introduced in every session of Congress since 1989.

The road to organizing for reparations begins with vocalizing our rights and with the realization that even today, the remnants of slavery create disparities in wealth, health equity, and opportunity.

EXERCISE: SAINT JEAN MALO ALTAR (CLAIMING REPARATIONS FOR RACISM AND SLAVERY)

While meditating at the altar of Malo, he has told me that in today's world, a large part of reparations is using funding from White institutions to build our own communities, sacred spaces of safety for BIPOC and AAPI folks. In his words, "We live in the shadows of the big house, but in our souls, we must move under the guise of liberation at all costs."

So work those jobs; let the words of those fucking assholes go in one ear and out the other. You're going to light their asses up with roots! Take that check and build a new haven—a Black Wall Street amid the rubble of exploitation.

Needs:

* 2–3 yards green fabric
* 1 green candle
* a framed image of St. Malo
* 1 jicara filled with water and ½ teaspoon fennel seeds (*Note:* Let sit uncovered overnight)
* 3 alligator claws placed in a large bowl of water

---

43. "H. R. 40," National African American Reparations Commission (NAARC), accessed January 4, 2021, https://reparationscomm.org/hr-40/.

* 9 yams
* 1 cup dried red beans and rice
* 1 raffia grass skirt
* a cauldron or other fireproof receptacle
* 1–2 charcoal disks
* 3 pieces each of frankincense and myrrh resins
* a pipe with lighter or matches
* 1 teaspoon each of dried chamomile and lavender
* 1 conch shell
* Psalms 140, 129, and 110 (see appendix C)

Instructions:

Choose a space indoors or outdoors. Place the fabric over the designated area and position the candle in the center with the framed image in front. The jicara should rest in front of the image. Arrange the other items at your discretion.

Put on the raffia skirt and place a lit charcoal disk inside the cauldron. Add the resins, then let sit for fifteen to thirty minutes, allowing the candlelight to guide your focus. Breathe in and out steadily to the count of five. As you do, reflect on ways your chosen career can contribute to community improvement. Brainstorm paths to repair the damage inflicted on your community through the Afrikan Holocaust. Consider ways to invest in BIPOC homesteads, scholarships, legal defense funding for the wrongfully incarcerated, partnerships with public schools, and active participation in parent-teacher organizations, even if that means becoming an angel donor to provide student essentials like clothes, shoes, paper, pencils, and books.

After the brainstorming session, recite Psalms 140, 129, and 110 three times each. Place a pinch of each dried herb into the pipe and begin to smoke until you feel a shift in your perception of reparations.

Winn-Dixie, Kongo, and Bottle Trees

In the children's novel *Because of Winn-Dixie* by Kate DiCamillo, an elderly Black woman named Gloria Dump has a tree in her yard covered with liquor bottles that hang from its branches. The spirit of her past lives are trapped in these bottles, ghosts that once possessed her into taking on the persona of a woman she didn't recognize. Her story is a powerful reminder of infusing the old ways into our lives as a part of our salvation and liberation.

Every year I teach this story to third-grade students, I feel the need to detour when asked, "What's a bottle tree?" Bottle trees originated in the Kongo region of West Afrika in the ninth century. Early accounts say they were used to ward off enemies, thieves, infertility, witchcraft, and malevolent spirits. If thieves passing outside a home saw a bottle tree with bones inside, the home wasn't burglarized. With our jars or bottles, we're trapping the spirit of systemic hate.

EXERCISE: BOTTLE TREE RITUAL FOR THE MAROON IN YOU

The following exercise is for dealing with systemic racism and the racists who manipulate it to their advantage. The malevolence White supremacy sources from the universal realm of anger, depression, turbulence, chaos, and oppression hates blue because it's the color of water, which these unruly spirits can't cross. Placing blue bottles on a tree allows you to catch and store errant energies that may have latched onto you throughout the day, or any energies trying to create imbalance in your life.

You can buy colored bottles, but I enjoy making mine. The drawback is that the coloring on your handmade bottles won't be waterproof, so you'll have to recolor them if they get wet.

Needs:

* newspaper
* a measuring cup
* 3 tablespoons Mod Podge
* 1 tablespoon water
* ¼ teaspoon blue food coloring
* a case of 24 mini swing-top glass bottles or clear glass beer bottles
* an aluminum foil–covered plate
* asafoetida (1 tablespoon per bottle)
* 3 frankincense incense sticks
* strips of paper (cut to Post-it size)
* a pen
* 1 gallon jug
* soapy water in a bucket
* a sturdy 3–4 foot live tree or indoor alternative
* Psalms 140, 129, and 110 (see appendix C)

Instructions:

Start by spreading newspapers across your work area, especially if working at your altar. Pour the Mod Podge into a measuring cup, then add the water. Slowly mix in the food coloring until the desired shade is achieved. Stir well, making sure the food coloring is fully absorbed.

Pour a small amount of the mixture into one of the glass bottles, enough to coat the bottom with a thin, opaque film. Swirl the bottle until fully colored, then pour the excess back into the measuring cup. Place the bottle upside down on the aluminum foil–covered plate and let it drain completely for seven to ten minutes before standing it upright. Complete these steps for however many bottles you like. (I like to do five at a time, but you can definitely do more.) When finished, allow the bottles to sit untouched for twenty-four hours.

After twenty-four hours, line the bottles up on the newspaper. Add a teaspoon of asafoetida to each. Light the incense and let the smoke spread throughout the bottles. Set the incense aside.

Take a strip of paper and write the name or situation blocking your success. Think of any radically motivated terrorism impacting your community and loved ones. Place the note inside a bottle and hang it on your tree. Recite Psalms 140, 129, and 110 nine times each. State your case as a descendant of a deprived group to St. Malo and ask him to fight with you to overturn discrimination.

Diving Deeper

When life makes you go "Hmmm…"

- If we considered the Afrikan Holocaust and its forced labor in terms of hourly wages, the resulting figure would be around $97 trillion.
- Twelve presidents before Abraham Lincoln owned slaves.
- From the periods of 1798–1802 and 1813–1817, 2 percent of the United States Treasury revenue collected came from the enslavement of Afrikan people.
- Insurance companies once offered policies on enslaved people and allowed banks to use enslaved people as collateral.
- The median wealth of Black households is $16,000 compared to White households at $163,000.
- The US census says 42 million people identify as Afrikan American or as being of Afrikan descent. If the $97 trillion figure from above was divided among their descendants, each person would earn a $2 million payout.

How could the United States ever afford that? Well, consider that in 2021, the defense budget totaled $740 billion.[44] Why can't the plantation use those funds to improve our lives? Fuck it, let's burn the big house down!

When we truly discuss reparations, we're channeling a collective outcry from both BIPOC people and their allies. My belief is that this country has never given us anything freely except hell. So why would this same country give us heaven in the form of reparations? The White elite must see a benefit for themselves in being antiracist. Unfortunately, that means sharing their umbrella of privilege, which many won't for fear it will minimize their superiority. A world without hate, where people are truly held accountable as the law of the land, diminishes proponents of White privilege and their American utopia.

When Black folks talk about repairing what was stolen in the Afrikan American Holocaust, we must include *all* people of color. How can we seek personal atonement while disregarding the importation of Chinese laborers to toil on southern sugar plantations, the internment of Japanese Americans during World War II, or the forced removal of Ottawas, Chippewas, Seminoles, Sioux, Klamaths, and Native Alaskans over centuries?

A poll conducted by the University of Massachusetts Amherst in 2021 indicated 72 percent of White Americans opposed cash reparations.[45] Some reasoned it was too difficult to determine the monetary value of slavery. Others believed reparations were a moot point since none of the people who were actually enslaved were alive to reap the benefit from the atrocities they endured. Still others believed that there was no ongoing legacy of slavery affecting the lives of Afrikan Americans today.

---

44. "What If All Enslaved Africans Were Given Repatriation When Slavery Ended," *MSN Video*, accessed July 25, 2024, https://www.msn.com/en-us/news/us/what-if-all-enslaved-africans-were-given-repatriation-when-slavery-ended/vi-BB1lwH2W.
45. Ashley V. Reichelmann and Matthew O. Hunt, "How We Repair It: White Americans' Attitudes toward Reparations," Brookings Institution, December 8, 2021, https://www.brookings.edu/articles/how-we-repair-it-white-americans-attitudes-toward-reparations/.

Nevertheless, let's examine the Homestead Acts of the 1860s and the Federal Housing Programs after World War II. In 1862, the Homestead Act provided 246 million acres of land-wealth for 1.5 million families over seven decades. It's estimated that 20–93 million Americans, mostly White, benefitted. And while many Whites considered the moral argument for Afrikan American reparations way too radical, the US government has pressured Germany to make reparations to victims of the Jewish Holocaust since World War II.

Many argue that the US government doesn't have the money to compensate for generations of moral impoverishment, which leads me to believe people of color should create our own repair by making the financial marketplace of America our puppet. We can build wealth by creating a society of people who take the time to read banned books, seek naturopathic modalities of healing, grow gardens in places where food deserts once existed, and recalibrate schooling to meet our needs. Our repair comes when we focus our stories on assessing colonization as the root cause of supremacy ideology. All BIPOC/AAPI people are our sisters and brothers, whether they own that fact or not. Colonization still washes minds. We can choose liberation over assimilation.

EXERCISE: DEATH TO THE COLONIZER'S WAYS

The following work won't kill colonizers, but it will begin the process of removing their shackles of job loss, emotional confusion, marital disrepair, and financial instability from our lives and placing them onto their wrists. Their loss will become your gain—yes, the energy from their loss will infuse your life with abundance!

Needs:

* 2 White fashion dolls, one male and one female
* a marker

* 1 piece of twine (long enough to tie around the necks or waists of both dolls at separate ends)
* a shoe box (large enough to house both dolls)
* soil (enough to cover both dolls when placed inside the box)
* 3 pieces of dragon blood resin
* a cauldron or other fireproof receptacle
* 1 charcoal disk
* 1 mason jar filled with urine gathered immediately after you wake up in the morning
* Psalms 119, 49, and 50 (see appendix C)

Instructions:

Take the dolls and write the name of the person oppressing your goals on each. (Both male and female dolls are used to symbolize the collective beneficiaries of slavery's White fragility movement.) Tie the twine around the neck or waist of each doll, securing them at separate ends.

Place the dolls inside the box, positioning the male on top of the female. Cover them with soil. Recite Psalms 119, 49, and 50 three times, then tell the buried stand-ins for your oppressor why you're banishing them beneath the earth. Explain the pain you feel and how you'll repair your life, and state the downfall you're sending them.

When finished, drive the box to a secluded area within a graveyard or heavily wooded area. Open the box, pour the urine over the soil, then close it again.

Leave the box and return home, healed. Wash and dry the jar for repurposing.

EXERCISE: THE BIG HOUSE IS ON FIRE RITUAL

As BIPOC folks, we know all too well when the colonizer's plantation mentality stands in the way of our success, treating us like unruly children instead of equals. This next exercise burns through that racism and creates a river of promise.

To be clear, this work isn't meant to burn down anybody's literal house, no matter how pronounced their bigotry. Again, we're simply opening a path out of a stubborn situation.

Needs:
* a cauldron or other fireproof receptacle
* 3 pieces of frankincense resin
* a sheet of paper with the image of a plantation
* a pen
* glue
* matches
* Psalm 110 (see appendix C)

Instructions:

Place the resin inside the cauldron and light it. Take the plantation image and hold it so the smoke caresses the entire sheet of paper.

On the back of the plantation image, write down the situation standing in the way of your human rights. When finished, cut the paper so your statement covers the same space as the plantation drawing.

For nine days, talk your shit—tell that representation of institutional racism exactly where it can go. On the ninth day, recite Psalm 110 nine times, then burn the image of the big house down and don't look back.

White Saviors/White Wardens

I'm not ashamed to say that even as a magickal person, I never feel completely safe in the presence of White women. I keep a picture of Tamla Horsford on my computer to remind me how quickly things can go wrong in relationships between BIPOC folks and White women.

On November 4, 2018, Tamla was found dead while attending an adult slumber party. Her lifeless body lay in the backyard of a property belonging to one of her fellow football booster moms. Initially, it was thought that she died as a result of falling from the balcony in a drunken state. Her death was ruled an accident due to ethanol intoxication. A second autopsy indicated abrasions on her body, which signaled foul play. Even after her family's attorney argued the case evidence and injury pointed toward homicide, and despite the family's independent findings, the case was closed in February 2019 due to a lack of evidence.

On the now-infamous sofa picture, there were seven women seated, posing, smiling, and leaning, in my opinion, away from Horsford. White women posing as if the forty-year-old mother of six had too much nerve believing she belonged there, believing her womanhood superseded her Blackness.

I've studied the slumber party image more times than you can possibly imagine. It's how I prepare to show up at a job where I've been the only BIPOC teacher for the past fifteen years. That image is my reminder that no matter how many smiles they shoot my way, I can't afford to blur the lines. It might cost me my job, my freedom, or, most important, my life. I didn't create racism, but living in this world, I recognize I need to abide by the rules of engagement and survival, unwritten as they are.

A Tale of Two Paraprofessionals

Recently, at my place of employment, a newly hired Black paraprofessional got into a debate with a White paraprofessional. The two women were on their lunch break and walking to purchase a cafeteria lunch. As they walked, they started joking about a party they had attended a week prior. Apparently both women had met men, and both had declined to take the conversations they had with these men any further, having found both too emotionally immature for their liking.

Their conversation moved into a discussion about which of these women would be the first to marry. The White woman insisted that she would be the first to wed because she was a Christian with morals and values, and she was young, thin, and White. Understandably, the Black woman questioned her reasoning, especially the part about race. The White woman pushed her and told her to lighten up—it was just a joke. Then she laughed and told the Black woman something to the effect that if they were going to continue being friends, she'd have to lay off on the Black bitchiness. The White woman pushed her again, even harder. The Black woman fell back hard, hitting her head against the wall and losing her footing. She then slid to the floor. The White woman pointed and laughed. She kept on reassuring the Black woman that she was truly sorry and didn't realize her strength. When the Black woman got up, she returned the push, and the White girl fell equally hard. The Black woman laughed. Angered and embarrassed, the White woman jumped up and scolded the Black woman with, "I will have your job! I will make it so you'll never see your child again. I will cry and scream. You know what happens when White women cry? You'll go to jail, get raped, eat trashy food, and die forgotten."

The Black woman ran to my room shaking, and through tears, she picked apart her story, explaining the moment when the White woman became her warden and no longer her savior. (Savior in the sense that before the violent clash, the White woman had made the classroom they shared a soothing space of sisterhood.) I reached for her hand and slowly, when there was a break between her thoughts and the racing ideas, she began to fashion stories about SROs, lynch mobs, and drowning in the Red River. It took forty-five minutes to get her to breathe with ease.

We both went to the principal's office. Together, we'd either set the whole plantation on fire or maroon ourselves so far away from there that when we were at work, nobody but us would know in our souls that we had quietly quit White women and all their shenanigans.

By the time we entered the principal's office, there were two police officers, the principal, the assistant principal, and the White woman in question. A room with five White people and the two Black women defending our self-worth, defending how we have come to be that close when we had only been acquainted for six months, and now here we were in a room showing solidarity in the face of the administration and this poor White woman.

The room of White people stared at us, scolding us with their scowls as if we were the monsters threatening to separate a mother from her child. For ninety minutes, both women talked over each other. The White woman paused only to cry, scream, and wring her hands. The Black woman rolled her eyes and sighed loudly, shifting in her chair, trying her best not to appear angry. We both recognized the officers' hands glued to their tasers.

I asked if we could see the camera footage. Schools have cameras. The entire room huddled around the principal's monitor, where it quickly became clear that the White woman was in the wrong. The Black woman interjected, "See, I was assaulted. I was assaulted and I defended myself." The White woman jumped up and let out a loud moan. She then reached for her keys dangling from her belt loop and threw them in the direction of the principal's head. No officer lifted a finger. They let her walk out of that room undone.

We never again heard anything about the footage or the altercation, and no one offered any apology for what happened. We were both seen as troublemakers who saved receipts. But even with all that, we were feared, and sometimes that's just as satisfying as being respected.

A week later, I gifted the Black woman, my sistah, a horseshoe. The talisman would strengthen her in moments when her humanity was being threatened. Over the next three months she told me she was beginning to gain traction in her life. She felt lucky and blessed instead of hopeless. She was managing her night school schedule and had settled on an agreeable babysitting schedule with her daughter's father's side of the family. At the job she felt a sense of peace, but even more than that, she told me she was happy to finally have a feeling of workplace humanity. She didn't feel like a rodent or an insect. She was a woman to be reckoned with, and she loved that feeling from the crown of her head to the soles of her feet.

EXERCISE: HORSESHOE HUMANITY AMULET

This is the amulet I created. When I want to keep my amulet extra close, I wear it in a crossbody bag or fanny pack.

Needs:
- 1–2 horseshoes
- 4–8 horseshoe nails
- Psalms 70, 115, and 132 (see appendix C)
- Hoyt's cologne
- 1 stick of palo santo incense

Instructions:

One at a time, hold the horseshoe(s) and nails in your dominant hand while reciting Psalms 70, 115, and 132 nine times each. When finished, place the horseshoe(s) and nails on St. Malo's altar (see page 96) and spritz with Hoyt's cologne. Light the palo santo, then run the smoke over the length of each object. Let the objects sit for twenty-four hours.

After twenty-four hours, place the objects inside your purse or use the nails to hang the horseshoe(s) above a door in your home. (Be sure to position with the opening pointing down.) Repeat once a month to keep the amulet charged.

Juju on the Fly

Eighteen years ago, the White principal at my children's magnet elementary school retired, and the school system led the search for her replacement. There were several young White women candidates who waltzed into a PTA meeting one evening, introducing themselves through their CVs and using Ebonics in the hopes of forming a connection with the room full of mothers. But we weren't looking for new friends. We wanted answers to our questions: How will you nurture our school culture? How will you engage with parents? What plans do you have to help low-income families who can't afford meals, tutors, after school care, or before school care?

Out of the five White women who graced us with their privilege, three didn't understand how parents with only a high school education could birth children with the mental capacity to pass a magnet school entrance exam. They literally kept saying how lucky these mothers were despite having a genetic predisposition toward lower intelligence. The other two came up with a harebrained scheme to encourage parents to pay for childcare with food stamps (off the record, of course).

The entire room erupted into shouts. I wasn't alone in reading their mannerisms as signs of their privilege and how they had come to blanket us under the warmth of fake atonement. Being our children's principal meant they'd absolve themselves of hate, White privilege. In their minds, they were relinquishing a morsel of privilege to the less fortunate.

A chair was thrown toward the staged speakers, and the melee soon boiled over into the streets. The White women drove away so fast they looked more like a motorcade that had wound up on the wrong side of town after a parade. After weeks of Black women protesting and writing letters to the school board, a Black woman was eventually hired for the job. When the new principal was announced at a school board meeting, nearly half of the White teachers present walked out. One of the PTA mothers whispered before the walkout, "The day I work for niggers is the day I slit my wrists and die."

The school went on to be a success because the parents invested in its survival. The parents became in-class aides, substitutes, and office workers and took on the job of before- and after-school care themselves. These women coordinated adult education courses, and athletics were no longer more important than academics. Repair happens when our survival becomes our wealth generations over.

EXERCISE: WEALTH AS SELF-ACTUALIZATION

Let's not wait for what's coming—let's start building an empowered vision of wealth today! Our wealth will center self-care, abundance, and upward mobility for our communities. We don't have to sell our souls or our bodies to thrive!

Needs:

* 1 each of the Scythe, the Mountain, and the Stars Lenormand cards
* 3 teaspoons dried calamus root
* glue
* a sheet of paper with the Dwennimmen adinkra symbol (see appendix D)
* a sheet of paper with the image of the job you want or the person(s) unjustly standing in your way
* a cauldron or other fireproof receptacle
* 1 charcoal disk
* 1–3 pieces of sandalwood resin
* Psalms 115, 139, and 150 (see appendix C)

Instructions:

Lay out the Lenormand cards in the following order: Mountain, Scythe, Stars. Sprinkle the calamus root on the cards.

Glue the adinkra symbol to the back of the job image so the images face opposite directions. Place a lit charcoal disk inside the cauldron, add the resin, and use the smoke to caress the image. Recite Psalms 115, 139, and 150 three times each day for nine days.

On the ninth day, burn the image while loudly stating your desires. Be firm about what you want, and my love, be prepared for what you get!

Chapter Six
Exu and His Holy Harlot, Pomba Gira:
Healing Black Love

Exu is a spirit from the Afro-Brazilian tradition. He is both a divine messenger and a gatekeeper between our world and the spirit world. Exu sits at the crossroads, waiting for us to choose the opportunity so he can unleash the consequences.

Exu is balance; he sits in the divine center, separating the polar outcomes: success and sorrow. Exu doesn't decide what comes, we do. He can glimpse into our story to preview the causes and effects, but he doesn't wish sadness into our lives, nor does he prevent our perceptions of evil from entering and decimating our intentions. We choose, and we get what we get. Sometimes what we get makes us throw a fit. As always, Exu laughs and cries in the same breath, both as a man and a boy.

Day cannot reprimand night, old age cannot steal the virility of youth, and fertility cannot question life as to the moment it becomes a being. Nor can it scold death for being the bridge to starting over in an unconscious state of déjà vu. Exu is the divine translator between humans and the gods, goddesses, and ancestors. He is sacred and profane, a beloved narcissist who understands his permission must be granted before there is traffic between thought, action, dreams, desires, will, and perseverance.

In the Afro-Brazilian tradition of Umbanda of which my Honduran grandfather was fond, exus are considered the spirits of frightening people, highly educated people, or people of superior esteem in their chosen career paths. In the New World, Exu is venerated as Eshu-Elegba in Lukumi, with 101 manifestations, or roads. As a divine trickster, he is similar to Papa Legba of Voodoo and Elegua of Santeria, where he removes obstacles and opens doors to new opportunities, but you, the querent, must *always* choose the desired door to unlock. He doesn't favor you or your choices, and he doesn't care if you believe you're deserving of a particular outcome. Whether savory or unsavory, our job as part of humanity is to evaluate each outcome and its effect on our lives. Exu humbles us by connecting our world with the spirit world. He knows the bounty behind all opportunities, and if we channel him through magick and praise words, he may soften our emotional, physical, spiritual, or psychological resolve as we work through the trauma of not only this life, but the repeated trauma from past lives.

How do we emotionally mature? How do we learn that a stove is hot? How do we learn that a racist chooses to stew in hate? We live, we learn, we experience, we run into errors, we regroup, and we catalog our experiences as lessons. These lessons test our durability and our ability to bounce back in a world riddled with as much violence as peace.

Exu represents male sexuality and virility. He is a vain connoisseur of wisdom and sex. His greeting is *Laroye*, the superb speaker and communicator. Monday is his day of the week, and red and black are his colors. He carries a walking stick that represents a phallus. In Brazil, he is the first Orixa to receive food and song offerings.

Pomba Gira

Now on to the love of Exu's life, his wife, Pomba Gira.

The Pomba Gira is another Afro-Brazilian spirit. I grew up hearing my grandfather beating his bata as he sang to the statue of this woman in a red dress. Her hands on her hips, a mocha-colored leg peeking from a thigh-high split, she was sexy and sassy in her red corset, gaudy makeup, and bangles. She also had flowers cascading throughout her hair and a tambourine waving in the air.

Pomba Gira wears a dagger under her garter. Her offerings are roses, flowers, coins, a skull, champagne, wine, sweet anise liquor, cigarettes, a mirror, costume jewelry, and lipstick. She is the sensual provocateur, the woman whose smile invites salacious trickery. She is sometimes called the female Esu or the bride of Exu. This is because you can always find her at the crossroads, figuratively and literally. She is referenced as a sacred harlot, the lady of the crosswalks of life whose garter sparkles under the streetlights.

Pomba Gira is the goddess of eroticism, death, and choices, and the patron hellraiser of women, crossdressers, sex workers, and transgender folks. She demands that those who love her receive fair and equal treatment and are never corralled with their backs against the corner. She is vengeance for all marginalized groups, and she is the power of women to demystify sexual desires while wielding those same desires in the form of a switchblade. In her opinion, all women deserve the most lavish luxuries of life. She isn't interested in procreation. She's interested in exonerating her children as they struggle to live life free of judgment.

EXERCISE: EXU AND POMBA GIRA ALTAR

Workings for Pomba Gira should be performed at midnight. Any offerings left in her honor should be placed at an intersection or crosswalk near a strip club or sex shop. A few of her most appreciated offerings are floral-scented oils, perfumes, red roses or wine (red is her favorite color), rum, tequila, whiskey, gin, vodka, and tobacco. She isn't a demure lady; she can outlast any man. So be very generous with your libations.

When I work with Exu and Pomba Gira's altar, I ask for aid in keeping my family happy and abundantly satisfied. Remember that when petitioning these two. If the result strengthens your relationships, Exu and Pomba Gira will wait for you at the crossroads since the choice you make will bring the consequences you deserve to push your story forward.

Needs:
* images or statues of Pomba Gira and Exu
* a bowl
* plain water
* 9–13 drops ylang-ylang oil
* 1 red penis candle
* 1 red vagina candle

Chapter Six

* a cauldron or other fireproof receptacle
* 1 charcoal disk
* 3 pieces of rose-scented resin
* 2–3 cups dried rose petals
* a wine glass
* 1 bottle of champagne or red wine
* a saucer or small plate
* palm oil (enough to coat over the saucer/plate)
* 1 slice of red velvet cake (covered and left on the altar overnight)
* cigars
* a wooden pipe
* 2–3 yards red-and-black checkerboard cloth
* 1 bottle of personal lubricant gel
* Psalms 140, 88, and 62 (see appendix C)
* 2–3 tablespoons dried peppermint leaves
* toys that stimulate the mind (e.g., Rubik's cubes, Uno, playing cards, checker/chess pieces, dominoes, dice)
* lingerie
* beauty supplies (e.g., lipstick, nail polish, perfume, makeup)
* a tissue
* *Optional:* sex toys

Instructions:

Place the images of Exu and Pomba Gira at oppositive ends of your altar. Fill the bowl with water and add the ylang-ylang oil. Place the candles in front of the water and light them.

Place a lit charcoal disk inside the cauldron. Add the resin. Sprinkle the rose petals around your altar, reserving a few to strew across your bedsheets. Pour a glass of champagne or red wine for Exu and Pomba Gira and place it on the altar. Coat the saucer with a thin layer of palm oil before putting the red velvet cake on top, then place it on your altar. Arrange the remaining altar objects (cigar, pipe, cloth) using your discretion.

Holding the personal lubricant gel, recite Psalms 140, 88, and 62 three times each. After the resin burns down, add pinches of the peppermint to the disk. As the smoke rises, pass each toy through it, then set aside.

Change into the lingerie and doll yourself up with your beauty supplies. Hold your desire in your mind; for example, you might think, *Exu and Pomba Gira, protect my family and marriage from financial loss. Allow my husband to advance in his job without anxiety or the temptation of other women. Allow him to remain in optimal health and to maintain a stiff penis, and may we both be forever emotionally satisfied, in bed and out.*

Once your intention is set, masturbate to orgasm. (You can use the optional sex toys for this step.) Wipe yourself with the tissue, then burn the tissue in your cauldron. Recite any one of the aforementioned psalms nine times as the tissue burns. Your prayers will be answered very soon.

The Pleasure Principles of Wealth

Pomba Gira's essence brings sensual abundance, pleasure, and wealth. She guides women as to the manner in which we should own our divine femininity. She reminds us that even as women, we should never negotiate our self-worth. In her divine feminine archetype, Pomba Gira lives to put a chokehold on the global patriarchy. She longs to empower women who fight for their sexual rights and bodily autonomy. She is the patroness of LGBTQIA+ people, who are also fighting for sexual liberation.

Pomba Gira exudes death, vengeance, and eroticism and refuses to view sex work as a shameful act. I have a sistah client who once said, "As a sex worker, we're often labeled idiots, whores with rocks in our heads, because why else would we be spreading our legs virtually? In truth, with two master's degrees, I know I'm smarter than more than half the dudes who DM me. I find myself editing their requests and sending them back to them. I tell them to resubmit the edited version. Petty, I know, but I get tired of the stereotype. I'm not a loser, I wasn't gang raped, and I have a beautiful relationship with my parents. I do me, and sex is my playground. I love that you introduced me to the goddess Pomba Gira. She doesn't condemn me; she accepts and celebrates my whorishness on all levels, baby!"

In the eyes of Pomba Gira, sex for pleasure and power are her soft spots. She isn't concerned with procreation, but if you're at your wit's end struggling to conceive, she has been known to take pity on you and bestow fertility on your womb.

EXERCISE: POMBA GIRA'S SENSUAL PROTECTION

In this working, you'll be doing a lap dance to heighten your sensual energy flow. If you need some ideas, it's fine to google "lap dance moves" before starting. Also, please note that the following working is very intense, so you should only perform it once a month.

Needs:

* a cigar
* a red lingerie bodysuit/teddy
* a red cape
* a red garter belt
* a pair of devil horns (large enough to wear)
* a pair of red high heels
* red lipstick
* rose water in a spray bottle
* a framed image or statue of Pomba Gira
* 1 red candle
* 1 alcoholic beverage (can be in a shot glass)
* a sturdy chair

* 1 rose
* a 3/5 domino

Instructions:

Light the cigar and cleanse your space by blowing smoke over all the items you'll be using, even the chair.

Now it's time for dress-up! Put on the lingerie, cape, garter belt, horns, heels, and lipstick, then spritz yourself with rose water all over. Place the image of Pomba Gira and the candle on your altar, then set the alcoholic beverage down next to the candle. Position the chair so it faces the altar from a few feet away.

Put on a sexy tune, preferably one that brings out your inner vixen. (If you can't settle on a song, you can borrow one of my favorites: "Love to Love You Baby" by Donna Summer.) Light the candle, then start performing your lap dance on the chair.

The moment you feel a surge of sexual electricity pulsating throughout your body, sit and repeat the following: *Pomba Gira, Patron Mother of women, crossdressers, sex workers, queer folks, and all outcasts and liberators of sexual freedom, we honor you. Protect your children from the heinous vibrations of those who seek to annihilate our right to exist, to breathe the same air, to laugh, and to love of our own choosing. For you, I dance to awaken our connection. I dance to speed you on your way. Protect us, oh beautiful, salacious Mother. Bring the wrath of your vengeance upon the head of anyone who tries to persecute us for our decisions. May they pay dearly until the moment of their last breath.*

Begin dancing again. When the energy shifts, this time, snuff out the flame. (This last dance seals the pact with Pomba Gira. It's how she places her field of protection around you and how you begin to thank her for her blessings.) Prepare for bed, taking off everything except the teddy and the garter.

The next day, take the alcohol and rose to a crossroads. Pour the alcohol out and leave the rose to rest in the same area. Carry the domino with you for nine days after each working. (This allows Pomba Gira to feel the very core of what angered you and lets her know how much time she needs to devote to your situation.)

You can reuse the tools from this working each month until you need to replace them. After snuffing out the cigar, you may want to keep it in a resealable plastic bag and place it in the freezer. You can keep the other items together in a box or container.

Diving Deeper

Pomba Gira speaks in passionate messages. She remembers the entirety of your life path, action by action. She will remind you of your successes and your failures. If she sees you shitting at the same watering hole you drank from weeks, months, or years ago, she will definitely remind you not to expect a clean bill of health.

If Exu represents machismo and sexual virility, Pomba Gira represents Foxy Brown, Christy Love, and the undercover mama disguised as a helpless prostitute. Pomba Gira has an insatiable appetite for sex, cigarettes, and sweets, which includes wine. She affirms the idea that all women and LGBTQIA+ people are beautiful and desired.

At the crossroads standing under the streetlight, waiting for the serial bullshitter to deny her the autonomy to fuck or be fucked with, Pomba Gira does as she damn well pleases. Be respectful and handle her with care; her wrath is legendary.

Pronouns She/Her or Ms. Luna

I once had a trans client, Luna, who had transitioned from male to female. "My parents didn't mind me being gay," Luna said, "but transitioning was too much. We argued all the time, and when I graduated with my PhD and neither Mom nor Dad showed up to watch me get hooded, I guessed we had come to the end of the road. I started my practice, completed my transition, and two years later, I was looking for love." That's when she met Tanner.

"We matched on Tinder," Luna told me. "He was Ryan Gosling kind of handsome, blond with blue eyes. He was tall. He spoke French, German, and Spanish with a Peruvian twang." Tanner was also a self-made man. He owned a restaurant and was the one the mayor called whenever a major player came to town and needed to be courted by the chamber of commerce. He also had a host of prominent friends, people who flew him places where NDAs changed hands as often as briefcases of money.

"He knew from the start about me being trans; I never hid it," Luna explained. "We were so in love for an entire year. I was spoiled with diamonds, pearls, red bottoms. Then shit changed the day after my thirty-second birthday.

"I showed him a wedding invitation—a mockup of our future wedding invitation. It had our names embossed in gold, with olive vines dangling around the edges. It was my way of popping the question. Tanner went from zero to a thousand in a split second. He called me a fucking freak and said he wasn't about to marry a freak. He kept asking who I sent it to, who else had seen this bullshit. Even though I told him I hadn't shown anybody, he slapped me and started punching and kicking me. He dragged me to the bathroom and began cutting off chunks of my hair. I tried to fight back, but he was so strong, so angry, and so violent. I decided crying might soften his heart, so I cried and prayed that he'd stop. Instead, he threw me out onto the streets, naked. He tossed my phone out the window and I called my colleague, Sylvia, who asked no questions. She drove me to her house, and later she told me if I wasn't going to call the police, I needed to cap him when he wasn't looking. She agreed to help, or she insisted I take it to Pomba Gira, and that's what I did."

Luna used the *I Curse You Until You Rot* work. Not only did she hold this man accountable for the pain and shame he wreaked on her life, but she also protected other trans women from his predations.

The Human Rights Campaign has tracked incidents of transgender violence since 2013. In 2023, 84 percent of victims of such violence were people of color, with a whopping 50 percent being Black trans women. Seventy-eight percent of the victims were killed by a gun, and 36 percent were killed by a romantic or sexual partner, a friend, or a family member. Finally, 50 percent were misgendered upon their death, either by authorities or in the press.[46]

Along with the *I Curse You Until You Rot* work, I also created a confusion oil recipe to help LGBTQIA+ people deal with homophobic rhetoric. This work is great for shutting down people who go around spouting shit.

EXERCISE: BLACK ARTS OIL

This Black Arts Oil creates confusion in the hearts and minds of bigots. I usually place a few dabs of it on cotton balls, then hide them around my space or the spaces of my adversaries.

Needs:

* 1 medium-to-large mason jar with lid
* 1 cup olive oil
* 13 drops patchouli oil
* 1 teaspoon black pepper
* 1 teaspoon cayenne pepper
* 1 teaspoon powdered valerian root
* 1 teaspoon powdered mustard seed
* 1 teaspoon sulfur powder

---

46. "Fatal Violence Against the Transgender and Gender-Expansive Community in 2023," *Human Rights Campaign*, 2024, https://www.hrc.org/resources/fatal-violence-against-the-transgender-and-gender-expansive-community-in-2023.

* 2–3 sprigs of Spanish moss
* 9 peppercorns
* 3 strands of a black dog's hair
* 1 bag of cotton balls
* Psalm 55 (see appendix C)

Instructions:

Pour the olive oil into the mason jar. Add the patchouli oil, then the peppers, valerian root, mustard seed, sulfur, moss, peppercorns, and finally the dog hairs. Stir, seal, and shake vigorously for five minutes. Afterward, place the jar in a cool, dark place. Stand facing the jar and recite Psalm 55 nine times. Allow the mixture to rest for two weeks before using.

I typically recite Psalm 55 again three times over any cotton balls I'm about to dab with the oil. For extremely irritating individuals, I sometimes leave the cotton balls soaking in the oil overnight; in these cases, I let the cotton balls drain on a towel-covered plate for twenty-four hours before using.

This oil is strong and highly potent, so feel free to use it creatively. For example, I've placed images of my targets inside baby food jars and filled the jars with oil to bind people from creating havoc in my life. When I do, I recite the psalm nine times, then turn the jar upside down in a cool, dark place.

EXERCISE: I CURSE YOU UNTIL YOU ROT

This was the working Luna did. It has two parts: a curse oil recipe and a ritual.

Needs:

* a towel or newspaper
* a medium-to-large mason jar with lid
* 1 cup olive oil

- ¼ teaspoon powdered myrrh
- 1 teaspoon powdered galangal
- 1 teaspoon powdered anise
- 1 teaspoon dried hyssop
- 1 teaspoon dried dill
- Psalms 9, 80, and 140 (see appendix C)
- aluminum foil
- 1 back-to-back separation candle
- a small paintbrush
- a cauldron or other fireproof receptacle
- 1 charcoal disk
- 1 teaspoon asafoetida

Instructions:

Lay out the towel or newspaper. Add the olive oil, myrrh, galangal, anise, hyssop, and dill to the mason jar, seal, and shake vigorously for five to seven minutes. Open the jar and recite Psalms 9, 80, and 140 over it three times each. Seal the jar again and place it on its head in a cool, dark place for two weeks before using.

After two weeks, place a piece of aluminum foil on a table, ensuring it's large enough to catch any spillage. Place the back-to-back separation candle on the foil. Using the paintbrush, coat the entire candle with your oil, then leave it to dry for forty-eight hours.

Once the candle has dried, place a lit charcoal disk in the cauldron, add the asafoetida, and repeat the psalms three times each. Tell the candle what you want to see happen to the person you're breaking away from.

Light the candle and meditate on your desired outcome—see it in your mind and believe it. Let the candle burn for fifteen minutes a day until it's no longer recognizable, then dispose of the remains at least nine blocks away from your home.

Marsha, Marsha, Marsha, the Star of Our Next Exercise

Marsha P. Johnson was born August 24, 1945. Johnson was a woman assigned male at birth. She described herself as a gay person, a transvestite, and a drag queen who used the pronouns she and her.

At age five, Marsha enjoyed dressing in women's clothing. During that same time, she experienced a sexual assault at the hands of a thirteen-year-old boy. Later, after graduating high school, Johnson moved from New Jersey to New York City with only fifteen dollars and a bag of clothes. Against all odds, Johnson was set to rewrite her story.

Marsha soon became an activist, sex worker, drag performer, and one of the subjects of Andy Warhol's art series *Ladies and Gentlemen*. She established Street Transvestite Action Revolutionaries (STAR), an organization that helped shelter homeless trans teens, with fellow activist Sylvia Rivera. Both had experienced homelessness and had to hustle to find sustenance and shelter. Before STAR found a brick-and-mortar home at 213 Second Avenue, it was housed in two hotel rooms rented by Sylvia and Marsha, who were known to sneak fifty people into both rooms.

Marsha also advocated on behalf of trans people of color within the radical organization Gay Liberation Front and the Gay Activists Alliance. In addition, she worked for the rights of queer people in prison and people with HIV/AIDS through education and healthcare promotion.

While many historical accounts credit Johnson as the one who threw the shot glass that set off the Stonewall Riots of June 28, 1969, she said that by the time she and Sylvia showed up, "the place was already on fire, and there was a raid already. The riots had already started."[47]

In the 1970s Marsha would find herself in and out of psychiatric hospitals, and with no way to earn a living outside of sex work, she continued to be arrested. In 1990, she was diagnosed with HIV. On July 6, 1992, her body was found in the Hudson River. Marsha's supporters were infuriated when police initially classified her death a suicide instead of a homicide.

---

47. Emma Rothberg, "Marsha P. Johnson," National Women's History Museum, 2022, https://www.womenshistory.org/education-resources/biographies/marsha-p-johnson.

Later authorities reclassified her death as a drowning from undetermined causes. Since 2012, the case has remained open.

In 2019, New York City announced Marsha P. Johnson and Sylvia Rivera, who died in 2002 due to liver cancer, would be honored with a monument to transgender women. In 2020, a Brooklyn waterfront park was also named in Marsha's honor.

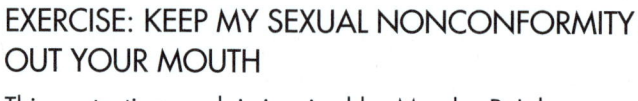

EXERCISE: KEEP MY SEXUAL NONCONFORMITY OUT YOUR MOUTH

This protection work is inspired by Marsha P. Johnson.

Needs:

* a framed image of Marsha P. Johnson
* framed images or statues of Pomba Gira and Exu
* 1 medium-to-large mason jar
* 2 cups olive oil
* 3 tablespoons dried rue
* 3 guinea peppers
* 15 drops bergamot oil
* Psalm 118 (see appendix C)

Instructions:

Set the images on your altar with Marsha's in the middle. Pour the olive oil into the mason jar, then add the herbs, peppers, and bergamot oil. Shake for five to seven minutes, then recite Psalm 118 nine times. Allow the oil to sit in front of Marsha's image for forty-eight hours.

Afterward, use your fingers to rub the oil all over Marsha's image. As you do, name the people you want to confuse. When finished, place the image back between Exu and Pomba Gira. Recite the psalm nine more times, then call out the name of the person(s) you want confused.

Repeat these steps—oiling Marsha's image, reciting the psalm, and calling out the names—for nine more nights. In no time at all you'll find confusion overtaking the individual(s) you named, and you'll be able to move about your life as you please.

Patron Saint of Sex Workers

If you're a sex worker and folks have been ridiculing your lifestyle or preventing you from making money, or you've been assaulted as a result of your job, this chica is for you.

About a year ago, a client of mine had worked her way up from stripping and prostitution to creating her own adult content website with photos, performances, and underwear for sale. She had posted a comment online about a patron of hers who happened to have seen her out at the movies. She was there alone killing time before meeting her best friend for a makeover day. This guy wouldn't stop smiling at her and eventually worked his way over to where she was sitting as the previews played. He asked for her autograph and she obliged. But then he asked for a date and if he could drive her home after the movie (he was an Uber driver). Then he started badgering her about making a movie of their own. She only escaped by lying and saying she needed the restroom before sneaking out of the movie.

No doubt this would've been unsettling for any woman. Yet there were folks chiming in in the comments that she shouldn't have felt creeped out. Folks were like, "He was just a fan," or "He was just hot and bothered over seeing his porn crush out in the wild." Some called her conceited and full of herself. Others even said she was in the wrong profession to be a narcissist. I mean, the rants were crazy.

Not wanting to get into an all-caps shouting match online, she phoned me and relayed the rest of the story, which she'd held back, fearing people would think she was looking for sympathy: The man had followed her toward the restrooms, waited until she came out, then screamed obscenities after her when she dashed toward the nearest exit. Minutes later, in the parking garage, she saw that he had followed her there too. It took her an hour to lose him before traveling home, a drive that under normal circumstances would take fifteen minutes. It remains the scariest moment in her life as a camgirl.

I told her I would craft a work that she could use to protect herself while performing. Pomba Gira reaffirmed for this sistah that she is entitled to sex, success, and safety, no matter what anybody dares to say.

EXERCISE: POMBA GIRA CAMGIRL

Online sex workers can use this ritual during performances for protection from harassment, both online and offline. If anyone tries to overstep your boundaries, they'll be consumed by blood, sweat, and tears. In addition, this working will reward you with a long list of high-end clients willing to pay top dollar for your services.

Needs:

- a mason jar with lid (large enough to set the candle on top)
- 1 cup avocado oil
- 13 drops ylang-ylang oil
- ½ cup honey
- ½ cup rose petals
- a framed image of Pomba Gira
- rose water in a spray bottle
- 1 red candle

Instructions:

Add the avocado and ylang-ylang oils, honey, and rose petals to the jar, then seal. Set aside.

Spritz the image with rose water and allow it to dry completely. Afterward, set it on a table near whatever camera you use to film your performances. Place the jar in front of the image and set the candle on top of it. Light the candle, then recite the following:

> *Beautiful St. Pomba Gira*
> *Protect me from assholes*
> *Protect me from creeps*
> *Protect me from johns who want to take advantage of me*
> *Protect me from brokeass fuckers*
> *Seeking to use my pussy theatrics to get off*
> *And then degrade me*
> *Talk shit about me*
> *Protect me from the ones who won't take no for an answer*
> *The rapists who dream of mutilating me because no one will have them*
> *Because no one will love the washed-up, pathetic, judgmental hypocrites they are*
> *Protect me, Mama*
> *Protect me*
> *And make my enemies, those who try to cross you*
> *Make them pay with blood, sweat, and tears*
> *And make them give up shitloads of that money*

Sit with the candle, staring into the flame for fifteen to thirty minutes. Then snuff out the flame. Repeat this work once a week.

Dr. Paschal Beverly Randolph

Another name I hold as a devotee of sexual liberation is Paschal Beverly Randolph. Placing Randolph's image between Exu and Pomba Gira on their altar allows me to answer questions about my emotional safety in relationships. With Randolph's help, I can discern if these relationships are safe spaces for love.

Born on October 10, 1825, Dr. Paschal Beverly Randolph was a Black medical doctor, occultist, Spiritualist, trance medium, and writer. Dr. Randolph utilized cannabis in an elixir he invented with his first wife, a Native American/Afrikan woman called Dowam Meskh. This elixir was said to provide mesmerizing abilities beneficial when scrying.

It has been widely purported that Randolph was the basis for the Marvel comic book character Dr. Strange. (Look up Dr. Randolph's image online and see for yourself—the similarities are uncanny!) Whether there's any truth to the matter, what isn't debatable is that this free man of color, born of mixed parentage, left home in his adolescence. He was penniless and spent his life up until the age of twenty working as a sailor. His travels led him through Europe to England and the distant lands of Persia. While in the Far East, his world expanded through mysticism and the occult. He studied the folk magick of every place he ventured, and even spent time in my hometown of New Orleans, where he immersed himself in conjure and Voodoo.

Randolph would go on to introduce the Ansairetic Mysteries into Western magick's lexicon, which led to the birth of sex magick. Randolph's incorporation of sexualizing magick was unheard of during his time. He authored over fifty books covering the topics of magick and medicine while also finding time to be a supporter of birth control, an independent publisher, and the founder of the Fraternitas Rosae Crucis Order in 1858. Randolph was also an abolitionist and devoted friend to Abraham Lincoln, so much so that some Rosicrucian papers detail that it was Randolph who authored the Gettysburg Address, not Lincoln.

It was said that throughout his life Randolph believed that had he been born White, his works would have been widely accepted and studied. But far too many learned people of his day disregarded his contributions. He was a man limited not by the inner workings of his mind, but by those who saw his brown skin as cause to negate this spiritual phenom.

Randolph died at the age of forty-nine from what was alleged to be a single self-inflicted wound to the head. This puzzled many people, as Randolph was known to have an aversion to death by suicide. Many years later, R. Swinburne Clymer, a Supreme Master of the Fraternitas, stated that a former friend of Randolph had admitted on his deathbed to killing him. The alleged murderer claimed that he took the conjurer's life due to jealousy and temporary insanity.

EXERCISE: DR. RANDOLPH'S VIEUX CARRÉ FLAME

You can honor the wonderfully gifted Black occultist Dr. Randolph through the following oil lamp ceremony. This working not only brings Randolph's protective energy to our Hoodoo erotica, but also adds an invaluable skill to our scrying repertoire. Ancient Kemetic people used oil lamps to scry when they wanted to communicate with deities and ancestors, find solutions to problems, or gain insight into the future.

For this working, your purpose is to commune with your ancestors and guardian spirit. Use it to ask for protection over your life or the lives of your loved ones, or as an extra oomph to your sex magick. (When using this work for sex magick, try performing it on the day you plan to make your move, alone or with a partner.)

Needs:

* 1 oil lamp with wick
* olive oil or coconut oil (enough to fill the lamp)
* a framed image of Dr. Randolph
* *Optional:* consciousness-raising tools (e.g., CBD edibles, marijuana, psychedelics) (*Note:* If none of those appeal to you, mix 1 to 2 teaspoons each of dried wild dagga, passion flower, blue lotus, and kanna to create a smokeable mixture)

Instructions:

First, scan your lamp to make sure there are no cracks in the glass and that the wick is long enough (at least eight inches long). Fill the lamp about two-thirds full with oil. (I find olive oil spooks malevolent energies from seeking a path to the flames, while coconut oil opens your third eye and heightens your connection to the spiritual realm.)

Once you've lit the lamp, place the image of Dr. Randolph behind it. Use the consciousness-raising tool of your choice to relax you as stare into the flames.

As you sit with the image, thank Randolph for his work in the occult and in the art of sex magick. Ask him to help you delve deeper into your understanding of yourself as a sexual being, spiritualizing your orgasmic potential and ability to commune with spirits and enveloping your loved ones with psychic protection. Ask him to open your third eye so you may experience the destiny marked by your journey through past lives.

Stare into the flames for fifteen to thirty minutes, listening and watching for any images; these are messages from Spirit. Don't be discouraged if you don't feel the connection after your first sitting, just trust that the veil is lifting.

Repeat this ritual for nine consecutive days, extinguishing the lamp after each session. Keep the image of Randolph in between Exu and Pomba Gira throughout—all three will remain hard at work solidifying transformation in your honor, even after you've snuffed out the flames.

Juju on the Fly

In 1982, author Alice Walker coined the term *colorism*. Colorism is the preference for and preferential treatment of people with lighter skin. Colorism is tied to White supremacy and is a divide that supports internalized racist oppression, the "White is right" trope that still survives today.[48]

A 2011 study on color consciousness found that mothers and grandmothers were often a girl's first source of skin tone socialization during childhood and adolescence.[49] When families connect negatively with darkness, so do the young children under their care. These children then go on to mature into a lifetime of self-hate. In 2020, 30 percent of Afrikan American girls ages twelve to sixteen reported that the media, family, peers, and so on regarded dark skin as not only unattractive but an indication of loudness, being hood, and obnoxiousness. Lighter tones were considered attractive and ladylike—less ghetto. Women between eighteen and twenty-four experienced colorism as a form of misogynoir, where women of darker hues were good enough for sex but never good enough to marry.

I remember dating a young man, Javier, who was as dark as me. He was freaking gorgeous, and every time we were together, I'd wrap my arm around his and admire our conjoined mahogany glow. I thought we were headed for forever. After all, he had popped the question. No, not marriage, but the other question: "You want to hang out for Mardi Gras?" I said yes, and we planned to meet up on St. Charles Avenue, where his family had staked out a spot.

But the closer the calendar got to Fat Tuesday, the clammier my love became. Even though we were the same hue, colorism reared its head between us. His great-grandmother, Louisa, was a light-skinned woman of French Creole descent. She was so light she had passed for White from birth to about the age of thirty, when she was outed by a White woman seeking the affections of Louisa's White fiancé. Her father was a White man known for raping Black women, and her mother "jet Black and simpleminded," as Javier tellingly put it. His grandmother married a Choctaw man, a surgeon,

....
48. "Colourism," Global Social Theory, n.d., https://globalsocialtheory.org/topics/colourism/.
49. JeffriAnne Wilder and Colleen Cain, "Teaching and Learning Color Consciousness in Black Families: Exploring Family Processes and Women's Experiences with Colorism," *Journal of Family Issues* 32, no. 5 (2010): 577–604, https://doi.org/10.1177/0192513 x10390858.

and his mama married a Haitian with money. Yes, he may have turned out as jet Black as his foremother, but he was rich, and for Javier and his family, wealth was the one thing that could make them ignore skin color.

One day Javier showed his mama my picture, a picture we took at a fair. My hair was wet because it had rained, and when I dried off, I was ashy as hell. He told me his mama took one look and threw the photo in her fireplace. She told him that's what you did to roaches, you exterminated them. You didn't let them roam around your house or take up space in your life.

Misogynoir surrounding dark-skinned women's sexual organs, desires, and sexual appetites creates an emotionally volatile atmosphere, where Black people are gaslit into adhering to divisive propaganda that cements itself into generational trauma. Sometimes that gaslighting comes from the tongues of other BIPOC people brainwashed and seduced by the colonizer's flights of fancy. Instead of fighting against White supremacy and its offshoots, these sellouts would rather act as overseers. As liberators, we must hold ourselves accountable for our healing. We must center a new dialogue around beauty and the acceptance of all our hues as desirable.

No, the Randolph work won't end colorism, but it will create space for emotional freedom. It allows our ancestors to help us not only paint our lives beautiful, but to divorce us from a supremacy mindset that shames us for our gorgeous skin.

Here are two works to bury colorism and embrace self-love.

EXERCISE: SCRY BYE, BABY, BYE BYE

This working uses a different scrying method to reveal a person or family's secrets.

Needs:

* 1 white candle
* 1 black mirror
* a glass of water
* a cauldron or other fireproof receptacle
* 1–2 charcoal disks

- 3 pieces of sandalwood resin
- a pen and paper
- steel wool (enough to wrap around the paper)
- a small mason jar
- 3 tablespoons soil from an ant hill (okay if it includes ants)
- 1 cup honey
- red cloth (large enough to cover the mouth of the mason jar)
- twine (enough to tie around the mouth of the mason jar)
- 3 large rubber bands

Instructions:

Place the following objects on your altar, ordered from left to right: the lit candle, the mirror, and the glass of water. Place a lit charcoal disk inside the cauldron. Add once piece of resin, then place the cauldron behind the mirror. Turn off any lights so the candle is your primary light source.

Sit in front of your altar and politely ask the mirror to reveal your target's secret shame. Stare into it and breathe in and out to a steady count of five until images begin to form. Use the pen and paper to record the secrets until images stop appearing.

Wrap the paper in the steel wool, then place inside the jar (you may need to fold the paper to make it fit). Add the soil and honey, then cover the mouth of the jar with the cloth. Tie the jar closed with the twine, secure it further with the rubber bands, and place it outside under a tree. Over the next three months, top up the jar with more honey and up to three additional teaspoons of ant hill soil. Leave the jar under the tree for the remainder of the year. All revelations should be clear by then. You can wash the jar out and reuse it after it has sat under the moonlight for three days.

EXERCISE: CHOCOLATE IN THE MIRROR SURE LOOKS GOOD

Use this working to regain control over your self-perception.

Needs:
* a sheet of stationery paper
* 3 ylang-ylang incense sticks
* perfume
* a mirror
* Psalm 71 (see appendix C)

Instructions:

Twenty-four hours before beginning this work, write the following affirmations on the stationery:

> I am a manifestation of beauty.
> My features invoke Goddess pride.
> My color is flawless.
> My size is flawless.
> No surgery can enhance the perfection coursing through these veins.
> I make it my business to tell all Black and Brown girls they're beautifully crafted.
> I come from a long line of beautiful, creative women who weave magick between candy yam thighs.
> There is nothing I would change about the skin I'm in.
> I am not a trend.
> My hair is not a trend.
> My glam does not begin or end with makeup.
> I take up space, barefaced, brainy, and with nappy beauty.
> My laughter is my joy.
> My body is my joy.

My health brings me joy.
My sex brings me joy.
I choose the pronouns I identify with.

The following day, spritz the stationary with perfume and light the three incense sticks. Standing nude in front of the mirror, recite Psalm 71 three times, then the affirmations nine times. Repeat this work for nine nights and watch as you regain full control over your self-perception.

Chapter Seven
Joseph and the Dirty South Headstand:
Protection

In Hoodoo, St. Joseph is syncretized with Obatala, the King of the White Cloth. Obatala is the Orisa of purity, wisdom, and truth. In Yoruba Orisa studies, Obatala is regarded as the moral compass for all Orisa and their devotees. He is known for his ability to listen impartially and to find clear, just solutions.

In the beginning of the universe, the highest god, Olodumare, sent sixteen Orisa to Earth to prepare it for humanity. Obatala, the architect of humanity, was tasked with molding all beings from clay. Once they were formed, Olodumare breathed life into them.

One story about Obatala reveals that even the Orisa aren't immune to human temptations. One day, while Obatala crafted beautiful obsidian works, Esu, the trickster, arrived with a plan. He pulled a bottle of palm wine from his satchel, hoping to tempt Obatala, who had never indulged.

At first, Obatala resisted. He smiled at his own craftsmanship and whispered, "Esu offers this wine as a challenge. He'll be disappointed when he sees the seal remains unbroken."

Obatala continued working, sculpting thousands more beings. But as the hours passed, his hands grew calloused, his throat parched, and his lips cracked. Convincing himself a single sip would do no harm, he took one. Then another. One swallow turned into two, which turned into three, which turned into the whole damned bottle.

Drunk but unaware, Obatala kept molding. He worked tirelessly, shaping hundreds of thousands of new figures before collapsing into a deep sleep. When he awoke the next morning, he was horrified to find his latest creations were misshapen and physically imbalanced.

My grandfather would say the lesson here is that no human is perfect. People gaze into the mirror, longing for unattainable heights. In the age of social media, that pursuit of perfection is even more relentless.

Ashamed, Obatala vowed to protect those he had unintentionally misshaped. He pledged himself as their patron Orisa, standing with those born with physical and mental impairments. As the embodiment of wisdom and purity, he demands that we hold ourselves to the highest moral standard. And when we fail, he teaches us to face the consequences with humility and the steady grace of an Orisa who wears white all day, every day.

My youngest son was born a child of Obatala, with the Orisa at his head. Obatala's children are meticulous in their appearance, treating their grooming with an artist's precision. When my son can't wear all white, he makes sure his undergarments, even down to his socks, are pure white. He drinks more water than soda, and he prefers soy milk. He bathes twice a day, cleansing himself from head to toe.

When night falls, my son seeks divination to determine if it's safe to leave the house and how long he may stay out. Like all Orisa, Obatala's initiation rites require consultation with Ifa to establish the initiate's taboos.

For the purpose of this chapter, taboos refer to specific foods they must avoid, colors they must not wear, and places they must stay away from lest they risk their safety. One universal taboo for all children of Obatala is abstaining from alcohol. Also, more often than not, they should wear white. Dressing in head-to-toe white helps keep their thoughts clear and prevents malicious energies from attaching to their physical bodies or spiritual essence.

Like St. Joseph, Obatala (also known as Oshagrinan) is the great messenger, forever blessed for his devotion to divinity. These different names or archetypes represent the various paths of an Orisa. As Oshagrinan, Obatala is an old man who hates noise, excessive questions, and those who refuse to stand for a cause greater than themselves. He has lived as long as he has because of his loyalty, wisdom, and discretion in overcoming obstacles. He prefers the solitude of night, working his magick under the cover of darkness—when the world sleeps, he plans.

Here are some basic facts about Obatala (Oshagrinan): His number is eight. His feast day is September 24, and his favorite color is white. He doesn't accept alcohol as an offering because it makes him overindulge, leading to chaotic outcomes. Instead, he welcomes offerings of cotton, powdered eggshells (cascarilla), cocoa butter, white rice, white custard, black-eyed peas, and sweet potatoes.

On the Flip Side

St. Joseph embodies the noble spirit of a man who accepts the role of stepfather to the holiest child known to humanity: Jesus, the Christ child. Throughout Mary's pregnancy, Joseph displays unwavering morality, loyalty, and spiritual dedication, ensuring both mother and child endure the hardships of traveling more than eighty miles from Nazareth to Bethlehem.

St. Joseph is often petitioned when someone wants to buy a home or get a job to improve their living situation. As St. Joseph the Worker, he passed his carpentry mastery to his stepson, Jesus, instilling the values of hard work, dedication, and loyalty to family and purpose.

In New Orleans, St. Joseph's influence is intertwined with Sicilian Americans, credited with bringing fava beans—known in Hoodoo as wishing or lucky beans—to the city. During the Middle Ages, Sicily endured a devastating drought that wiped out much of the population. When every other crop failed, the fava bean thrived, preventing further loss of life. Since then, it has been revered as a symbol of good fortune.

Even today the legacy of Sicilian migration lives on in its music, food, and money. "In the mid-1800s Sicilian citrus farmers migrated to the American gulf coast to trade oranges and lemons."[50] Many Sicilians worked as hired hands to southern plantation owners while others became grocers, peddlers of fruits and vegetables. The merging of Sicilian and New Orleans cuisine gave birth to the muffuletta sandwich. By the 1900s, more than forty thousand Sicilians had entered the United States through New

---

50. Lucia Re, "Italians and the Invention of Race: The Poetics and Politics of Difference in the Struggle over Libya, 1890–1913," *California Italian Studies* 1, no. 1 (2010), https://doi.org/10.5070/c311008862.

Orleans. By 2000, there were 250,000 Italian descendants living in the New Orleans area.[51]

In addition to pasta and red sauce, seafood and Worcestershire sauce became staples of the Sicilian diet. Before 1922, Sicilians and Blacks worked side by side in the food service industry. These restaurant jobs would later open the door to camaraderie in the form of jazz, which afforded Black musicians the freedom to play in Italian restaurants. However, in 1891, after the lynching of Sicilian men in New Orleans following a police officer's murder, Sicilian immigrants across the country would argue for the right to be treated with the same rights as other White groups. In 1922, an Alabama judge decreed that a Sicilian immigrant was "inconclusively White."[52] This precedent opened the door for extreme forms of anti-Black racism. Many believed that solidarity with Black people would prevent them from capitalizing on all that White privilege had to offer. Today, much of the city's Italian population maintains the same socioeconomic segregation of their forebears.

My grandfather would joke, "It's only on St. Joe's Day that they give up the mantle of racism—the separate and unequal. They come down off that high horse and strut through the streets second lining alongside Black folks like it's a family reunion. They act like there was never a divide. We standing at the altar together, whispering to fava beans and remembering how only colored folks know how to survive with beans in their belly. As White as they want to be, it's the colored in them that understands how to eat whatever the earth birth."

---

51. Re, "Italians."
52. "The Weakness of the 'Whiteness' Literature," Reason, May 31, 2019, https://reason.com/volokh/2019/05/31/the-weakness-of-the-whiteness-literature/.

EXERCISE: ST. JOSEPH'S ALTAR PROTECTING US FROM OUR NEIGHBORS

This working is for anyone searching for a new home, trying to close on a home, or even trying to get an unruly person out of your home.

Needs:

* 2–3 yards brown cloth
* a cauldron or other fireproof receptacle
* 1 charcoal disk
* 1 piece each of frankincense, myrrh, and amber resin
* 1–3 slices of bread on a saucer or small plate (covered)
* a small bowl of dried fava beans on a saucer or small plate
* 4 lucky hand roots on a saucer or small plate
* a framed image or statue of St. Joseph
* 2 brown candles
* 2 green candles
* a large crucifix
* a glass of white wine
* Psalms 76, 48, and 93 (see appendix C)

Instructions:

Lay the cloth over your altar, then place the lit charcoal disk inside the cauldron. Add the resin.

Pass the saucers of bread, fava beans, and lucky hand root through the smoke for three to five minutes until each is thoroughly cleansed. When finished, place them back on the altar. Arrange the remaining objects on the altar using your discretion.

Recite Psalms 76, 48, and 93 three times to finish the ritual.

Sundown in America

Sundown towns are towns or cities that exclude non-White people, most frequently Afrikan Americans, from staying after sunset.[53] This form of racial segregation was enforced by threats of mob violence, public lynchings, and housing discrimination.

The birth of sundown towns is historically documented as during Reconstruction. Whenever the subject of sundown towns came up, my grandfather would suck his teeth and sigh out, "The signs, they told you to get your ass out of dodge before the sun sputtered out its last snuffle of glow. They wanted you gone before the sky sunk behind the trees, or you could expect man, woman, or child to be dangling from those same trees, shielding the sun from their sin. You'd dangle for days as a reminder to other Negroes: Stay too long and lose your life."

St. Joseph's spiritual leadership gave him the ability to patiently and meticulously find shelter for his pregnant wife so their son could be born with a roof over his head. Hallelujah!

When folks want to buy, rent, or sell a home or apartment, they petition St. Joseph, who has a specific ritual that must be followed with sincerity.

EXERCISE: HOME MY HOME, DIVINE AND SWEETLY PROTECTED

This ritual helps protects your home from race-baiting neighbors, better known as vigilantes of hate.

Needs:

* a towel
* 1 pack of cotton balls
* Florida water in a spray bottle
* Psalms 79, 80, and 82 (see appendix C)
* 1 medium-to-large mason jar with lid

---

53. "Sundown Town | Meaning & History," Britannica, July 31, 2024, http://www.britannica.com/place/sundown-town.

* 3 tablespoons olive oil
* a framed image of your current home or the home you desire (*Note:* In lieu of an image, you can frame the home's address or a computer-generated map of its location)
* a cauldron or other fireproof receptacle
* 1 charcoal disk
* 3–6 pieces of palo santo resin

Instructions:

Lay out several cotton balls on your towel and spritz them lightly with Florida water. Recite Psalms 79, 80, and 82 three times, then drop the cotton balls into the mason jar. Add the olive oil.

Sit the uncovered jar on top of the framed image. Place the lit charcoal disk inside the cauldron, then add the resin. Recite the psalms again three times as you sit with the smoke, imagining a field of protection encircling your home and all its inhabitants. Let the resin burn out completely.

Repeat this work nightly for twenty-seven nights. If your cotton balls need to be replenished, you can change them out with fresh ones.

After twenty-seven nights, seal the jar and place it and the image in a cool, dark place. Let them rest there forever or until you move.

Option:

* When you're traveling through unfamiliar places, you can carry a few cotton balls in your pocket for protection.

Diving Deeper

While the number of all-White municipalities or neighborhoods may have decreased after the Civil Rights movement, certain discriminatory housing practices and modern-day versions of sundown cities still exist today.

A 2022 *Newsweek* article relayed the account of a Black truck driver passing through Vidor, Texas, an allegedly notorious sundown town. To date, Vidor is 98 percent White, with 20 percent of those Whites living in abject poverty. Vidor's poverty rate is the highest in all of Texas. Vidor also has a serious problem with methamphetamine addiction, which plagues a large population of the town's poor.

As the city of nearby Beaumont desegregated, "White flight" made Vidor a haven for many. In 1993, a federal mandate to desegregate a housing project (and, with it, allow in John DecQuir Sr., the first Black resident to live there since 1920) was met with protests, public rallies, and death threats. "Vidor is an alligator oasis, home to half a million alligators—a swampland prone to floods."[54]

The truck driver, Mr. Gideon, captioned a video documenting his harrowing experience traveling in and out of the city of Vidor. His TikTok has been viewed over 875,000 times. While driving along headed to his company's drop-off, Gideon says he saw Confederate flags and a doll fashioned in the image of a Black man that was wrapped in a Confederate flag and hung from a tree by its neck. When he finally arrived at the drop-off, Gideon claims a security guard issued a "code red." At this time, he overheard the guard saying to whoever was on the other end of the walkie-talkie that he didn't want to be responsible for Gideon's safety. In a matter of minutes, another man showed up. This man unloaded Gideon's haul and sent him on his way with a warning. "Dude, you might want to get up out of here as soon as possible; we're at sundown. You want to leave here now. Don't stop until you at least get to Beaumont." The man also

---

54. Shira Li Bartov, "Black Truck Driver Tells Horrifying Story of His Night in a 'Sundown Town,'" *Newsweek*, May 12, 2022, https://www.newsweek.com/black-truck-driver-tells-horrifying-story-night-sundown-town-texas-viral-tiktok-1706156.

informed Gideon that "police turn a blind eye to the town's happenings."[55] Gideon left and didn't stop to sleep until he had entered the Beaumont, Texas, city limits.

Nadia's Story

Three years ago a client of mine, Nadia, phoned me at 4:30 a.m. on a Friday begging me to help her daughter, who was two weeks into dorm life at an Indiana university. According to Nadia, her daughter had been awakened every night to what appeared to be a seance in the halls. She noticed her roommate leading the charge: There were chalk drawings on the floor near her bed and candles leading from her bed out into the hall. My client's daughter was terrified, and instead of choosing to scope the scene out decided to hide under the covers with her cell phone pressed firmly against her ear, whispering to her mother or sister until morning.

The last straw was when the daughter returned from class to find a dismembered Black doll under her sheets. The doll was smeared with ketchup, and it's pelvic area was ripped open. Inside was a glob of slime filled with dead cockroaches.

Shortly after removing the doll, the daughter became violently ill and was rushed to the hospital just in time to remove an extremely large fibroid-like cyst from her uterus. The daughter had never suffered from fibroids before.

After talking with both mother and daughter for an hour, we decided leaving school wasn't an option. The daughter refused to entertain the idea of enrolling anywhere else, so we decided to work *Soldiering Through Sundown Towns* with modifications to protect the integrity of the work, as she was still sharing a room with a roommate well versed in magick herself.

Following is the working we used, plus two more to keep you and your family safe from harm in unfriendly environments.

---

55. Bartov, "Black Truck Driver."

EXERCISE: SOLDIERING THROUGH SUNDOWN TOWNS

This is a working you can do for protection should you find yourself in a sundown town. (Trust me, they're still out there!)

Needs:

* a cauldron or other fireproof receptacle
* 1 charcoal disk
* 3–6 pieces of amber resin
* Psalms 79, 80, and 82 (see appendix C)
* a shoe box
* 2–3 cups soil
* 1–2 cups Spanish moss
* a package of green army men
* a sheet of paper with the image of the location you'll be traveling through (*Note:* In lieu of an image, you can use the location's address or a computer-generated map of it)
* modeling clay
* 3 teaspoons olive oil
* Florida water in a spray bottle
* a small statue of St. Joseph

Instructions:

Place the lit charcoal disk inside the cauldron. Add three pieces of resin. As the smoke rises, recite Psalms 79, 80, and 82 three times, adding more resin as needed.

Add a layer of soil to the bottom of the shoebox, then add a layer of Spanish moss. Bury the army men in the soil and moss so that only their top halves are visible.

Take the location image and spit on it to seal your Ase, the power of your desired intent; this gives you dominance over your travels. Fold the paper into as small a square as possible, then set it aside.

Form the modeling clay into a ball. Now take your paper and push it inside the clay ball. Rub the olive oil all over the ball to coat.

Now's the time to ask St. Joseph for protection. Lay it all out and explain what that protection looks like for you. Once St. Joseph has heard the fullness of your heart, place the ball inside the box, cover it with more Spanish moss, then spritz it three times with Florida water. Place the St. Joseph's statue inside the box, making sure the statue faces the moss ball. Cover the shoe box and leave it in a cool, dark place. Feed the ball weekly with three teaspoons of olive oil and three spritzes of Florida water. Continue with the feeding until your space becomes a soothing atmosphere.

EXERCISE: LIBERATION'S HOMECOMING

This work protects your space, home, and car as you travel through sundown towns or other areas where you might not be welcome.

Needs:

- a spray bottle
- Hoyt's cologne
- Florida water
- Psalms 79, 80, and 82 (see appendix C)
- a mason jar
- 1 framed image of St. Joseph
- 3 tablespoons filé powder
- 3 tablespoons powdered ginger
- 1 cup soil
- 1 floor mat (to be placed either in your car or inside your home at the front door)

Instructions:

Place a mixture of one part Hoyt's cologne and one part Florida water into the spray bottle. Hold the bottle in your hands while reciting Psalms 79, 80, and 82 three times each. Set the bottle aside.

Take the image of St. Joseph and place it inside the mason jar (you may need to fold it or cut it down to make it fit). Add the filé, ginger, and soil, then repeat each psalm over the open jar three times.

Place the jar behind the front door of your home. Using the Hoyt's cologne/Florida water solution, spritz the inside of the jar and both sides of the floor mat daily for nine days. Afterward, sprinkle a portion of the jar's contents under the mat. Replenish once a week as needed.

EXERCISE: KEYS 2 YOUR LIFE

This work heightens your safety and ensures that every time you unlock the doors to your home, success embraces you long before the woes of the world.

Needs:

* keys to your current or future home
* a spray bottle
* Hoyt's cologne
* 1 hand towel
* Psalms 79, 80, and 82 (see appendix C)

Instructions:

Lay out your towel and place the keys on it. Recite Psalms 79, 80, and 82 three times each. Place Hoyt's cologne inside the spray bottle. Spritz the keys on the front and back sides. Recite the psalms again, three times each, over the keys. Allow the keys to dry overnight while they rest on your altar. When you retrieve the keys the next morning, ask St. Joseph to allow you to forever open the doors of your home to abundance, protection, and a haven to recharge and reinvigorate your self-worth. Repeat this work once a week. You can also anoint your car keys for protection as you travel.

Cruising Through Life While BIPOC

So often, BIPOC people discern time by where they were when the death of one of our own happens with malice, leaving behind the most gruesome set of memories that cause PTSD to sear into our DNA. It happens, and there are those among us who rationalize PTSD by bonding with our captors. We watch murder or brutal beatings and somehow, out of fear or an internalized need to belong, we find the words to empathize with or defend White supremacy while critiquing its victims.

We find ourselves asking questions like *Why didn't any of the nine parishioners attending Emanuel African Methodist Episcopal Church have a gun of their own? Why wasn't there a shootout at the church instead of a massacre?* We blame the nine dead—Reverend Clementa Pinckney, Cynthia Hurd, Reverend Sharonda Coleman-Singleton, Tywanza Sanders, Ethel Lance, Susie Jackson, Reverend DePayne Middleton-Doctor, Reverend Daniel Simmons, and Myra Thompson instead of Dylann Roof. (When asked why he was doing it, Roof chillingly replied, "I have to do it."[56])

We ask why Sandra Bland didn't just signal a lane change. Why did she go word for word with the officer and refuse to get out of her car or put out the cigarette? Why did she hang herself with a plastic bag? Did it have something to do with her epilepsy? Why did Trayvon Martin wear a hoodie at night, looking suspicious? Why did he leave home for candy and a fruit juice cocktail? What about Eric Casebolt, who was captured on video in McKinney, Texas, engaging in racially motivated excessive force

---

56. "Dylann Roof Tells Jury, 'I Still Feel Like I Had to Do It,'" *ABC News*, January 10, 2017, https://abcnews.go.com/US/jurors-hear-closing-arguments-dylann-roof-trial/story?id=44673859.

against Dajerria Becton, an unarmed fifteen-year-old girl? Officer Casebolt was caught on video forcibly pushing Becton to the ground, handcuffing her and grabbing Becton by her hair.

This is part of the reason I've included my Required Reading for Spiritual Disruptors (see page 407). It gives us a fighting chance to reverse-engineer our mental eugenics and our cultural insensitivity toward the BIPOC community.

On February 23, 2020, the murder of Ahmaud Arbery while jogging through a suburban South Georgia neighborhood made national headlines. His assailants—William Bryan Jr., Travis McMichael, and Gregory McMichael—claimed they thought Arbery was a burglar and proceeded to shoot him three times when Arbery attempted to defend himself from his attackers. The entire confrontation was recorded by William Bryan Jr. on his cell phone.[57]

When I heard the news about Ahmaud Arbery, I was sitting next to my son as he weighed the choice between graduate school at Syracuse or the University of California, Berkeley. The television screen played the story on repeat, the anchor's voice echoing, "We don't yet have a motive, but we have the suspects in custody."

I remember the photo of Arbery's bright, smiling face spliced with the image of his final moments. I remember the embrace my son and I shared, the weight of the fury passing between us. Our words, raw and incendiary, felt swallowed, drifting downward into silence.

We already knew the motive. It was the consequence of cruising through life while BIPOC. It was the same story, recycled and set in another part of the country, but it still carried the same stench. When White people are pushed out due to their socioeconomic standing, BIPOC people are scapegoated. We become the villains, marked for control through imprisonment, coerced into conformity, or eliminated entirely.

---

57. Richard Fausset, "What We Know About the Shooting Death of Ahmaud Arbery," *The New York Times*, August 8, 2022, https://www.nytimes.com/article/ahmaud-arbery-shooting-georgia.html.

Abraham Lincoln's Emancipation Proclamation on January 1, 1863, freed more than 3.5 million enslaved Afrikans. This disruption of the social order was what prompted individuals like Henry J. Hearsay, a former Confederate army major and editor of the *New Orleans Daily Democrat* and *Shreveport Times*, to believe, "If Negroes listen to the screeds of agitators in the North, the result will be a race war, and race wars mean extermination."[58]

As my son and I rewatched the media coverage of Arbery's final moments, we reflected on the trust we place—sometimes too willingly—in America's promise that we can live freely. Everyone should have the right to jog, pause to admire a home under renovation, or simply exist without fear. I love window shopping, sightseeing, and wandering into open spaces. Should I be maimed or killed just for being human?

Refusing to let America throw stones and hide its hands, I turned to my magick. It became my way of reclaiming liberation—no more asking, and damned sure no more begging.

Hoodoo dominoes, as part of my work with St. Joe, offer BIPOC folks a way to find their tribe. They affirm that we don't have to live as prisoners in our homes. Instead, they serve as a blessing, easing our spirits and offering sacred respites of hope and solitude.

Hoodoo dominoes also bring energy to our Hoodoo practice. With a few of the saints, I only need to carry a single domino. Yes, you heard me right, one solitary domino.

EXERCISE: ST. JOE BENEATH THE BED

In Hoodoo, dominoes are used for divination and to carry one's luck on the road. Some folks use a pocketed domino as a reminder to pray to an ancestor or saint. Others use it as a talisman or amulet to increase their power over a situation, or to protect their sacred space.

....
58. "The Negro Motorist Green Book," AutoLife, University of Michigan, accessed December 21, 2023, http://www.autolife.umd.umich.edu/Race/R_Casestudy/Negro_motorist_green_bk.htm.

In this working, you'll use a domino partly as a reminder that we have great work taking place behind the scenes, partly as a tool to focus our attention.

Needs:

* 1 medium-to-large shoe box
* soil collected from the site of a bank or your new or current home (enough to fill the shoe box nearly full)
* a small statue of St. Joseph (precleaned with liquid black soap)
* 1 medium-to-large mason jar with lid
* 1 cup olive oil
* 2 tablespoons Five Finger Grass (cinquefoil)
* 9 drops cinnamon oil
* 9 drops bergamot oil
* 9 drops vanilla oil
* 7 fava beans
* pen and paper
* a 5/3 domino to bring good news swiftly

Instructions:

Fill the shoebox with soil, leaving two to three inches clear at the top.

Bury the statue upside down (on its head) in the middle of the box with the bottom exposed. (If the bottom is barely poking out, remove small portions of the soil at a time.) Pour the olive oil into the mason jar, then add the Five Finger Grass (for speedy outcomes with financial security), cinnamon oil (for luck), bergamot (to bring abundance to any desires), vanilla (to sweeten your luck), and fava beans. This mixture is your St. Joe oil. Seal the jar tightly and set aside.

With the pen and paper, write your petition to St. Joe. Be very clear about what you want; don't assume the spirit knows what you desire. For example, if you're closing on a new home, provide the address, its cost, and, if possible, a picture of it. If you're asking to remove a person from your current home, attach a small photo of them to your letter.

Fold the petition into a small square and bury it in the soil. Holding the jar of St. Joe oil, recite the following three times: *St. Joe, please bring me my wants, and please don't taunt. I need what I need: a home with my name on the deed. Hurry! Hurry! I have no time to waste. I don't want to live on the streets or under a bridge; I just want to live in peace.*

Shake the jar vigorously, then open it and apply a quarter-size amount of the oil to the statue's bottom. As you do, recite the incantation three more times. When finished, place the box under your bed. Repeat the working once a week until the desired outcome is reached.

EXERCISE: ST. JOE, DO ME A FAVA

This exercise is another working that uses a domino. It's for cases where you're trying to find gainful employment.

Needs:

* a pen
* a sheet of paper with an image of St. Joe
* 7 fava beans
* a small coin purse
* 1 gold candle
* a 5/3 domino
* the St. Joe oil you made in the previous working

Instructions:

Begin by writing your petition to St. Joe on the back of the image: Ask him for the new job by name. Discuss the salary you'd like to earn and any other nonnegotiable. (*Note:* Don't ask for a job you know you're not qualified for just to chase a dollar. St. Joseph will see right through your ploy and reward you with confusion.)

Wrap the fava beans (to represent luck and abundance) inside your petition. Place the wrapped letter and beans inside the coin purse.

Light the candle (symbolizing success and wealth). Holding the coin purse, envision yourself working in the career of your dreams. Imagine wealth pouring into your bank account, enough to bless your life and the lives of those you love. Recite the following: *St. Joe, St. Joe, I work hard for my money. I work even harder when I'm happy. I need to move on, but my money's looking funny. Help me find work; not only my pockets, but my soul hurts. I got to leave, I got to go. St. Joe, St. Joe, bring me the luck of the fava bean. St. Joe, St. Joe, as you stand on your head, don't fill me with dread. Don't be mean. Don't be mean. Make it so, make it so. St. Joe, St. Joe, make me the luckiest so and so.* Perform this meditation for fifteen minutes.

Finally, there's the domino effect. The 5/3 domino is a sign of good news soon to come. It opens us up to the fortune we've been waiting for all our lives. Rub a pea-size amount of the oil on the domino and tuck it in your pocket or bra. (You don't need to put it in a satchel. Let it breathe.) During the day, take it out for five minutes, look at it, and reflect on the work you've entered into.

Do your candle work, incantation, and domino reflection daily until the job is yours.

EXERCISE: ST. JOSEPH ON THE ROAD

One way Black travelers used to protect themselves on the road was by reading *The Negro Motorist Green Book*. The Green Book, an annual guidebook for Afrikan American motorists, was published by Victor H. Green, a Black letter carrier. He created the Green Book to help Black motorists avoid the dangers of traveling, noting which restaurants, gas stations, and tourist attractions were friendly to Afrikan Americans and which should be avoided. He also offered general advice, including a tip for Black drivers to always keep a chauffeur's cap at the ready—if stopped, they could then say "they were delivering a car for a White person."[59]

A friend of mine once said we needed to bring back the Green Book in some form. "If we know beforehand, then St. Joseph ain't got to work that hard to protect us," she said. This working won't bring the Green Book back, but it will provide you with its sacred protection.

Needs:

* a spray bottle
* 13 drops of frankincense essential oil
* 2 cups plain water
* a glue stick
* a sheet of paper with the image of St. Joseph
* a sheet of paper with the image of *The Negro Motorist Green Book*

Instructions:

First, add the frankincense oil and water to the spray bottle. Close and shake to combine, then set aside.

---

59. "The Negro Motorist Green Book."

Using the glue stick, paste the images together back to back. Lightly spritz both sides with frankincense solution, then fold the paper into a small square. Close your eyes and envision yourself traveling with an entourage of your ancestors flanking you. Hold that image until you feel totally comforted, then place the image in your pocket or glove compartment. Go about your day unencumbered by other folks' hatred.

A Young Person's Work

In Marion County, Florida, on June 2, 2023, thirty-five-year-old Ajike Owens, a Black woman, was shot and killed after a heated exchange with a White neighbor. It was reported that earlier in the day, the neighbor, Susan Lorincz, allegedly threw a roller skate at Owens's children, hitting one of them in the foot.[60] The children told their mother. When Owens went with her ten-year-old son to confront Lorincz, she was shot moments after she knocked on the door.

In Kansas City, Missouri, on April 13, 2023, sixteen-year-old Ralph Yarl, a Black teen, mistakenly knocked on the door of eighty-four-year-old Andrew Lester, a White man. Yarl was sent to pick up his younger brothers but mistakenly showed up at the wrong home. Without warning, Lester shot Yarl in the head and arm. Bleeding profusely, Yarl sought help at three different homes before someone finally assisted him. Neighbors eventually found him lying injured in the street. The teen now suffers from a traumatic brain injury and says his brain doesn't process dense information like it once did.

My mama says, "Bought sense is worth more than told sense." Laws designed to bury history's horrors are nothing more than blackface minstrel jokes, mocking BIPOC people as if we've drifted too far from Emmett

---

60. Bill Hutchinson and Deena Zaru, "Family of Ajike Owens Calls for Murder Charges after Suspect Charged with Manslaughter: 'We Are Deeply Disappointed,'" *ABC News*, June 27, 2023, https://abcnews.go.com/US/florida-woman-charged-fatal-shooting-ajike-owens-mother/story?id=100390462.

Till, Addie Mae Collins, Denise McNair, Carole Robertson, and Cynthia Wesley. But while our blood still stains the streets, we see America for what it is: a two-faced, rabid ghoul, exposing itself without shame.

I remember Halloween 2024, when one of my fourth-grade students sat in tears. "The racists are killing us," he said. "They kill Black daddies and mommies, and they kill children too. Halloween ought to be canceled until the real monsters are locked up."

I tried to explain that Black people don't live in fear. We live in love, always protecting one another. That's liberation. The same tools used to steal our lives can also be wielded for protection.

I told him: Always travel in groups and stick with people older than you—people wise enough to use their phones for more than dance crazes, restaurant meals, and cruise ship tickets. I reminded him, "You already know how America was founded. We studied it. You know how your ancestors got here. It wasn't on a cruise ship, but on a slave ship, one that many claim was divinely sanctioned to 'civilize' monsters. You already know the truth: The monsters are real, and they are unpredictable."

EXERCISE: WHIPPING THE DAYLIGHTS OUT OF RACISM (A YOUNG PERSON'S WORK)

The following St. Joseph work helps children protect themselves with the magick of Black and Brown people. Depending on your child's age, they can either perform the ritual on their own, or you can work through the steps together. The masked pinata represents fear, control, and avoidance. St. Joseph will beat a path through these forces to keep your child sound and in step with their higher purpose.

Needs:

* tape
* a sheet of paper with the image of St. Joseph
* a toy baseball bat
* a Halloween mask (the scarier the better!)

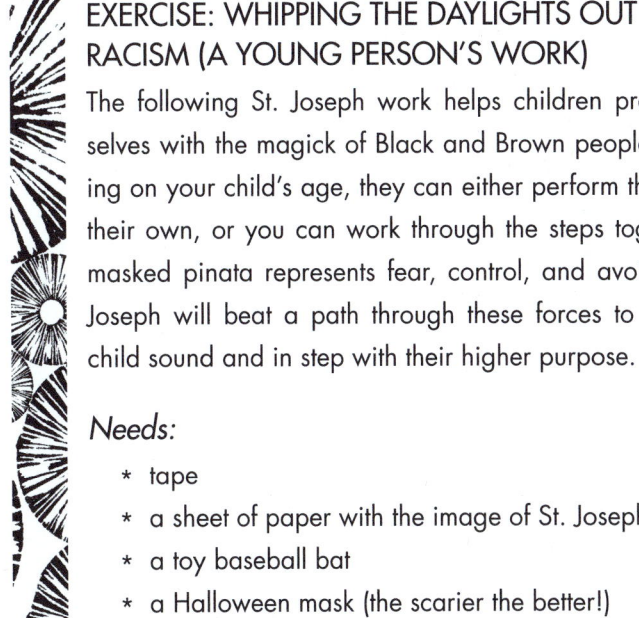

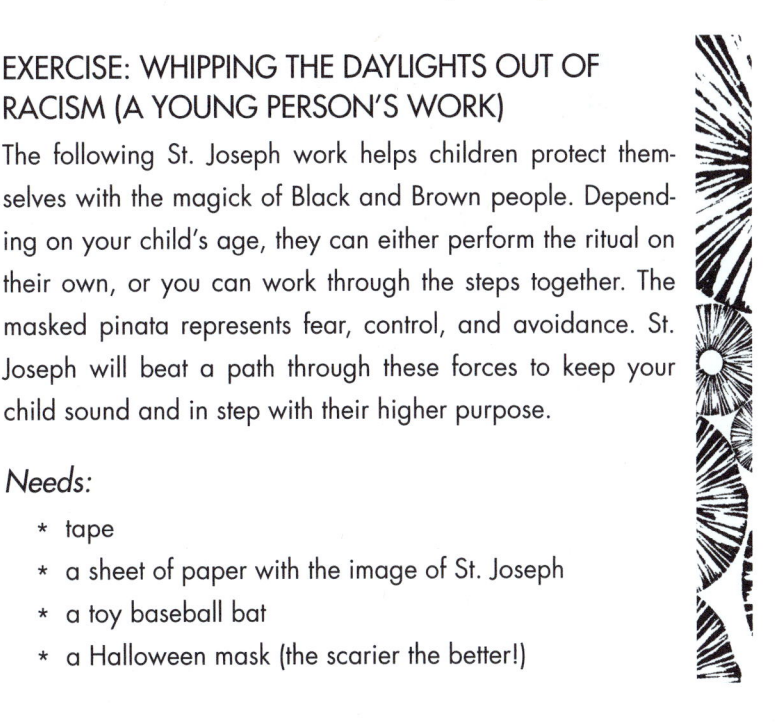

- an empty donkey pinata
- 3 pieces of twine, at least 12 inches long
- 3 sticks of Seven Afrikan Powers incense
- Psalm 119 (see appendix C)

Instructions:

Tape the printed image of St. Joseph to the bat, then place the mask on the pinata. Hang the pinata up with the twine, preferably outside.

Light all three incense sticks. Allow the bat to sway through the trail of smoke, making sure the image of St. Joseph soaks in an abundance of it. Recite Psalm 119 three times, then beat the pinata to a pulp. (No need for blindfolds; you want to see where each strike lands.)

Once the release is complete, bag up the mask and pinata remains and throw them away. Repeat this work as often as needed.

Juju on the Fly

After creating a ritual for children—who should never be left out of discussions on combating supremacist ideology—it struck me that they must also witness their parents actively protecting the home while reclaiming their autonomy to live freely.

Protection is a family affair. It takes collective energy to stamp out the violent intentions of our oppressors, whether we're minding our own business at home or enjoying life around town.

If you're an elder in a household with children, let them watch you, move with you, and participate as you carry out these works. Give them the chance to bless the land, spit into the soil, burn cowries kissed with whispered words of protection. Build a force field infused with the intentions of every villager living, breathing, eating, and existing in your home.

EXERCISE: ST. JOE AT 4 (PART 1)

A week after Hurricane Katrina, my husband and I traveled back to our hometown of New Orleans to check on not just our home but also the homes of relatives. When we arrived at my mother's rented shotgun home, White people were looting and stealing from not just her home, but from all the homes on her block. Many had been promised by the homeowners the legal rights to the property without first allowing the relocated Black and Brown renters the legal right to remove their belongings. This ritual work will protect a home and its occupants from being illegally tossed out of their property while securing it from theft or vandalism.

Needs:

* dousing rods
* a cauldron or other fireproof receptacle
* 1 charcoal disk
* 3 pieces of myrrh resin
* 4 green satchels or drawstring bags
* 3 tablespoons guinea peppers or peppercorns, divided
* 3 tablespoons red brick powder, divided
* 1–3 cups vetiver, divided
* a shovel or gardening trowel
* Psalms 79, 80, and 82 (see appendix C)
* 4 small statues of St. Joseph

Instructions:

Holding your dowsing rods, walk the perimeter of your home while asking St. Joe to stand guard at the Four Corners, protecting you from White supremacy, hate, racism, sexism, homophobia, transphobia, and ableism. Ask that your home become a safe haven where all marginalized hopes and dreams flourish. Walk the perimeter three times or until the rods are pointed straight ahead and not crossed.

Place a lit charcoal disk inside the cauldron, add the resin, then walk the perimeter again nine times. When finished, divide the guinea peppers, red brick, and vetiver among the satchels. Tighten the satchel strings and set aside.

Dig four holes at each corner of your home's perimeter. Make the holes deep enough to drop the statues in on their heads and drop those into the holes as well. Re-cover each hole with soil, then recite the psalms three times each as you walk the perimeter of your home, changing direction each time you complete the circuit. Recite Psalms 79 and 80 when you're walking clockwise, Psalm 82 as you walk counterclockwise.

Walk the perimeter of your home in the same way once a month, always reciting Psalms 79 and 80 clockwise and Psalm 82 counterclockwise. This keeps the protection flowing.

EXERCISE: ANYBODY SEEN MY MAN JOJO? (PART 2)

During the illegal property seizure, in the week after Hurricane Katrina, we were able to question what the fuck was going on. We were told that the assumption was that the former occupants had died by drowning or that they wouldn't have enough money to return, and if they did, they wouldn't be able to afford the price hike. The new rent would increase from $350 a month to $2,000 a month. This ritual work will protect the user from any undercurrents of price gouging and hatred directed at a physical home and/or its occupants.

Needs:
* pen and paper
* Psalms 82, 33, and 58 (see appendix C)

* a shovel or gardening trowel
* 1 small statue of St. Joseph
* 1 framed image or small statue of the Black Madonna
* 1 framed image or small statue of a baby
* 2 small angel statues
* a bowl filled with ¼ cup Florida water and ¼ cup plain water

Instructions:

Write the name of the person(s) attempting to push you out of your home through nefarious measures. (If you have photos of the trifling bastards, tape them to any of the images or to the base of any of your statues.) Writing vertically on your paper, write *no justice equals no peace*. Writing horizontally, jot down your desires for restitution. Be clear about what you want to happen.

Recite Psalms 82, 33, and 58 three times each. Next, dig a hole in your yard and bury your petition with the statue of St. Joseph, making sure the statue is on its head. Place the Black Madonna and the baby at opposite ends of a windowsill facing the hole where you buried St. Joseph.

Once you see positive change manifest in your life, dig up St. Joseph and place the whole family together on the windowsill. Add the angels, who'll serve as security, on either side of the family. Keep the bowl of Florida water solution near the window along with a sheet of paper listing the names of every person living in your home. Feel free to include any pets. If you so choose, you can even include a statute resembling your pet or their photo.

Chapter Eight
La Madama's Bridge Over Slave Waters:
Financial Success and Nationalism

Using La Madama for financial success and nationalism aligns with her wisdom, guidance, and ability to confront oppressive institutions, navigating their systems while creating a pathway to independence for her Maroon people. La Madama operated at the intersection of White supremacist ideas about power, resources, rights, and protection, blurring the lines of exclusion while securing survival for those in her care.

Since BIPOC people's earliest interactions with White supremacy, structural racism, and capitalism, liberation for those labeled three-fifths human has been systematically obstructed, replaced with poverty, underfunded education, and deteriorating healthcare, with medical professionals often failing to culturally prioritize our safety and well-being.

In the article "Structuring Poverty: How Racism Shapes Child Poverty and Child Adolescent Health," the authors state, "Unequal access to power, resources, rights, and protection by race reinforces notions of White racial dominance, White supremacy, and radical subjugation provides the social hierarchy that capitalism requires and exploits for profit accumulation."[61] The disenfranchisement of racial minorities has long been enforced through laws and violence, a reality La Madama understood all too well. Racism and capitalism together have sustained a socioeconomic hierarchy built on radical subjugation, beginning with the transatlantic slave trade and cementing the racialized wealth gap. Racial capitalism refers to the interconnection between capitalism and racism, which creates structural advantages in social power, rights, and privileges for certain classes of people.

---

61. Nia Heard-Garris et al., "Structuring Poverty: How Racism Shapes Child Poverty and Child and Adolescent Health," *Academic Pediatrics* 21, no. 8 (Supplement 2021): S108–16, https://doi.org/10.1016/j.acap.2021.05.026.

When structural racism merges with capitalism, resources are distributed along racial lines, perpetuating poverty, educational inequity, housing instability, and disparities in healthcare access.

La Madama

La Madama is the spirit of enslaved women and all their descendants. She is a powerful psychic and extremely protective of children and women. She is a staunch supporter of family stability. By venerating La Madama, we strengthen the connection to our Afrikan ancestry. On the plantation, La Madamaesque women were proficient mediums, diviners, and healers. They were oracles who easily communicated with Spirit, detailing to would-be insurrectionists the perfect moment to escape. La Madama is a spy deceitfully dressed in the cloak of a cook, a nursemaid, or a simple house domestic.

One of the most popular versions of La Madama appears in an apron and headscarf, a scarf tied around her neck and a wicker basket atop her head. La Madama clutches a broom that she uses to sweep away psychic maladies and physical vileness. She is the spirit of conjure women. Her historical ties bind her legacy to the Santeria and Lukumi practitioners, and she is a prominent Spirit energy in Cuba.

La Madama is honored by those who divine with bones and playing cards. She is the root worker who healed the sick, delivered babies, and helped those suffering from separation guilt, as many enslaved families were forever fractured when members were sold away, in many instances never to be heard from again.

La Madama is a road opener who dismantles generational trauma. She makes it so that all parties can breathe and find happiness, if not together then apart. She also paves the way for your financial success in times of stress and dire need.

Her offerings include molasses, whiskey, brown sugar, cigars, water, dark liquors, and a candle the color of her aprons, which can be red, white, orange, yellow, or blue. You can keep La Madama's image in a child's room to help your young one sleep through the night. Winning the lottery or choosing numbers that bring you financial stability is her calling card. Before bed, you can ask her to show you your next day or week's destiny. She'll allow you a small glimpse of what's to come.

EXERCISE: LA MADAMA ALTAR—BRIDGE OVER TROUBLED WATERS

Start your work with La Madama by building an altar and performing the following ritual.

Needs:

* a small saucer with a portion of last night's dinner
* 1–2 red or rainbow-colored aprons with the ties cut off
* a framed image or statue of La Madama
* a glass of plain water
* a small whisk broom
* 1 candle (same color as the aprons)
* a cauldron or other fireproof receptacle
* 1 charcoal disk
* 1–3 teaspoons each of the following dried herbs: peppermint, sage, rue, rosemary, and marjoram
* pen and paper
* Psalms 5, 122, and 76 (see appendix C)

Instructions:

The night before the working, set aside a portion of your dinner on a saucer. Cover and leave overnight.

Lay down the aprons to form your altar space. Set down the dinner portion, La Madama image, water, whisk broom, and candle on the altar, letting La Madama dictate how she wants her items placed. (As the energetic embodiment of all those enslaved women, La Madama is free to decide her whereabouts and the whereabouts of her tools.)

Once you've placed everything to her liking, place a lit charcoal disk inside the cauldron. Add a pinch of each herb, then use the pen and paper to write your petition. Detail how you envision your financial success playing out in the next week, month, year, or five years. Explain who you need protection from and why. Finally, thank La Madama with praise words, then fold the note into a small square. Hold it against your heart while sitting quietly with La Madama for ten minutes.

When the ten minutes are done, read your petition out loud nine times, then recite Psalms 5, 122, and 76 three times each. Leave the petition on your altar as is or frame it. As financial change happens, cross those items off your list.

Options:

* Instead of burning a pinch of each herb, burn a teaspoon of any one of them.
* Sit quietly with La Madama for fifteen to thirty minutes longer after writing and reading your petition out loud.

Harriet Tubman

I venerate the ancestress Harriet Tubman through the image of La Madama. Both are formidable women who refused to be denied their ability to conjure freedom by any means necessary. Harriet Tubman transformed the lives of Black people suffering under the Afrikan Holocaust.

So, who is Harriet Tubman? If we were to rely on Kanye West's unflattering statement about her, we might mistakenly believe her only contribution was moving enslaved people from one plantation to another, implying her work wasn't about liberation but simply shuffling human property around to keep plantations running. *Bullshit.*

Harriet Tubman escaped enslavement on September 17, 1849, alongside her brothers, Ben and Henry. When they changed their minds and returned, she pressed forward alone, traveling ninety miles from Maryland to Pennsylvania. She later returned to the South, freeing over three hundred enslaved people.

She carried a gun, both for protection and to prevent hesitant runaways from second-guessing their path to freedom. She used herbal tinctures to quiet young children and babies, soothing their cries during the treacherous journey to Canada. And in all her years of work, Ancestress Harriet never lost a single passenger aboard her freedom train.

During the Civil War, she served as a nurse, cook, and laundress, tending to both soldiers and enslaved people. By 1863, she led a spy and espionage network for the Union, contributing to the formation of Black Union regiments.

In 1896, she bought land in Auburn, New York, to establish the Harriet Tubman Home for Aged and Indigent Colored People. Pneumonia claimed her life on March 10, 1913.

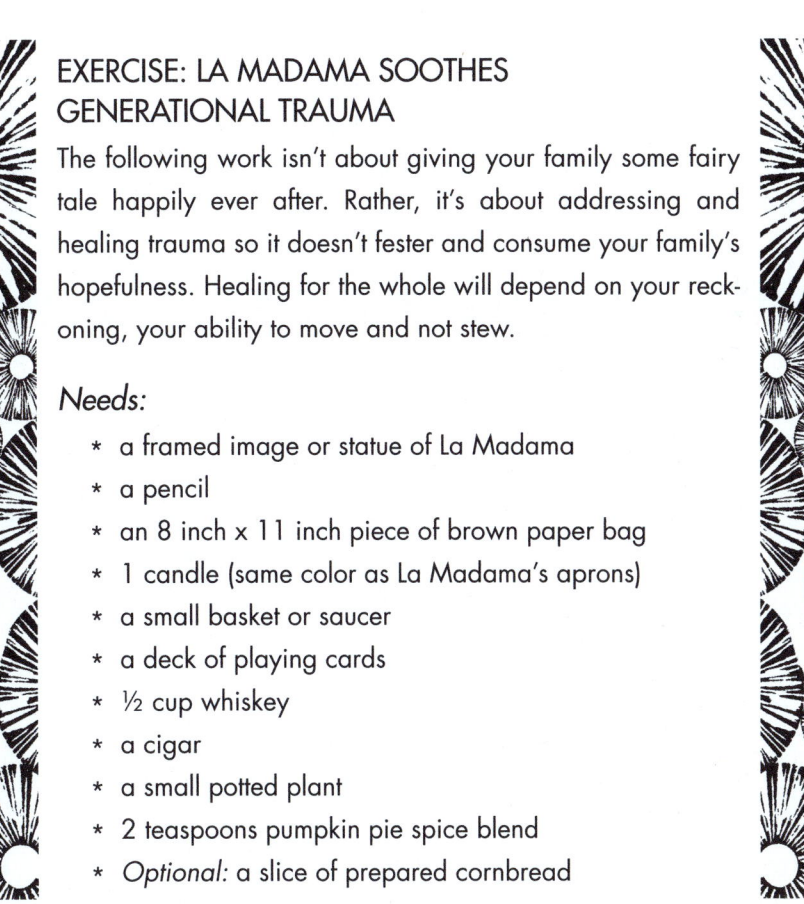

EXERCISE: LA MADAMA SOOTHES GENERATIONAL TRAUMA

The following work isn't about giving your family some fairy tale happily ever after. Rather, it's about addressing and healing trauma so it doesn't fester and consume your family's hopefulness. Healing for the whole will depend on your reckoning, your ability to move and not stew.

Needs:

* a framed image or statue of La Madama
* a pencil
* an 8 inch x 11 inch piece of brown paper bag
* 1 candle (same color as La Madama's aprons)
* a small basket or saucer
* a deck of playing cards
* ½ cup whiskey
* a cigar
* a small potted plant
* 2 teaspoons pumpkin pie spice blend
* *Optional:* a slice of prepared cornbread

Instructions:

Place the image of La Madama on your altar. Then, using the pencil and brown paper bag, write La Madama a letter. Ask her to heal each person in your family over time and to sweeten their hearts so they recognize any hurt they've caused others and make amends in their personal healing journey. Be clear about what defines each person's state of trauma as you see it.

When finished, light the candle and place the deck of cards into La Madama's basket. Sprinkle the cards with the pumpkin spice blend. Light the cigar and blow three puffs into the air, then set aside.

Place the whiskey and optional cornbread next to La Madama. Read the letter out loud once, pause to consume a mouthful of the whiskey and/or cornbread, then reread the letter. Repeat this process three times.

After you've completed the readings, fold the letter into a small square and bury it in the soil of your potted plant. Water the soil lightly, then sit staring into the candle flame for fifteen to thirty minutes. As you do, ask La Madama to show you the way in your dreams.

Sit with your candle for fifteen to thirty minutes each night for nine nights. La Madama will come, but be prepared to cry before you heal.

Option:

* For added protection, you can carry any one of the following dominoes: the 1/1 domino, 5/5 domino, or the 5/1 domino. By carrying this domino in your purse, pocket, or wallet, you'll ensure that the field of healing surrounds you at all times. Breathe on the domino whenever you need an extra burst of healing energy.

Diving Deeper

The original GI Bill ended in 1956 having provided educational training to eight million World War II veterans. It also facilitated 4.3 million home loans, totaling $33 billion, fueling an era of economic expansion.

However, this period also widened the racial wealth gap, deepening economic disparities between Black and White households in America. While many veterans received life-changing benefits, approximately 1.2 million Afrikan Americans were systematically denied key provisions under the GI Bill. This exclusion prevented them from receiving low-cost home loans, first-time home buyer assistance, college tuition waivers, and unemployment insurance, locking them out of wealth-building opportunities that shaped the nation's middle class.[62]

My grandfather Lonzo Coulter (or PawPaw, as I called him) would tell me stories of watching White men and Black men enter government offices having equally put their lives on the line for America with hopes of returning home to enjoy a slice of her pie. The Black men left these brick buildings with a few crumbs and not enough filling to decipher what kind of pie they were eating.

My grandfather had dreamed of attending cooking schools in foreign countries and then returning home to open a restaurant specializing in cuisine from Morocco, Ghana, Brazil, Cuba, Jamaica, and Haiti. "I stood there, pleading my case. I was due twenty dollars a week in unemployment compensation. I, just like other Black soldiers, was told to go out and pick a house on a street of our choosing and a check would be cut. We were treated like children, made to window shop only to be told the home of our choosing was either too much house for Negroes, or the neighborhood was more suitable for White GIs. When we got irate, the reasoning changed to us being ineligible because, unbeknownst to us, we had been dishonorably discharged, like a shitload of other Black men all across this country.

....
62. Erin Blakemore, "How the GI Bill's Promise Was Denied to a Million Black WWII Veterans," History, June 27, 2019, https://www.history.com/news/gi-bill-black-wwii-veterans-benefits.

"You know, I believe our community would be much better off if our people had been given the chance to instill the values of financial planning and education in our children. Imagine our children knowing what it feels like to live for generations in homes owned by their families. Imagine the pride. Imagine how that pride would bleed over into the community, schools, and businesses. Imagine the money flowing to and fro, by us, for us, and to us. With all that growth, America wouldn't have to lie about life, liberty, and happiness 'cause we'd all have access to them, and we'd fight to keep it strong by policing anybody who dared take them away from us."

When I think about opportunities to garner generational wealth as a BIPOC person, two events seriously weigh heavy on my mind: the 1912 Tulsa Race Massacre and the very recent closing of Raleigh, North Carolina's Liberation Station Bookstore.

According to the article "Tulsa Race Massacre: Fact-Checking Myths and Misconceptions," when a Black male, nineteen-year-old shoe shiner Dick Rowland, attempted to enter the South Main Street elevator but tripped and attempted to break his fall, he may have inadvertently grabbed hold of the White seventeen-year-old elevator operator, Sarah Page.[63]

Page screamed, and eyewitnesses alleged that Rowland was trying to sexually assault Page. Others alleged that the two knew each other since the White owner of the shoeshine parlor often arranged for his Black workers to ride that particular elevator to the top floor, where the colored "restrooms" were located. This elevator ride usually occurred once a day for Rowland and Page, putting them in each other's company and making it hard for many to believe Page felt threatened by a man she encountered regularly. Nevertheless, the *Tulsa Tribune* fanned the flames with an inflammatory front page identifying Rowland as "Diamond Dick." It further alleged that he was a stalker. There was also an editorial called "To Lynch a Negro Tonight." The front-page article was titled, "Nab Negro for Attacking Girl in Elevator."

....

63. Lakshmi Gandhi, "Tulsa Race Massacre: Fact Checking Myths and Misconceptions," NBC News, May 30, 2021, https://www.nbcnews.com/select/news/tulsa-race-massacre-fact-check-ncna1269045.

Sarah Page never pressed charges against Rowland, but the eyewitness allegations and racist newspaper article were enough to get him jailed.[64] Later, fifteen hundred White men swarmed the courthouse, and rumors of lynchings ensued. When a mere seventy-five armed Black men, many of whom were WWII veterans, offered to help guard Rowland, it fueled the false belief that a large-scale insurrection of Blacks from all over the region was occurring. This "White hysteria" set off a two-day White supremacist terrorist attack from May 31 to June 1, 1921. More than twelve hundred houses were burned and bombed, 215 were looted, and two newspapers, a library, a hospital, churches, hotels, stores, and other Black-owned businesses were decimated.

In today's economy, it's estimated that White rioters destroyed more than $200 million worth of property. At the time of the massacre, Greenwood was the wealthiest Black enclave in the nation. After the massacre, ten thousand people were left homeless.

In the hours after the riots, all charges against Dick Rowland were dropped, as it was decided that he did in fact stumble and stepped on Page's foot accidentally. Kept in jail during the riots, Rowland would later leave Tulsa, never to return.

The desire back then was to keep money circulating within their own community, so Blacks collectively funneled money into their businesses, creating a self-sustaining system where goods and services were reinvested for the betterment of Black people. We're talking about self-sustaining barber shops, salons, restaurants, taverns, pool halls, movie theaters, grocery stores, doctors' offices, and law offices.

In the spirit of Tulsa and the thriving communities decimated by White supremacy, I created this work to help us recognize the best institutions to break financial bread with. I've never been one of those people pretending to be desensitized by racial unrest. I want to shop where I'm celebrated and encouraged to dream big.

....
64. "The Tulsa Race Massacre: Facts about the Attacks and the Coverup," History, May 30, 2021, https://www.history.com/news/tulsa-race-massacre-facts.

EXERCISE: WALKING AROUND LIKE I OWN THE WORLD

Get ready, wealth is on the way!

Needs:

* a red satchel or drawstring bag
* ½ cup cornmeal
* 13 drops peppermint oil
* Psalm 32 (see appendix C)
* a sheet of paper with the image of La Madama
* a purse (*Note:* Choose a style and color you'll enjoy wearing regularly)

Instructions:

Place the cornmeal in the satchel. Add the peppermint oil. Holding the satchel, recite Psalm 32 nine times, then place the image inside (you may need to fold or cut down the paper to make it fit). Ask La Madama to protect your peace as you shop, eat out, do your banking, and so on.

Place the satchel inside your pillowcase and sleep with it there for nine nights. After the third night, keep the satchel in the purse during the day. This purse is now your blessings bag—whenever you wear it, savings will find you. Keep the purse fed by reworking this exercise every two weeks, sprinkling the used cornmeal around the perimeter of your home each time.

EXERCISE: MOLASSES WHISKEY

After completing this work, ask yourself and your family, "How can we help generate self-sufficiency within our community?" Then, with La Madama's guidance, be about the business of doing it!

Needs:
- a shot glass
- whiskey
- 1 teaspoon molasses (blackstrap is best, but any variety will do)
- 9 dimes
- 1 each of the Ace of Diamonds and Ace of Clubs playing cards
- 1 red candle
- 1 white candle
- 1 blue candle
- a framed image of the US flag
- Psalms 5, 122, and 76 (see appendix C)

Instructions:
Place the shot glass on your altar. Fill it halfway with whiskey, then add the molasses. Using the dimes, form a triangle around the glass. Place the candles in the following order: red at the top of the coin triangle, white to the left, and blue to the right. Set the flag image in front of the triangle. On both sides of the flag, place the playing cards, the Ace of Diamonds to the left and the Ace of Clubs to the right. Light the candles, then recite Psalms 5, 122, and 76 three times each.

Ask La Madama to protect you and ensure that you receive payment for the labor of your ancestors. May your payment come in the form of financial freedom—having enough money to purchase a dwelling, invest in education, and aid your family in a deeper, more meaningful understanding of generational wealth.

SASHA AND MALCOLM

My boyfriend (now my husband) of six years, Malcolm, and I decided we wanted to open a vegan/vegetarian restaurant. We decided to test the waters by first starting with a food truck. We're both college educated. I have a degree in restaurant and hotel management, and then I went back to earn a marketing degree. Malcolm has a degree in business law, and he eventually went to culinary arts school. We were in northern Louisiana with a dream to bring Cajunized soul food with a vegetarian twist to this particular region.

About a month into our business launch, we heard through a local newspaper that there was to be a nighttime music and wine festival, and so we thought, what better way to get our brand out there? We had gone through the necessary clearances to have our truck stationed as part of the festival and thought we were set. We were prepared to let our food do the talking. We had a menu rich in vegan and Louisiana favorites. We had vegan shrimp po' boys, vegan pulled pork sandwiches, vegan red beans and rice with vegetarian sausage, cauliflower chicken with barbecue dipping sauce, and sweet potato fries. We even made homemade ginger beer.

Within the first two hours, we made $6,000. I believe our long lines, compared to the other shorter lines of customers, started fucking with the pride of the other truck owners, and the next thing we knew, somebody had called the police. Get this: The police were told that we were using butter infused with marijuana to keep folks running back to our lines. I have locs and so do my husband, my sister, and her husband, who were both assisting us with trips to the market to purchase more food when we were running low. Yes, we smoke marijuana from time to time, but we don't lace our food with marijuana. Not only is that against the law, but that shit don't jive with our ethics. The people buying our food chose a healthier alternative when it came to what went in their mouths. I wouldn't sneak weed into someone's food and run the risk of seriously causing them physical harm.

The police took the White side and arrested us. We were let go within twenty-four hours, but we wound up spending every cent we earned to get out of jail, and we had to trash a shitload of bad food. We tried to sue the event coordinator and just wound up getting shitted on by our own attorney, who thought for an up-and-coming business we were making more potential enemies than friends.

I saw your book at a local bookstore and decided to email you. You emailed back, and I got a divination and a financial working that we used inside the food truck and will use in our restaurant. (We're saving for it now!) Your ritual business reading has been on point, and along with financial gain, we now have a well-rounded sense of camaraderie with other BIPOC people who are also starting out with a fresh businesses in the same area. We have each other's backs so the money earned by one becomes a win for us all. Even more important, we've become protectors of each other. We make sure we hire security that looks like us, we're strapped just in case, and we have friends out there videoing our events, because dirty people don't stop playing dirty—they're always looking to get it in. We come strapped with Hoodoo, and as my husband says, "With ancestors guarding our backs, they damned if they do and damned if they even thinking about jumping funny."

EXERCISE: SWEEP OUT THE BROKE AND SWEEP IN THE HOPE

This work counters the conspiracy to keep Black and Brown people living below the poverty line. It clears a path to spiritually align our truth with that of our highest need.

Needs:

* a bowl
* 3 tablespoons ground cinnamon
* 3 tablespoons chili powder
* soil from the grave of an ancestor/elder of yours
  (*Note:* If you don't have access to the grave soil of

an ancestor, place soil from your yard and a sheet of paper with the image/name of the ancestor and their birth and death dates inside a mason jar and use instead)
* 3 tablespoons sulfur powder
* Psalms 5, 122, and 76 (see appendix C)
* 1 spray bottle
* plain water
* 3 tablespoons Hoyt's cologne
* 3 tablespoons Kananga water
* a broom and dustpan

Instructions:

In the bowl, combine the cinnamon, chili powder, soil, and sulfur powder. Recite Psalms 5, 122, and 76 three times over the mixture, then set aside.

Fill your spray bottle halfway with plain water. Add the Hoyt's cologne and Kananga water, seal the bottle tightly, and shake vigorously nine times. Spritz the broom's bristles nine times as well.

Sprinkle the contents of the bowl onto the floor of your business or wherever transactions will be made. (Sasha placed a portion of the mixture in a satchel, then hid the satchel inside her food truck.) Allow the mixture to sit for twenty-four hours before sweeping it up with the broom. Repeat once a month.

As folks travel, their feet will remind them where the best-kept secrets are, and they'll keep coming back and recommending you to others. Watch business boom!

Generational Wealth

Generational wealth is the transfer of financial assets from one generation of family members to the next. It can include cash, stocks, bonds, and other investments, as well as real estate and family-owned property and businesses.[65] Generational wealth provides financial security and opportunities for future generations.

I define it here, in part, because for years, BIPOC communities have understood that the Tulsa Race Massacre was driven by more than just jealousy—it stemmed from fear. White supremacy saw the self-determination of Tulsa's Black residents as a threat, a rising consciousness that could spread to other Black communities. When Black Wall Street was bombed, America annihilated its own, ensuring Black people remained at the bottom of the socioeconomic ladder.

This brings me to another moment of White supremacy: Liberation Station, a bookstore in Raleigh, North Carolina. It opened its doors on June 19, 2023, with the mission of promoting Black literacy, especially among young readers. Less than a year later, on April 13, 2024, it shut down.

Owner Victoria Scott-Miller reported threats of violence, including death threats and hate mail. One caller even described her son's clothing and whereabouts, detailing times when he was alone inside the shop.

At the bookstore's grand opening, nearly four thousand people attended. Victoria and Duane Miller, the store's owners, said the aim was to serve the community and prepare their own children "for the world they will one day inherit."[66] Liberation Station specialized in children's books by underrepresented Black authors.

Miller alleged that the threats began with conservative objections to books taught in Raleigh schools, including *The Absolutely True Diary of a Part-Time Indian*, *Gender Queer*, and *George and Lawn Boy*.

The owners alerted their landlord to the escalating hate. But in a city that's 28 percent Black, many accused Scott-Miller of lying, accusing *her* of using racial intimidation. The landlord's response, according to the bookstore's owners, was to begin showcasing the spot to potential new tenants.

....

65. "Generational Wealth Overview," *MSN*, 2024, https://www.msn.com/en-us/money/personalfinance/generational-wealth-overview-examples-and-faqs/ar-AA1otB6e.
66. David Menconi, "Liberation Station, N.C.'s First Black-Owned Children's Bookstore, Comes to Downtown Raleigh," Visit Raleigh, June 14, 2023, https://www.visitraleigh.com/plan-a-trip/visitraleigh-insider-blog/post/liberation-station-opens-raleigh-nc-black-owned-children-book-store/.

EXERCISE: PIGGY'S BELLY OF COINS

This work is about collecting your money on your terms and deciding how to further invest it in all things BIPOC.

Needs:

* an extra-large piggy bank for each person in your home
* a sheet of paper with a 4 inch x 6 inch image of La Madama for each person in the home
* Psalm 1 (see appendix C)

Instructions:

Fold each La Madama image into a square small enough to slip inside the banks. When finished, recite Psalm 1 as you shake each bank. Ask La Madama to protect your wealth and to bless those who receive it while empowering you with their sacred abundance.

Distribute the banks to your family members. When the banks are full, use the money to invest exclusively in BIPOC businesses. Repeat every time you fill a bank.

Options:

* Put the money in a savings account called Ujamaa Savings Account (Cooperative Economics). You can save it up for a year, then make a collective family purchase from a BIPOC business.
* If you have children, use the banks as a learning opportunity. For example, you could talk about the importance of buying BIPOC or tell them about Black Wall Street and how buying BIPOC helps continue its legacy.

CYNTHIA

I started off in my house teaching only women nude Kemetic yoga, and then that moved into a combo male and female class. When the hookups started becoming bad for business (and what I mean by that is that folks were about to come to blows more often than being about the business of sutras), I decided to move into couples' yoga for an over-thirty-five crew. Later, I added sexercise with a little more of an aerobic impact.

A few months into my new plan, a White couple showed up. A few weeks after that, another White couple showed up. Nobody cared; as long as they were allies, not anthropologists, they were welcome. Not to mention, inclusive businesses earn more notoriety and money.

But it wasn't long before, I admit it, I struggled with their attendance. I stopped giving a fuck about the money. I had so much anxiety and so many sleepless nights. I felt like a fuckup when I looked into the eyes of other BIPOC people. They were beginning to look like anthropologists.

Then one day, the two women asked to film a class. They enthusiastically shared with me that they were going overseas to visit relatives and wanted to still feel connected to their new Black friends.

Using the term "new Black friends" was the first hiccup, but more than that, my antenna was on high alert about the filming. I should've been more proactive in tossing them out on their asses, but you know how a Black person struggles with reverse racism. I didn't want to be that Black person accusing White people just because they're White. I wanted to lay all our cards on the table and judge them for the here and now. I also believed that if I didn't do something, it'd become an all-out assault on every Black and Brown body, not just in that room but in our community.

In my mind, I was going off, but I knew the ramifications in real life if I played the angry Black woman. So I took six cleansing breaths in and out of the Tonglen meditation method, and then I stared her in the eyes, and with a very intimidating smile I said, "Girl, where do they do that at? Not here; we're assed out in a safe space. How safe would it be if I let you film us and parade our asses around like modern-day Sarah Baartmans and Ota Bengas? Not here, and if you don't mind handing your bags to my sistah, she will place them in a cubby. Record with your mind."

I could tell these White people had never anticipated the word no leaving my lips. They were more than stunned. One of the men said he was mortified. He thought she, his wife, posed a perfectly sane question, and that her reasoning could not and should not be disputed. My husband was by now leading the rest of the class in their sutras, as I had asked; his patience level wouldn't have been able to withstand this level of Whiteness. I told both couples to enjoy the day or leave, because my frequencies were rapidly turning sour. The women started to cry, and one told me I should be ashamed because she was a cutter, and her anxiety tonight would have her slicing through dinner straight into bathtime. I told my secretary to refund the payment for that day's lesson. Just then, one of the men whispered to the other a catchphrase I felt like he must've been sitting on for a minute: "You keep it, soul sistah. Think of it as your people's reparations." They left, giggling.

I didn't hear of them again until about six months later. One of my client friends was at a pharmaceutical conference, and this White naturopathic doctor spoke during a breakout session about this exclusive heaven-on-earth experience. She spoke about a place where the intersection between food as medicine and grounding through nude exercises gave new meaning to holistic healing. My client immediately thought of me and retorted, "I feel fabulous, because I'm already there. My husband and I have an amazing nude sexercise class that infuses Kemetic yoga with tantra and aerobics." The doctor gave her a bullshitting smirk, then went on to explain how she had met this couple, a one-of-a-kind pair who had moved to Mexico and opened this quaint space that infused all that. She swiped on her phone to show the owners of this delectable experience, and my client damned near fainted. It was the White couple who got pissed at me for not letting them film my routine. They were using my entire program. The fraudsters were draped in Kente cloth from head to toe. Their matted hair was beaded, and they wore adinkra arm bracelets. The doctor, who didn't notice my client's shock, told her she couldn't show her any moves to verify if they were, in fact, copycats because no cameras of any kind were allowed in class, and that included cell phones.

I don't own a monopoly on exercise, but I feel like stealing the work of BIPOC people and repackaging it with a White face just to make it eclectic is cultural appropriation, not appreciation. I felt like I needed to protect my business, so I went all Juju on the Fly on them. I wanted the copycat business to fold and for any wealth generated to go to the indigenous people of the land they were berating with lies. Then I wanted the energy to feed into my business so that it would prosper, and with that, I wanted to become a health ambassador to BIPOC couples longing to spice up their sex lives.

Thank you so much, Iya. In six months, my client called to say that the rip-off business had folded. It had something to do with drugs and the misappropriation of funds. My life changed too—this homegirl opened a second studio!

Juju on the Fly

Now, my love, it's time to affirm your success. The following work opens a portal, allowing us to invite financial success and abundance into our lives, as well as infusing us with the creative wherewithal to become wealth magnets.

EXERCISE: ABUNDANCE CORNBREAD WITH WEALTH BECOMES ME AFFIRMATIONS

When my grandfather baked cornbread, he would often remind me that food, when whispered to, can open a portal to a world of our choosing. With each turn of phrasing, each bite and swallow, we can transform our sorrow into a space of grace and spiritual upliftment. This ritual work will fill your heart and your daily life with the power to thrive even through the most dire situations.

Needs:

- a framed image or statue of La Madama
- Psalms 5, 122, and 76 (see appendix C)
- a sheet of paper
- scissors
- 1 9-inch round cake pan or cast-iron skillet
- oil or butter (for greasing the frying pan)
- a large bowl
- 1 cup cornmeal
- 1 cup all-purpose flour
- ⅔ cup sugar
- 1 teaspoon salt
- 3½ teaspoons baking powder
- 1 teaspoon cayenne pepper
- 1 tablespoon peppercorns
- ⅓ cup vegetable oil
- 1 cup milk
- 1 egg
- 9 dimes

Instructions:

Place the image of La Madama on your altar. Print out or copy Psalm 5 onto a sheet of paper, then use the scissors to cut out each line. Set the paper strips aside.

Grease the pan and preheat your oven to 400 degrees. In the bowl, mix the cornmeal, flour, sugar, salt, baking powder, cayenne, and peppercorns until well combined. Add the vegetable oil, milk, and eggs. Mix thoroughly.

Begin adding the lines of Psalm 5, stirring between every line. When finished, pour the batter into the pan. Bake for twenty-five minutes or until the cornbread is golden brown and a toothpick inserted in the middle comes out clean. Remove from the oven and set it on your altar.

Place the nine dimes in a circle around the cornbread. As it cools, recite Psalms 5, 122, and 76 three times each. When finished, speak the names of the perpetrators/thieves standing in the way of your success. Be firm when stating what you'd like to see happen to them. Allow the cornbread to sit on your La Madama altar for twenty-four hours before placing it at the foot of a tree.

Over the next nine days, recite the following affirmations daily three times before bed and three times before you leave for work.

I am wealth.
Wealth becomes me.
I create financial abundance from my ideas.
Wealth becomes me.
My hard work allows me to reap the rewards of a flourishing business.
My hard work allows me to reap the rewards of a flourishing peace of mind.
Worry about money does not consume me.
Money adores me.
I am a delicious money magnet.
I sing the praise of joy.
Joy sings the praise of my abundance.
Wealth looks good on me.
I wear abundance, and it ain't never going out of style.

Hold the image of La Madama in your arms and repeat the following: *Mama La Madama, now that you know the theft that stands in my way, I want you to hear how I call upon abundance to free me from poverty and wants that lie outside my realm of financial ability.*

Chapter Nine
St. Expedite:
Hurry Up and Be Prepared

Who doesn't want fast results when working the juju out of their Hoodoo? Enter St. Expedite, the patron saint of urgency. Some call him the saint of nerds, hackers, and students. Others say the Roman Catholic Church considers him too pagan to be officially recognized.

In New Orleans, St. Expedite mirrors the Northside Skull and Bone Gang, a city staple since 1819. Each year on Mardi Gras, the Gang reminds us to hurry up and get our lives in order, because after revelry comes death. And if we must hurry, we must also make sure our lives are well spent. That urgency, the push toward rebirth—that's classic St. Expedite.

In Ifa, initiation follows a formal process: praise words, song, and dance, followed by the reading of destiny. This reading reveals past life choices that will resurface, as well as the trauma or joy you're rushing toward based on your recent actions.

During my Itan, St. Expedite's energy surrounded me. One of the Iyanifas even said, "St. Expedite walks with you as a reminder never to linger too long at one pitstop. Life's journey is arduous for the soul. Just as sorrow doesn't last forever, neither does joy. Experience each life like a sponge soaking up water. And when that life is over, transition like a sponge relieved of liquid—free." I've come to understand that to birth my dreams, I must welcome the challenges and lessons that shape my soul's journey.

My favorite tale about St. Expedite goes like this: During the 1700s, a box containing bones arrived at a French monastery. The nuns receiving the box saw the word *EXPEDITE* written all over it, which some historians believe was intended to ensure the corpse received a speedy delivery. But the nuns thought differently; they assumed the bones inside were all that remained of the long-lost St. Expedite, a centurion thought by some to be martyred in 303 in Turkey as a result of his conversion to Christianity.[67, 68]

The nuns began praying to the bones. As their prayers were answered quickly, the corpse's speedy heroics spread for generations to come. He would become known as the saint who moves faster than the speed of sound, so you better make sure you're sure when you petition him—you might get more than you prayed for.

Tomorrow Isn't Promised

St. Expedite's statue is of a young Roman Centurion squashing the daylights out of a crow with his right foot. A ribbon with the inscription *cras* ("tomorrow" in Latin) is expelled from the bird's mouth. In Italian, *cras* is supposedly the sound of a crow in pain. Italian folktales speak of how crows as well as ravens are forever cawing about tomorrow.

St. Expedite destroys our yearning to procrastinate. He reminds us that satisfaction in life comes from getting to the root of our problems. Tomorrow is promised to no man, woman, child, or creature. We have to act promptly, as if our destiny depends on it. Success happens right now, when we champion a belief in our divine right to the same privilege as White humans. Our lives matter, our rights matter, our humanity matters, and St. Expedite wastes no time in granting us the win in a world set on cheating us out of a basic right to live our truth.

As much as he is the saint of fast solutions, he is also the saint of deadlines, which include work projects, homework assignments, commitments, and so on.

---

67. Karen Williams, "St. Expedito's Role in South Louisiana Catholicism, in New Orleans, and in the Italian-American Community near Independence, Louisiana," Folklife in Louisiana, accessed August 1, 2025, https://www.louisianafolklife.org/LT/Articles_Essays/lfmexpedito.html.
68. Frank Lewis, "St. Expedite, 'the Patron Saint of Procrastinators,'" *Mazzolini Artcraft* (blog), May 2019, https://mazzoliniartcraft.com/blog/st-expedite-the-patron-saint-of-procrastinators/.

EXERCISE: ST. EXPEDITE ALTAR

St. Expedite is the bringer of fast luck and often sought by gamblers, number runners, and lottery players. Folks work with St. Expedite when they need situations or challenges in their lives to change quickly. It could be getting your car out of the shop, hearing back from a college or university your child applied to, or finding out about the promotion you're up for.

There's no limit to expediency in your life. Just remember to give St. Expedite a slice of lemon pound cake and a glass of water after he's speeded you on your way.

Needs:

- 2–3 yards gold fabric
- 1 yard red fabric
- a framed picture or statue of St. Expedite
- 1 red candle
- 1 gold candle
- a bottle or can of beer
- a glass of water
- a checkbook
- a knife
- 9 fake gold doubloons
- 9 black feathers
- a bell
- a large mason jar filled with twenty fake dollar bills
- a glass of dried barley
- a pair of dice
- a tarot deck
- 5–10 deposit slips from your bank
- Psalms 1, 35, and 118 (see appendix C)

Instructions:

Cover your chosen altar space with the gold fabric first, then layer the red fabric over it. Place the image in the center and allow the candles to stand guard on both sides of it. Place the beer to the left and the glass of water to the right. The checkbook should lie in front of the image, and the knife should rest on top of the checkbook. Placement of the remaining objects is up to you; remember, be creative.

Once you've decorated your altar, recite Psalms 1, 35, and 118 three times each. Your space is now open to expedient magick.

Diane's Story

After Hurricane Katrina, Diane, a client of mine, and her family were living somewhere in the Rocky Mountain region. In Diane's words, "The feds had a plan to save the lives of all the poor Negro citizens of New Orleans who were stupid enough to live in a city that close to water and had no car or no plan to swallow what they couldn't swim through."

Once the world heard the residents of New Orleans were getting the keys to Uncle Sam's wallet—I'm talking vouchers, food stamps, and free medication—New Orleans "refugees" were worth more than a mouth full of Cash Money Millionaires grills. I'm laughing now, but Diane's story wasn't funny. As stories about the aftermath of Katrina go, her tale didn't live in the realm of a monolith.

On August 29, 2005, Katrina made landfall as a Category 4 hurricane at Plaquemines Parish. That's forty-five miles southeast of New Orleans.[69] While the city didn't receive a direct hit, the levees buttressing the industrial Seventeenth Street Canal collapsed beneath the storm's surge.[70] The

....

69. National Weather Service, "Hurricane Katrina – August 29, 2005," National Weather Service, last modified August 29, 2005, https://www.weather.gov/bmx/katrina_08292005.
70. Brantly Keiek, "Remembering Hurricane Katrina: Gulf Coast Reflects on Devastation and Resilience 19 Years Later," WGNO, August 29, 2024.

waters of Lake Pontchartrain and Lake Borgne overwhelmed the city. In the end, 20 percent of the city was submerged in massive flooding.[71]

When the levees were demolished, ten thousand poor, mostly Afrikan American residents were displaced. Many were housed in warehouses to await their next destination. Being "stuck" during Katrina had different connotations for people born and raised in New Orleans versus those just passing through or watching the disaster on TV. Many residents had lived blocks away from where they grew up, or sometimes even in the same house where they were born. New Orleans is more than a location on a map; it's an extension of our DNA.

Many didn't have the money to evacuate or didn't trust that the city wouldn't do them dirty if they left and tried to come back. As much as we love the city, and we do love the city real hard, we ain't afraid to kiss and tell the truth, even when it hurts. We don't trust politicians and we don't trust banks—chalk it up to institutionalized racism.

Katrina was a reckoning, a moment when people realized that, in the wake of a catastrophic disaster, it would take forever for New Orleans to recover. Amid the chaos, a scheme emerged: mass adoptions.

It's almost absurd to think about. While thousands of children languish in foster homes and adoption centers for years, entire families—Mom, Dad, six kids, grandparents, even pets—were taken in within minutes, all through a simple three-page Katrina adoption form.

Diane, through tears, recalled every word of that form. It listed names, medical history, schooling, work, background, next of kin, and the financial aid you were requesting or already receiving. "I run my mouth plenty and ask all sorts of questions, not just when I'm nervous. That's how come I know what every page of those forms said, and how come I got the read on our adoptive White folks. They wanted to know about bank accounts, if you previously rented or owned a home, and lastly, if you had burial insurance. You were also supposed to list the monetary amounts for the burial insurance. The adopting families got the money, all of it."

---

71. Sarah Pruitt, "How Levee Failures Made Hurricane Katrina a Bigger Disaster," History, August 27, 2020, https://www.history.com/articles/hurricane-katrina-levee-failures.

Once the papers were signed, any money meant for the adoptees went directly to the families who took them in. They received thousands of dollars every month, while the adoptees themselves were treated like servants.

According to Diane, this adoptive family didn't want big, athletically built Black men riding in the same van or truck as their teenage daughters. The wife even laughed while saying, "We Christians, but not that kind of Christian." That meant Diane's husband and two brothers got rerouted on a bus that was supposed to meet up with the rest of the family after ladies and the elderly got settled in.

It sounds stupid because it was. But for many, the only way out was through adoption or a shelter, and adoption sounded like the better choice. "I had so many people to worry about," Diane recalls. "My eighty-five-year-old, diabetic mother; my eighty-nine-year-old, paraplegic, wheelchair-bound daddy; me, sixty and blind 'cause of diabetes; and my daughter, thirty years old and pregnant."

The men were loaded onto buses filled with other Black men, all promised that as soon as the women, children, and elderly were settled in their forever homes, their families would send for them. (That phrase, "forever homes," makes my skin crawl. It made Black people sound like stray dogs, desperate to claw their way out of a shelter, fighting not to be put to sleep.)

Diane's family waited. And waited. But the men never came. It took an entire year before they were reunited with her two brothers and her daughter's husband. A whole damn year. That ain't right.

It was during that year Diane's family realized the truth: Their adoptive family weren't just Christians. They were KKK Christians—the kind who wore white sheets and pillowcases draped over their bodies in church. They trapped Diane's family in a barn crowded with horses, cows, and pigs. And filth: Animal shit. Human shit. Forced to work the farm from sunup to sundown, they never did see the inside of their adoptive family's house.

Diane's daughter, Sherilitha, had her baby in that barn they were forced to call home. Diane had to feel her way to the umbilical cord. "I had to coo that throbber to rest," she sobbed as she recalled the story. "Those White folks had never seen a blind midwife. My mama was there, up in age, but prepared to guide my hands when guiding was needed. She sang and moaned and chanted the psalms required. Wasn't no fanfare for the little one."

The husband kept questioning whether a baby would slow the family down in their daily work. At one point, he even suggested putting the little girl up in *their* home. Diane immediately saw it for what it was: a way to ensure none of them tried to run.

"It's just a thought," he said. "Wouldn't want you distracted."

Diane nearly lost her mind. Her mama and daddy erupted, cussing and shouting. The White man just smiled. "Don't worry," he assured them, "it was only a suggestion. No need to risk high blood pressure over it."

Diane's mama turned to the wife, pleading for Sherilitha to be let go so she could raise her baby like any mother should. But the wife refused. "She'll need money to live that kind of life," she said, "and we're not ready to make that kind of investment in a young woman with a newborn baby born in the middle of nowhere." She reminded them that Sherilitha didn't know her way around, that some folks in town "weren't as hospitable to Blacks" as they were.

Diane's mama was desperate, hoping Sherilitha and the baby could get a message to someone, anyone, if they got out. But the wife ended the conversation with finality: "Splitting up a family is never part of God's plan. You live together, you die together. Amen."

It must've been when the baby was a month old that Sherilitha came up with a plan. She had been calling on St. Expedite all night, and the moment she drifted off to sleep, he appeared to her in a dream. He told her how to pay him back once they got out.

To this day she won't say how, but somehow, Sherilitha got her hands on matches, a gas can, and plenty of rags: shitty rags, pissy rags, clean rags, dirty rags. You name it, she had it. All by herself, Sherilitha contorted her body and squeezed through a weatherworn slab of dry, rotting wood at the back of that locked barn-prison. Once outside, she scurried to the far ends of the farm and started a fire, a trail of flames leading straight to their adoptive family's car.

Then—an explosion! It could be heard for miles. Within minutes, firetrucks, police cars, and neighbors had swarmed the farm. Sherilitha screamed, dragging two paramedics toward the barn, shouting about padlocks and enslaved Black people. The next thing Diane remembers, they were inside an ambulance. Through its windows, Diane's mama watched the scene unfold, the adoptive parents staring in horror as their money train fled.

It was hard for Diane to dredge up the trauma, but she begged me to share it. In our last chat, Diane sighed and said, "I believe somebody will heal from my family's story. Maybe it's a cautionary tale, but listen, that place was as close to hell as I ever want to be again. Working for food, working for your prescription medicine, taking hose-pipe baths, and then drinking from that same hose. I was a slave, a modern-day slave, and I'd tell anybody that."

When she and her family got back to New Orleans and reunited, they gave Expedite his due. She said, "Right after we paid him, jobs came our way, and we were able to start working toward owning a home for all of us. We even started a Hurricane Fund, just so if we were ever in the position where we had to evacuate New Orleans, we wasn't putting ourselves up for no kinda fucking adoption. We all have had enough plantation living for a thousand lifetimes."

EXERCISE: POMEGRANATE TO THE RESCUE

The entirety of this work is completed inside a cold, dark cabinet.

Needs:

* paper and pen
* 1–2 yards red fabric
* a framed image or statue of St. Expedite
* 1 battery-operated candle
* a bowl of whole pistachios
* a glass of pomegranate juice

* 1 bottle of frankincense oil
* 9 black feathers
* Psalm 115 (see appendix C)

Instructions:

With the pen and paper, write out your troubles. Tell St. Expedite about the forces working against you, and remind him that this theft of time, money, and/or sanity must be avenged. Write their names nine times each; if you know their addresses, write them nine times each as well. Fold this letter into a small square and place it inside the bowl of pistachios. Set the bowl aside.

Position the cloth inside a cold, dark cabinet (you may need to fold it to get it to fit). Place the image of St. Expedite in the center, turn the candle on, and place the candle in front of the image. Place the glass of juice in front of the candle, the bowl of pistachios to the left of the image, and the frankincense oil to the image's right. Scatter the feathers across the altar, then sit and recite Psalm 115 nine times.

Each day over the next nine days, take a feather, sprinkle it three times with the oil, and leave it at the steps or walkway leading to a church, intersection, railroad, bus stop, courthouse, cemetery, school, hospital, or body of water. As you place the feather, know you're assured that St. Expedite is on the move. The leaving of the feathers lets him know you're keeping track of human time. While spiritual time is quite different, we recognize and appreciate St. Expedite's haste, not just in our work but in global affairs. This is why we leave the cabinet altar in place until the desired outcome is achieved. (Check daily just in case you need to change out the candle batteries.)

EXERCISE: ST. EXPEDITE, COME FAST AND IN A HURRY, SWEETEN MY WORRY

This exercise takes place over nine days. I like to have extra candles on hand so I don't have to halt the work by stepping out to buy more.

Needs:

* a framed image or statue of St. Expedite
* a vase filled with fresh flowers (a gift to the saint for fierceness and the kindness used to carry our intentions with speed)
* 1 red candle (for speed)
* pen and paper
* 1 refrigerated lemon pound cake (for sweet reward)
* a glass of water
* a psalm that reminds you of speed (see appendix C)
* a 6/6 domino (for abundance)

Instructions:

Place the image in the center of your altar with the flowers on either side. Light the candle and place it on the opposite side of the photo.

Using the pen and paper, write a short letter to St. Expedite telling him what you need speed to relieve. Close by telling the saint about the cake and water he'll receive once he's fulfilled his duty to you. Place your letter in front of the image, then end by reciting any psalm that reminds you of speed nine times. Let the candle burn for an hour each day for nine days, and carry the domino with you for the duration of the work. Spend a few minutes a day rubbing the domino in your hands and breathing into it.

If St. Expedite feels your request is worth his speed, you'll have your reward after nine days. At this time, St. Expedite will expect his reward, so place the cake and water on your altar and allow it to sit for three days. Afterward, leave the offerings at the foot of a tree.

If after nine days your request isn't granted, you can keep petitioning for two more sets of nine days. If there's still no luck, St. Expedite has determined your case doesn't deserve his expediency.

DAMON LASLO

I was one of those people who believed in atheism. I saw a YouTube dude talking about religion being a scared person's answer to everything they hadn't learned to comprehend yet. Since the beginning of time, folks have been making up shit for the shit they didn't have the background knowledge to decipher.

I was a college student a day away from graduation when I gave up on religion; nobody was making me believe anymore. I even donated my Bible—the one I sifted through during breaks, when I was forced to fly home, sit in a pew of my childhood church, and digest Southern Baptist ramblings about hellfire—to a thrift store. I had stumbled out of the matrix, and I was good with my freedom as an atheist. I had long since grown tired of churches, all of them, and at thirty-four years old, living on my own, I just believed in hustling.

I made my money as a used car salesman by day and an up-and-coming record producer by night. I had all these DJ events lined up, and because I wanted to make a name for myself, I'd DJ and have clients pay me in gas money before the event. The total for hyping the crowd and spinning records was always handled a day after the event. It's human nature to have this get-over spirit. We all go through it at times, some worse than others.

Some clients kept asking for more time on the wheels of steel or tried to barter with sexual favors. I got offered blowjobs from men and women; I'm an equal opportunity DJ over here. It was fucking wild the number of drugs they tried to let me hold down. I wanted my money, though. I can buy my own weed. I wasn't about to be known as the DJ who accepts drugs or sex over money.

I got a girl I fucks with. She's into crystals and incense. She convinced me to get a reading. St. Expedite turned out to be my savior. It was funny to me at first. I was just going along because she promised a whole lot of anal play. She walked me through how to work with St. Expedite, and she watched me for nine days do the shit. The whole purpose was to see if he could make it rain in my life. All I know is money started rolling in right after the nine days was up. Checks, cash, PayPal, CashApp, Venmo. People found a way to get me paid.

My girl advised me to do the ritual once a month and to take a portion, however much I decided, and leave it inside a church. The atheist in me was like, let's see what happens when I don't do the work. Shit, when I didn't do it, my pockets were fucked up. I was the brokest joke you ever want to see. I guess St. Expedite got more hustle than me—leaving niggas played on purpose is all kinds of foul.

I guess these days I'm a part-time atheist. I only believe in the spirits who show me what they're working with.

EXERCISE: WHEN IN ROME

You'll be making cards during this work to expedite payment. I like to create a big batch at a time, just to have plenty on hand whenever my life needs financial speed.

Needs:

* 1 bottle of red wine
* 1 store-bought pound cake
* a bowl filled with 6 garlic bulbs
* a toy crow or a framed image of a crow
* Psalm 145 (see appendix C)
* a 4 inch x 6 inch piece of cardstock

- a sheet of paper with a 4 inch x 6 inch image of St. Expedite
- glue
- tape
- a pen

Instructions:

At your St. Expedite altar, place the red wine and pound cake in front of his image. Place the bowl of garlic bulbs to the left of the image and the toy crow to the right. Recite Psalm 145 nine times over the garlic bulbs.

Take the cardstock and glue the image of St. Expedite to one side of it. Set it aside to dry. Once dry, write your name and the following on the opposite side of the cardstock: *Thank you always, St. Expedite!* The card is now complete.

How do you use these cards? If you're expecting payment from a client and you're worried they might try to finagle their way out of it or pay you beneath your worth, tape the card to the outer closed lid of your laptop. Position it so that when your computer opens, it's as if St. Expedite is staring at you from behind your computer's open outer lid. (This placement will look funny and probably remind you of a jack-in-the-box each time you open your computer, but it's worth it!) You can also tape a card inside your mailbox.

Once the card is in place, recite Psalm 145 nine times again, this time toward the image. Ask St. Expedite to ensure you get the outcome you desire.

On the ninth day after this work, scatter the garlic bulbs near six banks around town, or all outside one bank—either way, your money is on the way.

PawPaw Ernest Herrera

My grandfathers on both sides of my family loved stories. My Honduran grandfather, Ernest Herrera, had an insatiable curiosity for the history of places. Fate placed him in fascinating locations as a longshoreman, and wherever he traveled, he sought indigenous remnants of a people's spiritual iconography.

PawPaw Herrera considered himself a connoisseur of trinkets, artifacts that defined the soul of a place. Among them, he believed statues of St. Expedite were deeply tied to Mercury, the Roman messenger god, as well as Elegua, Baron Samedi, and Bonsu, all messenger tricksters.

He often told me that as Voodoo customs evolved, St. Expedite became more prominent. The greater the need for spiritual work to transcend the earthly plane, the more he was called upon to usher in transformation and to clear the path for renewal.

I've seen this reverence firsthand. In St. Louis Cemetery, folks petition Mama Marie Laveau at her tomb, leaving behind trinkets, St. Expedite statues, and prayer cards, hoping to double the speed of their petitions. I've watched them place a small sampling of pound cake atop her tomb, grinning into the night, surrendering their anguish and dismay to the spirit realm. A prayer whispered into Queen Marie's ears, carried swiftly by St. Expedite, soaring through the haunting breeze, a ritual weaving the Loa's mysteries with remnants of Catholicism. If that ain't New Orleans, child, then I don't know what is.

SHANTE

I'm Shante, and I can only tell you my side of the story. We were on a tour of St. Louis Cemetery. It was late at night, and Terrance was joking about the St. Expedite photo prayer card that one of the ladies on the tour handed out to people. He was making a rap song about the saint's name, and I spent ten minutes trying to get him to chill. We were in New Orleans celebrating our seven years of marriage. Terrance had gotten that itch folks talk about, and a year prior we were on the verge of divorce. I busted his ass with two White women in my bed. His ass was sandwiched in between them, all cozy and giggly like a cooing baby. They were filming porn. I thought I was in the middle of somebody's nightmare—it was fucking surreal! I thought about getting an OnlyFans account and fucking his best friend on camera to get back at him. But I couldn't do it. I couldn't be that reckless, that nasty on purpose. So I opted for therapy, which brought us back to each other. We even decided that each year we would celebrate our recommitment. That's how we wound up in New Orleans, standing in front of Marie Laveau's tomb with Terrance rapping.

TERRANCE

Look, I could've thought of a zillion things to do in New Orleans, but Shante wanted to visit cities of the dead. I thought it was funny, and when the guide kept it moving and we were left behind, I thought it was the perfect time to show her there was nothing to this hocus pocus. I took the envelope concealing the St. Expedite card from my pocket, and inside was a string of twine with nine knots. The instructions said to leave coins from your pockets and let the string touch the coins and the card as they lie on top of the tomb. On the back of the envelope, it said, "Return home and leave out on a windowsill either one slice of flat bread, a bowl of six figs, or a glass of red wine. Repeat Psalm 34 and let St. Expedite bring you quick luck, happiness, and success." I told St. Expedite I didn't want to have any attraction or sexual urge for women besides Shante. Shante wanted a warning: Whenever women were on the verge of playing, I'm on the hunt to be dicked down. I thought it was funny as hell. What kinda magick can make that happen?

Two weeks later, we were back in Dallas, and Shante came with me to this party. This woman we both knew as a maneater tried to shoot her shot. Titties were all glistening and glittering. What you know, your boy wasn't moved by none of it!

Shante walked her cousin downstairs to the lobby. Her cousin was waiting for her fiancé, who was unsure of how to get to the party. In no time at all, Shante was texting me. She was asking me if I was okay or if I needed her help since she was just downstairs. At first, I thought it was Shante spying on me, but it happened when we were at our jobs way across town—in two separate directions. Shit like that kept happening and still happens six years later.

St. Expedite works. I don't know how, but our marriage was hanging on by a thread before him, and now we work through anything.

EXERCISE: AT THE ENDS OF MY ROPE

How often do we find ourselves at the ends of a very-life-altering rope? I remember a time when a client was being harassed at work for wearing her hair naturally. My client was a woman who had earned three master's degrees and two PhDs. This Afro-Brazilian wonder woman, most days, wore beaded braids. Her boss didn't like it, and when performance evaluations were handed out, my client often received low scores. The boss claimed her hair was a nuisance and made the corporation look like a ghetto. This corporation sold yoga wear, and most days employees were expected to show up at work dressed as if they are stepping into a yoga studio, with messy buns and all. Yet my client's braids were too ethnic. This ritual will soothe your heart and mind while expeditiously clearing a path of divine ease.

Needs:

* glue
* a sheet of paper with the image of St. Expedite
* a sheet of paper with the image of Marie Laveau's tomb
* Psalm 34 (see appendix C)
* a piece of twine with 9 knots
* a glass of red wine

* 1 slice of flatbread, divided into 4 pieces
* 4 figs
* 9 dimes

Instructions:

Glue the image of St. Expedite to the back of the image of Marie Laveau's tomb, then allow them to dry. Over the next twenty-four hours, recite Psalm 34 three times (once in the morning and once at night) while holding the glued image.

The next day, place the image on the altar and take up the twine. While holding it, rub each knot as you tell St. Expedite exactly what brought you to the end of your rope and what he can do to fix it.

When finished, wrap the twine around the bottom of the wine glass and prop the image up against the glass. After a week, leave the bread and pour the wine at the foot of a tree. Rest the twine and figs on top of the bread. Recite Psalm 34 once and walk away, tossing the dimes over your left shoulder as you do.

Repeat the entire ritual as often as needed.

Juju on the Fly

Keep in mind, St. Expedite is known for his swift interventions. He's the saint to petition when dangerous, life-threatening situations arise, including money matters. St. Expedite will also help you with school exams, remodeling, home repairs, car repairs, legal issues, divorce settlements, and child custody cases.

All that said, remember that magick takes time to clear a path through the user's devotion. So how devoted you are will determine the swiftness of your petition.

It's advisable to feed St. Expedite either as he journeys or right after he's completed your task. I've met folks who feel more comfortable propriating him after the deed is done, but they forget. Their happiness at having turned the tide in their lives causes excitement that can fog their memory. St. Expedite could read this as a slight, causing him to renege on your success and crush it beneath his heel like he did that crow. Nobody got time for that sheesh.

EXERCISE: THE NEED FOR SPEED

This is another working for those times you need movement in a situation.

Needs:

* 1 yard gold or red fabric
* a large vase of water
* 6 garlic bulbs on a saucer
* 1 cup barley flakes in a mason jar
* a framed image or statue of St. Expedite
* 1 white battery-operated candle
* 9 roses
* 1 cup of any of the following: pine nuts, almonds, walnuts, or pistachios
* pen and paper
* Psalm 24 (see appendix C)
* frankincense oil

Instructions:

Lay the fabric in a cool, dark cabinet (you may need to fold it to get it to fit). Place the water on the left, the garlic bulbs and barley flakes on the right, and the image of St. Expedite in the center. Place the candle toward the very front so you can easily access it later. The roses and nuts can go wherever you like.

Using the pen and paper, write a letter explaining to St. Expedite why he should take on your case. Don't be shy; tell it like it is, then read the letter out loud to his image. When finished, place the letter on the altar and recite Psalm 24 three times.

Each morning for the next nine days, add three to nine drops of frankincense oil to the barley flakes, seal, shake, then leave the jar uncovered. Turn on the candle and recite Psalm 24 three times. In the evenings, before you go to bed, turn off the candle and recite Psalm 24 three times again.

After nine days, discard the water, garlic bulbs, barley flakes, roses, and nuts at the foot of a tree. Recite the psalm once more before leaving. In a very short time, you'll see doors opening in your life, moving your situation with speed. Repeat as often as needed—St. Expedite loves a chance to flex his speed!

Chapter Ten
Black Herman the Magic Man:
Protecting Your Activism

The Master of Illusion, Benjamin Rucker (1892–1934), was an Afrikan American stage magician known by his stage name, Black Herman. He blended magic with a strong separatist and militant political message, using his performances to uplift Black pride and empowerment.

Born in 1892 in Amherst, Virginia, it didn't take long for Herman to establish himself as the most prominent Afrikan American magician of his time. In Harlem, he headlined shows at Marcus Garvey's four-thousand-seat Liberty Hall, and in 1923, he sold out the venue for an entire month.

On stage, Herman captivated audiences by weaving magical occultism with a belief in superstition, drawing spectators into his illusions while advancing his political ideology. He had learned his craft from Prince Herman, a master illusionist with whom he toured in medicine shows. In addition to performing magic, they sold a "secret African remedy," a tonic rumored to contain alcohol and common Hoodoo spices.

After Prince Herman's death in 1909, seventeen-year-old Rucker decided to continue the magic but abandon the medicine show. He took the name Black Herman in honor of both Prince Herman and Alonzo Moore, another renowned Afrikan American magician.

In the South, Black Herman performed exclusively for Black audiences, while in the North, he entertained mixed-race crowds. A Black nationalist and activist, Herman spent his free time among revolutionary thinkers like Marcus Garvey and Booker T. Washington. Conversations between them led all three to take up Hoodoo talismans to ward off racism during their travels and speaking engagements, selling these conjure objects to Black audiences. According to Black Herman, the Black race could elude Klansmen simply by outliving them.

Little is known of Herman's early life, except that as a teenager, he wrote of enduring five years of hunger and wandering. During this time, he developed the uncanny ability to speak the language of animals, becoming an expert interpreter and ventriloquist.[72] Herman infused his tricks with powerful origin stories, weaving magic into narratives of survival and resistance. One of his most captivating routines, the Rope Escape, was said to be an illusion inspired by Afrikan shores, symbolizing the cunning and defiance that allowed enslaved people to elude captivity.

Beyond magic, Herman's tonics became part of the spectacle. His brother and assistant would position themselves among the audience, performing dramatic feats that convinced onlookers they were in a state of possession. Herman would then spiritually exorcise the demon, sometimes releasing a snake, other times a lizard that slithered through the crowd. This spectacle reinforced the belief that consuming Herman's tonic could protect one's body from a full-blown infestation by malevolent spirits.

Mediums also provided spiritual readings at his shows, allowing audience members to check the temperature of their own soul state. Herman's employment of these mediums eventually led to multiple arrests. But he never viewed them as setbacks. Instead, he saw them as evidence of Afrikan American oppression and proof his power was so strong, no jail could hold him.[73]

Secrets of Magic Mystery and Legerdemain

The act Black Herman was most famous for was called Buried Alive. It was such a compelling illusion that it kept audiences in suspense for weeks.

To accomplish the feat, Herman would slow his pulse by applying pressure to his underarm. A doctor of his choosing, secretly in on the act, would declare him dead before he was interred in Black Herman's Pri-

---

72. "Black Herman—Magic Biography," MagicTricks, accessed August 1, 2025, https://www.magictricks.com/black-herman.html.
73. "Black Herman's Secrets of Magic, Mystery, & Legerdermain," Internet Archive, July 12, 2021, https://archive.org/details/black_hermans_secrets_of_magic_mystery_and_legerdermain.

vate Graveyard. (This was all performed in full view of the audience.) As the coffin was lowered into the ground, Herman would make his unseen escape. For days, sometimes weeks, crowds would gather, watching the burial site and wondering about Herman's fate.

But while one town sat in agonizing suspense, Herman was already staging the same spectacle somewhere else. By the time the original coffin was exhumed, revealing a living, breathing Herman, another town was holding its breath, waiting for their turn to see the master illusionist reappear before their very eyes.

In 1925, Herman published *Secrets of Magic, Mystery, and Legerdemain*, which contained a semifictionalized autobiography, beginner illusions, astrology advice, lucky numbers, and Hoodoo customs and practices.

Black Herman died in 1934 at the age of forty-two, collapsing from a heart attack in Louisville, Kentucky. But because of the legendary success of his Buried Alive trick, many refused to believe he was truly gone. People traveled from far and wide, desperate to glimpse the body they were convinced would rise within days or weeks. The belief was so strong that the city eventually relocated his body to the railway station, as crowds refused to leave.

Herman's assistant, Washington Reeves, saw one final opportunity in the illusion: Even after Herman's death, Reeves charged a dime for admission to view Black Herman's corpse.

Many visitors took this as their chance to poke Herman's body with a pen, hoping to reveal the truth with their own eyes: Was the great Black illusionist truly dead, or was he causing trouble somewhere across town in the name of liberation?

Fun fact: The famed jazz musician Sun Ra (Herman Blount) was named after Black Herman!

EXERCISE: BLACK HERMAN ACTIVISM AND PROTECTION ALTAR

Following is the set-up for an altar to Black Herman for protection and support for your activism. Following this exercise is a working to empower you even further.

Needs:

* 2–3 yards black satin fabric
* a sheet of paper with the image of Black Herman
* 3 black candles
* a black top hat
* a black magician's wand
* a set of dousing rods
* a deck of black playing cards
* 1 rabbit's foot
* 9 shot glasses filled with either whiskey, gin, vodka, or rum
* 9 chicken feet painted black, red, green, blue, yellow, orange, purple, white, and pink
* 3 lucky hand roots
* Psalm 139 (see appendix C)

Instructions:

Lay the black satin over your desired altar space. Place the image of Black Herman in the center and the candles in a circle around the image. Place the top hat in front of the candles. To the left, place the shot glasses in a circle. To the right, place the chicken feet in a circle. You can place all the other items wherever you like.

Recite Psalm 139 nine times. Black Herman's altar is now ready for use.

EXERCISE: BLACKER THAN A HUNDRED MIDNIGHTS

In this work, you'll write down the names of people working against your activism. I'm talking about folks who are experts in throwing stones and hiding their hands—the social media comrades. You know, the ones who adorn themselves in your pain but have the audacity to scold you for standing up for yourself and your community.

Needs:

* a black top hat
* 3 cups soil from your yard
* 1 cup asafoetida
* ½ cup sulfur powder
* 3 pieces of hematite
* 3 pieces of black obsidian
* a marker
* 1–3 bay leaves
* a 4 inch x 6 inch framed image of yourself
* Psalm 91 (see appendix C)

Instructions:

Fill the hat with the soil, the asafoetida, and finally the sulfur. Push the hematite and obsidian pieces into the soil.

Using the marker, write the names of the individuals on the bay leaves. When finished, cover the leaves with soil and place your image on top of the mound.

Recite Psalm 91 three times, then recite the names listed on the leaves. Let them know that they're bound to suffer every time they even try to stand in the way of BIPOC progress. Their hopes and dreams will be buried alive until the day they recognize your humanity and right to live as privileged a life as they do.

Replace the soil mixture and bay leaves after one hundred nights.

Magickal Activism

According to *Merriam-Webster*, *activism* is defined as a doctrine or practice that emphasizes direct, vigorous action, especially in support of or opposition to one side of a controversial issue.[74] As an educator and self-appointed spiritual disruptor, I've had my fair share of run-ins with those who believe in sanitizing a world gone to shit. These dangerous-minded individuals see educators who teach historical truth as enemies, accusing them of liberalizing children's minds instead of celebrating knowledge. To them, teaching history forces White children to see themselves not as allies in unearthing truth, but as bullies upholding systemic racism, passing its tenets down generation after generation.

Every year, we hold a book fair at my school where I buy books for my kids, relatives, students, and friends' children. My love for books has helped nurture five avid readers in my own home, children who have lost themselves in the pages of *Goosebumps; Fear Street; The Bluest Eye; Roll of Thunder, Hear My Cry; Bud, Not Buddy; The Watsons Go to Birmingham; The People Could Fly; M.C. Higgins, The Great; Monster; Slam;* and *Lockdown*. They've ridden intergalactic spaceships, battled fearsome wizards, witnessed revolutions, felt the weight of socioeconomic depravity, and experienced racism firsthand through literature. They've come to understand that White privilege is an idea to challenge, not an acceptable way of being.

Yet this year, the school's book fair taught me a different kind of lesson, one about erasure. During my non-teaching period, I stepped into the book fair, eager to cross the threshold into worlds of fantasy, history, laughter, fright, and heartbreak. But what I found were shelves covered in construction paper with bold capitalized signs: *NOT FOR SALE!* When curious little fingers still tried slipping beneath the flaps, yellow tape—crime scene tape!—was deployed across entire shelves.

I gasped.

---

74. James Haskins et al., *Conjure Times: Black Magicians in America* (Walker & Company, 2001).

After ensuring no students were in the library, I let out a sharp, undeniable, "What the fuck!" My principal rolled her eyes, her silence speaking louder than words—racists gonna racist, after all. The librarian squinted over her glasses, then said something that landed like a slap: "America is tired of degenerates spilling their nasty, wicked, ungodly business around for good, Jesus-fearing families to see. America is fighting back."

I laughed, but the sound landed somewhere between humor and insanity. My principal asked if I was okay. I caught myself, then responded, "So, America's return to Christian values begins with banning books like *Under My Hijab*; *The Double Life of Pocahontas*; *The Drinking Gourd*; *Celia Cruz, Queen of Salsa*; *Between Us and Abuela: A Family Story from the Border*; and *A Dream Come True: Coming to America from Vietnam–1975*. You ladies are tripping, and I mean hard. This isn't a book fair, it's a crime scene. This is where freedom of speech comes to die."

Needless to say, I spent the rest of my off period buying as many banned books as my pocket change allowed, and I came back every single day that week. I even posted on social media, calling local book lovers to come, buy banned books, share banned books, read banned books in public spaces. Because my heart was screaming the truth: It's time to stop scrolling for tragedies and start recognizing the travesty unfolding before our very eyes.

In Duval County Public Schools, a district that encompasses Florida's largest city of Jacksonville where 70 percent of the students are of color, these same students are being told by the government that there's an inherent need to stop the "leftist indoctrination" in our public schools.[75] A proposed bill, HB1467, seeks to dissolve leftist influence by requiring a certified media specialist to review and approve every book available to students. It also introduces an "age-appropriate" qualifier, imposing additional scrutiny on books addressing racism, discrimination, sexism, and LGBTQIA+ rights.

---

75. Douglas Blair, "I'm a Former Teacher. Here's How Your Children Are Getting Indoctrinated by Leftist Ideology," The Heritage Foundation, 2019, https://www.heritage.org/education/commentary/im-former-teacher-heres-how-your-children-are-getting-indoctrinated-leftist.

This racist rhetoric seeped into a district where 40 percent of students are economically disadvantaged—an area that once advocated for inclusive classroom libraries meant to reflect diverse populations, ethnicities, religions, and gender identities. But by 2022, a shift in ideology had taken hold. Just as culturally sensitive books were delivered, the governor pivoted from inclusivity to political demoralization.

In response, Floridians mobilized, forming the Florida Freedom to Read Project in June 2022, a movement aimed at raising awareness through education, connecting parent organizations across Florida to defend students' access to information and ideas within schools. If you want to join the fight against book banning, contact the Freedom to Read Foundation at www.ftrf.org.

EXERCISE: BAN ON FIRE

This ritual targets laws that ban our rights and the people who create such laws.

Needs:

* a cauldron or other fireproof receptacle
* 1 charcoal disk
* 3 pieces of dragon's blood resin
* tape
* a sheet of paper with the shortened name of the target law or an image of the person spearheading that law
* 2 matches
* Psalm 140 (see appendix C)
* a knife

Instructions:

Place a lit charcoal disk inside the cauldron. Add the resin, arranging the pieces in a circle. Take the sheet of paper and tape the matches to the back of it. (Cross the matches and point the matchheads downward so they act as the feet of the paper.) Lay the knife over the cauldron.

Once the resin has completely burned out, lay the paper on top of the knife over the mouth of the cauldron. Recite Psalm 140 three times. Remove the knife, light both matches, and drop the paper into the cauldron to burn. (Cover the cauldron with a fireproof lid if the flames get too wild.) Leave the cauldron covered overnight.

For the next nine nights, continue to burn any remnants of the paper. Each time, recite Psalm 140 three times. Continue in this manner until there's nothing left of the paper except tiny pieces of ash. On the morning after the ninth day, take the spiritual residue and leave it near a courthouse, library, or school.

Diving Deeper

During March and April of 2022, I began reading my students *Bud, Not Buddy* by Christopher Paul Curtis, the story of a ten-year-old Black boy living in Flint, Michigan, during the Great Depression. After escaping a horrifying foster home, Bud sets out in search of the man on a flyer, a musician he believes to be his father.

For a month, I planned lessons around clips of the author discussing his journey as a writer and how this book became an instant classic among Black children who had never experienced the Great Depression firsthand. It was a story packed with adventure and misadventure, deeply rooted in poverty and social conditioning.

And while some might argue about White supremacy's relevance, my husband's grandmother had a different take on it. "I saw White folks eating their dogs. Wasn't no man's best friend then, when you got a bellyache. That's about the time your best friend starts looking like a week's worth of stew meat."

I read *Bud, Not Buddy* to a class of twenty-two fifth graders, who listened as images of life during the Great Depression faded in and out across my Promethean board. Their eyes followed the map of America, slowly understanding that there was nowhere to outrun hunger pains, dirty clothes, and smelly bodies. They realized that Black and White people alike lived with sickness until the moment they either forgot they were sick, reasoned with the pain, or died. There was no White America or Black America, just an entire nation equally let down.

At the end of each chapter, we processed how the story shaped our faith in this country. Those fifth graders unpacked loss in ways adults often fear to confront.

A few days into reading, the principal told me the book was too depressing for children at this age. They needed as many happy friendship stories as possible. Loss, like the Great Depression, was too heavy a concept.

I stopped reading for a week, to collect the tools for my ABRACADABRA *Sigil Warfare Ritual*, which I share in the following pages. But by the next week, parents had begun emailing me and begging me to continue reading whatever that book was that had boys and girls alike wanting to know if Bud finally found a sliver of happiness. Out of twenty-two students, nine were BIPOC, but it was two White moms who bought me class copies. The children had spoken. They had mobilized their parents in ways racist rhetoric would find impenetrable. These children, if given the chance, will grow to become not just allies but accomplices to a world rooted in compassion, not division.

Activism in Doses

One is never too old or too young to become an activist. I firmly believe that Black Herman understood the art of dosing: the delicate balance between revelation and restraint.

When you give a baby medicine, you disguise the sour beneath the sweet. Herman mastered this principle through showmanship, using sleight of hand to mesmerize his audience. He knew they would hang on his every word, eagerly awaiting the moment of awe. But as they waited, they would also absorb the bitter truth of their oppression. Through his illusions, they learned the importance of fighting back. Remaining silent and passive was an unconscionable act of self-malice, reducing one to a thing to be taunted and misused.

Within Herman's world of magic, his audience came face-to-face with the reality that Black people had been robbed, victimized, and discarded like soulless animals. And yet, Black Herman rallied them, urging them to challenge the lies, demanding to be recognized as humans, unlike the rabbit pulled from the depths of his top hat.

Teaching kids to be activists requires a similar kind of creative "dosing," helping kids take small, intentional steps to support their community. For kids that may look like:

- Keeping their neighborhood clean. Planting flowers one seed at a time.
- Volunteering with a parent at a local food bank.
- Learning about their future voting rights.
- Researching products, toys, and businesses that support their community.
- Investigating websites that feature people who look like them but fail to invest in their education, neighborhoods, or Black-owned businesses. (Activist kids learn early on that their economic impact is powerful.)

Kids spend a large part of their waking hours maneuvering through school. Student activists can take action by:

- Running for student government, or creating one if none exists.
- Starting an underground newspaper or a safe space to challenge conservative narratives.
- Tutoring peers, ensuring no future thinkers are left behind.
- Leading school boycotts of products, services, and companies that fail to serve their community.

Even very young children working under the guidance of a trusted adult can start being an activist by:

- Recycling or signing petitions for a community recycling hub.
- Creating birdhouses to foster an appreciation for nature.
- Building libraries filled with banned books.
- Writing letters to government officials, or creating videos voicing their stance.

Across communities, students can organize book clubs to study banned books, launch podcasts discussing social justice issues, and practice self-care through therapy and friendships. I encourage young activists to ease into verbalizing their spiritually disruptive nature by researching platforms like change.org or resist.bot, both of which can help them formulate informed conversations with media outlets and legislators.

Activism isn't just about protest. It's about reclaiming the narrative, realigning hearts with minds, and dismantling divisions, regardless of race, gender, or identity.

EXERCISE: TROUBLE THE WATER

In this working, you'll be creating a shirt empowered with protection for your activist gatherings. The day before you undertake it, make sure to place the decal onto the T-shirt using the package directions.

Needs:

* a mason jar
* 1–2 cups soil from your yard
* 3 tablespoons camwood powder
* 3 tablespoons dried mandrake root
* 3 sticks of Seven Afrikan Powers incense
* 1 white t-shirt in your size with an iron-on decal of a panther (*Note:* You can find BIPOC decal sellers

online, or make your own decal with printable iron-on paper)
* Psalm 140 (see appendix C)
* 2 yards black satin fabric
* 3 black satin ribbons
* 1 black candle

Instructions:

On your Black Herman altar, fill the jar halfway with soil. Add the camwood, more soil, then top with the mandrake root. Light the incense sticks and stand them up in the jar, leaving the tops exposed so they can burn to the midway point undeterred.

Lay the shirt flat on the altar, place the black candle in the center of the panther's face, and recite Psalm 140 three times. Remove the candle and wrap the shirt in the satin. Tie the shirt tightly with the ribbons, then place it near Black Herman's image. Light the candle, and let it burn for fifteen minutes.

Leave the shirt on the altar for nine nights, repeating the psalm over the shirt each night. Light the candle at each sitting for fifteen minutes.

After the ninth night, you can wear the shirt under your clothes whenever you participate in activist gatherings. Each time after the shirt is washed, repeat the entire working.

EXERCISE: ABRACADABRA SIGIL WARFARE RITUAL

Working with Black Herman, this ritual is sigil warfare and seeks to open the eyes of divisive individuals.

Needs:

* a cauldron or other fireproof receptacle
* 1 charcoal disk

* 3 pieces of dragon's blood resin
* paper and pen
* a sheet of paper with the Akofena adinkra symbol (see appendix D)
* a large mason jar
* 3 tablespoons camwood powder
* 3 tablespoons valerian root
* 1–2 cups soil
* 3 sticks of seven Afrikan Powers Incense
* 1 black plate
* Psalm 142 (see appendix C)

Instructions:

Place a lit charcoal disk inside the cauldron, then add the resin. On the opposite side of the Akofena adinkra symbol, write the following:

ABRACADABRA
ABRACADABR
ABRACADAB
ABRACADA
ABRACAD
ABRACA
ABRAC
ABRA
ABR
AB
A

Rub the paper in your hands until it's hot to the touch, then set it aside.

Add the camwood powder and valerian root to the mason jar, then drop in the adinkra symbol (you may need to fold the paper to get it to fit). Fill the jar to the top with soil. Light the incense sticks and stand them up in the jar, leaving the tops exposed so they can burn to the midway point undeterred.

Place the jar on top of the black plate, then recite Psalm 142 three times. Petition Black Herman to make divisive folks see the world through your eyes.

Repeat the lighting of the resin and incense sticks and psalm recitation every night for nine nights. Afterward, discard the perishable items at the foot of a tree. All other items can be repurposed for future workings.

Global Sparks That Reignited a Movement

On May 25, 2020, the world watched a horrific act of violence when Minnesota police officer Derek Chauvin pressed his knee into the neck of George Floyd for nine minutes and twenty-nine seconds, resulting in Floyd's death. Bystanders filmed the entire scene, which happened in broad daylight.

George Floyd's death became the Molotov cocktail thrown around the world. In the summer of 2020, as we experienced the first waves of a deadly pandemic and historic levels of unemployment, people took to the streets in protest of Black people killed by overpolicing. Hashtags catalogued the lives lost: Breonna Taylor, Tamir Rice, Freddie Gray, and so very many others.

In the same year as Floyd's killing, demonstrators in Belgium scaled a statue of King Leopold II, whose reign of terror (1865–1909) killed and maimed millions of Kongolese people. His statue was defaced, and a flag was hoisted representing the Democratic Republic of the Kongo. Defying COVID restrictions, people around the globe took to the streets in London, Seoul, Sydney, Monrovia, Rio de Janeiro, and in Syria, where a mural honoring Floyd was painted. To our brothers and sisters abroad, the stories of people of color dying in police custody reignited flare-ups in places like western Europe, where systemic inequalities haunt both Afrikan and Middle Eastern immigrants.

CARMEN WILLIAM

Remember the Rhodes Must Fall Campaign? I was there during the sit-in. I kept thinking anybody who defends Cecil Rhodes is a dumbass, Black or White. I even knew a couple of sistahs named Rhodesia growing up. Somebody didn't do their homework. The name of the now modern-day Zimbabwe was coined by European settlers employed by the British South Africa Company looking to honor their founder and director.[76]

Cecil Rhodes was a racist who paved the road to apartheid and restricted voting rights and land ownership. His statue is White folks' reminder that they have a right to see us as animals. It's an illusion made a reality by the color of our skin. Anatomically, we the same except for the color. Rhodes has said straight out of his own mouth, "I contend that we're the first race in the world, and that the more of the world we inhabit, the better it is for the human race." He wanted to make the Anglo-Saxon race one empire. His dream was the unification of British rule for the recovery of the United States. If White people believing in supremacist ideology can unite under the same supremacist umbrella, why can't BIPOC and AAPI people and our allies and accomplices unite to make a huge dent in the fight against our annihilation?

I'm so glad I found you on social media. I don't know what I would've done without that Herman on the Mainline work. I guess I'd still be talking that ADOS shit and analyzing my survival through a separatist lens. Even a fool can see that don't serve nobody but the supremacists. It helped me work through my own misgivings about even entertaining my struggle was any kin to Black and Brown people globally. Now my goal is to create kinship bonds with as many Black and Brown folks as I can worldwide.

....

76. Ben Johnson, "Cecil Rhodes," Historic UK, accessed August 1, 2025, https://www.historic-uk.com/HistoryUK/HistoryofEngland/Cecil-Rhodes/.

EXERCISE: HERMAN ON THE MAINLINE

This is the working Carmen did. It helps deal a death blow to White supremacy.

Needs:

* 1–2 feet of parchment paper
* Psalm 139 (see appendix C)
* a permanent marker
* 2 fashion dolls, one male and one female (to represent structural/institutional racism and people who strive to blot out our desire for equality)
* 1 piece of twine (long enough to tie around the necks or feet of both dolls at separate ends)
* a fly swatter
* a black shoe box (*Note:* The box and lid should be painted black inside and out)
* molasses
* honey
* corn syrup

Instructions:

Lay out the parchment paper and place all of your tools on top of it. Recite Psalm 139 three times, then use the marker to write the following on both dolls: *Liberation, Freedom, Salvation.* Tie the twine around the neck or feet of each doll, securing them at separate ends.

Holding the dolls by the middle of the twine, beat them with the fly swatter. As you beat them, discuss the barriers they're placing in the way of global activism. Tell the dolls how you would like to see the situation resolved. Explain what concessions you're willing to make, if any. Repeat the beating and discussion each night for nine nights, telling the dolls that with each working of this exercise, White supremacy is dealt a death blow while Pan Afrikanism thrives! Allow the dolls to rest in the covered shoebox after each beating.

The day after the ninth night, remove the dolls from the box and place them on the parchment paper. Coat them with the molasses, honey, and corn syrup. Repeat Psalm 139 nine times, then hang the dolls from a tree or fence near your home.

Juju on the Fly

I attend medical school overseas, so I'm familiar with dealing with racial barriers. The world witnessed the death of George Floyd during the day. My mother said Rodney King's ordeal happened at night, and she was outraged back then, but George Floyd's case upset her even more. With George Floyd, it felt like racism was openly mocking us. It seemed like it was taunting us, showing that even with cell phones and social media, we were still treated as if we were pests to be crushed while the world watched.

We felt powerless, questioning if the alleged counterfeit money justified his death. We wondered if the White woman was responsible for the twenty-dollar scam. I even heard my mother's preacher say, "God was tired of George's scams and called him home."

Why did no one speak up about the blatant racism affecting our very right to live, all over a supposed fake twenty-dollar bill? Who among us hasn't tried to trick a vending machine with a dollar attached to a string? It's a prank, not something one should die for—maybe it deserves community service, but not death.

Overseas, we cried out, "Defund the police." We knew it was unlikely to happen, but saying it was like a way of telling the police, "We're fed up with you killing us and profiting from it through social media campaigns instead of facing consequences like desk duty or being fired." They profit, shrug it off, and we end up burying our fathers, brothers, uncles, sisters, mothers, aunts, and friends.

America pretends to be civilized, but it's all a lie—a performance, a puppet show. Meanwhile, we're the puppets, always forced to dance for the master's approval. George Floyd's murder made every Black and Brown person confront racism. People all over the world joined the conversation, sharing what it means to live in our skin. The names for White supremacy might be different, but the cost has always been the same. Our ancestors paid it, and we, their descendants, are still paying it.

Floyd's death forced us to confront enemies we had buried deep in memory, not out of fear, but out of necessity. We didn't think we could change what had already happened or stop what was coming. All we could do was try to be the best version of ourselves. But George Floyd, lying dead in the street in broad daylight, pushed us to make promises. We pledged to finish our medical degrees, return to our communities, and fight to ensure the conspiracy to destroy Black and Brown bodies before 2045 wouldn't happen. Not while we're here to stop it.

We printed pictures of colonial murderers—names and faces as far back as we could remember. We defaced them, poking out their eyes or coloring them bloodred with markers. Then, in solidarity against colonialism, we burned the images and danced like our lives depended on it, moving to the beats of our favorite rappers, singers, and island rhythms. Once a month, we came together to cleanse our spirits, starting the slow process of healing wounds that run deeper than flesh. Deeper than bone.

With all the restrictions, even simple things like getting tampons or a new laptop charger are a challenge. Living under the shadow of White supremacy makes it even harder for people to visit family or send money. You jump through endless hoops just to buy four rolls of off-brand toilet paper. America doesn't reward you for choosing a life outside the box; instead, it punishes you by embargoing your adopted home of Cuba. America won't send me to medical school for free, expecting me to repay the gesture by honoring who invested in me. But I made it out of nothing, and in gratitude, I plan to treat underserved communities. Dreamers come in every color and from every background, and it's unfair to kill a dream just because my skin tone doesn't fit their idealized story.

My little sister, who's in the fourth grade, decided to protest Thanksgiving at her school this year. She waited for an after-school faculty meeting and brought a scroll she'd made to read aloud. My mom stood in the back of the library, fingers crossed, as my sister began: "Instead of buckle hats and cardboard tomahawks, we should recognize Thanksgiving for what it truly is: a National Day of Mourning. Otherwise, we're just celebrating oppression and genocide between bites of turkey, stuffing, and baked macaroni. If we want to be progressive and unified, we must stop spreading lies. The pilgrims didn't come with good intentions. What they wanted was the land, already occupied, and they pretended to be allies. The truth is easy to find online. Start with *Everything You Know about Thanksgiving Is WRONG* by Decoded MTV News. After reading and watching, you can visit nativegov.org to learn whose land you live on. Then, encourage your students to write letters apologizing for the devastation caused by genocide. Thank you for hearing me out."

My mom was so proud. No, the school didn't get rid of the buckle hats or cardboard tomahawks—were you expecting it to? This is America. But my mom and sister took action and invited a First Nations speaker to my sister's class anyway. The speaker later visited the library to meet students from all grades and share his ancestors' story, from the beginning to the tragic loss of so many lives. He used puppets to tell the story, and my sister said her entire class was in tears. Not a single dry eye, no matter the race—Black, White, and Brown alike.

EXERCISE: BLOOD IN YOUR EYE

This working helps remove the blocks, people, or institutions preventing justice.

Needs:

* a sheet of paper with the image of the person or institution blocking your right to justice
* a sheet of paper with the image of a pair of open eyes

* Psalm 140 (see appendix C)
* scissors
* glue or tape
* a cauldron or other fireproof receptacle
* 1 charcoal disk
* 3 pieces of dragon's blood resin
* 6 tablespoons dried calamus root
* a top hat
* a magician's wand

Instructions:

Place the images on the table and recite Psalm 140 over them three times. Using the scissors, cut the eyes out individually, then glue or tape them to the image of the target person or institution. Set aside.

Place a lit charcoal disk inside the cauldron. Add the resin and calamus root. Put the image inside the hat, then tap the outside of the hat nine times with the wand. Recite Psalm 140 three more times.

Ask Black Herman to spit blood in the eyes of anyone who stands in your way. (Be sure to say their names.) Recite the psalm three more times. Sit, focusing your attention on the individual or institution, for fifteen minutes or until the smoke burns out.

Repeat this work nightly for the next nine nights. On the morning after the ninth night, burn the photo in your cauldron and sprinkle the ash on or near a train track or at the foot of a tree.

Chapter Eleven
Mother Catherine Seals:
Protecting Our BIPOC Women

Mother Catherine Seals (1887–1930) built her home in the Lower Ninth Ward of New Orleans during the Jim Crow era. She was determined to create her own spiritual society, one that welcomed marginalized outcasts from all races.

After being shunned by White faith healers, she carried out her revenge by buying out an entire block—what is now Charbonnet Street. To keep out nosy intruders, Mother built a ten-foot wall around her property. Mother's work was considered dangerous Black magick because her temple housed more than three hundred people under one desegregated roof, a radical act in an era when racial separation was key to maintaining the institution of hate.

Mother Catherine was a fierce protector of women escaping violent marriages because she had endured three brutal unions herself. Her last marriage left her paralyzed. Seeking healing, Mother visited Brother Isaiah, a well-known White faith healer. But he rejected her outright, saying, "I don't heal Black people."

Devastated, Mother Catherine went home and prayed for deliverance. Her prayers were answered when she found Mother Leafy Anderson, who became her mentor in all things spiritual. Upon Anderson's death, Mother Catherine took leadership of New Orleans' Spiritual Movement, carrying forward her mentor's legacy. By 1924, she was renowned as a staunch defender of women and children. Even poor White families sought her aid, desperate for relief from dire straits and sickness, even tuberculosis. She became a heroine to the discarded, the abused, the forgotten. She called them the Innocent Blood: victims of unfortunate circumstances, born into struggle. "Like Jesus—innocent, and out of wedlock."

Mother Catherine was noted for the effective use of praise words coupled with simple ingredients like castor oil and Epsom salt, her mainstays to bring about efficacious healing.

Work Mama Blessed Be

About three years ago, I was at work, printing copies of forms for a meeting scheduled later that day when a notification popped up on my computer: The copier was jammed. I sighed. Another trip down the darkened hall to the copy room to fix the issue. I'd done this countless times. The outdated machine was notorious for its malfunctions, but my boss refused to put it out of its misery.

On this particular morning, after turning on the copy room light and clearing the crumpled paper from the tray, I was met with something entirely unexpected: The floor was covered in black-and-white photographs, all images of Mother Catherine Seals. I hadn't googled her or sent any prints to the machine.

Even stranger, just days before, I'd shared a heartfelt laugh with a dear friend who had pointed out my striking resemblance to Mama Catherine. When my sistah-friend collaged a side-by-side image of Mama Catherine and me, I responded with a simple "Ase." I was flattered. I had always been deeply familiar with Mama Catherine, having seen her image many times. Every time I looked into her eyes, I felt a growing connection to Spirit. That's why I kept her image enshrined in my library near my ancestral egun staff, Epsom salt, castor oil, and witch hazel. Her eyes spoke of healing and protection.

I picked up one of the images and told Mama Catherine that I accepted the call to work with her. She would become my patron saint of Hoodoo. There was no other explanation for eighteen copies of her image strewn across the copy room floor. This was no coincidence; it was Mother's Hoodoo initiating me, welcoming me.

EXERCISE: MOTHER CATHERINE SEALS ALTAR FOR THE INNOCENT

This altar is the seat of protection for women and children, most often those fleeing abusive situations. I especially love this altar as a work for single mothers or mothers going through divorce who are still in deep need of protection as they maneuver through life as the sole providers. I have used this altar with male clients seeking Mother Catherine's guidance in protecting the entirety of their families from patriarchal deceit in the areas of healthcare, daycare, and education.

Needs:

* 3 yards red fabric
* a sheet of paper with the image of Black Hawk
* a sheet of paper with the image of Mother Catherine
* 1 red candle
* 1 red Black Hawk head candle
* a tin bucket filled with the following: a plant of your choosing, a Native American warrior statue, arrows, spears, a saucer of tobacco resting atop cornhusks with chia seeds sprinkled on top, and a small American flag
* a glass of water with 1 teaspoon each of Epsom salt and castor oil stirred in
* a bota bag filled with water
* a cauldron or other fireproof receptacle
* 1 charcoal disk
* 1 teaspoon dried chicory
* a tambourine (real or a toy)
* a first aid kit
* a small infant doll

* a sheet of paper with the names of no more than nine women or children who require Mother's attentiveness to their health or the health of their relationships
* Psalm 31 (see appendix C)

Instructions:

Lay the fabric across your desired altar space. Place the images of Mother and Black Hawk in the center and the candles on either side of the images. Place the tin bucket on Black Hawk's side and the water glass and bota bag on Mother's side.

Working at the front of your altar, place a lit charcoal disk inside the cauldron. Add pinches of the chicory. All other items can be placed on the altar using your discretion. You can also place any medications you or your family members take on the altar, as well as any doctor's orders or appointment reminder cards. Doing this helps Mother direct her attention to the specific areas and family members that need specialized healing.

Recite Psalm 31 nine times, knowing that once you're finished, your altar space will be reborn.

EXERCISE: WRITING TO MOTHER

Letter writing is an excellent way to open a line of communication with Mother Catherine. It allows you to focus your intentions toward her healing ability. Your letter becomes words of praise and hope. I had a client tell me writing to Mother Catherine reminded him of his Catholic upbringing and participating in the Stations of the Cross. He saw his letter as a prayer. He even kept his letters in a binder marked "Bible of Sacred Healing."

Needs:
* pen and paper

Instructions:
Write a letter to Mother on one side of a sheet of paper asking her to heal each and every issue plaguing the people listed in the previous exercise. Then, make a smaller list of just the women's names and drop it inside the Epsom salt/castor oil water. Replenish the list and water weekly.

Black Women as Passing Fancies

A sistah once came to me in tears seeking guidance about her ex-husband, a White man who had decided he was done with what he called his "liberal experiment": being married to a Black woman. Three children later, my client found herself on the receiving end of his verbal insults, compounded by those of his newly acquired White wife. Their three children, aged six, nine, and twelve, had been disowned by their father, and it was agonizing for her to explain to them why he had chosen to abandon their family.

"How does one explain White privilege in matters of the heart?" she asked me. "This man once let love rule, claimed he saw no color for years, and then woke up one day as if breaking out of a coma only to look into the faces he kissed, the ones he swore to protect, and spit on us. Literally and figuratively—he called us 'nigger' more times than I ever read the word in *Huckleberry Finn*. I'll never understand, not in a million years, what he even saw in me to drag me through that hell."

We had a long conversation about self-preservation and the importance of choosing oneself. We explored the dynamics of mistaken identities, the layered ways White privilege plays out, even in intimate spaces like the bedroom. Eventually, we reached a breakthrough. She admitted that there had been early signs of trouble, indications that she was a sexual novelty to him, a passing fetish. She realized there had always been an expiration date for their so-called love.

She confessed their sex life often involved role-playing scenes of racial power dynamics. He had cast himself as the racist slave master, consumed by lust for her Black body, while she played the submissive object of his desire. These moments weren't true intimacy. They were a twisted performance where his lust was never meant to be confused with love.

EXERCISE: DRYING CHICKEN FEET

Before preparing the following Mother Catherine Seals work, you need to procure chicken feet. Two are required for the work, but you can prepare more to have on hand for future workings.

You'll be drying these chicken feet out before working them into your magick. You can use a dehydrator or your oven's lowest setting, but I prefer the salty container method.

Needs:

* 1 plastic container with lid (large enough to hold and seal the chicken feet without any overlapping)
* iodized salt (consecration of items)
* Psalms 7, 9, 14, 53, and 72 (see appendix C)

Instructions:

Pour a layer of salt into the container to cover the bottom completely. Arrange your chicken feet on top of the first layer, making sure the feet aren't touching or overlapping. Pour more salt on top to completely cover the feet.

Once the feet are covered, recite Psalms 7, 9, 14, 53, and 72 in the order listed, then place the feet in a cool, dry place. Three times a week, repeat the psalms over the closed container. Your feet will be ready to check for stiffness in six weeks.

EXERCISE: PROTECT ME AND MINE, MOTHER CATHERINE

This work helps heal, protect, and release your target person.

Needs:

- a framed image or statue of Mother Catherine Seals
- a bowl filled with ½ cup rubbing alcohol
- 1 egg
- a white satchel or drawstring bag
- 1 teaspoon asafoetida
- 1 tablespoon Epsom salt
- 1 red candle
- a bowl filled with ½ cup castor oil
- Florida water (bless your body)
- 2 dried chicken feet
- an image of your target for healing
- a brown paper bag
- *Optional:* 1 towel

Instructions:

Place Mother's image in the center of your altar. Lay the egg in the bowl with the rubbing alcohol, gently turning it so the entire egg is washed with alcohol. Add the asafoetida and salt to the satchel, then carve the name of the person in need of healing onto the candle three times. Light the candle and place it in front of Mother's picture.

Place the chicken feet in the castor oil bowl. Breathe over the oil and say the person's name you want healed. Recite the psalms from the earlier chicken feet work over the oil. Set aside.

Retrieve the egg from the alcohol and begin touching your entire body with it; you can do this in the nude or seminude. (This is a cleaning movement, a wiping away from your flesh.)

Once you've cleansed your entire body, place the egg in the brown paper bag. Ask Mother Catherine for protection, healing, and for release for the person in dire need. Sprinkle the Florida water into your hands and rub it over your entire body.

Place the chicken feet near the image of your target. (You can place them on a towel to dry off from the oil.) Light the candle and sit for fifteen minutes before extinguishing it. Wear the satchel to bed or place it inside your pillowcase. Say the name of the person you're targeting for healing, and keep repeating their name until you drop off to sleep.

In the morning, place the egg inside a brown paper bag and dispose of it. Leave the satchel in front of Mother's picture, but for nine nights, wear it or place it back inside your pillowcase every night.

Over the next few days, think about the healing you're sending into the world whenever you bathe. Also, use the castor oil as a healing full-body moisturizer. (Your body is healing your target with blessed oil.) You can repeat this work in its entirety once a week.

Diving Deeper

One of my favorite Instagram pages for uncovering almost forgotten incidents in Afrikan history is @AfricanArchives. This page recently shed light on a particularly haunting story from Louisiana's prison culture, a cautionary tale of female incarceration.

Before the Civil War, most prisoners were White. This makes sense, as most people of color were enslaved. At first glance, this fact seems historically predictable. But when you dig deeper, patterns of rebellion and punishment emerge. Many enslaved people, men and women alike, were imprisoned for acts of defiance like inciting resistance, assaulting White oppressors, arson, and the poisoning or attempted poisoning of slave masters.

For enslaved women, punishment was even more brutal. Those accused of rebellion, violence, or subversion were forced into the same cells as men, a system rife with exploitation and abuse. Historical records document cases of these women becoming pregnant—some by male inmates, others by prison officials themselves. This dark chapter in history serves as a reminder of the unrelenting violence enslaved people endured, both within and outside the prison walls.[77]

In 1848, Louisiana signed into law a rule that the children born from Afrikan Americans enslaved and serving life sentences became the property of the state. The mothers of these children were allowed to raise them until they reached the age of ten. After that, the children were auctioned. Many would either be repurchased by prison officials or by companies owned by individual stakeholders in penitentiary welfare. The proceeds of these auctions were used to fund schools for White children.

Everybody hitched their wagon to the promise that there was always freedom, a light at the end of the tunnel. It was whispered from the planter to the enslaved that if a woman or girl birthed fifteen babies, she would earn her freedom or serve a reduced sentence. But in reality, leaving the jail usually meant you were bought and sold as a domestic or a house concubine.

My grandmother would reach down, grab a handful of earth, and channel a heart-wrenching tale about the children born in prisons. In each tale, these children lived their whole lives struggling to get back inside the cages they called home. Their mothers were forced to endure rape after rape, only to have maybe ten or twelve live births. The moment they could no longer birth babies, these women were tossed into an open grave. My grandmother said sometimes, if you held the soil up to your ear, you could still hear the cries of newborns. If you listen during a thunderstorm, you'll hear women and little girls as young as twelve screaming in tongues to at least let them heal, to at least let them expel the placenta before planting another seed.

---

77. "5 Ways Prisoners Were Used for Profit throughout US History," *PBS News*, February 26, 2020, https://www.pbs.org/newshour/arts/5-ways-prisoners-were-used-for-profit-throughout-u-s.

Grandmama was keen to remind me that the soil remembers, and some days, when I felt young enough to run barefoot, the soil would whisper through the soles of my feet the names of the many babies who died there, killed by mothers refusing to let their babies become another man's mule.

MONICA

Katravion got accepted in this middle school that was more White than Black. The first day he came home looking like somebody had stolen his joy. He had always been a happy child full of excitement about track, soccer, and baseball. He wanted to become a drummer or become the first Black boy to win a gold medal in the sport of skateboarding. He was a Lupe Fiasco fan.

When he came home, I just thought he was experiencing the middle school blues. I thought he was struggling with how to fit into middle school. Since middle school was never that much fun for me, I thought it was just a rite of passage for him. I thought he'd feel his way through or suffer for three years and find his tribe in high school. I thought, when he continued to come home, I'd give it a few days before phoning his dad, who was overseas wrapping up his last six months in the military.

The next thing I knew, Katravion was a month in when he came downstairs for dinner, plopped into his dad's chair, and sighed out, "I hate that school. I'm the only Black kid in all my classes. I don't see another Black person until lunch, when me and the three other Black students sit together. The White kids think it's okay to call us offensive names—names that annoy the crap out of me. When we tell the resource officer, he asks us to repeat the whole altercation word for word. He grins while staring at us. He listens as we say 'nigger' and makes us say it over and over again. He says it's so he can discern if the Blacks are just causing problems or if they have a verified case of racism. Mama, I really, really hate that school."

We talked it out for hours, me and my son. We talked for six hours, and the next day I met with the principal and the resource officer. They assured me it was kids being kids. The principal even said my son and his friends need tougher skin in middle school. She tried convincing me that it was about teaching children to have tougher skin for high school. The other Black parents said I was making the situation worse; they kept saying they weren't about that BLM stuff. The other Black parents told me I was going to cause a scene and have their kids more singled out than in. They kept reminding me of the school's letter grade and how lucky our kids were to have it on their academic resume.

I decided to drop my son from that school. I found a Black magnet school and even found a Black homeschool where he thrived and found friendships with students who are proud to be BIPOC, children like him who didn't live for the White gaze.

A week after I dropped Katravion out of that school, one of his Black friends from Racism Middle tried to hang herself in her closet. Her mother had luckily found her in time. The mother called me, and I put her on speaker so Katravion could hear. Through her tears, she kept on saying how sorry she was. How Black folks got to stick together, how she had heard that all her life and just thought her parents and grandparents wanted to keep her stuck in a bygone era. She didn't want to believe that people can still hate like that over something as uncontrollable as skin color.

Listening to your children, showing them you care, supporting them, and helping them find support through counseling and positive interactions—this was something I had to learn and something we all have to learn and accept. Your tea helps me release the anxiety of feeling like a narcissistic mama who wanted a better life for her son at all costs without paying attention to the emotional PTSD I was putting him through. That tea helped me step back, breathe, and relax. It helped me to brainstorm and establish safeguards and parameters so that I can better mother Katravion in this world where Black lives don't matter enough—the face of this new world that I didn't order. Your elixir and that bath...I can't forget that bath, girlfriend. They both helped me to release all of this womb pain until I was finally ready to unleash a new me. I even found this confidential mental health support service for me and my son, and when I tell you they got us, they really got us. All you do is text CONNECT to 741741, the Crisis Text Line.

Sometimes sipping tea while listening to a voice of reason realigns a person to their personal liberation, and that's okay if that liberation doesn't show up on an Instagram feed for followers of people lying to prove your life is better than mine.

EXERCISE: HEALING ELIXIR FOR THE TROUBLED SOUL LIVES

This is the tea I recommended for Monica. The instructions for the bath are on the next page.

Needs:

* a large mason jar or pitcher
* ½ cup pomegranate juice
* ½ cup beetroot juice
* ½ cup pineapple juice
* 1 orange, sliced
* 1 lemon, sliced
* honey, agave, or other sweetener
* ½ cup calendula petals
* Psalm 18 (see appendix C)
* *Optional:* ice cubes

Instructions:

Add the juices to the jar, then the sliced fruit and honey to taste, and finally place the calendula petals on top to garnish. Recite Psalm 18 three times, then refrigerate for an hour. After the hour, you may drink the tea throughout the day. This elixir tastes best when consumed one to three days after making.

EXERCISE: SOUL LIVES BATH

You can prepare this bath for yourself and anyone else in your life who needs it. Monica prepared it for herself in her bathroom, and she helped her son prepare it in his bathroom. They both also shared the elixir.

Needs:

* 1 orange, sliced
* 1 lemon, sliced
* 6 tablespoons Epsom salt
* 13 drops lavender oil
* 1 cup pomegranate juice
* 1 cup beetroot juice
* 6 tablespoons Florida water
* 1–2 cups calendula petals
* Psalm 18 (see appendix C)
* *Optional:* 3 sticks of lavender incense

Instructions:

As you run your bath water, drop in the sliced fruit, Epsom salt, lavender oil, juices, and Florida water. Top it off with the calendula petals. Recite Psalm 18 three times, then step in and revive your soul.

Option:

* Burn three lavender incense sticks as you bathe.

Is Birthing Black Babies Killing Black Mothers?

In a February 17, 2023, article titled "New Study Finds Even the Wealthiest Black Mothers and Their Babies Are More Likely to Die in Childbirth," journalist Dominique Fluker notes that childbirth risks vary by race and parental income, which disproportionately affects Black and Brown families regardless of their socioeconomic standing.[78] The study combined income tax data; birth, death, and hospitalization records; census results, and social security data. Results indicated Black and Brown mothers aren't protected through pregnancy, even if they're relatively affluent. Mortality rates for high-income Black families appeared the same as those for the lowest income White families. Even Black mothers among the top 10 percent of earners still faced health risks like premature births. The study went on to show that Black women are more than three times more likely than their White counterparts to give birth to underweight babies.

This study wasn't the first indication of the alarming state of Black childbirth in America. In 2022, there were 22 maternal deaths for every 100,000 live US births. For Black and Brown women, the numbers were 49.5 deaths per 100,000.[79]

The Black maternal health crisis led to legislative action in the form of the Preventing Maternal Deaths Act of 2018. Under the act, medical guidelines are being rewritten to ensure doctors and nurses have the tools to prevent complications like hemorrhaging. The overall goal is to lower the infant mortality rate among BIPOC women by eliminating racist care practices from prenatal medicine.

---

78. Dominique Fluker, "New Study Finds Even the Wealthiest Black Mothers and Their Babies Are More Likely to Die in Childbirth," *Essence*, February 17, 2023, https://www.essence.com/lifestyle/parenting/childbirth-deadlier-for-black-families/.
79. Sabrina Malhi, "Childbirth Deadlier for Americans, Especially Black Women, Study Finds," *Washington Post*, June 5, 2024, https://www.washingtonpost.com/health/2024/06/04/us-maternal-mortality-rate-higher-other-countries/.

EXERCISE: SCREAM AWAY THIS MESS

Like the exercise on page 59, this is a type of scream water to help you relieve the pain of every vile happening you've ever seen. Note that this scream water will be used in the following working.

Needs:

* a small pot
* 1 cup plain water
* a jar of baby food
* Psalm 149 (see appendix C)
* 1 teaspoon dried licorice root

Instructions:

Put the water on the stove to boil. Once the water is boiling, remove it to an unused burner to cool. Add the licorice root and let steep for two minutes, allowing it to transform the water into a medicinal fluid.

After two minutes, recite Psalm 149 over the water three times, then begin to scream into the pot. Scream at every vile event you've either witnessed or been part of.

Once you've purged the trappings of White supremacy, let the water cool completely, then pour it into the baby food jar in preparation for the next work.

EXERCISE: MOTHER ME, MOTHER

This is a powerful work to protect those in need using the scream water from the last work. You'll need a very large cauldron and the names and images of those needing help.

Needs:

- a cauldron or other fireproof receptacle (extremely large with cover)
- 2 cups sand
- 2 cups soil from a women's shelter
- 2 cups soil from a graveyard
- 2 cups soil from a church
- 2 cups soil from a bank
- 90 stick pins
- images of the women and/or children needing protection (*Note:* In the absence of images, use index cards with their names written on them, one name per card)
- marker and paper
- 1–2 charcoal disks
- 3–6 pieces of amber resin
- 1 large chain and lock (large enough to wrap around and lock the cauldron)
- 2 yards red cloth
- Psalm 91 (see appendix C)
- a small baby food jar of scream water

Instructions:

Layer the inside of the cauldron with sand, then add the soils in the following order: women's shelter, graveyard, church, and bank. Insert the stick pins into the images, then drop them into the cauldron.

With the marker and paper, write out what you'd like to see happen to the person(s) responsible for causing peril in the life of the mother and/or child. Use one-word answers, for example, *jail, bankruptcy, sickness, relocation,* or fired.

When finished, fold the paper as small as you can, spit on it, and shove it into the soil until you can no longer see it. Place a lit charcoal disk on top of the soil, then add the resin. Place the images inside the cauldron away from the burning charcoal. Recite Psalm 91, then beg Mother to please protect the people in the photo.

Their safety is assured once the charcoal is completely burned and you're done reciting the psalm. Cover and chain the cauldron so that the chain crisscrosses the top and underbelly. Lock it securely and cover it with the red fabric.

For nine nights, unlock the cauldron and repeat the resin burning and psalms each night, relighting and covering thereafter. On the close of the ninth night pour the scream water into the cauldron. Lock the cauldron and let it sit undisturbed for three months. Repeat the entire work if necessary after the three months.

GENEVA

I was nineteen, and I had a doctor provided by welfare. He was a White man in his sixties who never once said a word to me at any of my visits. He talked to me through a White nurse who was rude and always popping off at the mouth. As if I wasn't a closed door away from the nurses' station, the nurse rambled on, "The first thing those people do when they find out what lives between their thighs is populate. They don't worry about how to feed them or teach them, they just push them out and let our taxes go up to eradicate the mess they made. They ought to be sterilized at birth." The coldness of the office's thermostat couldn't compare to the freezing temperatures of their stares. Their whispers, how quickly their smiling "good mornings" turned to eyerolls of disgust when the Brown woman standing in front of the window asked for a sign-in form because the kiosk machine was spitting out identification cards right and left.

At thirty weeks, I was sitting in my journalism law class when I started feeling bloated and nauseous. My vision blurred so much I thought my glasses were dirty. I reached for my pouch on the back of my chair to retrieve a wet wipe. My stomach was in a rage. So I ran to the bathroom, anticipating vomiting. I was at the point in this pregnancy when any smell more potent than my baby powder deodorant turned my stomach into a bitter rival. But instead of vomiting, I started feeling dizzy.

Ever since I found out I was pregnant, I had started wearing my phone in a crossbody purse. That way it's always there. No looking, searching through a knapsack at the most crucial of moments—like now.

The dizziness was winning. I had managed to back up against the wall where I could guide my body into a soft slide down to the floor. I pulled out my phone, and before I could dial, I heard two of my classmates rushing toward me, yelling my name. I woke up in the hospital room. My doctor was standing there explaining to the staff how I was, in his medical opinion, an overly dramatic young girl. I was nineteen and actually thought college and a baby were a good idea, he suggested. "I guess she thought she'd turn out like a Hallmark movie—all nappy-headed, proper speaking, and earning six figures by the closing scene." The nurses were laughing. The doctor was laughing. I closed my eyes to hide my tears.

It took another woman in the recovery room with me to recommend that I see a different doctor—find someone who was a team player. She whispered, "You need to leave that racist piece of shit right here with his Becky Sues." She went on to inform me that he had been her doctor years ago, and neither of her twins survived thanks to his negligence. She said he looked her in the eyes and said matter-of-factly, "I would be sorry for your loss, but your people don't mourn long before you're back at it making another baby, making more trouble for the rest of us honest taxpayers." She didn't know the cause of her children's deaths, not even to this day. She couldn't prove he was negligent, and she was too poor to afford anyone who would challenge him. But she swore he grinned as he turned to leave her room. Leaving her in tears was the joy of his life.

When my fiancé arrived, I told him about the Black doctor, the one the woman was now seeing; we agreed to see him ASAP. A week later, now at home, I passed out and was rushed to the hospital. I was diagnosed with HELLP syndrome, had an emergency C-section, and suffered a life-threatening liver condition. I woke up in an ICU bed. I was tubed up for three months after my baby's birth. I didn't get to kiss her until she was a week into her fourth month. The kiss may have been late, but I thanked God she was alive.

EXERCISE: SCREAM 2 KEEP FROM CRYING

I use Scream Water to cleanse my mental palate. Scream Water is my space to vent and expel the toxic energy my body is clinging to after experiencing tons of microaggressive discourse. I often tell folks there is no such thing as a minuscule racist moment. Even though the word *microaggression* exists, I use it to delineate how folks with privilege tend to differentiate between what is "really racist" and what is a BIPOC person just "pulling the race card" because they don't like being ostracized or coming in last in life. Scream Water allows me to keep it real away from the very folks who are determined to summon the angry Black woman just so they can cancel my feelings as gripes, conflating my reaction to my oppression. I scream because I am tired of being told to "put my big girl panties on and walk it off." Some days I want to walk ass-out as I scream into the wind, "Your words and your actions hold no power over me. Not now, not ever, fucker."

Needs:
- a large mason jar with lid
- 2 cups plain water
- Psalm 149 (see appendix C)
- 3 teaspoons dried licorice root
- 3 teaspoons dried witch hazel
- 3 teaspoons Epsom salt

Instructions:

Pour the water into the jar. Add the dried licorice, witch hazel, and Epsom salt, seal the jar tightly, and shake vigorously for five minutes. Open the jar and recite Psalm 149 over the water.

Begin screaming into the water, allowing all your anger and disgust to reverberate into it. With each scream, speak and release your truth, telling the water how racism has impacted your emotional, physical, and psychological movements. Think about every time you've been mistreated, oppressed, and invalidated by institutions of systemic oppression.

When finished, reseal the jar and take it to the physical location that harbors your pain (e.g., the doctor's office). Pour the water around the perimeter, or as close as you can get it. Trash the paper, cleanse the jar with black soap and water, and allow it to sit collecting moonlight for nine nights. Before reusing the jar, recite the psalm again nine times.

Option:
- In lieu of the actual location, you can drop a photo of the location or a piece of paper with the address written on it into the jar. Place the jar on Mother's altar and let it stay until your situation is rectified. Then, after you feel emotionally vindicated, toss the water into the street.

Juju on the Fly

Did you know that 50 percent of enslaved pregnant mothers lost their babies due to stillborn deaths or a lack of consistent medical care?[80] Children born alive usually succumbed to death within a year due to a failure in childhood postnatal care. When enslaved people, especially women, were conveniently allowed medical treatment, it was only done to protect the economic interest of the plantation's owner. A healthy mother meant the potential of fifteen live births during her lifetime. Being born onto the plantation also meant the child didn't have to be trafficked from Afrika.[81] In other words, plantation owners had the potential to earn from one womb fifteen new slaves and still gain the benefit of owning the mother. The investment in the wombs of Black women meant a lifetime of human returns, which equaled a lifetime of generational profit long after the importation of Afrikans was abolished.

When we examine the stories of the mothers of gynecology—Anarcha, Betsey, and Lucy—we're transported to 1840. Back then, a racist man named J. Marion Sims, dubbed the father of gynecology, experimented on these women, causing them to suffer vaginal fistulas that allowed urine and stool to leak through holes in the walls of their vaginas.[82] Sims experimented on these women without their permission, restraining them to the operating table without anesthesia or any form of pain medication. It's because these enslaved women were forced to undergo these painful surgeries that today many White doctors believe Black and Brown people can withstand high amounts of pain and therefore should be undertreated. According to the US Department of Health and Human Services, 40 percent of Black and

---

80. Deirdre Cooper Owens and Sharla M. Fett, "Black Maternal and Infant Health: Historical Legacies of Slavery," *American Journal of Public Health* 109, no. 10 (October 2019): 1342–45, https://doi.org/10.2105/AJPH.2019.305243.
81. Haywood L. Brown et al., "Black Women Health Inequity: The Origin of Perinatal Health Disparity," *Journal of the National Medical Association* 113, no. 1 (February 2021): 105–13, https://doi.org/10.1016/j.jnma.2020.11.008.
82. Sarah Kuta, "Subjected to Painful Experiments and Forgotten, Enslaved 'Mothers of Gynecology' Are Honored With New Monument," *Smithsonian Magazine*, May 11, 2022, https://www.smithsonianmag.com/smart-news/mothers-of-gynecology-monument-honors-enslaved-women-180980064/.

Brown people receive worse care when advocating for pain reduction than their White counterparts. Even when Black patients are given pain medication, it's at low doses, thereby saving more potent relief for White-bodied patients.[83]

J. Marion Sims spent five years operating on the mothers of gynecology, along with nine other women whose names are lost to history. Sims repeated the same procedures on all these women, with Anarcha enduring thirty surgeries! Yes, Sims is the inventor of the speculum, a gynecological instrument used during vaginal exams, but his lasting and most detrimental impact is as a racist who exploited the health of Black women and justified it as a way of safely improving the health of White women. Now, run tell that!

Several years ago, Veronica Maria Pimentel, an obstetrician and gynecologist, petitioned a coalition of twenty-four professional groups to recognize the systemic racism underlying the fields of obstetrics and gynecology.[84] In 2020, the American College of Obstetricians and Gynecologists, along with twenty-four groups, issued a joint statement doing just that. The statement also recognized Anarcha, Betsey, and Lucy's incalculable contributions.[85]

....

83. "Black Americans Are Systematically Under-Treated for Pain. Why?," Frank Batten School of Leadership and Public Policy, University of Virginia, June 30, 2020, https://batten.virginia.edu/about/news/black-americans-are-systematically-under-treated-pain-why.
84. Veronica Maria Pimentel and Deirdre Cooper Owens, "Recognizing Lucy, Betsey and Anarcha: A Live Conversation," presented by American College of Obstetricians and Gynecologists (ACOG), February 2021, https://www.acog.org/.
85. Eva Chalas, "The American College of Obstetricians and Gynecologists in 2020: A Clear Vision for the Future," *Obstetrics & Gynecology* 135, no. 6 (June 2020): 1251–54, https://doi.org/10.1097/AOG.0000000000003899.

EXERCISE: WOMB SONG TEA

This tea will call on the spirits of Mother Catherine Seals and all the other mothers of gynecology to protect your womb space.

Needs:

- plain water
- a tea setting (cup, spoon, and saucer)
- 1–2 reusable tea bags or 2 5 inch x 5 inch pieces of cheesecloth and 5–9 inches of twine
- 1 teaspoon dried basil
- 1 teaspoon dried lemon balm
- 1 teaspoon dried calendula
- 1 teaspoon each of any two of the following dried herbs: fenugreek, black cohosh, motherwort, Jamaican dogweed, Dong Quai, red raspberry, nettle, or red clover
- 1 teaspoon blackstrap molasses or agave
- Psalms 37 and 55 (see appendix C)

Instructions:

Set the water to boil. Add the herbs to your reusable tea bags or cheesecloth and close. Once the water boils, pour a portion into the cup, add the tea bags, and cover with the saucer. Let the tea steep for five to seven minutes.

After the tea has steeped, stir in the molasses, then recite Psalm 37 three times and Psalm 55 three times. Next, call out the names of Anarcha, Betsey, Lucy, and Mother Catherine Seals. Ask that they protect your womb space and provide an abundance of emotional, physical, and spiritual healing.

Close your eyes for five minutes and envision your healing story as it is now being rewritten, then enjoy the tea.

Chapter Twelve
Zora Neale Hurston:
Learning to Honor Our Past

Zora Neale Hurston (1891–1960) was born sometime in January 1891, though historians debate whether her birthplace was Notasulga, Alabama, or Eatonville, Florida.[86] She was the daughter of two formerly enslaved parents: John Hurston, a pastor, and Lucy Ann Potts Hurston.

Following her mother's death, Hurston's father remarried, and she found herself shuffled between relatives, navigating instability at a young age. To ensure her own financial survival, Hurston worked numerous odd jobs, including a stint as a maid for an actress in the Gilbert and Sullivan group.

In 1920, Hurston earned an associate's degree from Howard University. She soon became a prominent figure in the Harlem Renaissance, her New York apartment serving as a gathering place for literary and cultural icons like Langston Hughes and Countee Cullen.[87] Her passion for anthropology led to a scholarship at Barnard College, where she studied under Franz Boas, one of the most influential anthropologists of his time.

Hurston's 1926 short story "Sweat" depicted a woman struggling to escape an unfaithful, exploitative husband. In 1928, she penned the essay "How It Feels to Be Colored Me," offering a bold reflection on race and identity drawn from her childhood experiences in a predominantly White area. Throughout her career, Hurston contributed regularly to folkloric journals and magazines, prioritizing *The Journal of American Folklore*, where she documented Black cultural traditions with unparalleled depth.

---

86. New-York Historical Society, "Life Story: Zora Neale Hurston (1891–1960)," Women & the American Story, accessed July 1, 2025, https://wams.nyhistory.org/confidence-and-crises/jazz-age/zora-neale-hurston/.
87. Zora Neale Hurston Digital Archive, Center for Humanities and Digital Research, University of Central Florida, launched 2006, https://chdr.cah.ucf.edu/hurstonarchive/.

In 1934, Hurston published her first novel, *Jonah's Gourd Vine*, which chronicled the life of a flawed pastor, Johnny Buddy Pearson, and his experiences as a Black man navigating faith and hardship. By 1937, after receiving a Guggenheim fellowship, Hurston traveled to Haiti, where she conducted anthropological research and laid the groundwork for her most widely acclaimed novel, *Their Eyes Were Watching God*. This novel traces a journey of self-reliance through the marriages and tragedies of Janie Mae Crawford, and it solidified Hurston's legacy in American literature.

During the 1930s, Hurston and Hughes collaborated on a play titled *Mule-Bone: A Comedy of Negro Life*. However, the partnership dissolved over creative differences, with disputes over authorship and credit leading to a public fallout between the two literary titans.[88]

In 1954, Hurston faced backlash for her criticism of the Supreme Court's landmark Brown v. Board of Education ruling, which ended segregation in schools. She argued that forced desegregation would lead to spiritual and cultural oppression for Black communities, a stance that made her a controversial figure in the Civil Rights era.[89]

Indigenous Afrikan Traditions

In 1928, after graduating from Barnard College with a degree in anthropology, Hurston became enthralled by indigenous Afrikan traditions. *Mules and Men*, a collection of Afrikan American folklore from all over the South, was her first book-length exploration of the Afrikan indigenous presence in America as experienced through its culture and spirituality. In 1935, Hurston's studies took her to Columbia University, where she worked toward a PhD in anthropology. A Guggenheim fellowship allowed

---

88. "A Bone to Pick with the Writing and Fallout of Mule Bone," The Henry Ford, February 4, 2025, https://www.thehenryford.org/explore/blog/a-bone-to-pick-with-the-writing-and-fallout-of-mule-bone.
89. Olivia Marcucci, "Zora Neale Hurston and the Brown Debate: Race, Class, and the Progressive Empire," *Journal of Negro Education* 86, no. 1 (Winter 2017): 13–24.

her the time to study Obeah, a diasporic Afrikan tradition common to Jamaica.

Hurston wanted to write a proper Voodoo book. It was her belief that racist, judgmental Christian academics chose to characterize Black indigenous practices as devil worship and Black magick.[90] *Tell My Horse* was a firsthand account of indigenous folkloric practices that Hurston wrote as a practitioner, not as an academic.

Hurston went on to publish more books, essays, stories, and academic papers. She taught at North Carolina Central University and other schools in the south for years. She died at the age of sixty-nine in 1960. She was buried in the Garden of Heavenly Rest Cemetery in Fort Pierce, Florida.

In 1975, after reading Hurston's *Mules and Men*, the acclaimed writer Alice Walker made it her lifelong duty to find the grave of Zora Neale Hurston, her favorite author, and give it a proper headstone. Walker's 1975 *Ms.* magazine essay, "In Search of Zora Neale Hurston," revived interest in Hurston's writings.

Today, Hurston is considered the preeminent voice in Afrikan American folklore. Her writings describe traditions of Afrikan diasporic religion as found in the Caribbean and the American South. It was Zora Neale Hurston who made the trek into Hoodoo and Voodoo cultures. It was Hurston who joined as a willing participant in ceremonies. She was a folklorist with charm and endearing love for the people and their practice at a time when White anthropologists portrayed Black indigenous spirituality as unruly, animalistic, and evil.

---

90. Wendy Dutton, "The Problem of Invisibility: Voodoo and Zora Neale Hurston," *Frontiers: A Journal of Women Studies* 13, no. 2 (1993): 131, https://doi.org/10.2307/3346733.

EXERCISE: ZORA NEALE HURSTON'S DECOLONIZE THE MIND ALTAR

It's time to decolonize your thoughts! You'll be creating a resting ancestor doll in this work, which requires some advance preparation.

Needs:

* 1–3 railroad spikes
* Florida water
* rum
* 1 Black doll (represents your ancestral stand-in)
* rosewater in a spray bottle
* a shoebox with lid (large enough to fit the doll)
* a paintbrush
* purple and black craft paint
* a straight pin
* 3 black candles
* a black lace dress or skirt cut to fit as an altar covering (*Note:* If you have a large space to cover, you may need two items of clothing. If you can't find a black lace dress or skirt, 1–3 yards of black lace fabric will do)
* a framed image of Mama Zora Neale Hurston
* a cauldron or other fireproof receptacle
* 1–2 charcoal disks
* 3–6 pieces of palo santo resin
* a shot glass of bourbon
* a pack of cigarettes
* glue
* sheets of paper with images of your ancestors or their names

- 1–3 teaspoons dried juniper
- fancy clothes for the doll (*Note:* I recommend keeping several outfits on hand for when your ancestors want to be changed)
- 1–3 drops Nag Champa oil
- Psalm 32 (see appendix C)

Preparation:

Before you start the working, cleanse your railroad spikes with Florida water, then pour a shot of rum over them. Spritz the doll with rosewater.

Next, paint the show box and lid, inside and out, with the black and purple paint. Leave to dry.

Finally, use the pin to carve *I have returned* onto each candle.

Instructions:

Lay the lace fabric over your altar space. Place the image of Mama Zora in the center and arrange the candles in a circle around the image. Light the candles. Place a lit charcoal disk inside the cauldron. Add the resin. Set out the remaining items using your discretion.

Glue the images or names of your ancestors to the inside of the box and/or top. Once dry, sprinkle the dried juniper inside the box, then lay down the black satin fabric so it covers the bottom.

Make sure your doll is dressed gorgeously, then rub the Nag Champa oil in her hair to cleanse and feed her spirit. Recite Psalm 32 nine times over the doll, then put her in her resting box to complete the work.

Baptizing the Decolonized Mind

Conjure and Hoodoo have both relied heavily on turning the words of the oppressor against them. This has been done by transforming their Bible into a book of spells that, when voiced from the throat chakra of the oppressed, becomes weaponized as a healing missile. Yes, the Bible was forced upon the enslaved, but for many who never forgot their Afrikan spirituality, the Bible became a way of turning the tables on White supremacy.

I grew up in New Orleans, born and proudly raised. My conjure, my Hoodoo, often overlaps with Santeria, Ifa, Lukumi, Akan practices, Muerterismo, Palo Mayombe, and Kongo-Bantu. My conjure isn't European witchcraft. Conjure's roots and traditions started in the Southern United States with Kongo-Bantu origins that were greatly impacted by Senegambian people who originated from the Bight of Biafra.

These people's migration brought a merging of cosmologies, a deeper comprehension of the universe and its problematic components. Hoodoo would become the emerging spark detailing how these groups of people would heal their loss, creating pathways to survival.

A young couple in their mid-twenties once came to me seeking guidance on the path of spirituality they should undergo for the future of their relationship and also the spiritual development of their children. They had just given birth to fraternal twins who were a month old at our first conversation. We laughed a lot, and then came the tears. The young man and his wife were at a spiritual impasse. They had found that growing up in the south and attending Christian churches had left a foul taste in their mouths. They felt disconnected from God and the feminine energy they believed was more prevalent in the universe's design than male dominance. They had attended college with several people who grew up initiated to Islam, Santeria, Palo Mayombe, Brujeria, Hoodoo, Vodoun, and so on, and they were intrigued. They wanted a fairer representation of spirituality; they had done religion and were tired of being chastised by the threat of hell's fire. The tears were a release, a testament to a decision made by their hearts long before their minds agreed to venture out in search of a spirituality that welcomed their evolution.

I told them that as a conjurer, I could share a plethora of paths and divine on the ones they should research and those they should avoid. I also divined upon a bath that would help them dissociate from feelings of shame centered around having a spiritual awakening as adults.

The couple felt like their own lineage had spent generations living happy lives as colonized deaf, dumb, and blind fools. They were willing to defect from all the praying elders who had brought them thus far. Yet this embarrassment at something their elders couldn't control would hinder the young couple from transforming their lives for the better. I had to teach them that our connection to God or Goddess is etched within our DNA. We don't unlearn our Afrikanness. For many, youth and elders alike, it's simply lying dormant. Enslavement may have force-fed a name better suited to a White sky God, but our deeply rooted knowing of a higher power that is Blacker than a hundred midnights is a knowing that disrobes its colonized robes when we catch the Holy Ghost, or in how we sing our troubles into our places of worship and then nail them to the figurative cross, exorcising them in the name of all that is sanctified and holy.

The couple had to learn that our elders know firsthand that our God is Black with hair of lambswool; that truth is embedded inside an Afrikan-centered acceptance that our God/Goddess is as Afrikanly hued as our memory will allow us to conceive.

The following bath I shared with them helped them readjust their idea of what it means to be Afrikan-centered. The work quelled any thoughts of divisiveness while helping them come to terms with our BIPOC survival instincts.

The elders speak a knowing of history and its racial battles; they prayed through enslavement, reconstruction, Jim Crow, civil rights. May we be grateful to those elders forever speaking salvation as a means of honoring our survival in a land that tried to dupe us into agreeing to forget. We were taught by force of whip to name our spirituality Christianity, but our elders know better. They know that there is no language barrier when our DNA speaks in an ancient tongue ready and willing to go to war with our transgressors. Our elders know how to pray into existence the code of their DNA, which says even on soil not of Afrika, we are all hers. She is the alpha and the omega, the womb of civilization, the Eden, Eve, Adam, serpent, apple, and Lilith. Our spirituality by any name has always been the truth talker and the fire starter. When we speak, our soul translates all matters of our bruised hearts, and the recording of words too ancient to decipher becomes a parable of tongues, a parable of drums.

EXERCISE: MAMA ZORA'S BATH

This is the bath I offered to the young couple. You'll need to first set up the altar to Mama Zora as shown in the previous exercise.

Needs:
* 6 tablespoons Epsom salt
* ⅓ cup Florida water
* 1 teaspoon dried lavender
* 1 teaspoon dried sage
* 1 teaspoon dried lemongrass
* 1 teaspoon dried mugwort
* Psalm 139 (see appendix C)

Instructions:
After setting up your altar, it's time to prepare your bath. Fill the tub with steaming hot water, then add the salt, Florida water, and herbs. Stir the contents nine times using your dominant hand while reciting the psalm, then leave the herbs to soak into the water for fifteen minutes undisturbed.

Later, when you step into your bath, think about the history of your people in this country. Think long and hard about how they arrived here, and ask those forgotten by time to reconnect you with your indigenous spiritual paths. Ask Mama Zora to lead you to a deeper awakening of your people's true spirituality.

Relax in the bath for fifteen minutes, get out, and dry off. Recite the psalm again one more time.

Your altar space for Mama Zora is now open. You can snuff out your candles, but leave the resin burning.

JOVANDA BEENE

I get tired of walking into big-chain bookstores and almost every book on the shelf is by a White author or a bot you can't even find in a fifteen-minute Google search. I don't want my Hoodoo coming from a White woman or man. I mean, I started to feel like these publishers were saying the only people with authority on all subjects are White people. These publishers are delusional and clearly making a claim about superiority. I started thinking publishers and editors were saying, if White people don't validate Hoodoo, then it ain't real magick.

I've also run into books where White women swear they have a right to Hoodoo because generations ago, an enslaved Afrikan woman took a liking to their always "abolitionist" relative and out of solidarity gave them the secrets of conjure on a silver platter. I call bullshit on all of that. I started tuning in to BIPOC-led and friendly social media pages where other BIPOC people do the work of finding the real galangal chewers, the descendants of Maroons. That's my tribe.

If you haven't never been whipped, maimed, raped, or watched your family stolen away, how the hell are you supposed to resonate with the pain and the trauma of oppression? I'm talking about a trauma that seeps into our DNA, festering, reminding us that the memory is alive and plotting its next annihilation attempt.

Diving Deeper

According to those outside the culture who attempt to write about Hoodoo, the practice is often inaccurately described as being in opposition to good, civilized Christians. Critics who seek to demonize Hoodoo argue that it falls outside biblical teachings because its origins trace back to the enslavement of West Afrikans from Kongo, Sierra Leone, and Ghana.

In her book *Mojo Workin': The Old African American Hoodoo System*, Katrina Hazzard-Donald, associate professor of sociology, anthropology, and criminal justice at Rutgers University, also notes the exploitation of Hoodoo, especially when it emerged as a "commercial enterprise right around World War I among people who were not believers or practitioners even though they were willing to sell it." She added, "What many people start to see is something that I call commercialized or tourist Hoodoo. It has been presented as the 'real authentic' Hoodoo."[91]

Prevalent misconceptions about Hoodoo often make headlines, reinforcing narratives like "Hoodoo is the work of the devil" or "Hoodoo is a form of witchcraft and should not be practiced by churchgoing folks." Whenever Black and White evangelicals feel the need to increase church membership and revenue, they push the idea that Hoodoo is just another non-Christian pathway to make a pact with the Devil.

Another common misconception is the refusal to acknowledge that Voodoo (or Vodoun, as it's called in Haiti) is a legitimate religion with initiatory practices rather than something inherently evil. In reality, Vodoun played a critical role in Haiti's liberation, a victory that many White evangelicals still struggle to accept. The powers that be understand the reckoning that would come if BIPOC people reclaimed their spiritual traditions, which is precisely why Hoodoo and Voodoo remain misunderstood and misrepresented.

As we've already learned, Hoodoo, in truth, is a fusion of beliefs and cultural practices, blending elements from West Afrikan religions, Native First Nations traditions, and European herbal knowledge. Since enslaved Afrikans were taken in large numbers from regions like Senegal and the Kongo, more than half of Hoodoo's customs originated from the minds of enslaved Kongolese conjurers, carrying their wisdom forward despite centuries of forced displacement.

....
91. Katrina Hazzard-Donald, *Mojo Workin': The Old African American Hoodoo System* (University of Illinois Press, 2012).

We Were Hoodoo Long Before We Were Christian

At the end of the Civil War, somewhere between 11 percent and 15 percent of Afrikan Americans were Christians; most Black people practiced Hoodoo.[92] It's because of this that White Christians encouraged Blacks to look toward Christianity for their salvation. Controlling the minds of angry, once-subjugated people—many of whom wanted revenge, not answers—needed to involve a belief that enslavement and Christianity could heal their moral and spiritual disconnect from White God and his White son.

Remember Haiti? Remember how Haitians relied on the strength of their Afrikan gods? Remember how they fought and won their liberation? White evangelicals weren't about to see Blacks using Afrikan Gods to even the score. White evangelicals condemned Hoodoo, encouraging Blacks to fall in line with Christianity and its oppressive rule that called the struggle of the Afrikans God's curse in condemnation of the children of Ham for seeing his father's nakedness.

To ensure Black ministers encouraged a move away from Hoodoo toward Christianity, many White evangelicals attended services at Black churches. They would sit in the back and serve as overseers, ensuring that the teachings were delivered in a way that kept the Afrikans serving at the foot of their masters and his most holy emissary, White Jesus. Napoleon Bonaparte is attributed with saying, "Religion is what keeps the poor from murdering the rich." I will go a step further and say that allowing oneself to serve another culture's God, one who does not resemble the oppressed but instead resembles their oppressor, keeps the oppressed confused, docile, and teeming with self-pity, self-loathing, and internalized racist oppression.

The first blending of Christianity with Afrikan beliefs came by incorporating psalms into Hoodoo incantations. In essence, Hoodoo adapted to the world it was given. It incorporates the tools that are accessible for the growth and understanding of the user. The person performing the conjure, by the mere existence of their BIPOC DNA, will render the practice not witchcraft

....
92. Laurie Maffly-Kipp, "African American Christianity, Pt. II: From the Civil War to the Great Migration, 1865–1920," The National Humanities Center, accessed December 9, 2024, https://nationalhumanitiescenter.org/tserve/nineteen/nkeyinfo/aarcwgm.htm.

or devilment, but Hoodoo through and through. When we speak, our voices join a chorus of ancestors stretching toward the beginning of time. The result is a symphony of liberation.

Hoodoo is a closed practice. There is folk magick for White-bodied individuals where some tools may overlap with Hoodoo, but make no mistake: Hoodoo belongs to those folks who have the seedling of oppression steeped within their DNA. Afrikans were transported across and around the globe as part of their enslavement, so Black and Brown DNA is far and wide. That's why I included all people of color in this book. Generations of oppression connect conjurers across states and across countries.

What do colonizers look like practicing the rights of the colonized? What happens when the Maroons they conjure awaken with a machete in hand? How do the colonizers expect that to end?

EXERCISE: BLACK MIRROR DECOLONIZING

In this work, you'll call on Mama Zora to help open your mind and decolonize your practice.

Needs:
* 1 purple candle
* a cauldron or other fireproof receptacle
* 1–2 charcoal disks
* 3–6 pieces of palo santo resin
* 1 black mirror
* Psalms 24 and 27 (see appendix C)

Instructions:
Light the candle and place it in the center of your altar. Place a lit charcoal disk inside the cauldron. Add the resin. Place both the mirror and cauldron to the right of the candle.

Turn off all the lights, close your eyes, and breathe slowly in and out for five minutes. When finished, open your eyes slowly and stare into the mirror while repeating the following: *Zora Neale Hurston, great mother of mine, open my heart, open my mind. Allow me to see the world of spirits and the world of ancestors. Open my third eye to the heart of the divine. Come Devil's Shoestring, come High John, come Low John, come Jezebel, come vetiver, come asafoetida, come calamus, come Queen Elizabeth, come licorice, come lucky hand, come mandrake, come valerian, come Solomon's seal. Mama Zora, lead me down the path of conjuration in your name, Ase!*

Recite Psalms 24 and 27 three times each. Conclude the working by sitting quietly and staring into the mirror for forty-five minutes or until you begin to see your story unfold.

EXERCISE: ANTHROPOLOGICAL HOODOO

This work creates a soil jar that helps connect you to both First Nations and Afrikan ancestors who struggled and fought against oppression. The more you engage with your jar, shaking it and thanking it in the mornings and evenings, the deeper and more efficacious your magick will become.

Needs:

* a map of First Nations peoples (*Note:* Maps are available at both www.nativegov.org and www.native-land.ca/)
* paper and pencil
* glue
* a sheet of paper with the Boa Me Na Me Mmoa Wo adinkra symbol (see appendix)
* a marker
* 1 bay leaf
* a large mason jar with lid
* 3 tablespoons dried calamus root
* 1–2 cups soil from your yard

- a cauldron or other fireproof receptacle
- 1–2 charcoal disks
- 3–6 pieces of sandalwood resin
- 1 purple candle
- Psalm 102, 9, and 29 (see appendix C)

Instructions:

First, use the websites listed to find out the names of the First Nations peoples who inhabited the land you reside on. Write them down on the paper along with the names of members of your family tree. Add the following regions to your paper as well: Senegal, Gambia, Guinea-Bissau, Mali, Angola, Kongo, the Democratic Republic of Kongo, Gabon, Ghana, Benin, Nigeria, Togo, and Cameroon. Glue the Boa Me Na Me Mmoa Wo adinkra symbol to the paper, then set aside.

Take the marker and write the following words on the bay leaf, one on each side: *Protection* and *Salvation*. Add the calamus root to the mason jar, then fill the jar halfway with the soil. Drop in the paper (you may need to fold it to get it to fit) and cover it with the remaining soil. Set aside.

Place a lit charcoal disk inside the cauldron. Then, add three pieces of resin. Light the candle and recite Psalms 102, 9, and 29 three times each.

Seal the jar tightly and begin shaking it as you ask the First Nations peoples on whose land you now reside to allow you to continue to connect with the deep magick of the ancestors (yours and theirs) so you may fight against the same oppressive forces they gave their lives to denounce. Thank them for the use of their lands, then sit with the soil for fifteen minutes before snuffing out the candle. Leave the jar resting on your altar.

Each time before you eat a meal, thank the First Nations peoples and the Afrikans for their undying love and will to survive. Thank them for the soil and the bodies of water that still remember BIPOC pain.

CONTESSA

I'm part of this paranormal team. We first met in high school—two Afrikan Americans, one Asian American, one Native American, and one Mexican American. We're also all females. At first being nineteen and college students meant most of our fans were men, nineteen to sixty-ish, I'd say. They would tune in with their porn star ideas, asking us to wear either nothing or tight-fitting shirts or yoga pants where they could see our camel toe. Forget the fact we all love ghost hunting. All these guys wanted was hoochie mamas, tits, and ass.

Then we had the haters—the White people who tuned in to say stuff like "I hope the ghosts lynch you," or "I hope the ghost of a confederate soldier reenslaves you," or stuff about Asians and COVID, or stuff about Mexicans and how ghosts won't be able to understand their accent, or making jokes about racist ghosts scalping Native Americans. For every laugh they got, there were people who called them out and challenged their ignorance with attacks of their own.

I've never seen White teen ghost hunters dealing with the hate we had to go through. We realized we had to block out all the comments, which sucks because we do have fans who see us as an inspiration, and we like interacting with those fans. Our goal is to show that indigenous practices create liberation for the oppressed; they allow us to separate from a lifetime of violence and hegemonic White terrorism. We want to show BIPOC and AAPI people that not every spirit is malevolent or a demon causing trouble. We want people like us to watch what we do and see how sometimes the spirit has an unfinished truth to leave behind, and the person who needs to hear it most is either ignoring the spiritual or can't open themselves up to accessing any plane besides this one; their frequency is only tuned in to this life. That's what makes our job important. We each bring an indigenous method of stepping into the void as equals, not as oppressive agents of inequality.

The Drag Star Hoodoo

My grandmother once told me the story of a half Chickasaw, half Haitian man named Cecil Leviathan Jones who used to dress in drag. Grandmama said when he was wielding his womanish ways, Cecil could put Josephine Baker to shame, and you know how fine she was. Cecil was six foot four without heels and his signature beehive hairdo. He went around the city dressed like a geisha. He was a towering blue-black man, and after World War II he allowed his sexuality to flutter like a monarch butterfly who, after traveling long distances, had finally reached the winter of their content.

He could talk for hours about meeting Josephine Baker at the Theatre Marigny in Paris, and he'd waste no time in telling you that her leading role in the operetta *La Creole* was *très magnifique*. Baker, the war heroine with all her gravitas, was his feminine idol, his muse. He would talk about her being named Chevalier of the Legion d'honneur. He'd go on about how she pinned inconspicuous notes detailing airfields and the whereabouts of German troops to special pockets sewn inside her bras and panties like a badass. Nobody dared strip-search her; she was a lady of high society, a woman of intrigue, resistance, and intelligence.

If you stayed long enough, Cecil would let you watch him perform his delectable transformation. When he stood there drenched in French perfumes and silks, the smells of lavender and jasmine permeating even the wall's pores, you forgot he was a man just twenty minutes before. When he shooed you away, you glimpsed the mason jars, the herbs, and the bones. You heard the phonograph, *"J'ai deux amours,"* and you knew salvation was on the way.

Cecil had met and fallen in love with a man from Japan; that's where he learned to dress in drag. But he was also a Hoodoo man potent in conjure. He had this way of using divination as part of his theater. The divulging of truth in each tachikata movement was prophetic. He was known to wear flowers, even when donning his manly attire. He would never go a day without a flower in his hair. His favorite was the purple blooms of the Queen Elizabeth root. He also wore a bracelet of High John and smelled of bergamot.

According to Grandmama, Cecil would say, "While Christianity don't like homosexuality, Hoodoo speaks through the soul. Hoodoo don't care who you fuck as long as it's consensual, as long as you ain't screwing an enemy to your survival."

Cecil saved many lives. Grandmama said that he made elixirs for children on the verge of death. "And ain't no mama nor daddy ever complained about the dresses he wore while doing it. Nobody never labeled him. We just let that beautiful man work his conjure. You let him bring your baby back from the brink of death, and you thanked him for it. He was a magick man with lipsticks and perfumes and finer fabric than any woman I knew, but he was still magick. Man knew his way around a sewing machine too."

Up until the day he died of pneumonia, Cecil had an empty bottle of sake on his nightstand, my grandmother said. "Sick and all, but he was saving souls. Matter of fact, he saved more souls than those thieving-ass preachers round the way."

MARIEL GARCIA

Hoodoo has helped me come to terms with my oftentimes stagnant mental health issues. Rituals that help me navigate crises at work with my asshole boss and keep me anxiety-free at home when family members are impatient with my boundaries. I sometimes feel that in this patriarchal system, we as Black folks aren't taught to believe in therapy. Well, I do. I sought out a BIPOC woman who was both a Hoodoo and a therapist. We use tarot and rituals to build healing modalities customized to my learning style.

My therapist introduced me to healing circles where bibliotherapy was a prominent tool, and that ritual you sent her, the Goofer Dust to the Rescue work, that right there sparked a major transformation in my life. With you and therapy, I kicked the alcohol abuse that was draining my life. After my child died in a hit-and-run while at college, the only way I could cope with the loss was with liquor. Then it all changed with therapy and rituals; my life was saved.

I wouldn't wish the pain of losing a child on nobody. Yet I had one White therapist say, "Mariel, you have two other children. Pull yourself together for them. In time, you'll forget the one who died." I couldn't believe the insensitivity. Every day I wake up working toward healing. I understand that it's a process that's never quite finished. Reiki and acupuncture have also helped to soothe the rage. I can cry during hot yoga and feel the release overcome me as my body transforms from sutra to sutra. I can succumb to the healing while knowing in my heart that the pain will probably never fully go away. I've made my peace with that.

At this point it's been six years, and I know no amount of time will turn the scab into smooth skin. Life will always be bumpy. Nevertheless, Hoodoo and therapy has allowed me to honor the spirit of my child and to know he is always with me. Together, he and I, we're working through his transition so he doesn't harbor ill will on the other side. I'm still learning not to harbor any on this plane. I'm a forever work in progress.

EXERCISE: GOOFER DUST TO THE RESCUE

There are times when clients come to me seeking aid in reversing ancestral trauma that has successfully kept their lives at an emotional standstill. In those times, I recommend this work because we are all affected by those who have gone before us. This trauma can manifest itself in the form of a fear of achieving success or a replaying of missteps from those of your lineage who found themselves in physically or emotionally challenging situations. Oftentimes, the ancestor's reaction to the situation is grounded in bouts of manic depression. This depression becomes imprinted upon the soulspace of the Spirit, resulting in a trauma that lives within succeeding generations.

Needs:

* a mason jar
* soil from a graveyard

- * 3 tablespoons chili powder
- * 3 tablespoons sulfur powder
- * 3 tablespoons cayenne pepper
- * 3 tablespoons black pepper
- * fingernail clippings
- * hair clippings
- * a crucifix
- * an ankh
- * paper and pen
- * Psalm 9 (see appendix C)
- * a sheet of paper with the Abode Santann adinkra symbol (see appendix D)

Instructions:

Fill the mason jar halfway with the soil, then add the chili powder, sulfur, cayenne, and black pepper. Mix well. Add the fingernail and hair clippings, then set aside.

Using the pen and paper, list as many of the names of your ancestors as you can remember. Bury the list and the adinkra symbol in the soil (you may need to fold them to get them to fit). Bury the crucifix and the ankh as well. Recite Psalm 9 nine times for twenty-seven nights, then nine times on and nine times off as often as you require the working.

Top the jar nightly and place it at your head before bed. As you sleep, the jar will remove ancestral trauma from your body, as well as any trauma you're experiencing in this lifetime. In the morning you may feel heavy as your body realigns itself. Don't worry, you'll start to feel lighter throughout the day. Place the jar in sunlight each morning, as this allows the trauma to be released and devoured by the radiance of protection.

EXERCISE: ANCESTRAL DOLL HEALING

This work will create a doll that's connected to your ancestors. Your ancestral doll will provide protection and healing for you, your family, and your community for as long as you need her.

Needs:

* 1 Afrikan or Afrikan-inspired doll
* a cauldron or other fireproof receptacle
* 1–2 charcoal disks
* 3 tablespoons dried lavender
* 3 tablespoons dried chamomile
* 1 white candle
* a mason jar
* plain water
* 3 tablespoons Florida water
* images of trusted ancestors or index cards with their names (one name per card)
* Psalm 29 (see appendix C)
* food offerings (e.g., candy)
* toys
* *Optional:* a wicker basket

Instructions:

Lay your doll on your Zora altar. Place a lit charcoal disk inside the cauldron, then add a pinch of the lavender and chamomile. As the herbs burn, recite Psalm 29 three times.

Fill the mason jar halfway with water, then add a tablespoon of the Florida water and stir. Light the candle and place it behind the mason jar. Arrange the images around the doll, then ask the ancestors to use it as a receptacle for generational healing.

Sit with your doll daily for five to fifteen minutes (or longer, if desired) to pick up on any information about unseen obstacles. You can also write it letters asking for protection for those you love and your community. Always open and close your time with your doll by reading the psalm three times.

Once a month, give your doll a gift of food or toys. Gifts don't have to be elaborate. For example, water is always a favorite gift as it aids the spirits in moving toward your doll. Food items can be discarded weekly, but you can keep toys in a wicker basket near the altar.

Remember, whenever you feel burdened, go to your doll. Take care of it, ensuring it's always clean and happy, and it will fight your toughest battles in this life and the next.

Joyce's Story

Working with the spirit of Mama Zora will allow you to embrace not only an Afrikan-centered mindset but a Pan Afrikanist ideology. It will foster solidarity with other people of color, recognizing that we're all flawed and oftentimes fall short of acknowledging our divine interconnectedness to the spirits of other colorful people.

Unfortunately, there are those among us who try to make knowledge of self a byproduct of sniffing too much incense and stuffing our bras with too many crystals. But Mama Zora teaches us to look past those with fragile egos and even more fragile self-love. They're the ones who stare in the mirror praying for the day God paints them White.

Even in spiritual communities, you have to be careful about predators or charlatans. Just because they're practicing an indigenous spirituality doesn't mean we should give over our complete agency to any person. I don't devalue any spiritual practice, but I'll always call out people who abuse spirituality for their own ends.

JOYCE

A girlfriend of mine, Shaquella, had this idea to help me with all the troubles that were piling up on my ass. I had a cheating boyfriend, a landlord who wouldn't stop raising the rent ever since the fucking pandemic, and my autistic son's fuckboy daddy was choking the sobriety out of my last nerve. I was drinking a bottle of wine a day and convincing myself that the surgeon general says wine is good for the heart. I know I was bullshitting myself and my liver.

The two men in my life who I expected to play fair with me were fighting to free themselves from my physical and emotional grasp. Shaquella had been going to see this Yoruba priest, a babalawo, who helped her clean up her life after her own divorce. Her husband Brandon was a cokehead. He had drained their bank account three times before she decided enough was enough. The babalawo released her from that situation.

I never knew what or how he did it. She told me it was personal; it was her medicine, for her and her alone. She was the only person who was supposed to swallow her medicine, which meant the whole situation wasn't my business. I know how to butt out just as easily as I know how to butt in.

I couldn't deny it: Shaquella looked good, and she was happy. She had a new job, a new apartment, and a different bank. It was like her entire life was now housed in a giant bubble of protection, and nobody who didn't mean her good could get to her.

When I went to see him, I didn't know what to expect—what would be my medicine? It started with the babalawo asking to meet me at midnight. He told me to show up in a slip and no other underwear. I thought that was a weird request between people who ain't never once met. But I kept thinking about Shaquella and her progress. I also thought about my son's father, who refused to keep a job just so he wouldn't have to have child support garnish his check.

I met the babalawo at his home. He did a reading, a divination, for me. I sat on a straw mat and listened as he laid my entire life out in front of me. At first, I thought Shaquella had told him shit, but then he went back to my childhood and the rape by my sister's boyfriend. I've never told anyone that story, not even my sister, who wound up married to this man.

I watched the opele fall and heard the babalawo's whispers. He sang to the shells, then he revealed the contents of my medicine, my prescription for healing. It was all making sense to me; I was prioritizing my next moves. Then he told me in addition to the steps he had already laid out, he had to give me a bath. He also informed me that he had to put medicine inside my vagina, and he then went on describing how the medicine would be transferred from him into my vagina. The medicine had to be put on the tip of his penis and then inserted inside my vagina. He tried to reassure me that's how Shaquella was made whole.

I couldn't, I wouldn't. I got my raincoat and checked the fuck out. I drove home in tears, not just for me but for Shaquella also. In our need to be healed from sadass, immature men, we were willing to allow another sorry-ass to use spirituality to pimp us. I almost gave up on spirituality. I left the Baptist church because of creeps, sleazeball men with religious authority looking to take advantage of women, convinced their sexual identity makes them second class in the eyes of God.

I knew what Shaquella was doing with him, and I knew it was embarrassing for her to say it out loud. I knew she was trying to rationalize the sexual assault as healing, but it was sexual assault.

I'm glad I met you through LlewellynCon. I was glad I got to experience a healer who respects that I don't know this world, and who patiently walks me through each lesson with a genuine concern for my wholeness. Setting up that altar for Mama Zora helped me explore myself as a spiritual being, and it allowed me to see I don't need a man reigning over me because I'm, by nature of my vagina, inherently evil or childlike. Mama Zora's altar work made me understand the role women play in all of this. I get how BIPOC women are the culture bearers of Spirit. My life is worth living these days, and my Black girl magick is alive and well.

My friendship with Shaquella ended; she felt like I was trying to stunt her growth. She accused me of liking her better when she was pathetic and depressed all the time. She even found out that she was pregnant from the babalawo, and that she wasn't the only woman carrying his seed, or his HIV.

It's estimated that 736 million women globally have been subjected to physical sexual violence at least once in their lifetime.[93] And this figure doesn't account for the terrible byproducts of sexual violence, like depression, anxiety, unplanned pregnancy, or disease. If you're the victim of sexual harassment or an assault, please seek help. Don't live in silence, no matter who the perpetrator(s) might be. The National Sexual Assault Hotline can be reached 24/7, and all conversations are confidential. That number is 1-800-656-4673.

EXERCISE: STOP THE FUSS, RELEASE THE ENERGY OF HARASSMENT

If someone has a physical or mental hold on you, whether in this plane of existence or another, this work helps you release it. We know trauma will seep into the soul and haunt us through our life paths if we don't stop and do the work of healing.

Needs:

* 1 black candle
* 3–6 tablespoons sea salt (white and pink)
* 1–2 charcoal disks
* 3–6 pieces of Nag Champa resin
* Psalm 31 (see appendix C)

Instructions:

Light the candle and place it in the center of your Zora altar. Add three pinches each of the white and pink sea salt to the cauldron, then a lit charcoal disk and three pieces of resin. Call out the names of those who are causing you trauma. As you do, take a pinch of salt into your palm and blow it out

---

93. "Facts and Figures: Ending Violence against Women," *UN Women*, accessed March 3, 2021, https://www.unwomen.org/en/what-we-do/ending-violence-against-women/facts-and-figures.

the front door or an open window. Close by reciting Psalm 31 three times.

Repeat this work for nine nights once a month until you feel resolved.

Juju on the Fly

In 1928, Zora Neale Hurston drove down to New Orleans in a gray Chevrolet to study with the best conjurers, root workers, and Hoodoo the city had to offer. Seven years later, after the publication of *Mules and Men*, Hurston reported, "Hoodoo was burning with a flame in America with all the intensity of a suppressed religion."[94] Because of forced conversions to Christianity, indigenous practices had to go underground. It is here where phrasing like "spirit possession" became "catching the Holy Ghost."

But today, many millennials are tired of life underground. More and more, they're inclined to live spiritually out loud. My grandmama said, "The young folks flee to the old ways, and the old folks clutch them Bibles, hoping the words magically assemble into the shape of Jesus himself and carry them home, away from this boring-ass circus of lying-ass hypocrites. They don't want to fight for their liberation. They want to die and sip on milk and honey, leaving the fist-fighting to God. Ain't that some foolishness?"

You can't stop the burning flame of Hoodoo. One of my clients was glad to offer reasons why he left the Baptist church: "The Black church is too judgmental, especially on the topic of sexuality. The Black church knows damn well it's full of queer folks, from the musical directors to the ushers, the deacons, deaconesses, choir members, even the reverend sometimes. The Black church needs to just say gay and walk away from hate. The more the church alienates with spiritual separatism, the more they lose out on worshippers. And don't get me started on women in the pulpit. If Jesus had females as part of his entourage, then why are women

---

94. Dawn Araujo-Hawkins, "Why Some Young Black Christians Are Practicing Hoodoo," The Christian Century, accessed January 13, 2021, https://www.christiancentury.org/article/features/why-some-young-black-christians-are-practicing-hoodoo.

excluded from teaching and ministering? In school, most of my teachers were women, so I know they were capable. Are men worried they're going to be outsourced out of a job? The disciple Mary Magdalene followed Jesus around as his star student so that she could teach his gospel one day. That's progressive spirituality, not sexism, not patriarchal dogma. I mean, she's regarded as his most beloved disciple in Gnostic literature. She's also considered the Apostle to the Apostles because she announced Jesus's resurrection to them. She knew before everybody that he had risen. How is that for a woman with power?"

I'm finding in my current clientele that answering the call of new age spirituality requires an indigenous approach to what came before Christianity. These indigenous spiritual atmospheres serve to connect devotees to the pulse of the universe not only through spiritual study, but also through cultural outreach and historical research. These systems heal the mind, body, and spirit. These systems free devotees from the last vestiges of a bygone era of oppression. When we give the colonizers back their religion, we live freer, more productive lives now and in our lives to come.

Many young people are finding a limited worldview in teachings from the pulpit. Today's issues aren't being addressed, and when they seek counsel from their ministers, many report being told, "You go to church to seek the kingdom of heaven, not to examine racial issues. If you stay home because you're angry with a pastor who stays clear of social issues, then you risk going to hell when you die." Many former churchgoers blamed this apolitical stance for their departure. One told me, "For every Black church that risked it all during the eras of Jim Crow and Civil Rights, we have way too many ducking and dodging in the era of BLM. They want our money but not our honesty."

Even more former churchgoers are finding that the Black church has become a never-ending lecture series of fire and brimstone attacks on everything and everyone except White supremacy and White privilege. The Black church has missed the mark for many at proving itself a healing space, a safe haven for the soul. Church for many continues to fail at aligning its membership with the changing values and mores of today—financial security, mental health, educational rights, sexual health, job security, reproductive rights, LGBTQIA+ rights, and so on. Truly answering the call for many requires falling in line with progress, even if it means switching from a rotary phone mentality to a cell phone sensibility.

EXERCISE: MAKING MY OWN LAND OF MILK AND HONEY

Stop people trying to dim your light and call on Mama Zora to bless your Hoodoo.

Needs:

- 5 stones (painted black, red, green, gold, and silver)
- 1 black candle
- a mason jar
- 1–2 cups soil from a graveyard
- 1–2 cups soil from a church
- a sheet of paper with the Nsoromma adinkra symbol (see appendix D)
- 1 dried chicken foot (painted black)
- 3 tablespoons ground cinnamon
- Nag Champa oil
- 3 cowrie shells
- Psalm 70 (see appendix C)
- a shakere

Instructions:

Begin by painting your stones. Allow them to dry completely before continuing.

Light the candle and place it in the center of your altar, then place the jar in front of it. Pour the soil from the graveyard and then the church into the jar. Push the Nsoromma adinkra symbol into the soil (you may need to fold it to get it to fit).

Sprinkle the cinnamon and thirteen drops of the oil onto the soil, then place the dried and painted chicken foot on top. Surround the foot with the shells. Surround the jar with the painted stones. Ask Mama Zora to bless your Hoodoo and open all doors to your spiritual success.

Whenever you want to trap someone who's trying to dim your light, bury their name deep in the soil, recite Psalm 70, then tap the shakere to give the message a boost. The dead will beat the shit out of their spirit, depleting their energy.

Chapter Thirteen
Mama Healer Henrietta Lacks:
BIPOC Healthcare

Rebecca Skloot's 2010 New York Times bestselling book, *The Immortal Life of Henrietta Lacks*, exposes the medical community's misappropriation and unethical experimentation surrounding the theft and harvesting of Lacks's cells. If you haven't read this book and you're a person of color, you should. If you consider yourself an ally or accomplice, you should read it too.

Skloot's book offers critical historical insight into the life of Henrietta Lacks (1920–1951), a Black woman who sought care at Johns Hopkins Hospital, where she was later diagnosed with cervical cancer. Born on August 1, 1920, Lacks came from a rural Virginia family of tobacco farmers. In 1941, she, her husband, and their five young children moved to Baltimore, Maryland, hoping for greater economic opportunity.

By the time Lacks arrived at Johns Hopkins, she was already suffering from immense pain and relentless cervical and vaginal bleeding. According to Skloot's book, Lacks had no idea her cervical cells would become a cornerstone of scientific experimentation.[95] Nor did she know that return visits would lead to doctors acquiring more cells under false pretenses. There was never any consent detailing an agreement between Lacks and Johns Hopkins, which meant not only was she unaware of her contributions, but her family was also kept in the dark.

Henrietta's cells, scientifically categorized as HeLa cells, were found to divide easily and indefinitely, making her contributions to science and healthcare enormously monumental. In 1953, HeLa cell growth patterns and cell immortality were proven.[96] Two years later, the cells were used to

---
[95]. *The Immortal Life of Henrietta Lacks by Rebecca Skloot: Study Guide*, Pembroke Notes (Dog Ear Publishing, 2013).
[96]. Skloot, *The Immortal Life of Henrietta Lacks*.

study the effects of radiation on human cells, and they were instrumental in creating a homogeneous single mutant cell.[97] In 1956, the HeLa cells were used to document the behaviors of cancerous and pharmacological responses on malignant cells.

By 1960, HeLa cells were being transported into outer space as science studied the effects of radiation on space travel. HeLa cells have been instrumental in scientific breakthroughs in the areas of polio, cancer, HIV, Ebola, tuberculosis, invitro fertilization, human genome studies, and the creation of COVID vaccines.

Time after time, as Henrietta returned to Hopkins, her cells were harvested with no intent on seeking a cure for her deteriorating health. Henrietta's family eventually learned about the HeLa studies years later, despite the fact that Henrietta's cells had been circulating around the medical community for more than sixty years. Pharmaceutical companies and other scientific organizations have made billions of dollars because of Henrietta Lacks.[98]

What we should remember about HeLa cells is that they can be studied continuously because they multiply easily, making them immortal, and because they can be shared in lab settings, many medical breakthroughs would not have happened without them. What we should remember about the woman whose cells were stolen is that she died being duped by a medical profession that had little to no regard for the afflictions of BIPOC women.

To try to scratch the surface of rectifying past wrongs, the National Institutes of Health (NIH) created the HeLa Genome Data Use Agreement. It requires researchers to use a controlled access database where members of the Lacks family serve on the committee and are instrumen-

....
97. Max Matza, "Henrietta Lacks: Family of Black Woman Whose Cells Were Taken Settle Case," *BBC News*, August 1, 2023, https://www.bbc.com/news/world-us-canada-66376758.
98. Justin Gamble, "Estate of Henrietta Lacks Reaches Settlement with Biotech Company for Nonconsensual Use of Her Cells in Medical Research," *CNN*, August 1, 2023, https://www.cnn.com/2023/08/01/us/henrietta-lacks-thermo-fisher-scientific-settlement/index.html.

tal members of the review board. This board requires beforehand knowledge of any publication using genome data from HeLa cells.

We Are the Daughters of Henrietta Lacks

I was sitting with a group of BIPOC women discussing the harmful stereotypes America uses to judge our physical and emotional resilience. One sister passionately argued that we're the daughters of Henrietta Lacks, showing up to doctors' offices only to be misdiagnosed or underdiagnosed, sometimes intentionally. She said, "They think we can handle it. We're strong Black, Brown, or Indigenous women. The fact that we survive is seen as proof of our resilience."

Another woman chimed in, saying, "These White doctors just pat us on the shoulder with that 'attagirl' look in their eyes as they dismiss us from their offices. They don't really want to help us, just pacify us. We're BIPOC babies sucking on confusion. If you listen to them, they'll tell you that BIPOC women don't feel psychological stress, that we're immune to pain, physical or emotional."

The elder in the group, an eighty-year-old woman, cackled as she shared her own experience. "I'll do y'all one better," she said. "I once had a White OB-GYN try to pay me what she thought was a compliment. She told me, 'Your Black women must be superhuman. You endure racism every day and still find time to laugh and smile. If I were in your shoes, I'd dream of burning this country to the ground every time I closed my eyes. Honestly, I couldn't handle it. I'd need refills of Thorazine just to cope.'"

The elder leaned forward and whispered, "I told her, with my eyes open or closed, I see this country burning. I'm so 'crazy' that I cry when I'm happy and laugh when I'm ashamed of myself for crying. You got a mind drug for that?"

Healing with Mama Henrietta helps you resist the systems that were designed to harm, ignore, dismiss, or exploit BIPOC and AAPI people. She knows how supremacist institutions operate to cause harm. With her guidance, we reimagine healing and reclaim ownership of our bodies.

EXERCISE: MAMA HENRIETTA ALTAR AND RITUAL

This work takes place over several days. You'll build an altar to Mama Henrietta and create a powerful, healing tea.

Needs:

- 2–3 yards pink satin fabric covered with pink lace
- a cauldron or other fireproof receptacle
- 3 red candles
- 1–2 charcoal disks
- 6–9 pieces of frankincense resin
- a framed image of Henrietta Lacks
- a framed image of a HeLa cell
- an emergency surgical kit
- a toy microscope
- a vase of red roses
- rose water in a spray bottle
- Psalms 138, 139, and 140 (see appendix C)
- 2 teaspoons each of the following dried herbs on a saucer: rosemary, parsley, oregano, and cayenne pepper
- a kettle or pot
- 1 teaspoon powdered turmeric
- 1 teaspoon ground cinnamon
- 1 teaspoon powdered ginger
- 3 tablespoons beetroot powder
- 2 teaspoons lemon juice
- 3 tablespoons elderberry juice
- 2–3 cups water
- 1–3 tablespoons agave
- 1 large mason jar or pitcher with lid
- a favorite cup or mug
- 2 star anise

Instructions:

Lay the fabric on your altar space. Set the cauldron in the center and the candles around it in a circle. Place a lit charcoal disk inside the cauldron. Add the resin. Place the image of Henrietta to the left of the candles and the HeLa cell image to the right. Arrange the other items (the emergency surgical kit, toy microscope, vase of roses, and rose water) as you see fit.

Recite Psalms 138, 139, and 140 over the saucer of dried herbs three times each, then allow the herbs to rest on the altar for three nights. After this time, the herbs are ready for use in healing recipes. (They serve as cancer-fighting immunity boosters.)

You can place them in a plastic zip-top bag or lidded container.

Next, make a tea by mixing the turmeric, cinnamon, ginger, beetroot powder, lemon juice, elderberry juice, and water in a kettle or pot. Set the blend to boil. Once it does, let it cool before pouring it into the mason jar. Add the agave to taste, seal the jar tightly, then shake vigorously for one to two minutes. Pour in your cup and drink. Any remaining drink can be stored in the refrigerator.

Once you've finished drinking, place a star anise on the charcoal and relax into the stillness of the scent. Sit with your altar space for thirty minutes. As you sit, ask Mama Henrietta to protect you from medical institutions that try to use you as a guinea pig or don't take your health or your loved ones' health seriously. Ask her to help you stand up to doctors who demean and minimize your pain. Ask her to protect you from racism in all areas of hospitals and elder care facilities. When finished, snuff out the candle and spritz yourself with the rose water before retiring to bed.

Consume the tea within three days, reciting the psalms as you drink it.

Can a Sistah Catch a Break?

The 2022 Winter Olympics saw White figure skater Kamila Valieva test positive for a performance-enhancing drug. The International Olympic Committee's (IOC) Court of Arbitration of Sports (CAS) ruled that, due to her age, the timing of the news, and the irreparable harm if she was suspended and later found innocent, there wasn't time for a full-fledged legal process.[99] Valieva was the gold medal favorite in the women's figure skating competition. In the end, she was allowed to compete.

But when Afrikan American sprinter Sha'Carri Richardson faced the same IOC, the outcome was quite different. Richardson, who used marijuana to cope with the loss of her biological mother a month before the 2021 Tokyo Summer Olympics, was forced to bow out. Sha'Carri, like Kamila, was a medal contender who days before her competition was denied entrance, whereas Valieva's proof of drug usage provided to the IOC in December of 2021 wasn't considered a disqualifiable offense. The IOC ignored Sha'Carri's mental health while in mourning and held her to a different standard.

Fast forward to the summer of 2024. Simone Biles, Jordan Chiles, and Rebeca Andrade made Olympic history at the Paris summer games as the first all-Black gymnastics podium winners. Andrade, at age twenty-five, won gold. Biles, at twenty-seven, earned silver, and Chiles, at twenty-three, took home the bronze. Biles later said, "We had an all-Black podium of girls, so I think that was amazing, Black girl magic. So hopefully it teaches all the young girls out there that you can do anything you put your minds to, so keep training hard."

Later, there was the backlash amid a decision by the IOC to strip Jordan Chiles of her bronze medal. The argument was that Chiles's appeal of her floor exercise difficulty rating came four seconds too late, voiding her right to third place and instead placing her in fifth. The IOC conceded and took her bronze metal standing, giving it to Ana Barbosu of Romania.

---

99. Akilah Cadet, *White Supremacy Is All Around* (Hachette UK, 2024).

Next came the racist rants and slurs hurled at Chiles, which caused her to close her social media accounts to protect her mental health. USA Gymnastics and the US Olympic & Paralympic Committee said in a joint statement, "Throughout the appeal process, Jordan has been subject to consistent, utterly baseless, and extremely hurtful attacks on social media. No athlete should be subject to such treatment. We condemn the attacks and those who engage, support, or instigate them. We commend Jordan for conducting herself with integrity both on and off the competition floor, and we continue to stand by and support her."[100]

Gina Chiles, Jordan's mother, also posted on social media. "The racist, disgusting comments are still happening in 2024. I'm tired of people who say it no longer exists."[101] In a recent *NBC News* report, Jordan had this to say: "The biggest thing that was taken from me was the recognition of who I was, not just my sport, but the person I am. No matter what, I'm always going to have those accolades with me, and I'm going to continue to shine bright in the ways that I'm going to shine bright, because the star is never going to get dimmed."[102]

Sisters all over social media went in. They blamed Jordan's medal loss on the fact that White folks can't stand when people of color stake their claim to something White folks thought they owned. My favorite comment was on Twitter, written by someone named Lethia C. "They think nobody with a hint of melanin was born to flip, hop, and jump better than them. Then come three colored women, Black Girl Magic popping all up in Paris! Sistah champions, and nobody got time for that. They gotta wait

....
100. Matt Steinke, "Joint Statement from USA Gymnastics and the US Olympic & Paralympic Committee Regarding the CAS Decision on the Women's Floor Final," USA Gymnastics, August 10, 2024, https://usagym.org/joint-statement-from-usa-gymnastics-and-the-u-s-olympic-paralympic-committee-regarding-the-cas-decision-on-the-womens-floor-final/.
101. Amber Raiken, "Jordan Chiles' Mother Slams 'Racist, Disgusting' Comments About Her Daughter on Social Media," Yahoo! Sports, August 12, 2024, https://sports.yahoo.com/jordan-chiles-mother-slams-racist-164855762.html.
102. David K. Li, "Jordan Chiles Looking for 'My Peace' and 'My Justice' After Bronze Medal Dispute," *MSN*, September 11, 2024, https://www.msn.com/en-us/sports/nba/jordan-chiles-looking-for-my-peace-and-my-justice-after-bronze-medal-dispute/ar-AA1qpA9J.

till it's all said and done and steal their medal back. The optics is the optics, three chocolate winners, and nobody White and full of hate wants to see them kind of optics. They'd rather claw their eyes out with a rusty ice pick. Colonizers working overtime all it is. And why America ain't saying, hell no? They can butt into everybody else's affairs, fund wars and not peace, but they ain't about to defend a Black woman over a you know I ain't got to write it."

EXERCISE: BEETROOT MENTAL HEALTH BOOSTER

Taking back agency over your own mental and physical health is essential. This work gives you the mental health boost you need.

Needs:

- 3 cups plain water
- 3 tablespoons beetroot powder
- 1 teaspoon turmeric
- 1 teaspoon ginger
- 1 teaspoon lemon juice
- 1–3 tablespoons agave or brown sugar
- 3 tablespoons schisandra berry powder
- a large mason jar or pitcher with lid
- a favorite cup or mug
- Psalm 27 and 140 (see appendix C)

Instructions:

Set the water to boil. Once it has, remove it from the heat and add the beetroot, turmeric, ginger, lemon juice, schisandra berry powder, and agave to taste. Stir for one to two minutes while still hot but not steaming, then pour into the mason jar and seal. Shake vigorously for one to two minutes, then pour into your cup.

Drink slowly as you clear your mind. Repeat the following mantra between sips:

> I was chosen by my ancestors to defy time and space. I'm not measured by societal standards, but by my ability to redefine the person I was yesterday and in yester lives. No one can take my soul, the very heart of my survival. I accept that I'm greater than any trinket offered by man and any amount of money given. Whether you recognize my accolades or seek to diminish my standing in life, the greatest achievement is that I'm here, in this body, challenging the errors of this world with poise, grace, and fists always ready to fight. I'm an uncut gemstone, dancing wildly, laughing continuously. Even through my tears, I welcome the winds of transformation. Shall we dance, world, shall we dance?

Recite Psalm 27 and 140 three times each once you've completed the mantra. Allow the remaining drink to cool to room temperature, then store it in the refrigerator.

Consume the drink within three days. As you do, repeat the mantra and the psalms.

Diving Deeper

In *Incidents in the Life of a Slave Girl*, Harriet Jacobs recounts how, at the age of twelve, White men began whispering vulgarities in her ear as a way of grooming her for the eventual act of rape. This calculated introduction to sexualized language was meant to strip away her innocence and brand her as a woman, both physically and mentally.

In the warped minds of White planters and rapists, Black women were seen as unholy temptresses who somehow provoked these so-called godly men into committing un-Christian acts. They rationalized their abuse by claiming to be under a spell or possessed by the devil. What else, they argued, could make them fornicate with a "beast"?

For centuries, Black women and men have been forced to confront the cruel reality that our very existence is marked as "exotic" and oversexualized, reducing us to objects devoid of humanity and feeling. During slavery, rape was not only a violent assertion of control but a way for White men to wield supremacy over the spirits, emotions, wombs, and souls of Black women. Historical accounts tell of Black women being made to sleep on pallets at the foot of their masters' beds. This arrangement allowed the master to leave his wife's arms in the middle of the night and freely rape the enslaved woman with no shame, no guilt, and no pretense of sin.

Not only did this arrangement enable the master's depravity, but it also fostered hatred and resentment between the White husband and his White wife. The wife, humiliated and infuriated, often retaliated with violence, tormenting, maiming, or even murdering the Black woman, her children, and at times her husband's other victims.

I've sat in undergraduate classes and listened to White professors insist that Black women and men saw rape as a sign of affection, a claim so abhorrent I couldn't make it up if I tried.

Afro Picks and Revolutionary Fists

I remember the moment I decided to stop perming my hair. Adjusting to my cropped baby Afro took a few weeks, and there were times when I felt on the edge of a nervous breakdown. I questioned myself constantly: Without the perm, would I still be considered pretty? Or would my true self finally be exposed: a dark-skinned, nappy-headed, gap-toothed girl?

What led me to ditch the perm? It happened after an interview I conducted for my undergraduate newspaper. I was speaking with Baba Kwame Ture, who was giving a lecture on Pan Afrikanism and the role of the All-African People's Revolutionary Party in fostering Black and Brown solidarity. During our conversation, Baba Ture and I drifted into a discussion about letting go of European beauty standards. He encouraged me to embrace myself as the Goddess had made me, full of natural wonder, grace, and beauty.

At one point, he pulled an Afro pick from his pocket, its handle engraved with a raised Black Power fist. That small image struck me deeply. It planted a seed in my mind, reshaping how I viewed not only my hair, but also the psychological weight I had internalized around it.

For years, I believed that straightened, permed hair made me more desirable. I thought it gave me an edge, helping me match the lighter-skinned sistahs who, to me, seemed to exist in an entirely different league when it came to beauty. I couldn't be White, but I could at least have "White girl hair." I thought my perms sent a signal to men that I was worthy. That I could be seen as a viable girlfriend, fiancée, or wife, not just the girl you slept with in a pitch-dark boom-boom room filled with the stench of semen and hot wings.

I hadn't realized how much emotional baggage—centuries of history, really—was tied to my hair. It wasn't until years later, with the help of a BIPOC therapist, that I began to unpack it all. She helped me see the link between my obsession with these beauty politics, my disappointing dating life, and the bouts of bulimia I struggled with through my late high school and early college years.

Legacy of Devalued Black Bodies

There's a story that echoes through my family, often brought up around Kwanzaa or Black History Month. It's the story of PawPaw Henri and how he always kept his thirteen children close to the family's plot of land. He didn't let them wander far—not out of strictness, but out of protection. Back then, there were tales of White men lurking, eyeing young Black girls as young as eight or nine. If they took a liking to them, that supposed "liking" turned into something far darker: rape. And it wasn't just one horrific act of violence. It was repeated, over and over again, whenever the man felt the urge to satisfy his twisted desires. There was no sheriff anywhere who would even consider arresting a White man for such acts.

To them, relieving those pressures—the ones tied to striving past "White mediocrity" to join the ranks of the elite—was all but excusable.

The women in PawPaw Henri's family lived in constant fear. My mother often recalled sleeping near the front door with a shotgun, praying it wouldn't jam if she had to fire it, and praying that God would have mercy on her soul if she ever had to use it. She spoke of the horror that came with imagining the possibility of having to carry and birth a child conceived out of hatred. "Growing up, they told me stories," she'd say. "You couldn't hang clothes out to dry unless you dressed like a man, with heavy clothes and a hat to hide your shape. You didn't want anyone noticing your womanhood. It was so much stress, so much anxiety, knowing you were helpless. I can't imagine being fully grown and still not having ownership over my own body."

The truth is, many BIPOC women still live under this kind of scrutiny, viewed by society under a distorted lens. In the media, we're too often portrayed as exotic vixens consumed by lust, caricatures born from the legacy of enslavement. And although slavery has ended, the exploitation of Black bodies, both physical and psychological, remains embedded in everyday life. In the medical industry alone, abuses against BIPOC women persist. We're treated as though we're incapable of deserving the same humanity as White women, whose femininity and sensuality are considered sacred and worthy of endless defense.

Many of my clients have shared stories about being spoken to—by doctors, lovers, and employers—as though they were feral animals in need of shame and submission. It's clear that our society, steeped in its biases, has no intention of valuing or respecting Blackness.

RHONDA

I remember watching an investigative story about Henrietta Lacks. I couldn't believe that medical professionals would watch you die as they harvested your cells. The exploitation of the marginalized has a long, depressing history. To think that Doctor George Gey harvested Lacks's tissue, all without her permission, and to read that was legal at that time blew my mind. Those cells have been doubling since the fifties, and they're still alive, multiplying globally. Over 55 million used, I read, in seventy-five thousand studies. I even read about a biotech company pulling in over $10 billion annually because of Henrietta's cells.

My mama is seventy-nine years old, and she has kidney disease. Whenever she goes to the doctor's office, she whispers in my ear how we need to pay attention to what her doctor says and what he does. I need to discern if true healing is taking place. Black people don't trust White coats unless the person in those coats looks Brown. We ain't too giddy about Black doctors acting White either; we can sniff them out a mile away. They're always the ones, my mama says, "talking to you like they ain't had no home training, just book learning."

Henrietta ain't the first sign of Black and Brown people being medical guinea pigs. What about all those Puerto Rican women sterilized just to test the potency of birth control pills? White folks went to a whole island, without any thought for human beings' reproductive rights regardless of color, to sterilize Brown women just to create a pill to satisfy the unhappy wombs of White women. We already know that with Black and Brown women dying in childbirth, there'll be many more Henriettas to come, unnamed, abandoned, and discarded by history.

Mama's White kidney doctor would try to scold her to tears. He was full of threats about sending her to live in an elderly care facility instead of with me and my family. He said she needed dialysis, or she was going to die. It was me who decided she needed a second opinion, a Black or Brown opinion. We got one, and he had us tweaking her diet, taking nature walks, and prescribing herbs and medicine that weren't working against her healing. Mama started to thrive. I hate to think what would have happened had we stayed with that other doctor. I'm blessed, though, that I don't have to find out.

EXERCISE: SASSY SARSAPARILLA TEA

This tea has helped my own mother by supporting her kidney function, lowering her blood pressure, stabilizing her cholesterol, and protecting her liver. It also helps relieve joint pain associated with arthritis and fights cancer-causing agents. Mom drinks this one to three times a week in addition to following her doctor's orders. This work also calls to Mama Henrietta for healing.

Needs:

- plain water
- a tea setting (cup, spoon, and saucer)
- 1–2 reusable tea bags or 2 5 inch x 5 inch pieces of cheesecloth and 5–9 inches of twine
- 1 teaspoon dried sarsaparilla
- 1 teaspoon dried catnip
- 1 teaspoon dried lemon balm
- Psalms 140 and 91 (see appendix C)
- honey, agave, or other sweetener

Instructions:

Set the water to boil. Add the herbs to your reusable tea bags or cheesecloth and close. Holding them in the palm of your dominant hand, recite Psalms 140 and 91 three times each over the tea bags, then place them in the cup. Once the water boils, pour a portion into the cup, cover it with the saucer, and let the tea steep for five to seven minutes. After the tea has steeped, stir in honey to taste and drink.

Fibroids: The Black Woman's Kryptonite

Most women receive a diagnosis of fibroids between eighteen and fifty years of age.[103] Fibroids are noncancerous tumors that cause extreme pain and excessive bleeding. It left untreated, they can also cause severe anemia, infertility, pregnancy complications, urinary tract infections, and kidney disease.[104] It's believed that women who have experienced sexual, physical, or emotional abuse in childhood may have an increased risk of developing fibroids.

Other contributing factors include age, a family history of fibroids, being overweight, hypertension, vitamin D deficiency, never having children, menopause, diets high in preservatives, and increased alcohol consumption, all of which raise phytoestrogen levels in the body. Even daily coffee intake has been linked to fibroid growth in young women, with continued enlargement as they age.

However, the research isn't all discouraging. Eating four or more servings of fruit per day can reduce the risk of developing fibroids by 10 percent and help prevent their growth over time.

Speaking from personal experience, my battle with fibroids led me to embrace a naturopathic approach that incorporated rituals and increased my intake of fruits. Over time, I noticed a change in my menstrual cycle, and through regular visits with my OB-GYN, I discovered my fibroids had shrunk to the size of a pea.

That was when I decided to embrace a kinder, gentler healing journey, incorporating yoga and meditation as a way to support my body spiritually and physically. Women who exercise two to five days per week, including 150 minutes of moderate-intensity aerobic exercise and 75 minutes of vigorous-intensity movement, can lower their chances of developing fibroids. But remember, since not all fibroids are equal in size or symptoms,

---

103. Dr. Nsisong Asanga, "No One Seems to Know Why Black Women Are Plagued with Fibroids. Here's What We Can Say for Sure," *Atlanta Black Star*, May 27, 2024, https://atlantablackstar.com/2024/05/27/why-black-women-are-plagued-with-fibroids-heres-what-we-can-say-for-sure/.
104. "Fibroids (Uterine Myoma)," Yale Medicine, October 30, 2022, https://www.yalemedicine.org/conditions/fibroids.

it's crucial that women seek medical treatment to develop a personalized healing plan that aligns with their individual needs.

According to research on fibroids, Black women are 10 percent more likely to develop fibroids than White women. Estimates suggest that 80 percent of Black women will experience fibroid-related challenges, compared to 70 percent of White women diagnosed by age fifty.

Some medical professionals attribute this disproportionate rise in fibroids among Black women to their lack of participation in scientific research, limiting access to targeted treatments and solutions. Others argue that family history, environment, and age play significant roles in fibroid development and growth patterns. However, studies show that BIPOC women living in protective and nurturing environments experience a decrease in fibroid growth and pain, highlighting the influence of stress and social conditions on reproductive health.

The National Library of Medicine links fibroid development to Black women's frequent use of hair relaxers, noting that the risk increases with each year of relaxer use. The study suggests that chemicals in relaxers, known as phthalates, disrupt hormone balance, creating a pathway for fibroid formation.

If BIPOC women are disproportionately affected by fibroids, why are we less involved in scientific research aimed at addressing the issue?

ANKARA

Of course Black women are underrepresented in clinical trials. All of my years of living with fibroids while Black and Brown, my mama Afrikan American and my daddy Cuban, I've never once been asked to join a clinical trial. You want the truth? I ain't never met nobody who has. I had to scream and holler about my period lasting four months on and four months off. Two weeks of heavy bleeding and two weeks of spotting. I had to scream inside the doctor's office to please tell me what's wrong. He suggested a hysterectomy as his one and final answer. That's what he tells a woman with no children and no man either. All those medical books in his office, and that's all he could come up with. I wasn't pissed, because pissed is too limited a word. I was livid. I wanted to flip his desk and strangle the shit out of him. I wanted to shove his nuts up his ass and tell him that's what fibroids feel like.

Welfare doctors rushed me in as quick as they rushed me out. Didn't nobody let me make up my mind. They didn't explain a hysterectomy or any other alternative. They just assured me it would take the pain away, and then I could go on with life.

MAISY HERNANDEZ

I had fibroids that hurt like hell. I had a doctor who swore it was because of my lifestyle, and then he said God was punishing me. He was a welfare doctor. He brought this big basket of birth control pills into the room every visit. He didn't ask if you wanted any. I kept telling him about the pain and the cramps. Never once did he look me in my eyes. He just kept his stares inside the manilla folder, where my three abortions were an eyesore. I had crabs twice. I was nothing more to him than a nasty woman with a nasty woman's disease. He didn't know those pregnancies and those crabs came from my mama's boyfriend. So, at sixteen, I ran away. It wasn't until I was thirty and unable to have children that I had a fibroid removed. My girlfriend encouraged me to get it done. When I tell you, it was the size of a newborn!

Last year, my girlfriend and I adopted twins. Two massage therapists living our lives happy, on our terms. My new doctor is Black and a lady. She encouraged me to go to therapy. I'm not better, but I'm getting there.

KETURAH HARRIS

A doctor told my mama Black women die at a rate 40 percent higher than White women from breast cancer. She had metastatic breast cancer; she died the same year she found out. The welfare doctor said she viewed hospitals as if she were an actress on a Broadway stage. He said in her world, being at the doctor's office was the only time anybody paid any attention to her.

He really thought he was putting my mama's mind at ease by telling her she's supposed to die once cancer sets in. Not because she's sick and the cancer is spreading, but because he really believed it was because she was Black and predisposed for death.

You try to go through those physicians' handbooks and look for names that look Black. I ain't gonna lie, I did, but now you can google BIPOC doctors. I just found that out. Trust, I'll be using it.

I started thinking about clinical trials and why we ain't in them. It's because the White people who run the trials don't ask us. They count us out with assumptions based on racist stereotypes. Some of us are on welfare. We get food stamps. We live in government housing. Is that any reason to underrepresent us? Are those reasons to underserve us?

Yvonne's Story

Growing up, a client of mine named Yvonne dreaded the start of her period each month. "All the blood, I just didn't want to have to change pads all day, dripping like a faucet," she told me. The day the blood came, so did the cramps, and then the fibroid pain a day later. "This pain was worse than the cramping at the start of my cycle. It was brutal and unrelenting." Yvonne would vomit and sweat profusely. "I had massive globs of vaginal wall membrane squirming their way out of me, and I was always in a fetal position in tears. It was graphic, I know, but true," she said.

Yvonne remembers being so sick in the tenth grade that she'd hide in the stall on the floor of her high school restroom, taking shallow breaths just to relieve the pain. "Sometimes the coolness of the floor would take my mind off the pain long enough for me to forget that I was wrapped around a toilet," she said. Many days she would skip the rest of school and return home.

I told her aunt about a bath and tea I used growing up, and she tried it. "What did I have to lose? I was willing to try anything," she told me.

She started with an Epsom salt bath and then drank a cup or two of huckleberry and burdock root tea. Along with fibroid relief, she said it also helped her manage her diabetes. "With your help, I was able to start my baths and teatimes a week to three days before the first signs of fibroid pain. Both the tea and the bath were game changers," Yvonne told me.

EXERCISE: HUCKLEBERRY, COOL MY MOOD

For all the sistahs suffering from fibroids, this tea is a game changer. It's eased my abdominal and lower back pain and quelled the nausea I experience with my fibroids. Enjoy it with a healing Epsom salt bath.

Needs:

- plain water
- a tea setting (cup, spoon, and saucer)
- 1 tablespoon dried huckleberry leaves
- 1 tablespoon dried burdock root
- 1–2 reusable tea bags or 2 5 inch x 5 inch pieces of cheesecloth and 5–9 inches of twine
- Psalm 138 (see appendix C)
- honey, agave, or other sweetener

Instructions:

Set your water to boil. Add the herbs to your reusable tea bags or cheesecloth and close. Holding them in your dominant hand, recite Psalm 138 over the tea bags three times. Once the water boils, pour a portion into the cup, add the tea bags, and cover with the saucer. Let the tea steep for five to seven minutes. After the tea has steeped, stir in honey to taste and drink.

Juju on the Fly

I was introduced to Ekeko by my Honduran grandfather, who said that Afro-Peruvians traveled across Spanish-speaking lands, learning from Indigenous culture bearers, whom he credits with birthing Ekeko's energy. According to PawPaw, Ekeko brings abundance to homes and businesses, understanding both worldly desires and essential needs.

Ekeko has been kind to my family, constantly reminding me that Black and Brown win together. When we recognize our shared goals, we can dismantle systemic oppression—and if nothing else, we can commit to fighting until the end. As Claude McKay wrote, "Pressed to the wall, dying, but fighting back!"[105]

The image of Pachamama (Mother Earth) is often flanking Ekeko, symbolizing that nothing in the universe is beyond our reach. Whether through spirit or physical will, abundance is always possible. I keep a green drawstring bag near Ekeko, occasionally placing images of a particular want or need inside. Sometimes, I write a letter to Pachamama and Ekeko, detailing a health procedure for myself or a loved one and the outcome I wish to manifest. When approached with respect and intention, their energy brings abundance beyond imagination.

My personal battle with fibroids lasted from middle school through the stage in my life when I began giving birth to my five children. One gynecologist once told me I had so many fibroids that I'd never give birth. Hearing that was terrifying. He even recommended a hysterectomy. But at nineteen, I refused to let a doctor dictate the course of my life. I knew there had to be a less drastic approach.

I sought a second opinion and began studying herbs. That's how I developed *Ekeko and Pachamama on the Fly* tea. It's a remedy that helped me cope when an extremely large fibroid attached itself to my amniotic sac. One doctor believed the fibroid would eventually collapse the sac, leading to a pregnancy loss, but another encouraged me to slow down, trust my body, and continue with the teas. And the teas worked—the fibroids started shrinking.

My baby girl, my firstborn, arrived in February 1996 weighing nine pounds, ten ounces. Every child I've had since has Ekeko and Pachamama to thank for their survival.

I fought back.

---

105. Claude McKay, "If We Must Die," Poetry Foundation, accessed July 31, 2025, https://www.poetryfoundation.org/poems/44694/if-we-must-die.

EXERCISE: EKEKO AND PACHAMAMA ON THE FLY

Sometimes BIPOC people shy away from doctor's visits for fear of what the diagnosis might be. This ritual lets you find your emotional safe zone so all news becomes bearable. It also helps ensure abundance and healthy outcomes, or outcomes that can be transformed for the better with each visit. Do the ritual three days before a doctor's visit.

Needs:

- a clay Ekeko (mouth should be open enough to fit a cigar or cigarette)
- a framed image of Pachamama
- a cauldron or other fireproof receptacle
- 1–2 charcoal disks
- 6 pieces of bergamot resin
- 3 cups plain water
- 2 tea settings (cups, spoons, and saucers)
- 2 reusable tea bags or 2 5 inch x 5 inch pieces of cheesecloth and 5–9 inches of twine
- 6 teaspoons dried chasteberry, divided
- a cigar or cigarette
- Psalm 139 (see appendix C)
- 1–3 teaspoons honey
- a man's wallet for Ekeko with a 1 dollar bill inside (*Note:* Every time you do this work, add another dollar to the wallet and donate clothing or toiletries to a women's shelter)
- an ashtray
- a glass of red wine

Instructions:

Place the Ekeko and Pachamama image next to each other on Mama Henrietta's altar. Set the cauldron in front of the

Ekeko, then place a lit charcoal disk inside the cauldron. Add three pieces of resin. Place the wallet with the dollar inside to the right of Ekeko. Place the cigar or cigarette to the left of Ekeko, inside the ashtray.

Set the water to boil. Add three teaspoons of the chasteberry to each of your reusable tea bags or cheesecloth pieces and close. Once the water boils, pour a portion in each cup, add the teabags, and cover the cups with the saucers. Let the tea steep for five to seven minutes.

While the tea steeps, light the cigar and allow it to rest in Ekeko's mouth. (Keep the ashtray nearby in case it falls out.) Recite Psalm 139 three times. Drink your tea after it's finished steeping, and set Ekeko's tea and saucer in front of him. Place the glass of red wine in front of the image of Pachamama.

At least three days a week, give Ekeko and Pachamama a glass of water. They're working overtime to give you abundance even when your crabby ass may not deserve it.

Variation:

* When I do this ritual, I like to ask Ekeko and Pachamama to make my doctors' lives and financial situations wonderfully balanced—that way, they won't try to rob or overmedicate me!

Conclusion

The 2023 documentary *Stamped from the Beginning* opens with a provocative question, "What's wrong with Black people?"[106] By the end, the answer becomes clear: There's nothing wrong with us at all. The real issue lies in a world built to silence and erase people of color. We're expected to navigate life unseen and unheard. When we challenge White supremacy or institutional racism, we're often labeled as un-American or accused of being ungrateful to the country that supposedly "civilized" us.

I wrote this book with two main goals in mind: to highlight how racism leaves lasting scars—emotional, physical, and psychological—and to share how I've relied on spirituality to find peace during moments of racial unrest, both in my own life and within my community. When supremacist terrorism is allowed to persist unchecked, it causes deep, indescribable trauma that wounds the soul and leaves us struggling to heal.

A Global Malignancy

If we tune in to media outlets, we quickly recognize that racism isn't confined within the borders of a single country—it's a global crisis. In America, we can chant names from memory or search them online to relive the injustices perpetuated by institutional racism, White supremacy, and privilege. But what about the Afrikans in Ukraine, caught on video being mistreated and denied safety as they tried to flee the war-torn country?

Video footage circulating the internet showed the heartbreaking reality of Afrikan migrants and students stranded at the Ukrainian border, often left in below-freezing weather while White Ukrainian nationals were given priority. White House political analyst April Ryan reported on Instagram in a February 27, 2022 post, "They said women and children are allowed

---

106. Ibram X. Kendi, *Stamped from the Beginning: The Definitive History of Racist Ideas in America* (Bold Type Books, 2016).

in, just not Black women and children."[107] One horrifying video showed a woman denied refuge in a hostel as she stood holding a two-month-old in the bone-chilling cold. There's footage of a Ukrainian police officer pushing Black women and their children off a train headed to transport White-skinned women and children to safety.

An Afrikan friend watching the perils in Ukraine told me, "Black skin, no matter where it lives, is always on foreign soil by default. Nobody cares how smart or rich we are. Black is a scapegoat for whatever crime or fucked-up ideas about why White poverty exists, why every White person alive ain't a member of the elite. We're the boogeyman for grown-up supremacists. We need a global Black and Brown wake-up call, because White supremacy fucks all BIPOCs globally."

Racism is truly a global malignancy. In 2021 as part of an *MSNBC* article, Yaqiu Wang wrote of Afrikan residents living in China being forcibly tested for COVID and forced into quarantine in designated hotel spaces.[108] Landlords evicted Afrikan tenants and forced many to live on the street. Also in 2021, during China's Lunar New Year celebration, CCTV broadcasted Chinese dancers performing Afrikan songs and dancing in blackface to celebrate the culture of their Afrikan residents. Egregious racism is systemic around the world, and we must not forget to take the fight to the streets, not just the streets of America, but the global streets.

As we turn our focus to American soil, we find a telling story in Baton Rouge. After Hurricane Katrina, a news article reported that Baton Rouge welcomed two hundred thousand New Orleans residents, most of whom were Black. Not long after, the article shifted its attention to rising crime rates and a struggling education system. All of these narratives stoked fear among the city's White residents, which planted the seeds for what came next.

---

107. "Crisis in Ukraine Shifts to a Rally of Support for African Students and Migrants," *TheGrio*, March 2, 2022, https://thegrio.com/2022/03/01/ukraine-african-students-migrants/.
108. Human Rights Watch, "From Covid to Blackface on TV, China's Racism Problem Runs Deep," Human Rights Watch, February 18, 2021, https://www.hrw.org/news/2021/02/18/covid-blackface-tv-chinas-racism-problem-runs-deep.

In the Midwest, some towns are already pursuing the creation of White ethnostates. Inspired by this, wealthy White residents of Baton Rouge began working toward their own all-White city. Their efforts succeeded when a lower court approved the separation of a majority-White area from the predominantly Black city to form St. George, a new city in southeast Baton Rouge. The vision for St. George was clear: a place with low crime, top-tier schools, a cleaner environment, and a strong sense of belonging and racial pride. Supporters pictured it as a utopia devoid of drugs, public disorder, and, of course, Blackness.

My grandfather used to say there was no such thing as true desegregation. He believed White people would always find a way to reestablish segregation, whether through economics, education, healthcare, or employment. Over the years, I've seen evidence of his words while teaching in public schools that claim to serve all students equally. In reality, school districts often set entrance criteria for magnet programs, AP classes, gifted tracks, and honors courses. When these requirements are unfairly applied, the result is predominantly White classrooms with only a sprinkling of Black students. These programs become safe havens for White students, isolating them from the rest of the school and the larger Black student body. Black students, by contrast, are too often dismissed as unteachable, unmotivated, or only interested in sex. They're routinely labeled as uninterested in education beyond high school.

In predominantly White schools, this bias takes another form: Black students are disproportionately labeled as having special needs or classified as emotionally disturbed, learning disabled, ADHD, dyslexic, oppositional, or often simply labeled "angry." But in many cases, their only "offense" is being born Black.

I Wrote This Book...

I wrote this book because there's no milestone, no coming-of-age moment, when we can sit our children down and say, *Okay, you're thirteen now, you're ready to deal with racism.* The journey of life doesn't offer that simplicity to those of us who are BIPOC. We're born into a world where we bear the heavy weight of systemic prejudice. From the moment we take our first breath, we're targets.

There's a story that stays with me, a story of survival and fierce motherly resolve. A woman living in Brooklyn, a descendant of the Choctaw lineage, shared with me how she went into labor while waiting for the subway. As she clung to the rails awaiting the paramedics, she had no idea she was about to deliver new life into a moment brimming with violence.

When the paramedics—White men clad in authority—finally arrived, one looked at her and sneered, "Boys, we've got a fucking Indian here. I thought Custer finished them before his last stand."

She recalled how they laughed at her, their taunts curling through the air like venomous smoke. They called her names like Pocahontas and threw careless insults about her not having insurance. One even accused her of wanting a free ride around the city, while another implied she was running from something sinister, perhaps even a crime. All this while she stood there, a biochemist and the wife of another brilliant biochemist, nine months pregnant with her belly protruding defiantly on her petite frame.

She told me how fear gripped her heart during that ride to the hospital, but how rage began to fill the cracks. That fury wasn't just her own—it was ancestral. She wanted it to pour into the veins of the child inside her womb, to teach her baby the sacred truth: survival for BIPOC people means more than assimilation. Survival must be rooted in not letting the world make us forget why we fight, why we thrive, and why we reclaim our humanity despite centuries of being denied it. Her anger didn't wane until the moment her husband and sister entered the delivery room, their presence flanked by ancestral spirits who came to wrap her in their love and balm her pain.

I wrote this book remembering women like her, hoping to refute the myth that our survival rests upon becoming what the oppressor wants us to be: soulless sellouts, forever reaching for the scraps of a system designed to deny us our worth. When we look at the hierarchy of humanity in this country, White men stand at the pinnacle, followed only by White women, who live in proximity to that power. But what about us? What about the rest of us who endure this violent legacy?

This work steps into sacred spaces and calls forth a council of modern-day spiritual disruptors, women and men united by a desire not just to heal themselves, but to nourish one another through the deep and sometimes messy process of collective healing. The weight of White supremacy has scarred every corner of our identities. Yet we can no longer hide in the shadows of pain or cling solely to survival as our narrative. To heal is to stand tall in the fullness of our stories, even the bloodied ones, even the haunting ones.

Make no mistake: Racism, wherever it blooms, is familiar to us because we live with its barbed truths every single day. But let us never diminish the experiences of those who don't call this soil home. The boats that carried our ancestors didn't stop at one shore. They scattered our families, our lineages, our languages across continents. When we call for justice, we can't afford to have our hearts clenched by borders or our minds strangled by supremacist thinking. This is why I say, fuck that sort of thinking. It's the twisted root of the enemy we are fighting.

And for those waving flags of separatism and buying into divisive rhetoric like the ADOS movement, I speak to you directly: My ancestors were chained to decks and tossed into rivers long before their tortured bodies settled into the soil of New Orleans. Their pain isn't shackled to one place—it vibrates across the map.

Our story can't be told within the confines of dividing lines or territorial hierarchies. Our strength lies in the shared breath of our multitude. By 2045, a reckoning is on the horizon—a world that will be bursting with Black and Brown beauty, with communities fully awake to the power of our collective liberation. For White supremacists, this is a horror story; for us, it's an ancient prophecy coming to bloom. But beware of the weaker minds among us, the ones swayed by the whispers of division, often sold to us by skinfolk who have found comfort in White supremacy's shadow. We must remain watchful and resilient.

I invite you into this space of transformation, a sacred circle where we rise together by engaging in the practices within these pages. Host them among your kin, your closest beloveds, and your community. Share them in workshops (I host several!) among seekers, disruptors, and fellow warriors. Know that every day you reclaim your joy, you honor your ancestors. Every day you put love and intention into healing yourself and those around you, you dismantle the chains of racism.

This journey isn't simply about survival. It's about thriving, about celebrating, and about restoring the sacred balance that has always belonged to us. Together, through sustenance, solace, and resilience, we will grow a culture of liberation so radiant and unyielding that we become the steady beats of an antiracist world. And in time, we will feel the glimmers of ancestral joy calling us home to the holiness of our collective power.

Let this work remind you: Every day is a holy day, and healing is the most radical act you can offer the world.

Saving Space for Ancestors

So much of ritual for the BIPOC community is about reclaiming our privilege—the right to live life on an equal playing field and to never again have to modify how we move out of fear of emotional, spiritual, or physical annihilation.

When we give voice to our stories, reshaping them on soil that is as Indigenous and Afrikan as it is European, we reclaim the narrative. We, on our own terms, dismantle ideologies designed to diminish our contributions, denying us the inherited ownership of the stories woven into the land, stories that expose America as violent, racist, and an imposter posing as a civilized nation.

Rituals allow us to atone for lives cut short while recognizing the significance of our fight and survival. We came, we saw, we fought, and we endured. Now, it's time to add your shero or hero to the compendium of liberation. This is truly our moment, and I invite you to invoke the power of ritual, reclaiming the fire of your voice.

Honoring Those Who Have Fallen

At this writing, I honor my fallen sisters and brothers, whose horrific stories don't leave me even as I sleep.

We remember the life of Sade Carleena Robinson.

Born on May 10, 2004, Sade tragically lost her life in 2024. She was a nineteen-year-old college student who went missing in Milwaukee, Wisconsin. On April 2, 2024, a severed human leg was discovered in a park, and preliminary DNA testing confirmed that it belonged to Sade. Maxwell S. Anderson, a White man Sade had just begun dating, was later charged with her murder and dismemberment.[109]

We remember the life of Sheryl Mae Turner.

Born on April 12, 2004, in New Iberia, Louisiana, Sheryl met Anthony Pierce Holland Jr., a White male, online. The two engaged in a romantic relationship over text messages. Turner planned to spend the evening with Holland on December 31, 2023. Three weeks later, on January 24, the Catahoula Parish Sheriff's Office received a call about a body floating in the Ouachita River. Deputies recovered the remains, a torso—no head or extremities connected. On February 23, with a DNA sample from her twin sister, Sheryl's remains were identified. Holland Jr., who was named a suspect, later admitted to killing Turner inside his residence and dismembering her body.[110]

We remember the life of Rasheem Carter.

Rasheem was a twenty-five-year-old Black man from Mississippi who went missing on October 2, 2022. Days before his disappearance, he expressed

---

109. David Clarey, "What We Know About the Missing 19-Year-Old Woman in Milwaukee," *Journal Sentinel*, April 12, 2024, https://www.jsonline.com/story/news/2024/04/10/what-we-know-about-sade-robinson-the-missing-19-year-old-in-milwaukee/73263866007/.
110. Anna Fischer, "New Details Emerge About Ouachita River Victim Sheryl Turner." *KATC News*, April 9, 2024, https://www.katc.com/iberia-parish/new-details-emerge-about-ouachita-river-victim-sheryl-turner.

to both his mother and the police that White men in his community were targeting him. A month later, Rasheem's remains were found in a wooded area south of Taylorsville, Mississippi. His head had been severed from his body, and the cause and manner of death remain undetermined.[111]

We remember the life of Justin Johnson.

Justin was a sixteen-year-old from Harrisburg, Pennsylvania, who lost his life after an alleged game of tag with other teens. Due to his sickle cell disease, Justin couldn't run or exert too much energy without risking his health. On a Friday evening, four teens came to Justin's home. The doorbell rang, and Justin was coaxed into what he thought was a game of tag with his future football teammates. Justin, fearing the chase had turned into a racist game of cat and mouse, ran back home. Johnson's security camera captured two White boys yelling, "Where did he go? He went to [expletive] Africa." Later that night, his father found him unresponsive on the floor.[112]

We remember the life of Derontae Martin.

A nineteen-year-old Black man, Derontae tragically lost his life on April 25, 2021. Martin and a group of friends traveled ninety miles south from St. Louis to the town of Fredericktown, a town that is over 90 percent White. They drove to the home of James Wade, a White man with racist views, to attend a party. Sometime during the party, Martin died of a gunshot wound to his left temple. Martin was right-handed, and at the time of his death, his right arm and hand were in a cast as the result of surgery. His body was found in Wade's attic. Initially, Martin's death was

---

111. Tesfaye Negussie, "A Year After Black Man Disappeared Under Mysterious Circumstances, Questions Remain," *ABC News*, October 2, 2023, https://abcnews.go.com/US/rasheem-carters-mother-speaks-1-year-after-disappearance/story?id=103660675.
112. Davi Merchan, "Pennsylvania Father Seeks Answers After Son Dies Following Alleged Game of Tag," *ABC7 Chicago*, May 2, 2024, https://abc7chicago.com/what-happened-to-justin-johnson-senior-assassin-game-video-central-dauphin/14751818/.

ruled a suicide. The finding was later challenged, and it was ultimately determined that Martin died by "violence."[113]

We remember the life of Sonya Massey.
Sonya, a thirty-six-year-old Black woman, tragically lost her life on July 6, 2024, in her home near Springfield, Illinois. Deputy Sean Grayson of the Sangamon County Sheriff's Office in Woodside Township, who is White, shot Massey three times. Her fatal blow was to the head. Grayson said he felt threatened by a pan of hot water she was removing from her stove. Massey's death was ruled a homicide. Grayson has been charged with first-degree murder, aggravated battery with a firearm, and official misconduct.[114]

We Can't Wait

The deaths of so many, both named and unnamed, continue to haunt us, as they should. We live in troubled times, made worse by calls to roll back America to a so-called heyday that was far from great for BIPOC people, as well as for poor Whites whose only salvation was the fact that they were born White. That privilege afforded them at least a head start in America's race toward achieving freedoms: economic, educational, spiritual, and social.

In times like these, BIPOC folks are realizing that we're all we've got. The potions, stories, and recipes shared here in the names of Hoodoo saints and root warriors offer us a modicum of grace. We can't wait and pray for America to get her act together; we must hold her down and whip her into submission. By the power of revolution, protection, flight, liberation, and a refusal to let "sick and tired" be our only anthem, we will reject the notion that giving up is our only choice. By the power of joy, we will

---

113. "Who Killed Derontae Martin?" Who Killed Derontae Martin?, accessed December 10, 2024, https://justicefordrontae.com/.
114. Amanda Holpuch, "US Opens Investigation into Killing of Sonya Massey," *The New York Times*, November 17, 2024, https://www.nytimes.com/2024/11/17/us/sonya-massey-shooting-investigation.html.

survive this incarnation of America and stand in our full glory when she rises from the ashes, a child born of blood whose color reflects survival.

May these Hoodoo saints, warriors, and ancestors guide you as you process the world you were given, a world you left behind and a world we will transform, dismantle, and ultimately heal in your honor and in honor of so many others, known and unknown. Ase.

Acknowledgments

Thank you to my mother, Patricia Dean, for allowing me to see the world of Hoodoo and Voodoo through your eyes. Thank you to my husband for encouraging me to tell my stories my way, an Afrikanist BIPOC way. Thank you for being my safe space in a world of askari. I love you, Nadir Bomani. To my children, Nzingha, Kambui, Camara, Naima, and Sekou, thank you for allowing me to see the promise of my second act. Your ability to move into sometimes turbulent, sometimes graceful first acts has helped me step gracefully into the role of mothering from afar, allowing you room to hiccup, throw up, or rejoice. Thank you, Jelani Bomani, Yeye's first grand-omo; this book was born to be your guide when life requires a nudge across the finish line. Thank you, daughter-in-love, Johari Bomani, for the magick of love and for believing in the power of all things occult as culturally relevant.

Thank you to Llewellyn Worldwide for believing in the importance of this work, especially at a time when systemic racism has not only the nation but the globe in a chokehold. We practitioners of indigenous magick realize the value in the ways of our forefathers and foremothers. We value the importance of unearthing that which racism seeks to suppress through Christian indoctrination. We were born to disrupt!

Thank you to Heather Greene, my acquisitions editor, who allowed me the freedom to let these words breathe. You didn't hold my hand. Instead, you walked closely behind me as my fairy guardian editor. Thank you to my agent extraordinaire, Kate Davids, for advocating the shit out of this manuscript. Thank you for allowing the spiritual disruptor in me to pitch a tent in your world. Thank you to J. Allen Cross for putting a battery in my back and introducing me to the world of representation back when X identified as Twitter.

Thank you, dearest reader, for your willingness to fight as BIPOC/AAPI people for our right to live, laugh, and love unapologetically using whatever fucking pronouns our spirit answers to—to hell with legislation. Long live every spiritual disruptor born and yet to experience the world! Ase, baby! I love you all so much.

—Iya Mawiyah

Appendix A
Hoodoo Chifforobe

In 1980, as I sat on the linoleum floor brushing my doll's hair, I watched my grandfather transform his cedar chifforobe into a cabinet of curios filled with Hoodoo tools and oddities. I was captivated, drawn into the glow of his ritual as he unlocked the doors, releasing the scent of Hoyt's cologne, Nag Champa, and palo santo.

He would read psalms and chant to Esu and Obatala before retrieving a specific tool or finding a substitute for a depleted item. The cedar's aroma remained fresh, as if it had been cut and shaped just hours before rather than years ago.

Below is a list of Hoodoo essentials I've compiled, a tribute to the time I spent watching my grandfather and listening to his firm advice: "These are items you should never run out of." After years of practicing Hoodoo myself, I can confirm that these items are invaluable when you need fast luck or are in a pinch.

Tools and Supplies

- aluminum foil
- Bible
- black soap (liquid)
- bowls
- brown paper bags
- candles—wax (black, white, green, brown, purple, blue, yellow, orange)
- candles—white battery operated
- cauldron
- charcoal disks
- coins (all denominations)
- dice

- dollar bills
- dousing rods
- food coloring
- journals
- Lenormand cards
- lodestones
- magnetic sand
- markers
- mason jars (all sizes)
- measuring cups
- newspapers
- paint brushes
- paint set (acrylic and nontoxic)
- paper (notebook/printer and sketch)
- parchment paper
- pens
- picture frames (8 x 10 inches or 5 x 7 inches)
- plastic bags (zip top)
- playing cards
- rusty nails
- shakere
- spray bottles
- straight pins
- tarot cards
- teakettle
- tea settings (cups, spoons, and saucers)
- twine

Herbs, Incense, and Other Natural Ingredients

- amber incense (resin and sticks)
- asafoetida
- bay leaves
- bourbon

- cayenne pepper
- champagne
- chili powder
- coconut oil
- cowrie shells
- Florida water
- frankincense incense (resin and sticks)
- gin
- High John the Conqueror root
- honey
- Hoyt's cologne
- myrrh incense (resin and sticks)
- olive oil
- palo santo incense (resin and sticks)
- pumpkin spice
- rum
- sea salt
- soil (ant hill, bank, church, home, graveyard, and women's shelter)
- water (rain, spring, tap, thunder, ocean, river, and blessed)
- wine (red and white)

Appendix B
Patricia Ann Dean's Gumbo Recipe with a Side of Black Hawk

This gumbo recipe is one that is enjoyed by my family, ancestors, and saints. Gumbo is one of those special New Orleans meals served as part of cultural celebrations to honor both the living and the dead. I also serve it whenever I want to connect with the spirits of Indigenous folks who were here long before the European invasion. But child, never fret: In the Crescent City, we eat gumbo whenever we damned well please, and you can too!

In addition to serving this dish once a year on the National Day of Mourning for Indigenous People (also known as Thanksgiving Day), I perform a protection work for Black Hawk. This work allows me to cover the entirety of my family and community in protection. Afterward we all share in a hearty meal of gumbo to seal our connection to each other, the universe, and the ideal of being our BIPOC sisters' and brothers' keepers.

Please note, this gumbo is cooked over two days, so plan accordingly!

Ingredients:

* 5 pounds shrimp (in shells and with the heads on)
* a knife
* 2–3 large bowls
* salt
* plain water
* plastic cling film
* 1–2 stock pots
* onion powder
* garlic powder
* black pepper
* cayenne pepper

* 2 large plastic zip-top bags
* 1–2 whole onions
* 1–2 garlic bulbs
* 6–8 sprigs of fresh parsley
* 1 green bell pepper
* 2 stalks of celery
* 2 pounds crabs
* 3 cast iron skillets
* vegetable oil
* 3–4 cups okra
* 5 cups sliced smoked sausage
* a spatula
* 1–2 cups flour
* a cooking spoon
* a strainer
* a ladle
* *Optional:* dry creole seasoning blend

Instructions:

Day One: Peel and devein the shrimp. This involves peeling the shell and tail from the shrimp, separating the head from the body, then using a knife to slice down the back center of the shrimp to remove the vein. Set the shells, heads, and tails aside for later use.

Place the shrimp in a bowl with a tablespoon of salt, then completely cover with water. Cover the bowl with plastic cling film and refrigerate.

Place the shrimp heads, shells, and tails in a stock pot, then completely cover with water. Add the onion powder, garlic powder, black pepper, cayenne pepper, and more salt, all to taste. Allow the shrimp trimmings to cook on medium heat for 1 to 2 hours, adding more water to keep the mixture submerged. Once the cooking time is up, move the pot to an unused burner and cover.

Next, dice the onion, garlic, parsley, bell pepper, and celery. Place them in a plastic zip-top bag and refrigerate.

Let's move on to cleaning your crabs: For each crab, first remove the top shell, then the gills, the yellow "mustard," the eyes, and the apron. Then, rinse the body thoroughly with cold water. Pat dry with paper towels, place in a plastic zip-top bag, and refrigerate.

Day Two: Place one of the skillets on a burner set to medium heat. As it heats up, slice the okra and sausage into 1- to 2-inch rounds. Add the okra to the skillet and cook until lightly brown before turning off the heat.

Place another skillet on a burner set to medium heat. Oil lightly with the vegetable oil, then add the sausage. Cook until lightly crisp before turning off the heat.

Use another skillet to begin building your roux: Add 2 to 4 tablespoons of cooking oil to the skillet. As the oil heats up, begin adding the flour 1 tablespoon at a time. Once all the flour has been added, stir occasionally while allowing it to cook to a dark color that you're proud of.

Place the strainer over an empty stock pot and strain the roux 2 tablespoons at a time. Then, strain the broth from the shrimp trimmings pot. You can pour it into the strainer or work a little at a time using the ladle; just be careful not to let any trimmings fall in. When the pot is halfway full, add the okra and crabs.

At this time, you can use the free okra skillet to sauté the refrigerated vegetables. Cook them on medium-high just until they release their aroma, then add them to the stockpot with the okra and crabs.

Check the pot's water level again; if you need more roux or broth, add it. Cook with the pot covered on medium-low for an hour.

Rinse the shrimp thoroughly, then add them and the sausage to the pot. If you need more water, add it. (I like my water level to be 1 to 2 inches from the top edge of the pot once all the ingredients are added.) Cook the gumbo for 30 minutes to 1 hour, seasoning more as needed. If you prefer, you can add a dry creole seasoning blend at this point, but try to add a few pinches at a time so you don't overseason the gumbo.

When finished, serve over white rice.

Variation:

* Save the okra tips to leave at the bottom of a tree. This will be an invitation to Black Hawk that you will need his watchful eye.

Black Hawk (1767–1838)

Food has always been an integral part of grounding practitioners to the world of the living and the world of Spirit. Traditional meals that cater to our BIPOC DNA also center our thoughts, actions, and desires, providing an overwhelming efficacy that illuminates both spheres of existence. In my family, gumbo provides that spiritual solace.

While you're stirring away at your gumbo, let me share more about Black Hawk and how he ties into our feast. First, if you make a regular habit of feeding Black Hawk, all those battles you don't see coming, he will have already slaughtered in their tracks. My grandfather would leave a bowl of gumbo near a tree or body of water as a thank you to Black Hawk, and with that, Black Hawk always delivered.

Black Hawk was a Sauk leader in the early 1800s. He was famous for his battle acumen and for halting the advancement of settlers on Native territory. In his role as chief during the Black Hawk War of 1832, he was well respected for his ability to protect his people from enemies on both the diplomatic front and on the battlefield. Also in that year, Black Hawk escaped capture but was betrayed and eventually jailed. He is credited with saying, "How smooth must be the language of the Whites, when they can make right look like wrong, and wrong like right."[115]

Black Hawk became a staple in New Orleans Hoodoo as a result of Spiritualist leader Mother Leafy Anderson, who indoctrinated Black Hawk's essence as part of her movement. He was her primary spirit guide and came to her in a vision while she was still living in Chicago. Mother Anderson said Black Hawk was to be known as the Spirit of the South. In the most Afrikan city in the United States, New Orleans, the iconography of Black Hawk is most prevalent in the appearance of Mardi Gras Indians, rootworkers, Voodoo practitioners, and all who hail him as a liberator.

In Louisiana, historical parallels between the treatment of Afrikans and Native peoples and their fights for liberation are undeniable. Forced enslavement of both groups under the same European tyranny forged inevitable alliances between Afrikans and Natives.

Native inhabitants often saw their own disillusionment and ill treatment with the Europeans repackaged in the story of the Afrikan. As enslaved Afrikans escaped the plantation, relying heavily on herbs and root staples of this new territory, many found alliances among the Natives, who interpreted the magick of this world's herbs and roots. In addition, many Natives protected, sheltered, and even intermarried the Afrikans, in need of their solidarity.

Black Hawk is a reminder of the role so many Native people played in the Afrikan's fight for freedom. My grandfather would say, "We have the Natives to think for cayenne. If you mixed cayenne pepper with gunpowder and laid it in a dog's path, them slave-catcher hounds would lose the scent. Paste it over the soles of your feet and you could run anywhere you wanted. Them dogs wouldn't want nothing to do with your tracks."

---

115. Paul G. Tomlinson, *The Trail of Black Hawk* (D. Appleton and Company, 1915).

EXERCISE: PROTECT US FROM GENOCIDE, OVERPOLICING, AND WHITE SUPREMACIST LEGISLATION

Black Hawk is often consulted for legal issues and social justice. This call to action should be renewed annually.

Needs:

* 1 straight pin
* 1 purple candle
* 1 brown candle
* a small clay or wooden bowl
* 3 tablespoons corn flour
* 4 Indian Head pennies
* 1 cigar
* 1 plastic zip-top bag
* 1 teaspoon ground cinnamon
* 1 tablespoon dried juniper berries
* 3 tablespoons dried marigolds
* 3 tablespoons dried cedar leaves
* 3 tablespoons sweet grass
* 1 charcoal disk
* a framed image of Chief Black Hawk
* 1 fireproof container
* 6/2 domino
* *Note:* If this work is performed in a family or community setting, each person must provide a set of the needs listed

Instructions:

Carve the first name of the governing official on the purple candle and the official's last name on the brown candle. If you do not know the official, or if your beef is with the police or specific legislation or a bill, then carve your whole name on the purple candle. On the brown candle, carve the police department's initials or the legislation or bill's abbreviation.

Place the corn flour in the bowl, then lay the coins on top. Light the cigar and blow smoke over the coins and candles, then light the candles. Put the cinnamon, juniper berries, marigolds, cedar leaves, and sweet grass ingredients in the plastic bag and mix them thoroughly using your fingers. Seal the bag and set aside.

Place a lit charcoal disk inside the cauldron, then tell Black Hawk your troubles in a loud, affirming voice. Let him know your role in what's transpired and the unlawful position the government is putting you in. Let Black Hawk know exactly what you'd like to see manifest to change your situation.

Begin sprinkling portions of your mixture onto the charcoal. Stop once you see a definitive line of smoke. Repeat the following as you work: *Chief Black Hawk, you know the ways of the United States government. You understand what it means to be lied to, lied on, and jailed. You'll have your revenge through me and my plight. You'll work, unseen by the law, to bring justice to not just me but all who seek you out in our war against those who don't know the meaning of honor.*

Sit for ten minutes, thanking Black Hawk for the gift of his enduring legacy in your life. Remind him that you've brought him gifts of corn flour, a cigar, and coins. After your time, snuff the candles, but let the charcoal burn out on its own.

Using the same tools, repeat the ritual daily for nine days. Each day, carry the 6/2 domino as a reminder that Black Hawk brings luck and justice.

Appendix C
The Psalms

The following pages include a list of Psalms used within this book to facilitate easy access for all your magickal endeavors.

Psalm 1

1 Blessed is the man that walketh not in the counsel of the ungodly, nor standeth in the way of sinners, nor sitteth in the seat of the scornful.
2 But his delight is in the law of the LORD; and in his law doth he meditate day and night.
3 And he shall be like a tree planted by the rivers of water, that bringeth forth his fruit in his season; his leaf also shall not wither; and whatsoever he doeth shall prosper.
4 The ungodly are not so: but are like the chaff which the wind driveth away.
5 Therefore the ungodly shall not stand in the judgment, nor sinners in the congregation of the righteous.
6 For the LORD knoweth the way of the righteous: but the way of the ungodly shall perish.

Psalm 3

1 LORD, how are they increased that trouble me! many are they that rise up against me.
2 Many there be which say of my soul, There is no help for him in God. Selah.
3 But thou, O LORD, art a shield for me; my glory, and the lifter up of mine head.
4 I cried unto the LORD with my voice, and he heard me out of his holy hill. Selah.

5 I laid me down and slept; I awaked; for the LORD sustained me.
6 I will not be afraid of ten thousands of people, that have set themselves against me round about.
7 Arise, O LORD; save me, O my God: for thou hast smitten all mine enemies upon the cheek bone; thou hast broken the teeth of the ungodly.
8 Salvation belongeth unto the LORD: thy blessing is upon thy people. Selah.

Psalm 4

1 Hear me when I call, O God of my righteousness: thou hast enlarged me when I was in distress; have mercy upon me, and hear my prayer.
2 O ye sons of men, how long will ye turn my glory into shame? how long will ye love vanity, and seek after leasing? Selah.
3 But know that the LORD hath set apart him that is godly for himself: the LORD will hear when I call unto him.
4 Stand in awe, and sin not: commune with your own heart upon your bed, and be still. Selah.
5 Offer the sacrifices of righteousness, and put your trust in the LORD.
6 There be many that say, Who will shew us any good? LORD, lift thou up the light of thy countenance upon us.
7 Thou hast put gladness in my heart, more than in the time that their corn and their wine increased.
8 I will both lay me down in peace, and sleep: for thou, LORD, only makest me dwell in safety.

Psalm 5

1 Give ear to my words, O LORD, consider my meditation.
2 Hearken unto the voice of my cry, my King, and my God: for unto thee will I pray.

3 My voice shalt thou hear in the morning, O LORD; in the morning will I direct my prayer unto thee, and will look up.
4 For thou art not a God that hath pleasure in wickedness: neither shall evil dwell with thee.
5 The foolish shall not stand in thy sight: thou hatest all workers of iniquity.
6 Thou shalt destroy them that speak leasing: the LORD will abhor the bloody and deceitful man.
7 But as for me, I will come into thy house in the multitude of thy mercy: and in thy fear will I worship toward thy holy temple.
8 Lead me, O LORD, in thy righteousness because of mine enemies; make thy way straight before my face.
9 For there is no faithfulness in their mouth; their inward part is very wickedness; their throat is an open sepulchre; they flatter with their tongue.
10 Destroy thou them, O God; let them fall by their own counsels; cast them out in the multitude of their transgressions; for they have rebelled against thee.
11 But let all those that put their trust in thee rejoice: let them ever shout for joy, because thou defendest them: let them also that love thy name be joyful in thee.
12 For thou, LORD, wilt bless the righteous; with favor wilt thou compass him as with a shield.

Psalm 6

1 O LORD, rebuke me not in thine anger, neither chasten me in thy hot displeasure.
2 Have mercy upon me, O LORD; for I am weak: O LORD, heal me; for my bones are vexed.
3 My soul is also sore vexed: but thou, O LORD, how long?
4 Return, O LORD, deliver my soul: oh save me for thy mercies' sake.

5 For in death there is no remembrance of thee: in the grave who shall give thee thanks?
6 I am weary with my groaning; all the night make I my bed to swim; I water my couch with my tears.
7 Mine eye is consumed because of grief; it waxeth old because of all mine enemies.
8 Depart from me, all ye workers of iniquity; for the LORD hath heard the voice of my weeping.
9 The LORD hath heard my supplication; the LORD will receive my prayer.
10 Let all mine enemies be ashamed and sore vexed: let them return and be ashamed suddenly.

Psalm 7

1 O LORD my God, in thee do I put my trust: save me from all them that persecute me, and deliver me:
2 Lest he tear my soul like a lion, rending it in pieces, while there is none to deliver.
3 O LORD my God, if I have done this; if there be iniquity in my hands;
4 If I have rewarded evil unto him that was at peace with me; (yea, I have delivered him that without cause is mine enemy:)
5 Let the enemy persecute my soul, and take it; yea, let him tread down my life upon the earth, and lay mine honor in the dust. Selah.
6 Arise, O LORD, in thine anger, lift up thyself because of the rage of mine enemies: and awake for me to the judgment that thou hast commanded.
7 So shall the congregation of the people compass thee about: for their sakes therefore return thou on high.
8 The LORD shall judge the people: judge me, O LORD, according to my righteousness, and according to mine integrity that is in me.

9 Oh let the wickedness of the wicked come to an end; but establish the just: for the righteous God trieth the hearts and reins.
10 My defense is of God, which saveth the upright in heart.
11 God judgeth the righteous, and God is angry with the wicked every day.
12 If he turn not, he will whet his sword; he hath bent his bow, and made it ready.
13 He hath also prepared for him the instruments of death; he ordaineth his arrows against the persecutors.
14 Behold, he travaileth with iniquity, and hath conceived mischief, and brought forth falsehood.
15 He made a pit, and digged it, and is fallen into the ditch which he made.
16 His mischief shall return upon his own head, and his violent dealing shall come down upon his own pate.
17 I will praise the LORD according to his righteousness: and will sing praise to the name of the LORD most high.

Psalm 9

1 I will praise thee, O LORD, with my whole heart; I will shew forth all thy marvelous works.
2 I will be glad and rejoice in thee: I will sing praise to thy name, O thou most High.
3 When mine enemies are turned back, they shall fall and perish at thy presence.
4 For thou hast maintained my right and my cause; thou satest in the throne judging right.
5 Thou hast rebuked the heathen, thou hast destroyed the wicked, thou hast put out their name for ever and ever.
6 O thou enemy, destructions are come to a perpetual end: and thou hast destroyed cities; their memorial is perished with them.

7   But the LORD shall endure for ever: he hath prepared his throne for judgment.
8   And he shall judge the world in righteousness, he shall minister judgment to the people in uprightness.
9   The LORD also will be a refuge for the oppressed, a refuge in times of trouble.
10 And they that know thy name will put their trust in thee: for thou, LORD, hast not forsaken them that seek thee.
11 Sing praises to the LORD, which dwelleth in Zion: declare among the people his doings.
12 When he maketh inquisition for blood, he remembereth them: he forgetteth not the cry of the humble.
13 Have mercy upon me, O LORD; consider my trouble which I suffer of them that hate me, thou that liftest me up from the gates of death:
14 That I may shew forth all thy praise in the gates of the daughter of Zion: I will rejoice in thy salvation.
15 The heathen are sunk down in the pit that they made: in the net which they hid is their own foot taken.
16 The LORD is known by the judgment which he executeth: the wicked is snared in the work of his own hands. Higgaion. Selah.
17 The wicked shall be turned into hell, and all the nations that forget God.
18 For the needy shall not alway be forgotten: the expectation of the poor shall not perish for ever.
19 Arise, O LORD; let not man prevail: let the heathen be judged in thy sight.
20 Put them in fear, O LORD: that the nations may know themselves to be but men. Selah.

Psalm 11

1 In the LORD put I my trust: how say ye to my soul, Flee as a bird to your mountain?
2 For, lo, the wicked bend their bow, they make ready their arrow upon the string, that they may privily shoot at the upright in heart.
3 If the foundations be destroyed, what can the righteous do?
4 The LORD is in his holy temple, the LORD'S throne is in heaven: his eyes behold, his eyelids try, the children of men.
5 The LORD trieth the righteous: but the wicked and him that loveth violence his soul hateth.
6 Upon the wicked he shall rain snares, fire, and brimstone, and a horrible tempest: this shall be the portion of their cup.
7 For the righteous LORD loveth righteousness; his countenance doth behold the upright.

Psalm 12

1 Help, LORD; for the godly man ceaseth; for the faithful fail from among the children of men.
2 They speak vanity every one with his neighbor: with flattering lips and with a double heart do they speak.
3 The LORD shall cut off all flattering lips, and the tongue that speaketh proud things:
4 Who have said, With our tongue will we prevail; our lips are our own: who is lord over us?
5 For the oppression of the poor, for the sighing of the needy, now will I arise, saith the LORD; I will set him in safety from him that puffeth at him.
6 The words of the LORD are pure words: as silver tried in a furnace of earth, purified seven times.

7 Thou shalt keep them, O LORD, thou shalt preserve them from this generation for ever.

8 The wicked walk on every side, when the vilest men are exalted.

Psalm 14

1 The fool hath said in his heart, There is no God. They are corrupt, they have done abominable works, there is none that doeth good.

2 The LORD looked down from heaven upon the children of men, to see if there were any that did understand, and seek God.

3 They are all gone aside, they are all together become filthy: there is none that doeth good, no, not one.

4 Have all the workers of iniquity no knowledge? who eat up my people as they eat bread, and call not upon the LORD.

5 There were they in great fear: for God is in the generation of the righteous.

6 Ye have shamed the counsel of the poor, because the LORD is his refuge.

7 Oh that the salvation of Israel were come out of Zion! when the LORD bringeth back the captivity of his people, Jacob shall rejoice, and Israel shall be glad.

Psalm 18

1 I will love thee, O LORD, my strength.

2 The LORD is my rock, and my fortress, and my deliverer; my God, my strength, in whom I will trust; my buckler, and the horn of my salvation, and my high tower.

3 I will call upon the LORD, who is worthy to be praised: so shall I be saved from mine enemies.

4 The sorrows of death compassed me, and the floods of ungodly men made me afraid.

5 The sorrows of hell compassed me about: the snares of death prevented me.

6 In my distress I called upon the LORD, and cried unto my God: he heard my voice out of his temple, and my cry came before him, even into his ears.

7 Then the earth shook and trembled; the foundations also of the hills moved and were shaken, because he was wroth.

8 There went up a smoke out of his nostrils, and fire out of his mouth devoured: coals were kindled by it.

9 He bowed the heavens also, and came down: and darkness was under his feet.

10 And he rode upon a cherub, and did fly: yea, he did fly upon the wings of the wind.

11 He made darkness his secret place; his pavilion round about him were dark waters and thick clouds of the skies.

12 At the brightness that was before him his thick clouds passed, hail stones and coals of fire.

13 The LORD also thundered in the heavens, and the Highest gave his voice; hail stones and coals of fire.

14 Yea, he sent out his arrows, and scattered them; and he shot out lightnings, and discomfited them.

15 Then the channels of waters were seen, and the foundations of the world were discovered at thy rebuke, O LORD, at the blast of the breath of thy nostrils.

16 He sent from above, he took me, he drew me out of many waters.

17 He delivered me from my strong enemy, and from them which hated me: for they were too strong for me.

18 They prevented me in the day of my calamity: but the LORD was my stay.

19 He brought me forth also into a large place; he delivered me, because he delighted in me.
20 The LORD rewarded me according to my righteousness; according to the cleanness of my hands hath he recompensed me.
21 For I have kept the ways of the LORD, and have not wickedly departed from my God.
22 For all his judgments were before me, and I did not put away his statutes from me.
23 I was also upright before him, and I kept myself from mine iniquity.
24 Therefore hath the LORD recompensed me according to my righteousness, according to the cleanness of my hands in his eyesight.
25 With the merciful thou wilt shew thyself merciful; with an upright man thou wilt shew thyself upright;
26 With the pure thou wilt shew thyself pure; and with the froward thou wilt shew thyself froward.
27 For thou wilt save the afflicted people; but wilt bring down high looks.
28 For thou wilt light my candle: the LORD my God will enlighten my darkness.
29 For by thee I have run through a troop; and by my God have I leaped over a wall.
30 As for God, his way is perfect: the word of the LORD is tried: he is a buckler to all those that trust in him.
31 For who is God save the LORD? or who is a rock save our God?
32 It is God that girdeth me with strength, and maketh my way perfect.
33 He maketh my feet like hinds' feet, and setteth me upon my high places.
34 He teacheth my hands to war, so that a bow of steel is broken by mine arms.

35 Thou hast also given me the shield of thy salvation: and thy right hand hath holden me up, and thy gentleness hath made me great.

36 Thou hast enlarged my steps under me, that my feet did not slip.

37 I have pursued mine enemies, and overtaken them: neither did I turn again till they were consumed.

38 I have wounded them that they were not able to rise: they are fallen under my feet.

39 For thou hast girded me with strength unto the battle: thou hast subdued under me those that rose up against me.

40 Thou hast also given me the necks of mine enemies; that I might destroy them that hate me.

41 They cried, but there was none to save them: even unto the LORD, but he answered them not.

42 Then did I beat them small as the dust before the wind: I did cast them out as the dirt in the streets.

43 Thou hast delivered me from the strivings of the people; and thou hast made me the head of the heathen: a people whom I have not known shall serve me.

44 As soon as they hear of me, they shall obey me: the strangers shall submit themselves unto me.

45 The strangers shall fade away, and be afraid out of their close places.

46 The LORD liveth; and blessed be my rock; and let the God of my salvation be exalted.

47 It is God that avengeth me, and subdueth the people under me.

48 He delivereth me from mine enemies: yea, thou liftest me up above those that rise up against me: thou hast delivered me from the violent man.

49 Therefore will I give thanks unto thee, O LORD, among the heathen, and sing praises unto thy name.

50 Great deliverance giveth he to his king; and sheweth mercy to his anointed, to David, and to his seed for evermore.

Psalm 24

1 The earth is the LORD'S, and the fulness thereof; the world, and they that dwell therein.
2 For he hath founded it upon the seas, and established it upon the floods.
3 Who shall ascend into the hill of the LORD? or who shall stand in his holy place?
4 He that hath clean hands, and a pure heart; who hath not lifted up his soul unto vanity, nor sworn deceitfully.
5 He shall receive the blessing from the LORD, and righteousness from the God of his salvation.
6 This is the generation of them that seek him, that seek thy face, O Jacob. Selah.
7 Lift up your heads, O ye gates; and be ye lift up, ye everlasting doors; and the King of glory shall come in.
8 Who is this King of glory? The LORD strong and mighty, the LORD mighty in battle.
9 Lift up your heads, O ye gates; even lift them up, ye everlasting doors; and the King of glory shall come in.
10 Who is this King of glory? The LORD of hosts, he is the King of glory. Selah.

Psalm 25

1 Unto thee, O LORD, do I lift up my soul.
2 O my God, I trust in thee: let me not be ashamed, let not mine enemies triumph over me.
3 Yea, let none that wait on thee be ashamed: let them be ashamed which transgress without cause.
4 Shew me thy ways, O LORD; teach me thy paths.
5 Lead me in thy truth, and teach me: for thou art the God of my salvation; on thee do I wait all the day.

6 Remember, O LORD, thy tender mercies and thy lovingkindnesses; for they have been ever of old.
7 Remember not the sins of my youth, nor my transgressions: according to thy mercy remember thou me for thy goodness' sake, O LORD.
8 Good and upright is the LORD: therefore will he teach sinners in the way.
9 The meek will he guide in judgment: and the meek will he teach his way.
10 All the paths of the LORD are mercy and truth unto such as keep his covenant and his testimonies.
11 For thy name's sake, O LORD, pardon mine iniquity; for it is great.
12 What man is he that feareth the LORD? him shall he teach in the way that he shall choose.
13 His soul shall dwell at ease; and his seed shall inherit the earth.
14 The secret of the LORD is with them that fear him; and he will shew them his covenant.
15 Mine eyes are ever toward the LORD; for he shall pluck my feet out of the net.
16 Turn thee unto me, and have mercy upon me; for I am desolate and afflicted.
17 The troubles of my heart are enlarged: O bring thou me out of my distresses.
18 Look upon mine affliction and my pain; and forgive all my sins.
19 Consider mine enemies; for they are many; and they hate me with cruel hatred.
20 O keep my soul, and deliver me: let me not be ashamed; for I put my trust in thee.
21 Let integrity and uprightness preserve me; for I wait on thee.
22 Redeem Israel, O God, out of all his troubles.

Psalm 27

1. The LORD is my light and my salvation; whom shall I fear? the LORD is the strength of my life; of whom shall I be afraid?
2. When the wicked, even mine enemies and my foes, came upon me to eat up my flesh, they stumbled and fell.
3. Though a host should encamp against me, my heart shall not fear: though war should rise against me, in this will I be confident.
4. One thing have I desired of the LORD, that will I seek after; that I may dwell in the house of the LORD all the days of my life, to behold the beauty of the LORD, and to enquire in his temple.
5. For in the time of trouble he shall hide me in his pavilion: in the secret of his tabernacle shall he hide me; he shall set me up upon a rock.
6. And now shall mine head be lifted up above mine enemies round about me: therefore will I offer in his tabernacle sacrifices of joy; I will sing, yea, I will sing praises unto the LORD.
7. Hear, O LORD, when I cry with my voice: have mercy also upon me, and answer me.
8. When thou saidst, Seek ye my face; my heart said unto thee, Thy face, LORD, will I seek.
9. Hide not thy face far from me; put not thy servant away in anger: thou hast been my help; leave me not, neither forsake me, O God of my salvation.
10. When my father and my mother forsake me, then the LORD will take me up.
11. Teach me thy way, O LORD, and lead me in a plain path, because of mine enemies.
12. Deliver me not over unto the will of mine enemies: for false witnesses are risen up against me, and such as breathe out cruelty.

13 I had fainted, unless I had believed to see the goodness of the LORD in the land of the living.

14 Wait on the LORD: be of good courage, and he shall strengthen thine heart: wait, I say, on the LORD.

Psalm 29

1 Give unto the LORD, O ye mighty, give unto the LORD glory and strength.

2 Give unto the LORD the glory due unto his name; worship the LORD in the beauty of holiness.

3 The voice of the LORD is upon the waters: the God of glory thundereth: the LORD is upon many waters.

4 The voice of the LORD is powerful; the voice of the LORD is full of majesty.

5 The voice of the LORD breaketh the cedars; yea, the LORD breaketh the cedars of Lebanon.

6 He maketh them also to skip like a calf; Lebanon and Sirion like a young unicorn.

7 The voice of the LORD divideth the flames of fire.

8 The voice of the LORD shaketh the wilderness; the LORD shaketh the wilderness of Kadesh.

9 The voice of the LORD maketh the hinds to calve, and discovereth the forests: and in his temple doth every one speak of his glory.

10 The LORD sitteth upon the flood; yea, the LORD sitteth King for ever.

11 The LORD will give strength unto his people; the LORD will bless his people with peace.

Psalm 31

1 In thee, O LORD, do I put my trust; let me never be ashamed: deliver me in thy righteousness.

2 Bow down thine ear to me; deliver me speedily: be thou my strong rock, for a house of defense to save me.

3 For thou art my rock and my fortress; therefore for thy name's sake lead me, and guide me.

4 Pull me out of the net that they have laid privily for me: for thou art my strength.

5 Into thine hand I commit my spirit: thou hast redeemed me, O LORD God of truth.

6 I have hated them that regard lying vanities: but I trust in the LORD.

7 I will be glad and rejoice in thy mercy: for thou hast considered my trouble; thou hast known my soul in adversities;

8 And hast not shut me up into the hand of the enemy: thou hast set my feet in a large room.

9 Have mercy upon me, O LORD, for I am in trouble: mine eye is consumed with grief, yea, my soul and my belly.

10 For my life is spent with grief, and my years with sighing: my strength faileth because of mine iniquity, and my bones are consumed.

11 I was a reproach among all mine enemies, but especially among my neighbors, and a fear to mine acquaintance: they that did see me without fled from me.

12 I am forgotten as a dead man out of mind: I am like a broken vessel.

13 For I have heard the slander of many: fear was on every side: while they took counsel together against me, they devised to take away my life.

14 But I trusted in thee, O LORD: I said, Thou art my God.

15 My times are in thy hand: deliver me from the hand of mine enemies, and from them that persecute me.

16 Make thy face to shine upon thy servant: save me for thy mercies' sake.

17 Let me not be ashamed, O LORD; for I have called upon thee: let the wicked be ashamed, and let them be silent in the grave.
18 Let the lying lips be put to silence; which speak grievous things proudly and contemptuously against the righteous.
19 Oh how great is thy goodness, which thou hast laid up for them that fear thee; which thou hast wrought for them that trust in thee before the sons of men!
20 Thou shalt hide them in the secret of thy presence from the pride of man: thou shalt keep them secretly in a pavilion from the strife of tongues.
21 Blessed be the LORD: for he hath shewed me his marvelous kindness in a strong city.
22 For I said in my haste, I am cut off from before thine eyes: nevertheless thou heardest the voice of my supplications when I cried unto thee.
23 O love the LORD, all ye his saints: for the LORD preserveth the faithful, and plentifully rewardeth the proud doer.
24 Be of good courage, and he shall strengthen your heart, all ye that hope in the LORD.

Psalm 32

1 Blessed is he whose transgression is forgiven, whose sin is covered.
2 Blessed is the man unto whom the LORD imputeth not iniquity, and in whose spirit there is no guile.
3 When I kept silence, my bones waxed old through my roaring all the day long.
4 For day and night thy hand was heavy upon me: my moisture is turned into the drought of summer. Selah.
5 I acknowledged my sin unto thee, and mine iniquity have I not hid. I said, I will confess my transgressions unto the LORD; and thou forgavest the iniquity of my sin. Selah.

6 For this shall every one that is godly pray unto thee in a time when thou mayest be found: surely in the floods of great waters they shall not come nigh unto him.
7 Thou art my hiding place; thou shalt preserve me from trouble; thou shalt compass me about with songs of deliverance. Selah.
8 I will instruct thee and teach thee in the way which thou shalt go: I will guide thee with mine eye.
9 Be ye not as the horse, or as the mule, which have no understanding: whose mouth must be held in with bit and bridle, lest they come near unto thee.
10 Many sorrows shall be to the wicked: but he that trusteth in the LORD, mercy shall compass him about.
11 Be glad in the LORD, and rejoice, ye righteous: and shout for joy, all ye that are upright in heart.

Psalm 33

1 Rejoice in the LORD, O ye righteous: for praise is comely for the upright.
2 Praise the LORD with harp: sing unto him with the psaltery and an instrument of ten strings.
3 Sing unto him a new song; play skillfully with a loud noise.
4 For the word of the LORD is right; and all his works are done in truth.
5 He loveth righteousness and judgment: the earth is full of the goodness of the LORD.
6 By the word of the LORD were the heavens made; and all the host of them by the breath of his mouth.
7 He gathereth the waters of the sea together as a heap: he layeth up the depth in storehouses.
8 Let all the earth fear the LORD: let all the inhabitants of the world stand in awe of him.
9 For he spake, and it was done; he commanded, and it stood fast.

10 The LORD bringeth the counsel of the heathen to nought: he maketh the devices of the people of none effect.
11 The counsel of the LORD standeth for ever, the thoughts of his heart to all generations.
12 Blessed is the nation whose God is the LORD; and the people whom he hath chosen for his own inheritance.
13 The LORD looketh from heaven; he beholdeth all the sons of men.
14 From the place of his habitation he looketh upon all the inhabitants of the earth.
15 He fashioneth their hearts alike; he considereth all their works.
16 There is no king saved by the multitude of a host: a mighty man is not delivered by much strength.
17 A horse is a vain thing for safety: neither shall he deliver any by his great strength.
18 Behold, the eye of the LORD is upon them that fear him, upon them that hope in his mercy;
19 To deliver their soul from death, and to keep them alive in famine.
20 Our soul waiteth for the LORD: he is our help and our shield.
21 For our heart shall rejoice in him, because we have trusted in his holy name.
22 Let thy mercy, O LORD, be upon us, according as we hope in thee.

Psalm 34

1 I will bless the LORD at all times: his praise shall continually be in my mouth.
2 My soul shall make her boast in the LORD: the humble shall hear thereof, and be glad.
3 O magnify the LORD with me, and let us exalt his name together.

4 I sought the LORD, and he heard me, and delivered me from all my fears.

5 They looked unto him, and were lightened: and their faces were not ashamed.

6 This poor man cried, and the LORD heard him, and saved him out of all his troubles.

7 The angel of the LORD encampeth round about them that fear him, and delivereth them.

8 O taste and see that the LORD is good: blessed is the man that trusteth in him.

9 O fear the LORD, ye his saints: for there is no want to them that fear him.

10 The young lions do lack, and suffer hunger: but they that seek the LORD shall not want any good thing.

11 Come, ye children, hearken unto me: I will teach you the fear of the LORD.

12 What man is he that desireth life, and loveth many days, that he may see good?

13 Keep thy tongue from evil, and thy lips from speaking guile.

14 Depart from evil, and do good; seek peace, and pursue it.

15 The eyes of the LORD are upon the righteous, and his ears are open unto their cry.

16 The face of the LORD is against them that do evil, to cut off the remembrance of them from the earth.

17 The righteous cry, and the LORD heareth, and delivereth them out of all their troubles.

18 The LORD is nigh unto them that are of a broken heart; and saveth such as be of a contrite spirit.

19 Many are the afflictions of the righteous: but the LORD delivereth him out of them all.

20 He keepeth all his bones: not one of them is broken.

21 Evil shall slay the wicked: and they that hate the righteous shall be desolate.

22 The LORD redeemeth the soul of his servants: and none of them that trust in him shall be desolate.

Psalm 35

1 Plead my cause, O LORD, with them that strive with me: fight against them that fight against me.
2 Take hold of shield and buckler, and stand up for mine help.
3 Draw out also the spear, and stop the way against them that persecute me: say unto my soul, I am thy salvation.
4 Let them be confounded and put to shame that seek after my soul: let them be turned back and brought to confusion that devise my hurt.
5 Let them be as chaff before the wind: and let the angel of the LORD chase them.
6 Let their way be dark and slippery: and let the angel of the LORD persecute them.
7 For without cause have they hid for me their net in a pit, which without cause they have digged for my soul.
8 Let destruction come upon him at unawares; and let his net that he hath hid catch himself: into that very destruction let him fall.
9 And my soul shall be joyful in the LORD: it shall rejoice in his salvation.
10 All my bones shall say, LORD, who is like unto thee, which deliverest the poor from him that is too strong for him, yea, the poor and the needy from him that spoileth him?
11 False witnesses did rise up; they laid to my charge things that I knew not.
12 They rewarded me evil for good to the spoiling of my soul.
13 But as for me, when they were sick, my clothing was sackcloth: I humbled my soul with fasting; and my prayer returned into mine own bosom.

14 I behaved myself as though he had been my friend or brother: I bowed down heavily, as one that mourneth for his mother.
15 But in mine adversity they rejoiced, and gathered themselves together: yea, the abjects gathered themselves together against me, and I knew it not; they did tear me, and ceased not:
16 With hypocritical mockers in feasts, they gnashed upon me with their teeth.
17 Lord, how long wilt thou look on? rescue my soul from their destructions, my darling from the lions.
18 I will give thee thanks in the great congregation: I will praise thee among much people.
19 Let not them that are mine enemies wrongfully rejoice over me: neither let them wink with the eye that hate me without a cause.
20 For they speak not peace: but they devise deceitful matters against them that are quiet in the land.
21 Yea, they opened their mouth wide against me, and said, Aha, aha, our eye hath seen it.
22 This thou hast seen, O LORD: keep not silence: O Lord, be not far from me.
23 Stir up thyself, and awake to my judgment, even unto my cause, my God and my Lord.
24 Judge me, O LORD my God, according to thy righteousness; and let them not rejoice over me.
25 Let them not say in their hearts, Ah, so would we have it: let them not say, We have swallowed him up.
26 Let them be ashamed and brought to confusion together that rejoice at mine hurt: let them be clothed with shame and dishonor that magnify themselves against me.
27 Let them shout for joy, and be glad, that favor my righteous cause: yea, let them say continually, Let the LORD be magnified, which hath pleasure in the prosperity of his servant.

28 And my tongue shall speak of thy righteousness and of thy praise all the day long.

Psalm 48

1 Great is the LORD, and greatly to be praised in the city of our God, in the mountain of his holiness.
2 Beautiful for situation, the joy of the whole earth, is mount Zion, on the sides of the north, the city of the great King.
3 God is known in her palaces for a refuge.
4 For, lo, the kings were assembled, they passed by together.
5 They saw it, and so they marveled; they were troubled, and hasted away.
6 Fear took hold upon them there, and pain, as of a woman in travail.
7 Thou breakest the ships of Tarshish with an east wind.
8 As we have heard, so have we seen in the city of the LORD of hosts, in the city of our God: God will establish it for ever. Selah.
9 We have thought of thy lovingkindness, O God, in the midst of thy temple.
10 According to thy name, O God, so is thy praise unto the ends of the earth: thy right hand is full of righteousness.
11 Let mount Zion rejoice, let the daughters of Judah be glad, because of thy judgments.
12 Walk about Zion, and go round about her: tell the towers thereof.
13 Mark ye well her bulwarks, consider her palaces; that ye may tell it to the generation following.
14 For this God is our God for ever and ever: he will be our guide even unto death.

Psalm 49

1 Hear this, all ye people; give ear, all ye inhabitants of the world:
2 Both low and high, rich and poor, together.
3 My mouth shall speak of wisdom; and the meditation of my heart shall be of understanding.
4 I will incline mine ear to a parable: I will open my dark saying upon the harp.
5 Wherefore should I fear in the days of evil, when the iniquity of my heels shall compass me about?
6 They that trust in their wealth, and boast themselves in the multitude of their riches;
7 None of them can by any means redeem his brother, nor give to God a ransom for him:
8 (For the redemption of their soul is precious, and it ceaseth for ever:)
9 That he should still live for ever, and not see corruption.
10 For he seeth that wise men die, likewise the fool and the brutish person perish, and leave their wealth to others.
11 Their inward thought is, that their houses shall continue for ever, and their dwelling places to all generations; they call their lands after their own names.
12 Nevertheless man being in honor abideth not: he is like the beasts that perish.
13 This their way is their folly: yet their posterity approve their sayings. Selah.
14 Like sheep they are laid in the grave; death shall feed on them; and the upright shall have dominion over them in the morning; and their beauty shall consume in the grave from their dwelling.
15 But God will redeem my soul from the power of the grave: for he shall receive me. Selah.
16 Be not thou afraid when one is made rich, when the glory of his house is increased;

17 For when he dieth he shall carry nothing away: his glory shall not descend after him.
18 Though while he lived he blessed his soul: and men will praise thee, when thou doest well to thyself.
19 He shall go to the generation of his fathers; they shall never see light.
20 Man that is in honor, and understandeth not, is like the beasts that perish.

Psalm 50

1 The mighty God, even the LORD, hath spoken, and called the earth from the rising of the sun unto the going down thereof.
2 Out of Zion, the perfection of beauty, God hath shined.
3 Our God shall come, and shall not keep silence: a fire shall devour before him, and it shall be very tempestuous round about him.
4 He shall call to the heavens from above, and to the earth, that he may judge his people.
5 Gather my saints together unto me; those that have made a covenant with me by sacrifice.
6 And the heavens shall declare his righteousness: for God is judge himself. Selah.
7 Hear, O my people, and I will speak; O Israel, and I will testify against thee: I am God, even thy God.
8 I will not reprove thee for thy sacrifices or thy burnt offerings, to have been continually before me.
9 I will take no bullock out of thy house, nor he goats out of thy folds.
10 For every beast of the forest is mine, and the cattle upon a thousand hills.
11 I know all the fowls of the mountains: and the wild beasts of the field are mine.

12 If I were hungry, I would not tell thee: for the world is mine, and the fulness thereof.
13 Will I eat the flesh of bulls, or drink the blood of goats?
14 Offer unto God thanksgiving; and pay thy vows unto the most High:
15 And call upon me in the day of trouble: I will deliver thee, and thou shalt glorify me.
16 But unto the wicked God saith, What hast thou to do to declare my statutes, or that thou shouldest take my covenant in thy mouth?
17 Seeing thou hatest instruction, and castest my words behind thee.
18 When thou sawest a thief, then thou consentedst with him, and hast been partaker with adulterers.
19 Thou givest thy mouth to evil, and thy tongue frameth deceit.
20 Thou sittest and speakest against thy brother; thou slanderest thine own mother's son.
21 These things hast thou done, and I kept silence; thou thoughtest that I was altogether such a one as thyself: but I will reprove thee, and set them in order before thine eyes.
22 Now consider this, ye that forget God, lest I tear you in pieces, and there be none to deliver.
23 Whoso offereth praise glorifieth me: and to him that ordereth his conversation aright will I shew the salvation of God.

Psalm 53

1 The fool hath said in his heart, There is no God. Corrupt are they, and have done abominable iniquity: there is none that doeth good.
2 God looked down from heaven upon the children of men, to see if there were any that did understand, that did seek God.
3 Every one of them is gone back: they are altogether become filthy; there is none that doeth good, no, not one.

4 Have the workers of iniquity no knowledge? who eat up my people as they eat bread: they have not called upon God.
5 There were they in great fear, where no fear was: for God hath scattered the bones of him that encampeth against thee: thou hast put them to shame, because God hath despised them.
6 Oh that the salvation of Israel were come out of Zion! When God bringeth back the captivity of his people, Jacob shall rejoice, and Israel shall be glad.

Psalm 55

1 Give ear to my prayer, O God; and hide not thyself from my supplication.
2 Attend unto me, and hear me: I mourn in my complaint, and make a noise;
3 Because of the voice of the enemy, because of the oppression of the wicked: for they cast iniquity upon me, and in wrath they hate me.
4 My heart is sore pained within me: and the terrors of death are fallen upon me.
5 Fearfulness and trembling are come upon me, and horror hath overwhelmed me.
6 And I said, Oh that I had wings like a dove! for then would I fly away, and be at rest.
7 Lo, then would I wander far off, and remain in the wilderness. Selah.
8 I would hasten my escape from the windy storm and tempest.
9 Destroy, O Lord, and divide their tongues: for I have seen violence and strife in the city.
10 Day and night they go about it upon the walls thereof: mischief also and sorrow are in the midst of it.
11 Wickedness is in the midst thereof: deceit and guile depart not from her streets.

12 For it was not an enemy that reproached me; then I could have borne it: neither was it he that hated me that did magnify himself against me; then I would have hid myself from him:
13 But it was thou, a man mine equal, my guide, and mine acquaintance.
14 We took sweet counsel together, and walked unto the house of God in company.
15 Let death seize upon them, and let them go down quick into hell: for wickedness is in their dwellings, and among them.
16 As for me, I will call upon God; and the LORD shall save me.
17 Evening, and morning, and at noon, will I pray, and cry aloud: and he shall hear my voice.
18 He hath delivered my soul in peace from the battle that was against me: for there were many with me.
19 God shall hear, and afflict them, even he that abideth of old. Selah. Because they have no changes, therefore they fear not God.
20 He hath put forth his hands against such as be at peace with him: he hath broken his covenant.
21 The words of his mouth were smoother than butter, but war was in his heart: his words were softer than oil, yet were they drawn swords.
22 Cast thy burden upon the LORD, and he shall sustain thee: he shall never suffer the righteous to be moved.
23 But thou, O God, shalt bring them down into the pit of destruction: bloody and deceitful men shall not live out half their days; but I will trust in thee.

Psalm 56

1 Be merciful unto me, O God: for man would swallow me up; he fighting daily oppresseth me.
2 Mine enemies would daily swallow me up: for they be many that fight against me, O thou most High.

3 What time I am afraid, I will trust in thee.
4 In God I will praise his word, in God I have put my trust; I will not fear what flesh can do unto me.
5 Every day they wrest my words: all their thoughts are against me for evil.
6 They gather themselves together, they hide themselves, they mark my steps, when they wait for my soul.
7 Shall they escape by iniquity? in thine anger cast down the people, O God.
8 Thou tellest my wanderings: put thou my tears into thy bottle: are they not in thy book?
9 When I cry unto thee, then shall mine enemies turn back: this I know; for God is for me.
10 In God will I praise his word: in the LORD will I praise his word.
11 In God have I put my trust: I will not be afraid what man can do unto me.
12 Thy vows are upon me, O God: I will render praises unto thee.
13 For thou hast delivered my soul from death: wilt not thou deliver my feet from falling, that I may walk before God in the light of the living?

Psalm 58

1 Do ye indeed speak righteousness, O congregation? do ye judge uprightly, O ye sons of men?
2 Yea, in heart ye work wickedness; ye weigh the violence of your hands in the earth.
3 The wicked are estranged from the womb: they go astray as soon as they be born, speaking lies.
4 Their poison is like the poison of a serpent: they are like the deaf adder that stoppeth her ear;
5 Which will not hearken to the voice of charmers, charming never so wisely.

6 Break their teeth, O God, in their mouth: break out the great teeth of the young lions, O LORD.

7 Let them melt away as waters which run continually: when he bendeth his bow to shoot his arrows, let them be as cut in pieces.

8 As a snail which melteth, let every one of them pass away: like the untimely birth of a woman, that they may not see the sun.

9 Before your pots can feel the thorns, he shall take them away as with a whirlwind, both living, and in his wrath.

10 The righteous shall rejoice when he seeth the vengeance: he shall wash his feet in the blood of the wicked.

11 So that a man shall say, Verily there is a reward for the righteous: verily he is a God that judgeth in the earth.

Psalm 59

1 Deliver me from mine enemies, O my God: defend me from them that rise up against me.

2 Deliver me from the workers of iniquity, and save me from bloody men.

3 For, lo, they lie in wait for my soul: the mighty are gathered against me; not for my transgression, nor for my sin, O LORD.

4 They run and prepare themselves without my fault: awake to help me, and behold.

5 Thou therefore, O LORD God of hosts, the God of Israel, awake to visit all the heathen: be not merciful to any wicked transgressors. Selah.

6 They return at evening: they make a noise like a dog, and go round about the city.

7 Behold, they belch out with their mouth: swords are in their lips: for who, say they, doth hear?

8 But thou, O LORD, shalt laugh at them; thou shalt have all the heathen in derision.

9   Because of his strength will I wait upon thee: for God is my defense.
10 The God of my mercy shall prevent me: God shall let me see my desire upon mine enemies.
11 Slay them not, lest my people forget: scatter them by thy power; and bring them down, O Lord our shield.
12 For the sin of their mouth and the words of their lips let them even be taken in their pride: and for cursing and lying which they speak.
13 Consume them in wrath, consume them, that they may not be: and let them know that God ruleth in Jacob unto the ends of the earth. Selah.
14 And at evening let them return; and let them make a noise like a dog, and go round about the city.
15 Let them wander up and down for meat, and grudge if they be not satisfied.
16 But I will sing of thy power; yea, I will sing aloud of thy mercy in the morning: for thou hast been my defense and refuge in the day of my trouble.
17 Unto thee, O my strength, will I sing: for God is my defense, and the God of my mercy.

Psalm 62

1 Truly my soul waiteth upon God: from him cometh my salvation.
2 He only is my rock and my salvation; he is my defense; I shall not be greatly moved.
3 How long will ye imagine mischief against a man? ye shall be slain all of you: as a bowing wall shall ye be, and as a tottering fence.
4 They only consult to cast him down from his excellency: they delight in lies: they bless with their mouth, but they curse inwardly. Selah.

5 My soul, wait thou only upon God; for my expectation is from him.
6 He only is my rock and my salvation: he is my defense; I shall not be moved.
7 In God is my salvation and my glory: the rock of my strength, and my refuge, is in God.
8 Trust in him at all times; ye people, pour out your heart before him: God is a refuge for us. Selah.
9 Surely men of low degree are vanity, and men of high degree are a lie: to be laid in the balance, they are altogether lighter than vanity.
10 Trust not in oppression, and become not vain in robbery: if riches increase, set not your heart upon them.
11 God hath spoken once; twice have I heard this; that power belongeth unto God.
12 Also unto thee, O Lord, belongeth mercy: for thou renderest to every man according to his work.

Psalm 63

1 O God, thou art my God; early will I seek thee: my soul thirsteth for thee, my flesh longeth for thee in a dry and thirsty land, where no water is;
2 To see thy power and thy glory, so as I have seen thee in the sanctuary.
3 Because thy lovingkindness is better than life, my lips shall praise thee.
4 Thus will I bless thee while I live: I will lift up my hands in thy name.
5 My soul shall be satisfied as with marrow and fatness; and my mouth shall praise thee with joyful lips:
6 When I remember thee upon my bed, and meditate on thee in the night watches.

7 Because thou hast been my help, therefore in the shadow of thy wings will I rejoice.
8 My soul followeth hard after thee: thy right hand upholdeth me.
9 But those that seek my soul, to destroy it, shall go into the lower parts of the earth.
10 They shall fall by the sword: they shall be a portion for foxes.
11 But the king shall rejoice in God; every one that sweareth by him shall glory: but the mouth of them that speak lies shall be stopped.

Psalm 67

1 God be merciful unto us, and bless us; and cause his face to shine upon us; Selah.
2 That thy way may be known upon earth, thy saving health among all nations.
3 Let the people praise thee, O God; let all the people praise thee.
4 O let the nations be glad and sing for joy: for thou shalt judge the people righteously, and govern the nations upon earth. Selah.
5 Let the people praise thee, O God; let all the people praise thee.
6 Then shall the earth yield her increase; and God, even our own God, shall bless us.
7 God shall bless us; and all the ends of the earth shall fear him.

Psalm 70

1 Make haste, O God, to deliver me; make haste to help me, O LORD.
2 Let them be ashamed and confounded that seek after my soul: let them be turned backward, and put to confusion, that desire my hurt.
3 Let them be turned back for a reward of their shame that say, Aha, aha.

4 Let all those that seek thee rejoice and be glad in thee: and let such as love thy salvation say continually, Let God be magnified.
5 But I am poor and needy: make haste unto me, O God: thou art my help and my deliverer; O LORD, make no tarrying.

Psalm 71

1 In thee, O LORD, do I put my trust: let me never be put to confusion.
2 Deliver me in thy righteousness, and cause me to escape: incline thine ear unto me, and save me.
3 Be thou my strong habitation, whereunto I may continually resort: thou hast given commandment to save me; for thou art my rock and my fortress.
4 Deliver me, O my God, out of the hand of the wicked, out of the hand of the unrighteous and cruel man.
5 For thou art my hope, O Lord GOD: thou art my trust from my youth.
6 By thee have I been holden up from the womb: thou art he that took me out of my mother's bowels: my praise shall be continually of thee.
7 I am as a wonder unto many; but thou art my strong refuge.
8 Let my mouth be filled with thy praise and with thy honor all the day.
9 Cast me not off in the time of old age; forsake me not when my strength faileth.
10 For mine enemies speak against me; and they that lay wait for my soul take counsel together,
11 Saying, God hath forsaken him: persecute and take him; for there is none to deliver him.
12 O God, be not far from me: O my God, make haste for my help.

13 Let them be confounded and consumed that are adversaries to my soul; let them be covered with reproach and dishonor that seek my hurt.

14 But I will hope continually, and will yet praise thee more and more.

15 My mouth shall shew forth thy righteousness and thy salvation all the day; for I know not the numbers thereof.

16 I will go in the strength of the Lord GOD: I will make mention of thy righteousness, even of thine only.

17 O God, thou hast taught me from my youth: and hitherto have I declared thy wondrous works.

18 Now also when I am old and gray-haired, O God, forsake me not; until I have shewed thy strength unto this generation, and thy power to every one that is to come.

19 Thy righteousness also, O God, is very high, who hast done great things: O God, who is like unto thee!

20 Thou, which hast shewed me great and sore troubles, shalt quicken me again, and shalt bring me up again from the depths of the earth.

21 Thou shalt increase my greatness, and comfort me on every side.

22 I will also praise thee with the psaltery, even thy truth, O my God: unto thee will I sing with the harp, O thou Holy One of Israel.

23 My lips shall greatly rejoice when I sing unto thee; and my soul, which thou hast redeemed.

24 My tongue also shall talk of thy righteousness all the day long: for they are confounded, for they are brought unto shame, that seek my hurt.

Psalm 72

1 Give the king thy judgments, O God, and thy righteousness unto the king's son.

2 He shall judge thy people with righteousness, and thy poor with judgment.
3 The mountains shall bring peace to the people, and the little hills, by righteousness.
4 He shall judge the poor of the people, he shall save the children of the needy, and shall break in pieces the oppressor.
5 They shall fear thee as long as the sun and moon endure, throughout all generations.
6 He shall come down like rain upon the mown grass: as showers that water the earth.
7 In his days shall the righteous flourish; and abundance of peace so long as the moon endureth.
8 He shall have dominion also from sea to sea, and from the river unto the ends of the earth.
9 They that dwell in the wilderness shall bow before him; and his enemies shall lick the dust.
10 The kings of Tarshish and of the isles shall bring presents: the kings of Sheba and Seba shall offer gifts.
11 Yea, all kings shall fall down before him: all nations shall serve him.
12 For he shall deliver the needy when he crieth; the poor also, and him that hath no helper.
13 He shall spare the poor and needy, and shall save the souls of the needy.
14 He shall redeem their soul from deceit and violence: and precious shall their blood be in his sight.
15 And he shall live, and to him shall be given of the gold of Sheba: prayer also shall be made for him continually; and daily shall he be praised.
16 There shall be a handful of corn in the earth upon the top of the mountains; the fruit thereof shall shake like Lebanon: and they of the city shall flourish like grass of the earth.

17 His name shall endure for ever: his name shall be continued as long as the sun: and men shall be blessed in him: all nations shall call him blessed.
18 Blessed be the LORD God, the God of Israel, who only doeth wondrous things.
19 And blessed be his glorious name for ever: and let the whole earth be filled with his glory; Amen, and Amen.
20 The prayers of David the son of Jesse are ended.

Psalm 76

1 In Judah is God known: his name is great in Israel.
2 In Salem also is his tabernacle, and his dwelling place in Zion.
3 There brake he the arrows of the bow, the shield, and the sword, and the battle. Selah.
4 Thou art more glorious and excellent than the mountains of prey.
5 The stouthearted are spoiled, they have slept their sleep: and none of the men of might have found their hands.
6 At thy rebuke, O God of Jacob, both the chariot and horse are cast into a dead sleep.
7 Thou, even thou, art to be feared: and who may stand in thy sight when once thou art angry?
8 Thou didst cause judgment to be heard from heaven; the earth feared, and was still,
9 When God arose to judgment, to save all the meek of the earth. Selah.
10 Surely the wrath of man shall praise thee: the remainder of wrath shalt thou restrain.
11 Vow, and pay unto the LORD your God: let all that be round about him bring presents unto him that ought to be feared.
12 He shall cut off the spirit of princes: he is terrible to the kings of the earth.

Psalm 79

1 O God, the heathen are come into thine inheritance; thy holy temple have they defiled; they have laid Jerusalem on heaps.

2 The dead bodies of thy servants have they given to be meat unto the fowls of the heaven, the flesh of thy saints unto the beasts of the earth.

3 Their blood have they shed like water round about Jerusalem; and there was none to bury them.

4 We are become a reproach to our neighbors, a scorn and derision to them that are round about us.

5 How long, LORD? wilt thou be angry for ever? shall thy jealousy burn like fire?

6 Pour out thy wrath upon the heathen that have not known thee, and upon the kingdoms that have not called upon thy name.

7 For they have devoured Jacob, and laid waste his dwelling place.

8 O remember not against us former iniquities: let thy tender mercies speedily prevent us: for we are brought very low.

9 Help us, O God of our salvation, for the glory of thy name: and deliver us, and purge away our sins, for thy name's sake.

10 Wherefore should the heathen say, Where is their God? let him be known among the heathen in our sight by the revenging of the blood of thy servants which is shed.

11 Let the sighing of the prisoner come before thee; according to the greatness of thy power preserve thou those that are appointed to die;

12 And render unto our neighbors sevenfold into their bosom their reproach, wherewith they have reproached thee, O Lord.

13 So we thy people and sheep of thy pasture will give thee thanks for ever: we will shew forth thy praise to all generations.

Psalm 80

1 Give ear, O Shepherd of Israel, thou that leadest Joseph like a flock; thou that dwellest between the cherubims, shine forth.

2 Before Ephraim and Benjamin and Manasseh stir up thy strength, and come and save us.

3 Turn us again, O God, and cause thy face to shine; and we shall be saved.

4 O LORD God of hosts, how long wilt thou be angry against the prayer of thy people?

5 Thou feedest them with the bread of tears; and givest them tears to drink in great measure.

6 Thou makest us a strife unto our neighbors: and our enemies laugh among themselves.

7 Turn us again, O God of hosts, and cause thy face to shine; and we shall be saved.

8 Thou hast brought a vine out of Egypt: thou hast cast out the heathen, and planted it.

9 Thou preparedst room before it, and didst cause it to take deep root, and it filled the land.

10 The hills were covered with the shadow of it, and the boughs thereof were like the goodly cedars.

11 She sent out her boughs unto the sea, and her branches unto the river.

12 Why hast thou then broken down her hedges, so that all they which pass by the way do pluck her?

13 The boar out of the wood doth waste it, and the wild beast of the field doth devour it.

14 Return, we beseech thee, O God of hosts: look down from heaven, and behold, and visit this vine;

15 And the vineyard which thy right hand hath planted, and the branch that thou madest strong for thyself.

16 It is burned with fire, it is cut down: they perish at the rebuke of thy countenance.

17 Let thy hand be upon the man of thy right hand, upon the son of man whom thou madest strong for thyself.
18 So will not we go back from thee: quicken us, and we will call upon thy name.
19 Turn us again, O LORD God of hosts, cause thy face to shine; and we shall be saved.

Psalm 82

1 God standeth in the congregation of the mighty; he judgeth among the gods.
2 How long will ye judge unjustly, and accept the persons of the wicked? Selah.
3 Defend the poor and fatherless: do justice to the afflicted and needy.
4 Deliver the poor and needy: rid them out of the hand of the wicked.
5 They know not, neither will they understand; they walk on in darkness: all the foundations of the earth are out of course.
6 I have said, Ye are gods; and all of you are children of the most High.
7 But ye shall die like men, and fall like one of the princes.
8 Arise, O God, judge the earth: for thou shalt inherit all nations.

Psalm 84

1 How amiable are thy tabernacles, O LORD of hosts!
2 My soul longeth, yea, even fainteth for the courts of the LORD: my heart and my flesh crieth out for the living God.
3 Yea, the sparrow hath found a house, and the swallow a nest for herself, where she may lay her young, even thine altars, O LORD of hosts, my King, and my God.

4 Blessed are they that dwell in thy house: they will be still praising thee. Selah.
5 Blessed is the man whose strength is in thee; in whose heart are the ways of them.
6 Who passing through the valley of Baca make it a well; the rain also filleth the pools.
7 They go from strength to strength, every one of them in Zion appeareth before God.
8 O LORD God of hosts, hear my prayer: give ear, O God of Jacob. Selah.
9 Behold, O God our shield, and look upon the face of thine anointed.
10 For a day in thy courts is better than a thousand. I had rather be a doorkeeper in the house of my God, than to dwell in the tents of wickedness.
11 For the LORD God is a sun and shield: the LORD will give grace and glory: no good thing will he withhold from them that walk uprightly.
12 O LORD of hosts, blessed is the man that trusteth in thee.

Psalm 88

1 O LORD God of my salvation, I have cried day and night before thee:
2 Let my prayer come before thee: incline thine ear unto my cry;
3 For my soul is full of troubles: and my life draweth nigh unto the grave.
4 I am counted with them that go down into the pit: I am as a man that hath no strength:
5 Free among the dead, like the slain that lie in the grave, whom thou rememberest no more: and they are cut off from thy hand.
6 Thou hast laid me in the lowest pit, in darkness, in the deeps.

7 Thy wrath lieth hard upon me, and thou hast afflicted me with all thy waves. Selah.
8 Thou hast put away mine acquaintance far from me; thou hast made me an abomination unto them: I am shut up, and I cannot come forth.
9 Mine eye mourneth by reason of affliction: LORD, I have called daily upon thee, I have stretched out my hands unto thee.
10 Wilt thou shew wonders to the dead? shall the dead arise and praise thee? Selah.
11 Shall thy lovingkindness be declared in the grave? or thy faithfulness in destruction?
12 Shall thy wonders be known in the dark? and thy righteousness in the land of forgetfulness?
13 But unto thee have I cried, O LORD; and in the morning shall my prayer prevent thee.
14 LORD, why castest thou off my soul? why hidest thou thy face from me?
15 I am afflicted and ready to die from my youth up: while I suffer thy terrors I am distracted.
16 Thy fierce wrath goeth over me; thy terrors have cut me off.
17 They came round about me daily like water; they compassed me about together.
18 Lover and friend hast thou put far from me, and mine acquaintance into darkness.

Psalm 89

1 I will sing of the mercies of the LORD for ever: with my mouth will I make known thy faithfulness to all generations.
2 For I have said, Mercy shall be built up for ever: thy faithfulness shalt thou establish in the very heavens.
3 I have made a covenant with my chosen, I have sworn unto David my servant,

4 Thy seed will I establish for ever, and build up thy throne to all generations. Selah.
5 And the heavens shall praise thy wonders, O LORD: thy faithfulness also in the congregation of the saints.
6 For who in the heaven can be compared unto the LORD? who among the sons of the mighty can be likened unto the LORD?
7 God is greatly to be feared in the assembly of the saints, and to be had in reverence of all them that are about him.
8 O LORD God of hosts, who is a strong LORD like unto thee? or to thy faithfulness round about thee?
9 Thou rulest the raging of the sea: when the waves thereof arise, thou stillest them.
10 Thou hast broken Rahab in pieces, as one that is slain; thou hast scattered thine enemies with thy strong arm.
11 The heavens are thine, the earth also is thine: as for the world and the fulness thereof, thou hast founded them.
12 The north and the south thou hast created them: Tabor and Hermon shall rejoice in thy name.
13 Thou hast a mighty arm: strong is thy hand, and high is thy right hand.
14 Justice and judgment are the habitation of thy throne: mercy and truth shall go before thy face.
15 Blessed is the people that know the joyful sound: they shall walk, O LORD, in the light of thy countenance.
16 In thy name shall they rejoice all the day: and in thy righteousness shall they be exalted.
17 For thou art the glory of their strength: and in thy favor our horn shall be exalted.
18 For the LORD is our defense; and the Holy One of Israel is our king.
19 Then thou spakest in vision to thy holy one, and saidst, I have laid help upon one that is mighty; I have exalted one chosen out of the people.

20 I have found David my servant; with my holy oil have I anointed him:
21 With whom my hand shall be established: mine arm also shall strengthen him.
22 The enemy shall not exact upon him; nor the son of wickedness afflict him.
23 And I will beat down his foes before his face, and plague them that hate him.
24 But my faithfulness and my mercy shall be with him: and in my name shall his horn be exalted.
25 I will set his hand also in the sea, and his right hand in the rivers.
26 He shall cry unto me, Thou art my father, my God, and the rock of my salvation.
27 Also I will make him my firstborn, higher than the kings of the earth.
28 My mercy will I keep for him for evermore, and my covenant shall stand fast with him.
29 His seed also will I make to endure for ever, and his throne as the days of heaven.
30 If his children forsake my law, and walk not in my judgments;
31 If they break my statutes, and keep not my commandments;
32 Then will I visit their transgression with the rod, and their iniquity with stripes.
33 Nevertheless my lovingkindness will I not utterly take from him, nor suffer my faithfulness to fail.
34 My covenant will I not break, nor alter the thing that is gone out of my lips.
35 Once have I sworn by my holiness that I will not lie unto David.
36 His seed shall endure for ever, and his throne as the sun before me.

37 It shall be established for ever as the moon, and as a faithful witness in heaven. Selah.
38 But thou hast cast off and abhorred, thou hast been wroth with thine anointed.
39 Thou hast made void the covenant of thy servant: thou hast profaned his crown by casting it to the ground.
40 Thou hast broken down all his hedges; thou hast brought his strong holds to ruin.
41 All that pass by the way spoil him: he is a reproach to his neighbors.
42 Thou hast set up the right hand of his adversaries; thou hast made all his enemies to rejoice.
43 Thou hast also turned the edge of his sword, and hast not made him to stand in the battle.
44 Thou hast made his glory to cease, and cast his throne down to the ground.
45 The days of his youth hast thou shortened: thou hast covered him with shame. Selah.
46 How long, LORD? wilt thou hide thyself for ever? shall thy wrath burn like fire?
47 Remember how short my time is: wherefore hast thou made all men in vain?
48 What man is he that liveth, and shall not see death? shall he deliver his soul from the hand of the grave? Selah.
49 Lord, where are thy former lovingkindnesses, which thou swarest unto David in thy truth?
50 Remember, Lord, the reproach of thy servants; how I do bear in my bosom the reproach of all the mighty people;
51 Wherewith thine enemies have reproached, O LORD; wherewith they have reproached the footsteps of thine anointed.
52 Blessed be the LORD for evermore. Amen, and Amen.

Psalm 90

1. Lord, thou hast been our dwelling place in all generations.
2. Before the mountains were brought forth, or ever thou hadst formed the earth and the world, even from everlasting to everlasting, thou art God.
3. Thou turnest man to destruction; and sayest, Return, ye children of men.
4. For a thousand years in thy sight are but as yesterday when it is past, and as a watch in the night.
5. Thou carriest them away as with a flood; they are as a sleep: in the morning they are like grass which groweth up.
6. In the morning it flourisheth, and groweth up; in the evening it is cut down, and withereth.
7. For we are consumed by thine anger, and by thy wrath are we troubled.
8. Thou hast set our iniquities before thee, our secret sins in the light of thy countenance.
9. For all our days are passed away in thy wrath: we spend our years as a tale that is told.
10. The days of our years are threescore years and ten; and if by reason of strength they be fourscore years, yet is their strength labor and sorrow; for it is soon cut off, and we fly away.
11. Who knoweth the power of thine anger? even according to thy fear, so is thy wrath.
12. So teach us to number our days, that we may apply our hearts unto wisdom.
13. Return, O LORD, how long? and let it repent thee concerning thy servants.
14. O satisfy us early with thy mercy; that we may rejoice and be glad all our days.
15. Make us glad according to the days wherein thou hast afflicted us, and the years wherein we have seen evil.

16 Let thy work appear unto thy servants, and thy glory unto their children.
17 And let the beauty of the LORD our God be upon us: and establish thou the work of our hands upon us; yea, the work of our hands establish thou it.

Psalm 91

1 He that dwelleth in the secret place of the most High shall abide under the shadow of the Almighty.
2 I will say of the LORD, He is my refuge and my fortress: my God; in him will I trust.
3 Surely he shall deliver thee from the snare of the fowler, and from the noisome pestilence.
4 He shall cover thee with his feathers, and under his wings shalt thou trust: his truth shall be thy shield and buckler.
5 Thou shalt not be afraid for the terror by night; nor for the arrow that flieth by day;
6 Nor for the pestilence that walketh in darkness; nor for the destruction that wasteth at noonday.
7 A thousand shall fall at thy side, and ten thousand at thy right hand; but it shall not come nigh thee.
8 Only with thine eyes shalt thou behold and see the reward of the wicked.
9 Because thou hast made the LORD, which is my refuge, even the most High, thy habitation;
10 There shall no evil befall thee, neither shall any plague come nigh thy dwelling.
11 For he shall give his angels charge over thee, to keep thee in all thy ways.
12 They shall bear thee up in their hands, lest thou dash thy foot against a stone.
13 Thou shalt tread upon the lion and adder: the young lion and the dragon shalt thou trample under feet.

14 Because he hath set his love upon me, therefore will I deliver him: I will set him on high, because he hath known my name.
15 He shall call upon me, and I will answer him: I will be with him in trouble; I will deliver him, and honor him.
16 With long life will I satisfy him, and shew him my salvation.

Psalm 93

1 The LORD reigneth, he is clothed with majesty; the LORD is clothed with strength, wherewith he hath girded himself: the world also is stablished, that it cannot be moved.
2 Thy throne is established of old: thou art from everlasting.
3 The floods have lifted up, O LORD, the floods have lifted up their voice; the floods lift up their waves.
4 The LORD on high is mightier than the noise of many waters, yea, than the mighty waves of the sea.
5 Thy testimonies are very sure: holiness becometh thine house, O LORD, for ever.

Psalm 97

1 The LORD reigneth; let the earth rejoice; let the multitude of isles be glad thereof.
2 Clouds and darkness are round about him: righteousness and judgment are the habitation of his throne.
3 A fire goeth before him, and burneth up his enemies round about.
4 His lightnings enlightened the world: the earth saw, and trembled.
5 The hills melted like wax at the presence of the LORD, at the presence of the Lord of the whole earth.
6 The heavens declare his righteousness, and all the people see his glory.

7 Confounded be all they that serve graven images, that boast themselves of idols: worship him, all ye gods.
8 Zion heard, and was glad; and the daughters of Judah rejoiced because of thy judgments, O LORD.
9 For thou, LORD, art high above all the earth: thou art exalted far above all gods.
10 Ye that love the LORD, hate evil: he preserveth the souls of his saints; he delivereth them out of the hand of the wicked.
11 Light is sown for the righteous, and gladness for the upright in heart.
12 Rejoice in the LORD, ye righteous; and give thanks at the remembrance of his holiness.

Psalm 102

1 Hear my prayer, O LORD, and let my cry come unto thee.
2 Hide not thy face from me in the day when I am in trouble; incline thine ear unto me: in the day when I call answer me speedily.
3 For my days are consumed like smoke, and my bones are burned as a hearth.
4 My heart is smitten, and withered like grass; so that I forget to eat my bread.
5 By reason of the voice of my groaning my bones cleave to my skin.
6 I am like a pelican of the wilderness: I am like an owl of the desert.
7 I watch, and am as a sparrow alone upon the house top.
8 Mine enemies reproach me all the day; and they that are mad against me are sworn against me.
9 For I have eaten ashes like bread, and mingled my drink with weeping,
10 Because of thine indignation and thy wrath: for thou hast lifted me up, and cast me down.

11 My days are like a shadow that declineth; and I am withered like grass.

12 But thou, O LORD, shalt endure for ever; and thy remembrance unto all generations.

13 Thou shalt arise, and have mercy upon Zion: for the time to favor her, yea, the set time, is come.

14 For thy servants take pleasure in her stones, and favor the dust thereof.

15 So the heathen shall fear the name of the LORD, and all the kings of the earth thy glory.

16 When the LORD shall build up Zion, he shall appear in his glory.

17 He will regard the prayer of the destitute, and not despise their prayer.

18 This shall be written for the generation to come: and the people which shall be created shall praise the LORD.

19 For he hath looked down from the height of his sanctuary; from heaven did the LORD behold the earth;

20 To hear the groaning of the prisoner; to loose those that are appointed to death;

21 To declare the name of the LORD in Zion, and his praise in Jerusalem;

22 When the people are gathered together, and the kingdoms, to serve the LORD.

23 He weakened my strength in the way; he shortened my days.

24 I said, O my God, take me not away in the midst of my days: thy years are throughout all generations.

25 Of old hast thou laid the foundation of the earth: and the heavens are the work of thy hands.

26 They shall perish, but thou shalt endure: yea, all of them shall wax old like a garment; as a vesture shalt thou change them, and they shall be changed:

27 But thou art the same, and thy years shall have no end.

28 The children of thy servants shall continue, and their seed shall be established before thee.

Psalm 107

1 O give thanks unto the LORD, for he is good: for his mercy endureth for ever.
2 Let the redeemed of the LORD say so, whom he hath redeemed from the hand of the enemy;
3 And gathered them out of the lands, from the east, and from the west, from the north, and from the south.
4 They wandered in the wilderness in a solitary way; they found no city to dwell in.
5 Hungry and thirsty, their soul fainted in them.
6 Then they cried unto the LORD in their trouble, and he delivered them out of their distresses.
7 And he led them forth by the right way, that they might go to a city of habitation.
8 Oh that men would praise the LORD for his goodness, and for his wonderful works to the children of men!
9 For he satisfieth the longing soul, and filleth the hungry soul with goodness.
10 Such as sit in darkness and in the shadow of death, being bound in affliction and iron;
11 Because they rebelled against the words of God, and contemned the counsel of the most High:
12 Therefore he brought down their heart with labor; they fell down, and there was none to help.
13 Then they cried unto the LORD in their trouble, and he saved them out of their distresses.
14 He brought them out of darkness and the shadow of death, and brake their bands in sunder.
15 Oh that men would praise the LORD for his goodness, and for his wonderful works to the children of men!

16 For he hath broken the gates of brass, and cut the bars of iron in sunder.
17 Fools because of their transgression, and because of their iniquities, are afflicted.
18 Their soul abhorreth all manner of meat; and they draw near unto the gates of death.
19 Then they cry unto the LORD in their trouble, and he saveth them out of their distresses.
20 He sent his word, and healed them, and delivered them from their destructions.
21 Oh that men would praise the LORD for his goodness, and for his wonderful works to the children of men!
22 And let them sacrifice the sacrifices of thanksgiving, and declare his works with rejoicing.
23 They that go down to the sea in ships, that do business in great waters;
24 These see the works of the LORD, and his wonders in the deep.
25 For he commandeth, and raiseth the stormy wind, which lifteth up the waves thereof.
26 They mount up to the heaven, they go down again to the depths: their soul is melted because of trouble.
27 They reel to and fro, and stagger like a drunken man, and are at their wits' end.
28 Then they cry unto the LORD in their trouble, and he bringeth them out of their distresses.
29 He maketh the storm a calm, so that the waves thereof are still.
30 Then are they glad because they be quiet; so he bringeth them unto their desired haven.
31 Oh that men would praise the LORD for his goodness, and for his wonderful works to the children of men!
32 Let them exalt him also in the congregation of the people, and praise him in the assembly of the elders.

33 He turneth rivers into a wilderness, and the watersprings into dry ground;
34 A fruitful land into barrenness, for the wickedness of them that dwell therein.
35 He turneth the wilderness into a standing water, and dry ground into watersprings.
36 And there he maketh the hungry to dwell, that they may prepare a city for habitation;
37 And sow the fields, and plant vineyards, which may yield fruits of increase.
38 He blesseth them also, so that they are multiplied greatly; and suffereth not their cattle to decrease.
39 Again, they are minished and brought low through oppression, affliction, and sorrow.
40 He poureth contempt upon princes, and causeth them to wander in the wilderness, where there is no way.
41 Yet setteth he the poor on high from affliction, and maketh him families like a flock.
42 The righteous shall see it, and rejoice: and all iniquity shall stop her mouth.
43 Whoso is wise, and will observe these things, even they shall understand the lovingkindness of the LORD.

Psalm 110

1 The LORD said unto my Lord, Sit thou at my right hand, until I make thine enemies thy footstool.
2 The LORD shall send the rod of thy strength out of Zion: rule thou in the midst of thine enemies.
3 Thy people shall be willing in the day of thy power, in the beauties of holiness from the womb of the morning: thou hast the dew of thy youth.
4 The LORD hath sworn, and will not repent, Thou art a priest for ever after the order of Melchizedek.

5 The Lord at thy right hand shall strike through kings in the day of his wrath.
6 He shall judge among the heathen, he shall fill the places with the dead bodies; he shall wound the heads over many countries.
7 He shall drink of the brook in the way: therefore shall he lift up the head.

Psalm 111

1 Praise ye the LORD. I will praise the LORD with my whole heart, in the assembly of the upright, and in the congregation.
2 The works of the LORD are great, sought out of all them that have pleasure therein.
3 His work is honorable and glorious: and his righteousness endureth for ever.
4 He hath made his wonderful works to be remembered: the LORD is gracious and full of compassion.
5 He hath given meat unto them that fear him: he will ever be mindful of his covenant.
6 He hath shewed his people the power of his works, that he may give them the heritage of the heathen.
7 The works of his hands are verity and judgment; all his commandments are sure.
8 They stand fast for ever and ever, and are done in truth and uprightness.
9 He sent redemption unto his people: he hath commanded his covenant for ever: holy and reverend is his name.
10 The fear of the LORD is the beginning of wisdom: a good understanding have all they that do his commandments: his praise endureth for ever.

Psalm 113

1 Praise ye the LORD. Praise, O ye servants of the LORD, praise the name of the LORD.
2 Blessed be the name of the LORD from this time forth and for evermore.
3 From the rising of the sun unto the going down of the same the LORD'S name is to be praised.
4 The LORD is high above all nations, and his glory above the heavens.
5 Who is like unto the LORD our God, who dwelleth on high,
6 Who humbleth himself to behold the things that are in heaven, and in the earth!
7 He raiseth up the poor out of the dust, and lifteth the needy out of the dunghill;
8 That he may set him with princes, even with the princes of his people.
9 He maketh the barren woman to keep house, and to be a joyful mother of children. Praise ye the LORD.

Psalm 115

1 Not unto us, O LORD, not unto us, but unto thy name give glory, for thy mercy, and for thy truth's sake.
2 Wherefore should the heathen say, Where is now their God?
3 But our God is in the heavens: he hath done whatsoever he hath pleased.
4 Their idols are silver and gold, the work of men's hands.
5 They have mouths, but they speak not: eyes have they, but they see not:
6 They have ears, but they hear not: noses have they, but they smell not:
7 They have hands, but they handle not: feet have they, but they walk not: neither speak they through their throat.

8 They that make them are like unto them; so is every one that trusteth in them.
9 O Israel, trust thou in the LORD: he is their help and their shield.
10 O house of Aaron, trust in the LORD: he is their help and their shield.
11 Ye that fear the LORD, trust in the LORD: he is their help and their shield.
12 The LORD hath been mindful of us: he will bless us; he will bless the house of Israel; he will bless the house of Aaron.
13 He will bless them that fear the LORD, both small and great.
14 The LORD shall increase you more and more, you and your children.
15 Ye are blessed of the LORD which made heaven and earth.
16 The heaven, even the heavens, are the LORD'S: but the earth hath he given to the children of men.
17 The dead praise not the LORD, neither any that go down into silence.
18 But we will bless the LORD from this time forth and for evermore. Praise the LORD.

Psalm 118

1 O give thanks unto the LORD; for he is good: because his mercy endureth for ever.
2 Let Israel now say, that his mercy endureth for ever.
3 Let the house of Aaron now say, that his mercy endureth for ever.
4 Let them now that fear the LORD say, that his mercy endureth for ever.
5 I called upon the LORD in distress: the LORD answered me, and set me in a large place.
6 The LORD is on my side; I will not fear: what can man do unto me?

7 The LORD taketh my part with them that help me: therefore shall I see my desire upon them that hate me.
8 It is better to trust in the LORD than to put confidence in man.
9 It is better to trust in the LORD than to put confidence in princes.
10 All nations compassed me about: but in the name of the LORD will I destroy them.
11 They compassed me about; yea, they compassed me about: but in the name of the LORD I will destroy them.
12 They compassed me about like bees; they are quenched as the fire of thorns: for in the name of the LORD I will destroy them.
13 Thou hast thrust sore at me that I might fall: but the LORD helped me.
14 The LORD is my strength and song, and is become my salvation.
15 The voice of rejoicing and salvation is in the tabernacles of the righteous: the right hand of the LORD doeth valiantly.
16 The right hand of the LORD is exalted: the right hand of the LORD doeth valiantly.
17 I shall not die, but live, and declare the works of the LORD.
18 The LORD hath chastened me sore: but he hath not given me over unto death.
19 Open to me the gates of righteousness: I will go into them, and I will praise the LORD:
20 This gate of the LORD, into which the righteous shall enter.
21 I will praise thee: for thou hast heard me, and art become my salvation.
22 The stone which the builders refused is become the head stone of the corner.
23 This is the LORD'S doing; it is marvelous in our eyes.
24 This is the day which the LORD hath made; we will rejoice and be glad in it.
25 Save now, I beseech thee, O LORD: O LORD, I beseech thee, send now prosperity.

26 Blessed be he that cometh in the name of the LORD: we have blessed you out of the house of the LORD.
27 God is the LORD, which hath shewed us light: bind the sacrifice with cords, even unto the horns of the altar.
28 Thou art my God, and I will praise thee: thou art my God, I will exalt thee.
29 O give thanks unto the LORD; for he is good: for his mercy endureth for ever.

Psalm 119

1 ALEPH. Blessed are the undefiled in the way, who walk in the law of the LORD.
2 Blessed are they that keep his testimonies, and that seek him with the whole heart.
3 They also do no iniquity: they walk in his ways.
4 Thou hast commanded us to keep thy precepts diligently.
5 O that my ways were directed to keep thy statutes!
6 Then shall I not be ashamed, when I have respect unto all thy commandments.
7 I will praise thee with uprightness of heart, when I shall have learned thy righteous judgments.
8 I will keep thy statutes: O forsake me not utterly.
9 BETH. Wherewithal shall a young man cleanse his way? by taking heed thereto according to thy word.
10 With my whole heart have I sought thee: O let me not wander from thy commandments.
11 Thy word have I hid in mine heart, that I might not sin against thee.
12 Blessed art thou, O LORD: teach me thy statutes.
13 With my lips have I declared all the judgments of thy mouth.
14 I have rejoiced in the way of thy testimonies, as much as in all riches.
15 I will meditate in thy precepts, and have respect unto thy ways.

16 I will delight myself in thy statutes: I will not forget thy word.
17 GIMEL. Deal bountifully with thy servant, that I may live, and keep thy word.
18 Open thou mine eyes, that I may behold wondrous things out of thy law.
19 I am a stranger in the earth: hide not thy commandments from me.
20 My soul breaketh for the longing that it hath unto thy judgments at all times.
21 Thou hast rebuked the proud that are cursed, which do err from thy commandments.
22 Remove from me reproach and contempt; for I have kept thy testimonies.
23 Princes also did sit and speak against me: but thy servant did meditate in thy statutes.
24 Thy testimonies also are my delight and my counsellors.
25 DALETH. My soul cleaveth unto the dust: quicken thou me according to thy word.
26 I have declared my ways, and thou heardest me: teach me thy statutes.
27 Make me to understand the way of thy precepts: so shall I talk of thy wondrous works.
28 My soul melteth for heaviness: strengthen thou me according unto thy word.
29 Remove from me the way of lying: and grant me thy law graciously.
30 I have chosen the way of truth: thy judgments have I laid before me.
31 I have stuck unto thy testimonies: O LORD, put me not to shame.
32 I will run the way of thy commandments, when thou shalt enlarge my heart.

33 HE. Teach me, O LORD, the way of thy statutes; and I shall keep it unto the end.
34 Give me understanding, and I shall keep thy law; yea, I shall observe it with my whole heart.
35 Make me to go in the path of thy commandments; for therein do I delight.
36 Incline my heart unto thy testimonies, and not to covetousness.
37 Turn away mine eyes from beholding vanity; and quicken thou me in thy way.
38 Stablish thy word unto thy servant, who is devoted to thy fear.
39 Turn away my reproach which I fear: for thy judgments are good.
40 Behold, I have longed after thy precepts: quicken me in thy righteousness.
41 VAU. Let thy mercies come also unto me, O LORD, even thy salvation, according to thy word.
42 So shall I have wherewith to answer him that reproacheth me: for I trust in thy word.
43 And take not the word of truth utterly out of my mouth; for I have hoped in thy judgments.
44 So shall I keep thy law continually for ever and ever.
45 And I will walk at liberty: for I seek thy precepts.
46 I will speak of thy testimonies also before kings, and will not be ashamed.
47 And I will delight myself in thy commandments, which I have loved.
48 My hands also will I lift up unto thy commandments, which I have loved; and I will meditate in thy statutes.
49 ZAIN. Remember the word unto thy servant, upon which thou hast caused me to hope.
50 This is my comfort in my affliction: for thy word hath quickened me.

51 The proud have had me greatly in derision: yet have I not declined from thy law.
52 I remembered thy judgments of old, O LORD; and have comforted myself.
53 Horror hath taken hold upon me because of the wicked that forsake thy law.
54 Thy statutes have been my songs in the house of my pilgrimage.
55 I have remembered thy name, O LORD, in the night, and have kept thy law.
56 This I had, because I kept thy precepts.
57 CHETH. Thou art my portion, O LORD: I have said that I would keep thy words.
58 I intreated thy favor with my whole heart: be merciful unto me according to thy word.
59 I thought on my ways, and turned my feet unto thy testimonies.
60 I made haste, and delayed not to keep thy commandments.
61 The bands of the wicked have robbed me: but I have not forgotten thy law.
62 At midnight I will rise to give thanks unto thee because of thy righteous judgments.
63 I am a companion of all them that fear thee, and of them that keep thy precepts.
64 The earth, O LORD, is full of thy mercy: teach me thy statutes.
65 TETH. Thou hast dealt well with thy servant, O LORD, according unto thy word.
66 Teach me good judgment and knowledge: for I have believed thy commandments.
67 Before I was afflicted I went astray: but now have I kept thy word.
68 Thou art good, and doest good; teach me thy statutes.
69 The proud have forged a lie against me: but I will keep thy precepts with my whole heart.
70 Their heart is as fat as grease; but I delight in thy law.

71 It is good for me that I have been afflicted; that I might learn thy statutes.
72 The law of thy mouth is better unto me than thousands of gold and silver.
73 JOD. Thy hands have made me and fashioned me: give me understanding, that I may learn thy commandments.
74 They that fear thee will be glad when they see me; because I have hoped in thy word.
75 I know, O LORD, that thy judgments are right, and that thou in faithfulness hast afflicted me.
76 Let, I pray thee, thy merciful kindness be for my comfort, according to thy word unto thy servant.
77 Let thy tender mercies come unto me, that I may live: for thy law is my delight.
78 Let the proud be ashamed; for they dealt perversely with me without a cause: but I will meditate in thy precepts.
79 Let those that fear thee turn unto me, and those that have known thy testimonies.
80 Let my heart be sound in thy statutes; that I be not ashamed.
81 CAPH. My soul fainteth for thy salvation: but I hope in thy word.
82 Mine eyes fail for thy word, saying, When wilt thou comfort me?
83 For I am become like a bottle in the smoke; yet do I not forget thy statutes.
84 How many are the days of thy servant? when wilt thou execute judgment on them that persecute me?
85 The proud have digged pits for me, which are not after thy law.
86 All thy commandments are faithful: they persecute me wrongfully; help thou me.
87 They had almost consumed me upon earth; but I forsook not thy precepts.
88 Quicken me after thy lovingkindness; so shall I keep the testimony of thy mouth.
89 LAMED. For ever, O LORD, thy word is settled in heaven.

90 Thy faithfulness is unto all generations: thou hast established the earth, and it abideth.
91 They continue this day according to thine ordinances: for all are thy servants.
92 Unless thy law had been my delights, I should then have perished in mine affliction.
93 I will never forget thy precepts: for with them thou hast quickened me.
94 I am thine, save me; for I have sought thy precepts.
95 The wicked have waited for me to destroy me: but I will consider thy testimonies.
96 I have seen an end of all perfection: but thy commandment is exceeding broad.
97 MEM. O how love I thy law! it is my meditation all the day.
98 Thou through thy commandments hast made me wiser than mine enemies: for they are ever with me.
99 I have more understanding than all my teachers: for thy testimonies are my meditation.
100 I understand more than the ancients, because I keep thy precepts.
101 I have refrained my feet from every evil way, that I might keep thy word.
102 I have not departed from thy judgments: for thou hast taught me.
103 How sweet are thy words unto my taste! yea, sweeter than honey to my mouth!
104 Through thy precepts I get understanding: therefore I hate every false way.
105 NUN. Thy word is a lamp unto my feet, and a light unto my path.
106 I have sworn, and I will perform it, that I will keep thy righteous judgments.

107 I am afflicted very much: quicken me, O LORD, according unto thy word.

108 Accept, I beseech thee, the freewill offerings of my mouth, O LORD, and teach me thy judgments.

109 My soul is continually in my hand: yet do I not forget thy law.

110 The wicked have laid a snare for me: yet I erred not from thy precepts.

111 Thy testimonies have I taken as a heritage for ever: for they are the rejoicing of my heart.

112 I have inclined mine heart to perform thy statutes alway, even unto the end.

113 SAMECH. I hate vain thoughts: but thy law do I love.

114 Thou art my hiding place and my shield: I hope in thy word.

115 Depart from me, ye evildoers: for I will keep the commandments of my God.

116 Uphold me according unto thy word, that I may live: and let me not be ashamed of my hope.

117 Hold thou me up, and I shall be safe: and I will have respect unto thy statutes continually.

118 Thou hast trodden down all them that err from thy statutes: for their deceit is falsehood.

119 Thou puttest away all the wicked of the earth like dross: therefore I love thy testimonies.

120 My flesh trembleth for fear of thee; and I am afraid of thy judgments.

121 AIN. I have done judgment and justice: leave me not to mine oppressors.

122 Be surety for thy servant for good: let not the proud oppress me.

123 Mine eyes fail for thy salvation, and for the word of thy righteousness.

124 Deal with thy servant according unto thy mercy, and teach me thy statutes.

125 I am thy servant; give me understanding, that I may know thy testimonies.
126 It is time for thee, LORD, to work: for they have made void thy law.
127 Therefore I love thy commandments above gold; yea, above fine gold.
128 Therefore I esteem all thy precepts concerning all things to be right; and I hate every false way.
129 PE. Thy testimonies are wonderful: therefore doth my soul keep them.
130 The entrance of thy words giveth light; it giveth understanding unto the simple.
131 I opened my mouth, and panted: for I longed for thy commandments.
132 Look thou upon me, and be merciful unto me, as thou usest to do unto those that love thy name.
133 Order my steps in thy word: and let not any iniquity have dominion over me.
134 Deliver me from the oppression of man: so will I keep thy precepts.
135 Make thy face to shine upon thy servant; and teach me thy statutes.
136 Rivers of waters run down mine eyes, because they keep not thy law.
137 TZADDI. Righteous art thou, O LORD, and upright are thy judgments.
138 Thy testimonies that thou hast commanded are righteous and very faithful.
139 My zeal hath consumed me, because mine enemies have forgotten thy words.
140 Thy word is very pure: therefore thy servant loveth it.
141 I am small and despised: yet do not I forget thy precepts.

142 Thy righteousness is an everlasting righteousness, and thy law is the truth.
143 Trouble and anguish have taken hold on me: yet thy commandments are my delights.
144 The righteousness of thy testimonies is everlasting: give me understanding, and I shall live.
145 KOPH. I cried with my whole heart; hear me, O LORD: I will keep thy statutes.
146 I cried unto thee; save me, and I shall keep thy testimonies.
147 I prevented the dawning of the morning, and cried: I hoped in thy word.
148 Mine eyes prevent the night watches, that I might meditate in thy word.
149 Hear my voice according unto thy lovingkindness: O LORD, quicken me according to thy judgment.
150 They draw nigh that follow after mischief: they are far from thy law.
151 Thou art near, O LORD; and all thy commandments are truth.
152 Concerning thy testimonies, I have known of old that thou hast founded them for ever.
153 RESH. Consider mine affliction, and deliver me: for I do not forget thy law.
154 Plead my cause, and deliver me: quicken me according to thy word.
155 Salvation is far from the wicked: for they seek not thy statutes.
156 Great are thy tender mercies, O LORD: quicken me according to thy judgments.
157 Many are my persecutors and mine enemies; yet do I not decline from thy testimonies.
158 I beheld the transgressors, and was grieved; because they kept not thy word.
159 Consider how I love thy precepts: quicken me, O LORD, according to thy lovingkindness.

160 Thy word is true from the beginning: and every one of thy righteous judgments endureth for ever.
161 SCHIN. Princes have persecuted me without a cause: but my heart standeth in awe of thy word.
162 I rejoice at thy word, as one that findeth great spoil.
163 I hate and abhor lying: but thy law do I love.
164 Seven times a day do I praise thee because of thy righteous judgments.
165 Great peace have they which love thy law: and nothing shall offend them.
166 LORD, I have hoped for thy salvation, and done thy commandments.
167 My soul hath kept thy testimonies; and I love them exceedingly.
168 I have kept thy precepts and thy testimonies: for all my ways are before thee.
169 TAU. Let my cry come near before thee, O LORD: give me understanding according to thy word.
170 Let my supplication come before thee: deliver me according to thy word.
171 My lips shall utter praise, when thou hast taught me thy statutes.
172 My tongue shall speak of thy word: for all thy commandments are righteousness.
173 Let thine hand help me; for I have chosen thy precepts.
174 I have longed for thy salvation, O LORD; and thy law is my delight.
175 Let my soul live, and it shall praise thee; and let thy judgments help me.
176 I have gone astray like a lost sheep; seek thy servant; for I do not forget thy commandments.

Psalm 121

1 I will lift up mine eyes unto the hills, from whence cometh my help.
2 My help cometh from the LORD, which made heaven and earth.
3 He will not suffer thy foot to be moved: he that keepeth thee will not slumber.
4 Behold, he that keepeth Israel shall neither slumber nor sleep.
5 The LORD is thy keeper: the LORD is thy shade upon thy right hand.
6 The sun shall not smite thee by day, nor the moon by night.
7 The LORD shall preserve thee from all evil: he shall preserve thy soul.
8 The LORD shall preserve thy going out and thy coming in from this time forth, and even for evermore.

Psalm 122

1 I was glad when they said unto me, Let us go into the house of the LORD.
2 Our feet shall stand within thy gates, O Jerusalem.
3 Jerusalem is builded as a city that is compact together:
4 Whither the tribes go up, the tribes of the LORD, unto the testimony of Israel, to give thanks unto the name of the LORD.
5 For there are set thrones of judgment, the thrones of the house of David.
6 Pray for the peace of Jerusalem: they shall prosper that love thee.
7 Peace be within thy walls, and prosperity within thy palaces.
8 For my brethren and companions' sakes, I will now say, Peace be within thee.
9 Because of the house of the LORD our God I will seek thy good.

Psalm 129

1 Many a time have they afflicted me from my youth, may Israel now say:
2 Many a time have they afflicted me from my youth: yet they have not prevailed against me.
3 The plowers plowed upon my back: they made long their furrows.
4 The LORD is righteous: he hath cut asunder the cords of the wicked.
5 Let them all be confounded and turned back that hate Zion.
6 Let them be as the grass upon the housetops, which withereth afore it groweth up:
7 Wherewith the mower filleth not his hand; nor he that bindeth sheaves his bosom.
8 Neither do they which go by say, The blessing of the LORD be upon you: we bless you in the name of the LORD.

Psalm 132

1 A Song of degrees. LORD, remember David, and all his afflictions:
2 How he sware unto the LORD, and vowed unto the mighty God of Jacob;
3 Surely I will not come into the tabernacle of my house, nor go up into my bed;
4 I will not give sleep to mine eyes, or slumber to mine eyelids,
5 Until I find out a place for the LORD, a habitation for the mighty God of Jacob.
6 Lo, we heard of it at Ephratah: we found it in the fields of the wood.
7 We will go into his tabernacles: we will worship at his footstool.
8 Arise, O LORD, into thy rest; thou, and the ark of thy strength.

9 Let thy priests be clothed with righteousness; and let thy saints shout for joy.
10 For thy servant David's sake turn not away the face of thine anointed.
11 The LORD hath sworn in truth unto David; he will not turn from it; Of the fruit of thy body will I set upon thy throne.
12 If thy children will keep my covenant and my testimony that I shall teach them, their children shall also sit upon thy throne for evermore.
13 For the LORD hath chosen Zion; he hath desired it for his habitation.
14 This is my rest for ever: here will I dwell; for I have desired it.
15 I will abundantly bless her provision: I will satisfy her poor with bread.
16 I will also clothe her priests with salvation: and her saints shall shout aloud for joy.
17 There will I make the horn of David to bud: I have ordained a lamp for mine anointed.
18 His enemies will I clothe with shame: but upon himself shall his crown flourish.

Psalm 133

1 Behold, how good and how pleasant it is for brethren to dwell together in unity!
2 It is like the precious ointment upon the head, that ran down upon the beard, even Aaron's beard: that went down to the skirts of his garments;
3 As the dew of Hermon, and as the dew that descended upon the mountains of Zion: for there the LORD commanded the blessing, even life for evermore.

Psalm 138

1 I will praise thee with my whole heart: before the gods will I sing praise unto thee.
2 I will worship toward thy holy temple, and praise thy name for thy lovingkindness and for thy truth: for thou hast magnified thy word above all thy name.
3 In the day when I cried thou answeredst me, and strengthenedst me with strength in my soul.
4 All the kings of the earth shall praise thee, O LORD, when they hear the words of thy mouth.
5 Yea, they shall sing in the ways of the LORD: for great is the glory of the LORD.
6 Though the LORD be high, yet hath he respect unto the lowly: but the proud he knoweth afar off.
7 Though I walk in the midst of trouble, thou wilt revive me: thou shalt stretch forth thine hand against the wrath of mine enemies, and thy right hand shall save me.
8 The LORD will perfect that which concerneth me: thy mercy, O LORD, endureth for ever: forsake not the works of thine own hands.

Psalm 139

1 O LORD, thou hast searched me, and known me.
2 Thou knowest my downsitting and mine uprising, thou understandest my thought afar off.
3 Thou compassest my path and my lying down, and art acquainted with all my ways.
4 For there is not a word in my tongue, but, lo, O LORD, thou knowest it altogether.
5 Thou hast beset me behind and before, and laid thine hand upon me.

6 Such knowledge is too wonderful for me; it is high, I cannot attain unto it.
7 Whither shall I go from thy spirit? or whither shall I flee from thy presence?
8 If I ascend up into heaven, thou art there: if I make my bed in hell, behold, thou art there.
9 If I take the wings of the morning, and dwell in the uttermost parts of the sea;
10 Even there shall thy hand lead me, and thy right hand shall hold me.
11 If I say, Surely the darkness shall cover me; even the night shall be light about me.
12 Yea, the darkness hideth not from thee; but the night shineth as the day: the darkness and the light are both alike to thee.
13 For thou hast possessed my reins: thou hast covered me in my mother's womb.
14 I will praise thee; for I am fearfully and wonderfully made: marvelous are thy works; and that my soul knoweth right well.
15 My substance was not hid from thee, when I was made in secret, and curiously wrought in the lowest parts of the earth.
16 Thine eyes did see my substance, yet being unperfect; and in thy book all my members were written, which in continuance were fashioned, when as yet there was none of them.
17 How precious also are thy thoughts unto me, O God! how great is the sum of them!
18 If I should count them, they are more in number than the sand: when I awake, I am still with thee.
19 Surely thou wilt slay the wicked, O God: depart from me therefore, ye bloody men.
20 For they speak against thee wickedly, and thine enemies take thy name in vain.
21 Do not I hate them, O LORD, that hate thee? and am not I grieved with those that rise up against thee?

22 I hate them with perfect hatred: I count them mine enemies.
23 Search me, O God, and know my heart: try me, and know my thoughts:
24 And see if there be any wicked way in me, and lead me in the way everlasting.

Psalm 140

1 Deliver me, O LORD, from the evil man: preserve me from the violent man;
2 Which imagine mischiefs in their heart; continually are they gathered together for war.
3 They have sharpened their tongues like a serpent; adders' poison is under their lips. Selah.
4 Keep me, O LORD, from the hands of the wicked; preserve me from the violent man; who have purposed to overthrow my goings.
5 The proud have hid a snare for me, and cords; they have spread a net by the wayside; they have set gins for me. Selah.
6 I said unto the LORD, Thou art my God: hear the voice of my supplications, O LORD.
7 O GOD the Lord, the strength of my salvation, thou hast covered my head in the day of battle.
8 Grant not, O LORD, the desires of the wicked: further not his wicked device; lest they exalt themselves. Selah.
9 As for the head of those that compass me about, let the mischief of their own lips cover them.
10 Let burning coals fall upon them: let them be cast into the fire; into deep pits, that they rise not up again.
11 Let not an evil speaker be established in the earth: evil shall hunt the violent man to overthrow him.
12 I know that the LORD will maintain the cause of the afflicted, and the right of the poor.

13 Surely the righteous shall give thanks unto thy name: the upright shall dwell in thy presence.

Psalm 141

1 LORD, I cry unto thee: make haste unto me; give ear unto my voice, when I cry unto thee.
2 Let my prayer be set forth before thee as incense; and the lifting up of my hands as the evening sacrifice.
3 Set a watch, O LORD, before my mouth; keep the door of my lips.
4 Incline not my heart to any evil thing, to practice wicked works with men that work iniquity: and let me not eat of their dainties.
5 Let the righteous smite me; it shall be a kindness: and let him reprove me; it shall be an excellent oil, which shall not break my head: for yet my prayer also shall be in their calamities.
6 When their judges are overthrown in stony places, they shall hear my words; for they are sweet.
7 Our bones are scattered at the grave's mouth, as when one cutteth and cleaveth wood upon the earth.
8 But mine eyes are unto thee, O GOD the Lord: in thee is my trust; leave not my soul destitute.
9 Keep me from the snares which they have laid for me, and the gins of the workers of iniquity.
10 Let the wicked fall into their own nets, while that I withal escape.

Psalm 142

1 I cried unto the LORD with my voice; with my voice unto the LORD did I make my supplication.
2 I poured out my complaint before him; I shewed before him my trouble.

3 When my spirit was overwhelmed within me, then thou knewest my path. In the way wherein I walked have they privily laid a snare for me.
4 I looked on my right hand, and beheld, but there was no man that would know me: refuge failed me; no man cared for my soul.
5 I cried unto thee, O LORD: I said, Thou art my refuge and my portion in the land of the living.
6 Attend unto my cry; for I am brought very low: deliver me from my persecutors; for they are stronger than I.
7 Bring my soul out of prison, that I may praise thy name: the righteous shall compass me about; for thou shalt deal bountifully with me.

Psalm 145

1 I will extol thee, my God, O king; and I will bless thy name for ever and ever.
2 Every day will I bless thee; and I will praise thy name for ever and ever.
3 Great is the LORD, and greatly to be praised; and his greatness is unsearchable.
4 One generation shall praise thy works to another, and shall declare thy mighty acts.
5 I will speak of the glorious honor of thy majesty, and of thy wondrous works.
6 And men shall speak of the might of thy terrible acts: and I will declare thy greatness.
7 They shall abundantly utter the memory of thy great goodness, and shall sing of thy righteousness.
8 The LORD is gracious, and full of compassion; slow to anger, and of great mercy.
9 The LORD is good to all: and his tender mercies are over all his works.

10 All thy works shall praise thee, O LORD; and thy saints shall bless thee.
11 They shall speak of the glory of thy kingdom, and talk of thy power;
12 To make known to the sons of men his mighty acts, and the glorious majesty of his kingdom.
13 Thy kingdom is an everlasting kingdom, and thy dominion endureth throughout all generations.
14 The LORD upholdeth all that fall, and raiseth up all those that be bowed down.
15 The eyes of all wait upon thee; and thou givest them their meat in due season.
16 Thou openest thine hand, and satisfiest the desire of every living thing.
17 The LORD is righteous in all his ways, and holy in all his works.
18 The LORD is nigh unto all them that call upon him, to all that call upon him in truth.
19 He will fulfil the desire of them that fear him: he also will hear their cry, and will save them.
20 The LORD preserveth all them that love him: but all the wicked will he destroy.
21 My mouth shall speak the praise of the LORD: and let all flesh bless his holy name for ever and ever.

Psalm 149

1 Praise ye the LORD. Sing unto the LORD a new song, and his praise in the congregation of saints.
2 Let Israel rejoice in him that made him: let the children of Zion be joyful in their King.
3 Let them praise his name in the dance: let them sing praises unto him with the timbrel and harp.
4 For the LORD taketh pleasure in his people: he will beautify the meek with salvation.

5 Let the saints be joyful in glory: let them sing aloud upon their beds.
6 Let the high praises of God be in their mouth, and a two-edged sword in their hand;
7 To execute vengeance upon the heathen, and punishments upon the people;
8 To bind their kings with chains, and their nobles with fetters of iron;
9 To execute upon them the judgment written: this honor have all his saints. Praise ye the LORD.

Psalm 150

1 Praise ye the LORD. Praise God in his sanctuary: praise him in the firmament of his power.
2 Praise him for his mighty acts: praise him according to his excellent greatness.
3 Praise him with the sound of the trumpet: praise him with the psaltery and harp.
4 Praise him with the timbrel and dance: praise him with stringed instruments and organs.
5 Praise him upon the loud cymbals: praise him upon the high sounding cymbals.
6 Let every thing that hath breath praise the LORD. Praise ye the LORD.

Appendix D
Adinkra Symbols

This pictorial index is meant to serve a guide to aid you in crafting your symbols for magickal use.

Abode Santann

Meaning: The universe is vast and always overseen by the all-knowing and those who have gone before

Akofena

Meaning: Sword of war

Ananse Ntentan

Meaning: A spider's crafty and creative web is a tool to outwit

Anyi Me Aye

Meaning: If you will not praise me, don't spoil my name

Boa Me Na Me Mmoa Wo

Meaning: Help me and let me help you

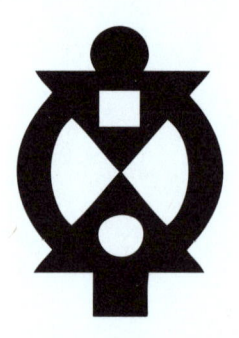

Dwennimmen

Meaning: Strength, wisdom, and learning with humility

Gyawu Atiko

Meaning: A symbol of valor and bravery

Nsoromma

Meaning: Child of the heavens

Odo Nnyew Fie Kwan

Meaning: Love does not lose its way home

Sankofa

Meaning: Go back and retrieve your past

Required Reading for Spiritual Disruptors

This reading list and the ritual that follows it was compiled with you in mind. The goal is to help BIPOC people, their allies, and their accomplices better understand, appreciate, and reconfigure allegiance to the culture of a people breaking chains, kicking ass, and taking names.

Set yourself a goal of reading at least one book a month. Take notes, write in the margins, dog ear pages, and keep a journal labeled *Required Reading for Spiritual Disruptors*. As you complete each chapter, make sure to write down any important takeaways.

Acts of Faith: 25th Anniversary Edition by Iyanla Vanzant
A Cup of Water Under My Bed: A Memoir by Daisy Hernández
African Holistic Health by Llaila O. Afrika
After the Rain: Gentle Reminders for Healing, Courage, and Self-Love by Alexandra Elle
A Kick in the Belly: Women, Slavery, and Resistance by Stella Dadzie
All the Black Girls Are Activists: A Fourth Wave Womanist Pursuit of Dreams as Radical Resistance by EbonyJanice Moore
The Altar Within: A Radical Devotional Guide to Liberate the Divine Self by Juliet Diaz
Angela Davis: An Autobiography by Angela Y. Davis
Assata: An Autobiography by Assata Shakur
Astrology for Mystics: Exploring the Occult Depths of the Water Houses in Your Natal Chart by Tayannah Lee McQuillar
As We Have Always Done: Indigenous Freedom Through Radical Resistance by Leanne Betasamosake Simpson
Baby of the Family by Tina McElroy Ansa
Bibliotherapy in the Bronx by Emely Rumble
Black Gods: Orisa Studies in the New World by Gary Edwards and John Mason
Black Indian (Made in Michigan Writer Series) by Shonda Buchanan

Black Magic: Religion and the African American Conjuring Tradition by Yvonne P. Chireau

Black Men and Depression: Saving Our Lives, Healing Our Families and Friends by John Head

Body Autonomy: Decolonizing Sex Work & Drug Use edited by Justice Rivera

The Book of Juju: Africana Spirituality for Healing, Liberation, and Self-Discovery by Juju Bae

Chains and Images of Psychological Slavery by Na'Im Akbar

Che Guevara Reader: Writings on Politics & Revolution by Ernesto Che Guevara

Christopher Columbus and the Afrikan Holocaust: Slavery and the Rise of European Capitalism by John Henrik Clarke

The Color Complex (Revised): The Politics of Skin Color in a New Millennium by Kathy Russell-Cole, Midge Wilson, and Ronald E. Hall

The Community of Self by Na'Im Akbar

Conjuring the Calabash: Empowering Women with Hoodoo Spells & Magick by Mawiyah Kai EL-Jamah Bomani

Countering the Conspiracy to Destroy Black Boys by Dr. Jawanza Kunjufu

The Delectable Negro: Human Consumption and Homoeroticism within US Slave Culture by Vincent Woodard

Devil Ain't Nothin' but a Five Letter Word: A Self-Help Journal to Transforming Fear by Iya Ifalola Omobola

Four Seasons of Mojo: An Herbal Guide to Natural Living by Stephanie Rose Bird

God Is a Black Woman by Christena Cleveland

God Is Red: A Native View of Religion by Vine Deloria Jr.

The Hate U Give by Angie Thomas

Hoodoo for Everyone: Modern Approaches to Magic, Conjure, Rootwork, and Liberation by Sherry Shone

How We Heal: Uncover Your Power and Set Yourself Free by Alexandra Elle

I Am Alfonso Jones by Tony Medina

The Immortal Life of Henrietta Lacks by Rebecca Skloot

Incantations Embodied: Rituals for Empowerment, Reclamation, and Resistance by Kimberly Rodriguez

The Isis Papers: The Keys to the Colors by Dr. Frances Cress Welsing

Jambalaya: The Natural Woman's Book of Personal Charms and Practical Rituals by Luisah Teish

King Leopold's Ghost: A Story of Greed, Terror, and Heroism in Colonial Africa by Adam Hochschild

The Language of Lenormand: A Practical Guide for Everyday Divination by Erika Robinson

Let the Circle Be Unbroken: The Implications of African Spirituality in the Diaspora by Marimba Ani

The Magical Art of Crafting Charm Bags: 100 Mystical Formulas for Success, Love, Wealth, and Wellbeing by Elhoim Leafar

The Marie Laveau Voodoo Grimoire: Rituals, Recipes, and Spells for Healing, Protection, Beauty, Love, and More by Denise Alvarado

Mexican Sorcery: A Practical Guide to Brujeria de Rancho by Laura Davila

Mojo Workin': The Old African American Hoodoo System by Katrina Hazzard-Donald

The Natural First Aid Handbook: Household Remedies, Herbal Treatments, and Basic Emergency Preparedness Everyone Should Know by Brigitte Mars

Negroes with Guns by Robert F. Williams

Ona Agbani: The Ancient Path by Iyalosa Apetebii Olaomi Osunyemi Akalatunde

On a Move: The Story of Mumia Abu-Jamal by Terry Bisson

Orishas, Goddesses, and Voodoo Queens: The Divine Feminine in the African Religious Traditions by Lilith Dorsey

Pagan Origins of the Christ Myth by John G. Jackson

Power of the Psalms by Anna Riva

Psychic Witch: A Metaphysical Guide to Meditation, Magick & Manifestation by Mat Auryn

Rootwork: Using the Folk Magick of Black America for Love, Money, and Success by Tayannah Lee McQuillar

Sacred Woman: A Guide to Healing the Feminine Body, Mind, and Spirit by Queen Afua

The Salt Eaters by Toni Cade Bambara

Sassafrass, Cypress & Indigo: A Novel by Ntozake Shange

Self-Care for Black Men: 100 Ways to Heal and Liberate by Jor-El Caraballo

Sensual Faith: The Art of Coming Home to Your Body by Lyvonne Briggs

The 1619 Project: A New Origin Story by Nikole Hannah-Jones

The Spirit of Intimacy: Ancient African Teachings in the Ways of Relationships by Sobonfu Somé

Stamped from the Beginning: The Definitive History of Racist Ideas in America by Ibram X. Kendi

Stolen Legacy by George G. M. James

Tarot for the Hard Work: An Archetypal Journey to Confront Racism and Inspire Collective Healing by Maria Minnis

Tarot for Troubled Times: Confront Your Shadow, Heal Your Self & Transform the World by Shaheen Miro and Theresa Reed

The 21 Divisions: Mysteries and Magic of Dominican Voodoo by Hector Salva

The Wake of the Wind: A Novel by J. California Cooper

White Supremacy Is All Around: Notes from a Black Disabled Woman in a White World by Akilah Cadet

Why I'm No Longer Talking to White People About Race by Reni Eddo-Lodge

William Styron's Nat Turner: Ten Black Writers Respond edited by John Henrik Clarke

Wisdom of the Natural World: Spiritual and Practical Teachings from Plants, Animals & Mother Earth by Granddaughter Crow

Woman Who Glows in the Dark: A Curandera Reveals Traditional Aztec Secrets of Physical and Spiritual Health by Elena Avila and Joy Parker

Women Writing Resistance: Essays on Latin America and the Caribbean edited by Jennifer Browdy de Hernandez

Working the Roots: Over 400 Years of Traditional African American Healing by Michele Elizabeth Lee

You Don't Know Us Negroes and Other Essays by Zora Neale Hurston

Yurugu: An African-Centered Critique of European Cultural Thought and Behavior by Marimba Ani

EXERCISE: READING LIFE AS A SPIRITUAL DISRUPTOR

This working can be done with any of the books on the list.

Needs:

* 3 sticks of Seven Afrikan Powers incense
* a journal with an image of St. Joseph glued to the inside cover
* 1 white candle
* 1 piece of black tourmaline
* a book of your choosing from the required reading list

Instructions:

Light a stick of incense; this is to help facilitate understanding from the astral realm. It also places you in communion with St. Joseph.

Pick up your tourmaline and touch it to the third eye region of your forehead, your lips, your throat, and finally your heart. Upon completion of this, place it near the candle. Light your candle, close your eyes, and ask St. Joseph to show you how to use what you'll learn to protect BIPOC people and to not allow the media and divisive colorful people to dilute your progress toward building strong relations with any and all survivors of colonization.

Now, you may've already read a chapter of your chosen book, or you can use this time to read. It's totally up to you. How long you choose to sit determines if the other incense sticks will be used.

Once the reading is over, answer the following questions in your journal for each chapter of each book. Feel free to add questions as they arise.

* Summarize the chapter in your own words. Use no more than two pages. Stick to the most pertinent ideas.

* How can you use the information presented in this chapter to improve your connection with other BIPOC people in your community?
* How can you address this information with the youth and elders of your community, who may be unfamiliar with these concepts?
* How will this information impact the future course of your spiritual development?
* How will you use this information to build solidarity between BIPOC folks globally?

Bibliography

"African American Hoodoo: More than Magic." 2013. *Futurity*. January 4, 2013. https://www.futurity.org/african-american-hoodoo-more-than-magic/.

"Akashic Records for Beginners: Access Your Soul's Journey." The Hermit and the Page, July 19, 2023. https://thehermitandthepage.com/akashic-records-for-beginners/#Introduction_to_Akashic_Records_For_Beginners.

Araujo-Hawkins, Dawn. "Why Some Young Black Christians Are Practicing Hoodoo." The Christian Century. Accessed January 13, 2021. https://www.christiancentury.org/article/features/why-some-young-black-christians-are-practicing-hoodoo.

Asanga, Dr. Nsisong. "No One Seems to Know Why Black Women Are Plagued with Fibroids. Here's What We Can Say for Sure." *Atlanta Black Star*, May 27, 2024. https://atlantablackstar.com/2024/05/27/why-black-women-are-plagued-with-fibroids-heres-what-we-can-say-for-sure/.

"Barbara Bush Calls Evacuees Better Off." *The New York Times*, September 7, 2005. https://www.nytimes.com/2005/09/07/us/nationalspecial/barbara-bush-calls-evacuees-better-off.html.

Bauer, Shane. "5 Ways Prisoners Were Used for Profit Throughout US History." *PBS News*. February 26, 2020. https://www.pbs.org/newshour/arts/5-ways-prisoners-were-used-for-profit-throughout-u-s.

Bernstein, David. "The Weakness of the 'Whiteness' Literature." Reason, May 31, 2019. https://reason.com/volokh/2019/05/31/the-weakness-of-the-whiteness-literature/.

"Black Girls Viewed as Less Innocent than White Girls, Georgetown Law Research Finds." Georgetown Law, June 27, 2017. https://www.law.georgetown.edu/news/black-girls-viewed-as-less-innocent-than-white-girls-georgetown-law-research-finds-2/.

"Black Herman: Politics and Magic." MagicTricks, 2024. https://www.magictricks.com/black-herman.html.

"Black Herman's Secrets of Magic, Mystery, & Legerdermain." Internet Archive, 2021. https://archive.org/details/black_hermans_secrets_of_magic_mystery_and_legerdermain.

"Black Woman Recounts How Black Men Were Treated at Ukraine Train Station." *CNN*, March 1, 2022. https://edition.cnn.com/videos/world/2022/03/01/sidner-naya-ukraine-poland-train-sot-dlt-vpx.cnn.

Blair, Douglas. "I'm a Former Teacher. Here's How Your Children Are Getting Indoctrinated by Leftist Ideology." The Heritage Foundation, 2019. https://www.heritage.org/education/commentary/im-former-teacher-heres-how-your-children-are-getting-indoctrinated-leftist.

Blakemore, Erin. "How the GI Bill's Promise Was Denied to a Million Black WWII Veterans." History, June 27, 2019. https://www.history.com/news/gi-bill-black-wwii-veterans-benefits.

Bodirsky, Monica. "The Lenormand Oracle: History and Practice." *Spiral Nature Magazine*, October 17, 2018. https://www.spiralnature.com/magick/lenormand-oracle-history-practice/.

Butler, Deanna. "The Devil, Abiaka: The Legacy of Sam Jones." Florida Seminole Tourism, September 21, 2023. https://floridaseminoletourism.com/the-devil-abiaka-the-legacy-of-sam-jones/.

Cadet, Akilah. *White Supremacy Is All Around*. Hachette UK, 2024.

Chenier, Cierra. "Jean Saint Malo: The Man, Maroon, & Martyr." *NOIR 'N NOLA*, July 30, 2018. https://www.noirnnola.com/post/2018/07/30/jean-saint-malo-the-man-the-maroon-the-martyr.

Chireau, Yvonne. "Root Doctors and Hoodoo Medicine." YouTube, February 18, 2022. https://youtu.be/icabuoWxPC0?si=JgZXZxfxclA4htEy.

Clarey, David. "What We Know About the Missing 19-Year-Old Woman in Milwaukee." *Journal Sentinel*, April 12, 2024. https://www.jsonline.com/story/news/2024/04/10/what-we-know-about-sade-robinson-the-missing-19-year-old-in-milwaukee/73263866007/.

"Colourism." Global Social Theory, n.d. https://globalsocialtheory.org/topics/colourism/.

Dier, Chris. "The Legend of Jean Saint Malo." Chris Dier, June 19, 2020. https://chrisdier.com/2020/06/19/the-legend-of-jean-san-malo/.

Ducharme, Jamie. "Why the COVID-19 Pandemic Is Prompting a National Existential Crisis." *Time*, December 29, 2020. https://time.com/5925218/covid-19-pandemic-life-decisions/.

Dutton, Wendy. "The Problem of Invisibility: Voodoo and Zora Neale Hurston." *Frontiers: A Journal of Women Studies* 13, no. 2 (1993): 131. https://doi.org/10.2307/3346733.

"Facts and Figures: Ending Violence against Women." UN Women. Accessed March 3, 2021. https://www.unwomen.org/en/what-we-do/ending-violence-against-women/facts-and-figures.

"Fatal Violence Against the Transgender and Gender-Expansive Community in 2023." Human Rights Campaign, 2024. https://www.hrc.org/resources/fatal-violence-against-the-transgender-and-gender-expansive-community-in-2023.

Fausset, Richard. "What We Know About the Shooting Death of Ahmaud Arbery." *The New York Times*, August 8, 2022. https://www.nytimes.com/article/ahmaud-arbery-shooting-georgia.html.

"Fibroids (Uterine Myoma)." Yale Medicine, October 30, 2022. https://www.yalemedicine.org/conditions/fibroids.

Fischer, Anna. "New Details Emerge About Ouachita River Victim Sheryl Turner." *KATC News*, April 9, 2024. https://www.katc.com/iberia-parish/new-details-emerge-about-ouachita-river-victim-sheryl-turner.

Fluker, Dominique. "New Study Finds Even the Wealthiest Black Mothers and Their Babies Are More Likely to Die in Childbirth." *Essence*. Updated February 17, 2023. https://www.essence.com/lifestyle/parenting/childbirth-deadlier-for-black-families/.

Fought, Leigh. *Women in the World of Frederick Douglass*. New York: Oxford University Press, 2017.

Frey, William H. "The US Will Become 'Minority White' in 2045, Census Projects." Brookings, March 14, 2018. https://www.brookings.edu/articles/the-us-will-become-minority-white-in-2045-census-projects/.

Gamble, Justin. "Estate of Henrietta Lacks Reaches Settlement with Biotech Company for Nonconsensual Use of Her Cells in Medical Research." *CNN*, August 1, 2023. https://www.cnn.com/2023/08/01/us/henrietta-lacks-thermo-fisher-scientific-settlement/index.html.

Gandhi, Lakshmi. "Tulsa Race Massacre: Fact Checking Myths and Misconceptions." *NBC News*, May 30, 2021. https://www.nbcnews.com/select/news/tulsa-race-massacre-fact-check-ncna1269045.

Garcia, J. L. A. "Racism and the Discourse of Phobias: Negrophobia, Xenophobia and More—Dialogue with Kim and Sundstrom." Philosophic Exchange, 2020. https://soar.suny.edu/handle/20.500.12648/7164.

"Generational Wealth Overview." *MSN*, 2024. https://www.msn.com/en-us/money/personalfinance/generational-wealth-overview-examples-and-faqs/ar-AA1otB6e.

"H.R. 40 Is Not a Symbolic Act. It's a Path to Restorative Justice." American Civil Liberties Union, May 22, 2020. https://www.aclu.org/news/racial-justice/h-r-40-is-not-a-symbolic-act-its-a-path-to-restorative-justice.

Hair, William Ivy. *Carnival of Fury: Robert Charles and the New Orleans Race Riot of 1900*. Louisiana State University Press, 2008.

Haskins, James, Kathleen Benson, Ellen Cipriano, and James Walker. *Conjure Times: Black Magicians in America*. Walker & Company, 2001.

Holpuch, Amanda. "US Opens Investigation into Killing of Sonya Massey." *The New York Times*, November 17, 2024. https://www.nytimes.com/2024/11/17/us/sonya-massey-shooting-investigation.html.

Hoskin, Maia Niguel. "It's Not Just Us: Why Racism Should Be Seen as a Global Issue." *The Community Voice*, March 3, 2022. https://www.communityvoiceks.com/2022/03/03/its-not-just-us-why-racism-should-be-seen-as-a-global-issue/.

"H. R. 40." National African-American Reparations Commission (NAARC). Accessed January 4, 2021. https://reparationscomm.org/hr-40/.

Hutchinson, Bill, and Deena Zaru. "Family of Ajike Owens Calls for Murder Charges after Suspect Charged with Manslaughter: 'We Are Deeply Disappointed.'" *ABC News*, June 27, 2023. https://abcnews.go.com/US/florida-woman-charged-fatal-shooting-ajike-owens-mother/story?id=100390462.

The Immortal Life of Henrietta Lacks by Rebecca Skloot: Study Guide. Pembroke Notes. Dog Ear Publishing, 2013.

"John Horse." The Great Seminole Nation of Oklahoma. Accessed July 14, 2024. http://seminolenation-indianterritory.org/johnhorse.htm.

Johnson, Ben. "Cecil Rhodes." Historic UK, 2017. https://www.historic-uk.com/HistoryUK/HistoryofEngland/Cecil-Rhodes/.

"Dylann Roof Tells Jury, 'I Still Feel Like I Had to Do It.'" *ABC News*, January 10, 2017. https://abcnews.go.com/US/jurors-hear-closing-arguments-dylann-roof-trial/story?id=44673859.

Lewis, Frank. "St. Expedite, 'the Patron Saint of Procrastinators.'" *Mazzolini Artcraft* (blog), May 2019. https://mazzoliniartcraft.com/blog/st-expedite-the-patron-saint-of-procrastinators/.

Li, David K. "Jordan Chiles Looking for 'My Peace' and 'My Justice' After Bronze Medal Dispute." *MSN*, September 11, 2024. https://www.msn.com/en-us/sports/nba/jordan-chiles-looking-for-my-peace-and-my-justice-after-bronze-medal-dispute/ar-AA1qpA9J.

Lockhart, P. R. "A New Report Shows How Racism and Bias Deny Black Girls Their Childhoods." *Vox*, May 16, 2019. https://www.vox.com/identities/2019/5/16/18624683/black-girls-racism-bias-adultification-discipline-georgetown.

Loewen, James W. *Sundown Towns: A Hidden Dimension of American Racism*. Simon & Schuster, 2006.

"The Lost City of Frenier." *Southern Gothic* (blog), March 26, 2018. https://www.southerngothicmedia.com/blog/2018/3/24/episode-003-the-lost-city-of-frenier.

MacGaffey, Wyatt. "Constructing a Kongo Identity: Scholarship and Mythopoesis." *Comparative Studies in Society and History* 58, no. 1 (2016): 159–80. https://doi.org/10.1017/s0010417515000602.

Madhubuti, Haki R., and Rose Buchanan. "Four Reasons for Using 'K' in Afrika." The State of History. January 27, 1994. https://soh.omeka.chass.ncsu.edu/items/show/692.

Maffly-Kipp, Laurie. "African American Christianity, Pt. II: From the Civil War to the Great Migration, 1865–1920." National Humanities Center. Accessed December 9, 2024. https://nationalhumanitiescenter.org/tserve/nineteen/nkeyinfo/aarcwgm.htm.

Malhi, Sabrina. "Childbirth Deadlier for Americans, Especially Black Women, Study Finds." *Washington Post*, June 5, 2024. https://www.washingtonpost.com/health/2024/06/04/us-maternal-mortality-rate-higher-other-countries/.

Matza, Max. "Henrietta Lacks: Family of Black Woman Whose Cells Were Taken Settle Case." *BBC News*, August 1, 2023. https://www.bbc.com/news/world-us-canada-66376758.

McKay, Claude. "If We Must Die." Poetry Foundation. Accessed July 31, 2025. https://www.poetryfoundation.org/poems/44694/if-we-must-die.

McQuillar, Tayannah Lee. *Hoodoo Tarot: 78-Card Deck and Book for Rootworkers*. Destiny Books, 2020.

"Measuring Religion in Pew Research Center's American Trends Panel." Pew Research Center, January 14, 2021. https://www.pewresearch.org/religion/2021/01/14/measuring-religion-in-pew-research-centers-american-trends-panel/.

Menconi, David. "Liberation Station, N.C.'s First Black-Owned Children's Bookstore, Comes to Downtown Raleigh." Visit Raleigh, June 14, 2023. https://www.visitraleigh.com/plan-a-trip/visitraleigh-insider-blog/post/liberation-station-opens-raleigh-nc-black-owned-children-book-store/.

Merchan, Davi. "Pennsylvania Father Seeks Answers After Son Dies Following Alleged Game of Tag." *ABC7 Chicago*, May 2, 2024. https://

abc7chicago.com/what-happened-to-justin-johnson-senior-assassin-game-video-central-dauphin/14751818/.

Mills, Kim, host. *Speaking of Psychology*, podcast. Episode 110. "The Invisibility of White Privilege, with Brian Lowery, PhD." American Psychological Association. Accessed November 7, 2024. https://www.apa.org/news/podcasts/speaking-of-psychology/white-privilege.

Morris, Bilal. "The Black Seminoles: How Fugitive Slaves Escaped to Mexico Before the Civil War." *NewsOne*, December 19, 2022. https://newsone.com/4467763/black-seminoles-mexico-free-blacks-slavery/.

Morrison, Toni. "Quotable Quote." Goodreads. Accessed July 31, 2025. https://www.goodreads.com/quotes/3228728-the-function-the-very-serious-function-of-racism-is-distraction.

"The Negro Motorist Green Book." AutoLife, University of Michigan. Accessed December 21, 2023. http://www.autolife.umd.umich.edu/Race/R_Casestudy/Negro_motorist_green_bk.htm.

Negussie, Tesfaye. "A Year After Black Man Disappeared Under Mysterious Circumstances, Questions Remain." *ABC News*, October 2, 2023. https://abcnews.go.com/US/rasheem-carters-mother-speaks-1-year-after-disappearance/story?id=103660675.

Pope, Sarah. "Traditional Foods of the Seminole Tribe of Florida." The Healthy Home Economist, February 11, 2012. https://www.thehealthyhomeeconomist.com/traditional-foods-of-the-seminole-tribe-of-florida/.

Porter-Mitchell, Juliette. "Story of John Horse, a Black Seminole Warrior." ArchBalt. Accessed July 14, 2024. https://www.archbalt.org/story-of-john-horse-a-black-seminole-warrior/?print=pdf.

Prasad, Ritu. "Serena Williams and the Trope of the 'Angry Black Woman.'" *BBC News*, September 11, 2018. https://www.bbc.com/news/world-us-canada-45476500.

Raiken, Amber. "Jordan Chiles' Mother Slams 'Racist, Disgusting' Comments About Her Daughter on Social Media." Yahoo! Sports, August 12, 2024. https://sports.yahoo.com/jordan-chiles-mother-slams-racist-164855762.html.

"A Rare Assemblage of Knuckle Bones for Gaming and Divination Discovered in the Ancient City of Maresha." The Friends of the Israel Antiquities Authority, August 18, 2022. https://www.friendsofiaa.org/news/2022/8/18/a-rare-assemblage-of-knuckle-bones-for-gaming-and-divination-discovered-in-the-ancient-city-of-maresha.

Re, Lucia. "Italians and the Invention of Race: The Poetics and Politics of Difference in the Struggle over Libya, 1890–1913." *California Italian Studies* 1, no. 1 (2010). https://doi.org/10.5070/c311008862.

Reichelmann, Ashley V., and Matthew O. Hunt. "How We Repair It: White Americans' Attitudes toward Reparations." Brookings Institution, December 8, 2021. https://www.brookings.edu/articles/how-we-repair-it-white-americans-attitudes-toward-reparations/.

Rich, Frank. "The Spoils of War Coverage." *The New York Times*, April 13, 2003. https://www.nytimes.com/2003/04/13/arts/the-spoils-of-war-coverage.html.

Rimer, Sara. "After Arrest, Town Shamed by '68 Killing Seeks Renewal." *The New York Times*, May 17, 2002. https://www.nytimes.com/2002/05/17/us/after-arrest-town-shamed-by-68-killing-seeks-renewal.html.

Rodriguez, Bianca. "Unforgettable Quotes by Marsha P. Johnson." *Marie Claire*, June 3, 2020. https://www.marieclaire.com/politics/a32745825/marsha-p-johnson-quotes/.

"Science in the Middle Ages—Rediscovering Its Latent Genius." Medievalists, February 13, 2021. https://www.medievalists.net/2021/02/science-in-the-middle-ages/.

"Sinister Manchac Swamp and the Chilling Curse of Julia Brown." Ancient Pages, August 25, 2021. https://www.ancientpages.com/2021/08/25/sinister-manchac-swamp-and-the-chilling-curse-of-julia-brown/.

"The State of Black Women in Corporate America." Lean In. Accessed October 9, 2020. https://leanin.org/research/state-of-black-women-in-corporate-america.

"Swamp Legends, Voodoo Queen of Manchac Swamp, Julia Brown." *Hollier on Da Bayou* (blog), July 24, 2018. https://hollierondabayou.blogspot.com/2018/07/swamp-legends-voodoo-queen-of-manchac.html.

"Syncretism (Orisha-Saint Correspondence)." NARKIVE Newsgroup Archive. Accessed July 12, 2024. https://alt.religion.orisha.narkive.com/PF8QMNbQ/syncretism-orisha-saint-correspondence.

"The Tulsa Race Massacre: Facts About the Attack." History, May 30, 2021. https://www.history.com/news/tulsa-race-massacre-facts.

"27 Inspirational Alex Elle Quotes on Love & Healing." Art of Poets, April 22, 2024. https://artofpoets.com/alex-elle-quotes/.

Welsing, Francis Cress. "The Cress Theory of Color-Confrontation." *The Black Scholar* 5, no. 8 (1974): 32–40.

"What If All Enslaved Africans Were Given Repatriation When Slavery Ended." *MSN Video*. Accessed July 25, 2024. https://www.msn.com/en-us/news/us/what-if-all-enslaved-africans-were-given-repatriation-when-slavery-ended/vi-BB1lwH2W.

"Who Killed Derontae Martin?" Justice for Derontae. Accessed December 10, 2024. https://justiceforderontae.com/.

"Working at the Intersection: What Black Women Are Up Against." Lean In. Accessed January 19, 2020. https://leanin.org/black-women-racism-discrimination-at-work.

NOTES

NOTES

NOTES

NOTES

NOTES

NOTES

To Write to the Author

If you wish to contact the author or would like more information about this book, please write to the author in care of Llewellyn Worldwide Ltd. and we will forward your request. Both the author and publisher appreciate hearing from you and learning of your enjoyment of this book and how it has helped you. Llewellyn Worldwide Ltd. cannot guarantee that every letter written to the author can be answered, but all will be forwarded. Please write to:

Mawiyah Kai EL-Jamah Bomani
℅ Llewellyn Worldwide
2143 Wooddale Drive
Woodbury, MN 55125-2989

Please enclose a self-addressed stamped envelope for reply, or $1.00 to cover costs. If outside the U.S.A., enclose an international postal reply coupon.

Many of Llewellyn's authors have websites with additional information and resources. For more information, please visit our website at http://www.llewellyn.com.